Cases on Talent Strategy in a VUCA Economy

Yusuf Hassan
https://orcid.org/0000-0001-6662-7402
Heriot Watt University, UAE

IGI Global
Scientific Publishing
Publishing Tomorrow's Research Today

Vice President of Editorial — Melissa Wagner
Director of Acquisitions — Mikaela Felty
Director of Book Development — Jocelynn Hessler
Production Manager — Mike Brehm
Cover Design — Jose Rosado

Published in the United States of America by
IGI Global Scientific Publishing
701 East Chocolate Avenue
Hershey, PA, 17033, USA
Tel: 717-533-8845 | Fax: 717-533-7115
Website: https://www.igi-global.com E-mail: cust@igi-global.com

Library of Congress Cataloging-in-Publication Data

Names: Hassan, Yusuf, 1992- editor
Title: Cases on talent strategy in a VUCA economy / edited by: Yusuf Hassan.
Description: Hershey, PA : IGI Global Scientific Publishing, [2026] | Includes bibliographical references and index. | Summary: "This book presents classroom-ready case studies on how organizations navigate talent management in the volatile, uncertain, complex, and ambiguous (VUCA) economy. Showcasing real-world and simulated scenarios, it explores strategies for rapid upskilling, agile development, cross-team collaboration, ethical workforce management, and sustaining culture amid change"-- Provided by publisher.
Identifiers: LCCN 2025038305 (print) | LCCN 2025038306 (ebook) | ISBN 9798337357768 hardcover | ISBN 9798337357775 paperback | ISBN 9798337357782 ebook
Subjects: LCSH: Corporate governance | Industrial management | Uncertainty | LCGFT: Case studies
Classification: LCC HD2741 .C37 2026 (print) | LCC HD2741 (ebook) | DDC 658.4--dc23/eng/20260112
LC record available at https://lccn.loc.gov/2025038305
LC ebook record available at https://lccn.loc.gov/2025038306

British Cataloguing in Publication Data
A Cataloguing in Publication record for this book is available from the British Library.

Table of Contents

Detailed Table of Contents

This chapter examines how talent management is conceptualized and enacted within large Indian cooperatives through a qualitative multi-case study. Drawing on publicly available reports and archival sources, it analyzes three prominent cooperatives, Amul, IFFCO, and NAFED, to explore how ownership structure, governance, and strategic purpose shape people practices. The findings show that talent in cooperatives extends beyond conventional high-potential employees to include system-wide capability, institutional memory, and member-linked competence. While industrial cooperatives adopt formalized learning platforms and leadership pipelines, federated and policy-facing cooperatives rely more on embedded routines, procedural rigor, and long-term employment relationships. The chapter contributes to talent management theory by extending it beyond corporate settings and offers practical insights for cooperative leaders and policymakers seeking to strengthen capability without diluting cooperative values.

This case study defines how talent management can be used to promote organisational resilience and business development in small technical service firms with reference to the Broadcom Technical Concepts LLC, Abu Dhabi. With its operations in a dynamic ELV systems integration industry, the organisation has used workforce flexibility, retention of skilled workers, and strategic redeployment to keep its operations running even when there is havoc like the COVID-19. The development of a complementary venture, ShowCraft allowed to utilize the available technical potential in the most efficient way and thus diversify without raising the number of employees. The research brings out the role of human capital as a strategic asset within uncertain settings as well as underscoring the existence of structured talent development and succession planning in providing a long term sustainability and scalability.

Preface

ABOUT THIS BOOK

In contemporary management discourse, few ideas have captured the imagination of scholars, practitioners, and policymakers as strongly as the notion that organizations now operate in a world defined by volatility, uncertainty, complexity, and ambiguity. The acronym VUCA, originally used within military strategic thinking to describe rapidly shifting geopolitical conditions, has increasingly become a useful lens through which the challenges of modern organizational life are interpreted. While the term itself may appear abstract at first glance, the realities it represents are visible across industries and institutional settings. Organizations today encounter technological disruption that reshapes markets at unprecedented speed, geopolitical developments that alter supply chains and investment patterns, demographic shifts that redefine workforce expectations, and societal pressures that compel businesses to reconsider their broader responsibilities toward stakeholders. These developments collectively produce an environment in which stability can no longer be assumed and where the ability to adapt often becomes the decisive factor in organizational survival.

Within such a context, the role of talent strategy has taken on renewed significance. Historically, discussions about strategy in management literature tended to focus primarily on market positioning, industry structure, or competitive advantage derived from resources and capabilities. Human resource management, although acknowledged as important, was often treated as a supporting function responsible for recruitment, performance evaluation, and employee administration. Over time, however, both research and managerial practice have recognized that talent is not merely a support mechanism for strategy but rather a central component of it. Organizations increasingly realize that the ability to attract, develop, and mobilize human capability is closely tied to their capacity for innovation, resilience, and sustained performance. The strategic management of talent therefore becomes not simply an HR activity but a core organizational priority.

Several influential discussions in practitioner-oriented scholarship have emphasized this shift. Analyses published in business outlets such as *Harvard Business Review* and *Forbes* frequently note that organizations facing volatile environments must cultivate workforces capable of learning quickly, collaborating across functional boundaries, and responding effectively to emerging opportunities and threats. For instance, research exploring how organizations manage uncertainty highlights the importance of building adaptive capabilities among employees and leaders, rather than relying solely on formal strategic planning processes (Bennett & Lemoine, 2014). Similarly, work on leadership in turbulent environments stresses the need for clarity of purpose and organizational coherence so that employees can navigate ambiguity while remaining aligned with broader strategic goals (Johansen, 2017). These insights collectively underscore a fundamental reality: strategy in the contemporary world cannot be separated from the people who enact it.

At the same time, talent strategy itself has undergone significant transformation in response to changing workplace dynamics. The nature of work has evolved dramatically in recent years due to digitalization, automation, and the expansion of knowledge-intensive industries. Organizations increasingly rely on employees who possess specialized expertise, creative problem-solving ability, and the capacity to collaborate across geographical and organizational boundaries. In such settings, traditional hierarchical models of management often prove insufficient. Employees expect greater autonomy, opportunities for learning, and meaningful engagement with their work. Organizations that fail to respond to these expectations frequently struggle to attract and retain skilled professionals.

The disruptions associated with the COVID-19 pandemic further accelerated many of these trends. Remote and hybrid work arrangements became widespread, forcing organizations to reconsider long-standing assumptions about productivity, supervision, and collaboration. As workplaces shifted toward digital platforms, leaders were compelled to rethink how performance is evaluated and how organizational culture can be sustained when employees are not physically co-located. Recent publications during this period emphasized that managing performance in distributed work environments requires greater emphasis on trust, outcomes, and communication rather than reliance on physical visibility or direct oversight (Gratton, 2021). These developments illustrate how talent strategy must continuously evolve in response to broader societal and technological shifts.

The central motivation behind this edited volume lies in the recognition that the challenges associated with talent strategy become particularly visible when examined through real organizational situations. While conceptual discussions provide valuable theoretical insights, they often leave readers wondering how these ideas manifest in everyday managerial practice. Teaching cases offer a powerful means of bridging this gap between theory and practice. By presenting detailed narratives of organizations confronting specific challenges, cases allow students and practitioners to observe how managers interpret complex circumstances, evaluate alternative courses of action, and implement strategic decisions under conditions of uncertainty.

The pedagogical tradition of case-based learning has long been recognized as one of the most effective approaches in management education. Rather than presenting knowledge in purely abstract form, case studies invite learners to engage actively with organizational situations. Students are encouraged to analyze the context in which decisions occur, identify the underlying problems faced by managers, and propose possible solutions based on theoretical frameworks. This interactive learning process mirrors the realities of managerial work, where decisions must often be made in environments characterized by incomplete information and competing priorities. For undergraduate and postgraduate students in business and management programs, exposure to well-designed teaching cases provides an opportunity to develop analytical reasoning, strategic thinking, and practical problem-solving skills.

The present book, *Cases on Talent Strategy in a VUCA World*, has therefore been designed primarily as a teaching resource that can support classroom learning in courses related to human resource management, organizational behaviour, strategy, and leadership. The chapters included in the volume present organizational narratives drawn from diverse industries and institutional contexts. Each case explores a specific dimension of talent strategy, ranging from performance management and leadership development to workforce capability building and talent retention. By examining these issues through detailed organizational examples, the book enables readers to observe how theoretical concepts discussed in academic literature become relevant in real managerial settings.

One of the cases included in this volume examines talent management within cooperative enterprises operating in the Indian context. Cooperatives occupy a distinctive organizational space where economic objectives intersect with community-oriented principles. Unlike conventional corporations, cooperatives are owned and governed by their members, who may be farmers, producers, consumers or workers depending on the sector. This ownership structure shapes the way managerial decisions are made and introduces a range of unique governance considerations. As the case demonstrates, talent management within cooperative organizations involves balancing professional management practices with democratic participation and community accountability. Employees and managers must not only deliver operational efficiency but also maintain trust with member-owners who rely on the cooperative for economic stability and collective representation. The case illustrates how large cooperatives attempt to attract professional talent, develop managerial capabilities, and sustain institutional legitimacy while operating in competitive markets. In doing so, it highlights the complexities that arise when organizational values and commercial imperatives intersect (Grashuis & Su, 2019).

Another case in the volume addresses the transformation of performance management systems in organizations adopting hybrid work models. The shift toward hybrid work has created both opportunities and challenges for managers. On the one hand, flexible work arrangements allow organizations to access broader talent pools and offer employees greater autonomy. On the other hand, they complicate the process of monitoring performance and maintaining team cohesion. The case explores how managers attempt to redesign evaluation frameworks that emphasize outcomes rather than physical presence. It also examines the role of digital collaboration tools, employee feedback mechanisms, and leadership communication in sustaining productivity within distributed teams. By presenting a detailed organizational narrative, the chapter encourages students to reflect on how performance management practices must adapt to evolving work arrangements.

A further case focuses on talent development strategies within technology-driven organizations. Firms operating in sectors characterized by rapid innovation often face intense competition for highly skilled professionals. Recruiting talented individuals represents only the first step; organizations must also create environments that support continuous learning and professional growth. The case illustrates how companies attempt to design training programs, mentorship systems, and leadership development initiatives that enable employees to keep pace with technological change. It also highlights the challenges associated with retaining high-potential talent in labour markets where opportunities for mobility are abundant.

A few chapters in this volume also explore the relationship between organizational culture and talent strategy. Culture shapes the informal norms and expectations that guide employee behaviour within organizations. Although often difficult to measure directly, cultural dynamics influence how individuals interpret organizational goals, interact with colleagues, and respond to leadership initiatives. Through case narratives drawn from different industries, the book illustrates how leaders attempt to cultivate cultures that encourage innovation, accountability and ethical conduct. In some cases, strong cultural alignment supports successful organizational transformation. In others, entrenched cultural assumptions create resistance to change, complicating efforts to implement new talent management practices.

Leadership development emerges as another important theme across the chapters included in this volume. Organizations operating in volatile environments require leaders who can navigate ambiguity, build collaborative relationships, and make strategic decisions under pressure. Developing such leadership capability requires deliberate investment in talent identification, mentoring, and experiential learning opportunities. Several cases therefore examine how organizations attempt to design leadership pipelines that prepare employees for increasingly complex managerial responsibilities. These narratives demonstrate that leadership development is not simply a matter of formal training programs but often involves providing individuals with opportunities to confront challenging assignments that broaden their perspective and enhance their decision-making capacity.

An important feature of this edited volume is the diversity of organizational contexts represented within the cases. Talent strategy challenges do not arise exclusively in large multinational corporations; they are equally relevant in cooperatives, technology firms, service organizations, and emerging business models. By presenting cases from multiple sectors, the book encourages readers to compare how different organizations respond to similar challenges. Such comparisons help illuminate the role that institutional context plays in shaping managerial decisions. What works effectively in one organizational environment may require adaptation in another due to differences in governance structures, market conditions, or cultural expectations.

From an educational perspective, the cases included in this volume are particularly valuable for undergraduate and postgraduate students who seek to understand how theoretical frameworks introduced in textbooks translate into practical decision-making scenarios. Many students encounter concepts such as strategic human resource management, leadership development, and organizational culture during their academic studies, yet they may struggle to see how these ideas operate within real organizations. Case-based learning provides a bridge between theory and practice by presenting situations in which managers must apply these concepts while confronting real constraints.

Instructors using this book may find that the cases encourage lively classroom discussion. Because case studies rarely present a single definitive solution, they invite students to explore multiple perspectives and debate the merits of different courses of action. One group of students might emphasize strategic alignment and efficiency, while another might focus on employee well-being or organizational culture. Through this process, learners develop the capacity to analyze complex organizational issues and appreciate the trade-offs inherent in managerial decision-making.

The cases also highlight the importance of contextual sensitivity in talent strategy. Organizations cannot simply replicate practices that appear successful elsewhere without considering their own unique circumstances. Factors such as industry dynamics, institutional environment, workforce composition, and organizational history influence how talent strategies are designed and implemented. By examining a variety of cases, students gain insight into the ways in which managers adapt general principles to specific contexts.

Another aspect that distinguishes the cases in this volume is their emphasis on strategic decision points. Each chapter presents a situation in which organizational leaders must evaluate alternative approaches to addressing a talent-related challenge. Readers are invited to consider the information available to decision makers at that moment and assess how different choices might influence organizational outcomes. This structure encourages students to move beyond passive reading and actively engage with the case material as analysts and decision makers. Taken together, the cases included in this edited book illustrate a central theme i.e., talent strategy is deeply intertwined with broader organizational dynamics. Decisions related to recruitment, training, leadership development and performance evaluation cannot be understood in isolation from the strategic environment in which organizations operate. By examining these relationships through detailed case narratives, the book provides readers with a richer appreciation of how talent management practices evolve in response to changing economic and institutional conditions.

REFERENCES

Bennett, N., & Lemoine, G. J. (2014). What VUCA really means for you. *Harvard Business Review*, *92*(1–2), 27–42.

Collings, D. G., & Mellahi, K. (2009). Strategic talent management: A review and research agenda. *Human Resource Management Review*, *19*(4), 304–313. DOI: 10.1016/j.hrmr.2009.04.001

Grashuis, J., & Su, Y. (2019). A review of the empirical literature on farmer cooperatives: Performance, ownership, and governance. *Annals of Public and Cooperative Economics*, *90*(1), 77–102. DOI: 10.1111/apce.12205

Gratton, L. (2021). How to do hybrid right. *Harvard Business Review*, *99*(3), 65–74.

Johansen, B. (2017). *The new leadership literacies: Thriving in a future of extreme disruption and distributed everything*. Berrett-Koehler.

Chapter 1
Agile Talent Management in a VUCA Public Sector:
Lessons From Case Studies of Talent Management

Jure Andolšek
http://orcid.org/0009-0001-7524-2878
School of Economics and Business, Ljubljana, Slovenia

Maša Košak
School of Economics and Business, Ljubljana, Slovenia

EXECUTIVE SUMMARY

In volatile, uncertain, complex, and ambiguous (VUCA) environments, public sector organizations face unprecedented talent challenges. This chapter examines how agile talent management and inclusive succession planning can sustain public institutions through rapid change, focusing on the case of Slovenia's civil service. Drawing on literature and real-world cases, it contrasts inclusive versus exclusive approaches to talent and highlights key practices—from early identification and development programs to knowledge transfer and retention strategies—that build workforce agility. The chapter includes insights from Slovenian private-sector organizations that have pioneered formal talent and succession systems, and compares them with international public-sector examples. Practical frameworks and recommendations are provided to help public leaders implement transparent, equitable talent strategies and ensure leadership continuity in the VUCA era.

DOI: 10.4018/979-8-3373-5776-8.ch001

INTRODUCTION

Public administrations across Europe are increasingly operating in volatile, uncertain, complex, and ambiguous (VUCA) environments. Rapid digital transformation, demographic shifts, fiscal constraints, and evolving citizen expectations challenge long-standing systems and governance traditions (OECD, 2021a; Pollitt & Bouckaert, 2017). These conditions are evident in the Slovenian civil service, where over a quarter of the workforce is nearing retirement and strategic workforce planning remains underdeveloped (OECD, 2021b). In such a context, talent management (TM) and succession planning (SP) emerge not merely as managerial trends, but as strategic necessities to ensure continuity, institutional agility, and capacity to deliver essential public services amid uncertainty (Thunnissen & Gallardo-Gallardo, 2017).

While "talent management" is traditionally associated with corporate environments, its relevance to public administration is increasingly recognized in both research and practice (Boselie & Thunnissen, 2017; Collings, Mellahi & Cascio,, 2019). Effective public-sector TM can foster leadership continuity, sustain institutional memory, and build organizational responsiveness to shifting policy demands (Kravariti & Johnston, 2020). However, translating these practices into public administration is not straightforward. Public law employment systems, political accountability, union negotiations, and rigid HR regulations often limit managerial discretion (Van der Wal, 2017; Ingraham et al., 2000). This chapter explores how public organizations; particularly in Slovenia, can navigate these constraints while implementing inclusive and ethical TM and SP practices suited for a VUCA world. It does so by examining both theoretical foundations and practical cases, ultimately offering frameworks for developing agile talent strategies in the public sector.

Despite increasing interest in TM and SP within public administration, the literature remains fragmented and under-theorized in several key respects. First, there is limited conceptual clarity on how inclusive and agile TM frameworks can be operationalized within the structural, legal, and cultural conditions specific to civil services; especially in post-socialist European countries like Slovenia (Kozjek & Franca, 2020). Second, while public-sector talent discussions often center on high-level policy objectives (e.g., OECD, 2021a; European Commission, 2023), they rarely offer actionable, empirically informed models based on lived organizational practices. Third, research tends to treat public and private sector HRM as categorically separate, thus neglecting the opportunity for constructive cross-sector learning — a gap this chapter directly addresses (Schuler, Budhwar & Florkowski, 2002).

This chapter responds to these gaps by offering an empirically grounded, theoretically informed, and context-sensitive analysis of agile TM and SP strategies in the Slovenian public sector. Drawing on structured insights from three large organizations in Slovenia (from the banking, insurance, and manufacturing sectors) the chapter identifies transferable practices, development models, and governance principles relevant to the public sphere. It introduces a framework for implementing inclusive, ethical, and development-focused TM systems that are responsive to the constraints and complexity of public employment systems. In doing so, the chapter contributes to the evolving literature on public-sector HRM by advancing a values-driven, cross-sectoral, and adaptive model of talent management appropriate for the realities of 21st-century governance.

THEORETICAL FOUNDATIONS OF TALENT MANAGEMENT IN THE PUBLIC SECTOR

TM encompasses the proactive strategies and practices an organization uses to attract, develop, and retain individuals with high potential to meet current and future needs (Al, Cascio & Paauwe, 2014). Several key conceptual dichotomies help frame TM in any context:

Inclusive vs. exclusive talent philosophy. An inclusive approach treats all employees as having talent worth developing, whereas an exclusive approach focuses on a select few "high potentials" or critical roles (Gallardo-Gallardo,2018). In public institutions, inclusive models are often favored to avoid elitism and uphold fairness (Dries & Kaše, 2023). Every employee is given opportunities to grow, aligning with public service values of equity. However, entirely inclusive models can dilute focus; evidence suggests that a blended approach may be necessary, especially in succession planning where targeted investment in future leaders is essential (Rothwell, 2010). An organization might, for example, offer general development programs to all staff (inclusive) while still running high-potential leadership tracks (exclusive) in parallel.

Subjective vs. objective notions of "Talent". Talent can be conceptualized subjectively as an innate quality or leadership charisma identifiable in certain individuals, or objectively as a set of observable competencies, qualifications, and performance indicators (Tansley, 2011). Public-sector employers, being bound by formal evaluation criteria and merit-based rules, tend to emphasize objective measures – e.g., demonstrated skills, years of experience, exam scores – when identifying talent (Oliveira et al., 2024). Still, the challenge in a VUCA context is to also recognize less tangible qualities like adaptability, learning agility, and resilience that may not show up in traditional appraisals. Incorporating both objective performance data and more subjective potential indicators can improve identification of future leaders who will thrive amid uncertainty.

Input vs. output focus. Some talent systems emphasize input (an individual's potential, motivations, and traits) while others emphasize output (current performance and results) (Meyers et al., 2020). Input-driven models look at who could succeed in bigger roles tomorrow, whereas output-driven models reward who is succeeding in their job today. Both perspectives hold merit. Potential matters for long-term planning, but past and present performance remains a key indicator of credibility—particularly in the public eye where accountability is high. Balancing these views, organizations often use performance as a baseline qualification and potential as a differentiator for advancement opportunities (Poocharoen & Lee, 2013). In a VUCA world, public organizations can't afford rigid choices. They need to stay flexible and combine different approaches, adjusting to fast changes, complex tasks, and uncertain future skill needs.

Underlying all these dichotomies is the principle that strategic talent management aligns individual growth with the strategic needs of the organization. As Collings and Mellahi (2009) argue, strategic TM involves deliberately mapping and developing employees' competencies to meet future organizational objectives. In a public-sector context, this means linking TM and succession efforts to the capability of institutions to carry out their public mandates in the years ahead. For example, if a government agency anticipates a greater need for digital skills or policy coordination, its talent strategy should cultivate those competencies among its staff today. Transferring private-sector talent models to government, however, is not straightforward. Public servants are often motivated more by intrinsic factors such as public service mission and job security than by the financial incentives common in the private sector (Vandenabeele, 2007). Civil services also operate under formalized rules that limit managerial discretion in hiring and promotions (e.g. standardized pay scales, tenure-based progression, open competition for positions). These constraints mean that any public-sector talent initiative must be carefully designed to fit within legal frameworks and to maintain transparency and meritocracy. Nonetheless, as the demands on government workforces intensify under VUCA pressures, many public organizations are seeking to adapt, finding creative ways to implement talent development and succession planning within the boundaries of civil service systems (Shet, 2024).

CASE CONTEXT: TALENT CHALLENGES IN SLOVENIA'S PUBLIC SECTOR

Slovenia's public administration provides a compelling context for exploring talent management in government. Like many post-socialist European countries, Slovenia inherited a centralized and rule-bound civil service system (Sommermann, 2025), which has only gradually begun shifting toward more strategic human resource management. Today, the public sector faces converging pressures: an ageing workforce, fast-changing skill requirements (e.g. digital competencies), and increasing competition for qualified personnel (Yoon, 2019). Recognizing these challenges, Slovenian policymakers have started to put TM and SP on the agenda, though implementation remains nascent.

One pressing issue is generational turnover. According to OECD analyses, the age structure of Slovenia's civil service is skewed toward older employees; a significant share of officials will reach retirement in the next 5–10 years (OECD, 2021b). At the same time, younger talent enters slowly, with only a small percentage of central administration staff under the age of 35. This dynamic raises the risk of knowledge loss and leadership vacuum if succession is not managed proactively. These demographic and skill challenges are not only HR issues but clear signs of a VUCA environment—volatile retirements, uncertain inflows of younger staff, complex legal frameworks, and ambiguous career paths. Seeing them through a VUCA lens highlights why Slovenia needs more strategic and flexible talent planning.

However, strategic workforce planning practices; such as forecasting retirements, identifying skill gaps, and preparing successors are still underdeveloped. Historically, workforce planning in the civil service has been more administrative (filling vacancies as they arise) than strategic (anticipating future needs) (OECD, 2021b). Nevertheless, recent reforms indicate a growing awareness of talent strategy. In 2023 the government introduced changes to better recognize and reward "acting" officials (those temporarily filling more senior roles), effectively institutionalizing a mechanism to support succession planning (Government of the Republic of Slovenia, 2025). By formalizing how acting appointments are handled and possibly giving credit for that experience, the civil service is beginning to create pathways for emerging leaders to step up when vacancies occur. This is one step toward a more agile approach, ensuring leadership continuity during transitions.

Another notable initiative is the »Partnership for Change« (slo: *Partnerstvo za spremembe*) program, a public–private knowledge exchange platform launched in 2015. This innovative program, co-led by the Ministry of Public Administration and the American Chamber of Commerce in Slovenia, allows public servants to undertake short mutual exchanges with private-sector companies (AmCham Slovenia, 2023). Participants spend time in a different organization to learn new ways of working, then bring back ideas to their home institution. By exposing civil servants to fresh perspectives and best practices from industry, the program enhances adaptability, innovation, and cross-sector understanding. It effectively broadens the development opportunities available to public employees beyond the confines of their own agencies, which is a key aspect of agile talent development in a VUCA world.

Despite such initiatives, Slovenia's public administration lacks some of the infrastructure seen in more advanced public-sector talent systems. There is no centralized talent pool or fast-stream program for high-potentials, no formal cross-ministerial rotation or succession program, nor comprehensive use of HR analytics to predict workforce trends. Talent management activities, where they exist, tend to be ad hoc or confined to individual ministries rather than system-wide. This places the Slovenian administration behind some of its OECD peers in terms of readiness for demographic and skill shifts. However, the early steps being taken – policy tweaks, pilot programs, and increased dialogue on the topic – suggest a foundation on which more integrated and strategic talent management initiatives could be built (referenca).

To explore how Slovenia might further develop an agile, inclusive talent strategy, it is instructive to look at both domestic and international examples. The next section delves into insights from several large Slovenian organizations in the private sector that have implemented robust talent management and succession planning practices. These cases, while from outside the public sector, offer concrete examples of how a systematic approach to managing talent can function in a Slovenian context. We will then compare these insights with practices from other public sectors internationally, before discussing recommendations for the Slovenian public administration.

INSIGHTS FROM SLOVENIAN TALENT MANAGEMENT CASES

While the public sector has unique constraints, it can draw lessons from successful talent management practices in other contexts. In order to gather practical insights, we examined the talent management and succession practices of three large Slovenian organizations in different industries – one in manufacturing, one in banking, and one in insurance. Each company employs several hundred to a few thousand people and operates within a broader international corporate structure. Information was collected through in-depth interviews with HR managers in each organization. The findings reveal how these organizations define and identify talent, develop high-potential employees, plan for succession, and strive to retain their key people. Their approaches, summarized below, highlight principles that can be considered in adapting talent strategies for the public sector.

DEFINING "TALENT" AND SUCCESSORS: INCLUSIVE VS. EXCLUSIVE APPROACHES

The philosophy of talent management varies across the organizations, reflecting each company's culture and strategic priorities. A fundamental question is whether "talent" is viewed broadly (inclusive approach) or as a designation for a select few (exclusive approach).

The manufacturing company has a highly formalized and exclusive approach, considering talent as a combination of strong current performance and high future potential. Only a select pool of employees – those who consistently exceed performance expectations and demonstrate leadership or expert potential – are formally designated as "talents." This company explicitly distinguishes its talent pool as the source for future leaders or key experts. The philosophy is that not everyone will qualify; instead, the organization invests deeply in those identified as having the highest impact potential.

The banking institution leans toward a hybrid approach, blending inclusive and exclusive elements. The leadership espouses the view that *every* employee has some potential for growth (an inclusive ethos of developing all staff). However, in practice they do identify a somewhat narrower group (approximately the top 3–4% of employees) who receive additional development opportunities as high-potentials. In other words, they start with inclusive assumptions and provide growth opportunities for all, but additionaly implement an exclusive tier for those who really stand out. This approach aims to ensure broad engagement in development while still concentrating resources on those most likely to assume critical roles.

The insurance company's approach is selective and somewhat exclusive, focusing specifically on young "high flyers." Their formal talent program targets employees roughly under the age of 30 who are deemed to have strong leadership promise. Every few years, a new cohort (up to about 30 individuals) is chosen for an intensive and highly structurised development program. This reflects a view that fresh perspectives from younger professionals are especially valuable, and investing in youth will secure the company's future leadership. It is exclusive in the sense that only a limited number can participate each cycle, but it's also transparent and structured, with clear criteria for selection (e.g. education level, performance, and managerial recommendations).

Despite these differences, all three organizations share a common understanding of what a *talent* is – employees with above-average performance and a demonstrated potential to take on more complex or higher-responsibility roles in the future. In all cases, talent is not defined solely by one's current job success; it is seen as a combination of current achievements, behavioral characteristics (such as initiative and adaptability), willingness to learn, internal motivation, and alignment with the company's long-term needs. For example, the manufacturing firm explicitly looks for individuals who not only excel in their present duties but also show openness to mobility (taking on different roles or assignments), ability to learn new skills (often including fluency in foreign languages for their international operations), and embodiment of the company's values. Talent, in their view, means the person could succeed in a significantly bigger role down the line – be it as a senior manager or a top technical expert.

Another commonality is that all three companies recognize dual career paths for advancement: a managerial path and a specialist (professional/technical) path.

This is important in defining talent because it acknowledges that leadership is not the only way an employee can contribute at a high level. For instance, the manufacturing company's talent pool includes not just would-be managers but also project leaders and technical innovators who are critical to R&D and operations. Similarly, the bank and insurance company each have parallel tracks so that a high-performing expert (for example, a data scientist or legal expert) can be considered "talent" and given development opportunities without forcing them into people-management roles if that is not their strength or interest. This practice of valuing both leadership and expert talent ensures inclusivity of different talent profiles and is highly relevant to public sector contexts, where not all crucial roles are managerial (e.g., a government might want to develop top policy analysts or IT specialists, not only future department heads).

The private-sector cases show that talent revolves around identifying employees who combine strong performance with future potential. The three Slovenian companies often navigated this by using clear criteria and a structured process to decide who is in the talent pool, attempting to make even an exclusive approach fair and merit-based. This balance matters even more in a VUCA world, where organizations need both broad engagement and focused investment to stay agile amid change.

IDENTIFYING TALENTS AND HIGH-POTENTIALS: PROCESSES AND CRITERIA

Identifying who qualifies as "talent" is a critical process that the companies approached with formal systems to ensure rigor and reduce bias. Each organization employed multi-step identification procedures combining performance evaluation with assessments of potential, often incorporating both managerial judgment and HR oversight.

The organisation in the manufacturing uses a 9-cell performance–potential matrix as the backbone of its talent identification. All employees are annually evaluated on two dimensions: their recent job performance and their future potential. Managers plot individuals into a 3x3 grid (often known as the "9-box matrix") ranging from low to high performance and potential. Those falling into the high-performing, high-potential boxes are flagged as potential talents. What sets this process apart is the robust calibration: multiple managers from different departments meet to review and debate the placements. Through these calibration sessions, they compare assessments to ensure that standards are consistent across the organization and not just reflective of one manager's opinion. This collective review helps mitigate individual biases and provides a more objective consensus on who truly stands out. Additionally, this firm has explicit criteria beyond performance metrics – for example, an individual's readiness to relocate or take on diverse assignments, and their alignment with corporate values, are factored into the potential rating. The outcome of the process is a designated talent pool: those who land in the top tiers of the matrix are officially recognized as "talents" and enter the talent development program (described later). This process is repeated yearly, allowing for new entrants and ensuring the talent pool remains dynamic. Notably, in this company talent identification is tightly linked with succession planning: as soon as someone is identified as a high-potential, management considers which future leadership or expert roles they might fill, and development plans are created accordingly.

The company in the banking sector is slightly more inclusive when it comes to developing talent itself, but selective in outcome – offers development opportunities to all employees, but some exclusive opportunities are only provided to a special few. It begins with an organization-wide premise that every employee should have a development discussion with their manager. In these discussions, managers identify individuals who have performed above expectations and exhibit ambition or exceptional capabilities. Annually, managers nominate these individuals to the high-potential list. About 3.5% of the workforce (a few dozen out of a few thousand employees) typically gets nominated. These nominations are then reviewed by the HR department and subjected to executive calibration: the senior management team discusses the nominations to validate that each person indeed fits the high-potential profile, considering factors such as sustained performance, leadership qualities or unique skills, and motivation level. The bank uses a set of criteria combining quantitative and qualitative data: performance appraisals, any available competency assessments, and the manager's qualitative input on the employee's drive and ability to take on more responsibility. Importantly, once an employee is selected into the talent pool, an individual development plan (IDP) is crafted for them (involving the employee, their manager, and HR). However, the bank makes it clear that being labeled a "talent" is not a guarantee of promotion; it is a commitment to development. This manages expectations and keeps the pressure constructive. The identification process is revisited each year, meaning someone not selected one year might be nominated the next if they show improvement, and vice versa.

The insurance industry company's talent identification process is the most structured of all three, and is periodic. Rather than continuous annual nominations, they run a talent identification cycle every few – approximately three – years (aligning with their strategic planning cycle). When a cycle opens, top management issues a call to all business units to propose candidates who meet specific criteria. These criteria typically include: under a certain age threshold (around 30 years old, as they focus on young talent), a solid record of performance, the requisite educational background or professional qualifications, and demonstrated motivation and loyalty to the company. Managers put forward candidates, who then undergo a multi-step assessment: this can involve psychometric tests (to evaluate cognitive abilities, personality traits, leadership potential), as well as the candidates writing a motivational letter or essay about their career aspirations and commitment to the company.

The use of a motivation letter effectively requires candidates to self-reflect and declare their interest in long-term growth within the organization. This step introduces an element of self-selection and commitment – only those truly interested in an accelerated development path will go through with it, which helps ensure engagement. An HR and executive panel reviews the test results and letters, and makes the final selection of up to 30 participants for the talent program cohort. Those selected are informed of their status and even sign a learning agreement, acknowledging the investment the company will make in them and their own pledge to actively participate (and often to remain with the company for a certain period after completing the program). This formal agreement underscores the reciprocal commitment in the talent relationship.

Across all three organizations, we see an emphasis on structured, multi-criteria evaluation to identify high-potentials. Performance (the track record of results) is universally a starting point – nobody with mediocre performance would be considered talent – but beyond that, aspects of potential are measured through different means: managerial judgment (all companies), collaborative calibration (manufacturing and banking), formal assessments and candidate input (insurance). These processes are documented and repeatable, lending credibility and transparency to what might otherwise be seen as a subjective or opaque selection. In the context of public administration, such formalization could be very valuable; civil servants are understandably wary of favoritism, so a clear methodology (e.g. using defined criteria and involving multiple evaluators) can help legitimize exclusive development opportunities.

It's also worth noting that the scope of inclusion differs: the bank's 3.5% figure indicates a relatively broad pool, whereas the insurance firm's 30-person cohort in a workforce of thousands is extremely selective. The manufacturing company did not quote a percentage, but implied a small top tier making it through the nine-box review. The appropriate scope likely depends on organizational needs and resources – a public sector might lean more toward the bank's model (a somewhat larger pool) to maintain a perception of inclusivity, unless resources force a tighter focus.

SUCCESSION PLANNING FOR KEY POSITIONS

In tandem with identifying general talent pools, the companies also engage in succession planning for specific key positions. Talent management and succession planning (SP) are closely related but not identical: TM often casts a wide net on people, whereas SP zooms in on roles. All three organizations recognized certain roles as *critical* (due to their impact or the risk that a vacancy would seriously disrupt operations) and took steps to ensure continuity for those roles.

A common approach within the three companies is to maintain a list of "key positions" for most important roles – for example, senior management, unique technical expert, or any position where the incumbent is one of few people with necessary know-how. For each key position, the organizations try to identify one or more potential successors and assess their readiness. However, among the three companies practices of SP varied in terms of how formal and transparent this process is.

In the banking sector example, SP is a formal, confidential process. For each critical role (such as department heads, regional managers, etc.), the leadership team, in consultation with HR, designates a primary and secondary successor. They use categories like "ready now," "ready within 1 year," or "ready in 2-3 years with proper development" to indicate how prepared each candidate is, and this informs what development or exposure that person might need. These succession plans are reviewed and updated on a regular cycle (approximately every two years, or sooner if a leadership change occurs). Importantly, in this bank successors are generally not informed that they have been earmarked for a specific role. The rationale is to avoid creating false expectations or complacency, and to preserve flexibility – if circumstances change, the organization doesn't want to be seen as breaking a promise. Only when a succession is imminent (for instance, a manager has announced retirement and the successor will likely step in) might the conversation become explicit with the individuals involved. Until then, the plans remain an internal tool for management.

The manufacturing company also conducts SP but in a somewhat informal and developmental manner. Instead of keeping a hidden list, their practice is to actively involve potential successors in the work of current job holders well ahead of any transition. For example, if a plant manager is expected to retire in a couple of years, the company might assign one of the talent pool members as that manager's deputy or have them lead significant projects under the manager's mentorship. Through this "deputizing" approach, the candidate gains first-hand experience, and the organization can observe their capability in a trial setting. While there may still be an internal understanding of "who would likely replace whom," the emphasis is on knowledge transfer on the job rather than waiting for a vacancy and then appointing someone. Successors in this environment might be aware that they are being groomed – it could be implied by the responsibilities they're given – but there isn't a formal declaration or guarantee. The succession "plan" is embedded in these developmental assignments and the presence of backup personnel for each key area.

The insurance sector company has the most formalized SP, at least for senior leadership roles, and in this case the identified successors *are* aware of their status (though it's not broadly advertised). For top executive positions within the company (and its subsidiaries), a slate of one or more "designated successors" is approved by the Supervisory Board. These individuals are often those who have come through the talent program or otherwise proven themselves. Being a designated successor is a confidential status (known to the individual and top management, but not announced to all staff). These people may receive extra leadership development or be included in higher-level strategic discussions to prepare them. The Supervisory Board's involvement indicates how seriously succession is taken – it's not just an HR exercise, but part of governance and long-term planning. Additionally, this company's succession strategy is linked to its multi-year talent cycles: after the talent program, graduates are often funneled into positions that put them next in line for leadership, creating a pipeline that the Board can oversee.

The noteworthy aspect here is the transparency (or lack thereof) toward the employees involved. The approaches range from completely opaque (banking, where successors usually do not know they are in a plan) to somewhat transparent (insurance, where successors know but it's kept discreet), to implicitly transparent through practice (manufacturing, where a successor might guess their status based on being chosen as a deputy). Each approach has pros and cons. Keeping it quiet can prevent people from feeling undue pressure or entitlement, but it also means those individuals might not realize the company is investing in them, possibly reducing their loyalty. Being open can motivate and prepare someone, but if handled poorly it could cause others to feel passed over or could backfire if plans change and a "promised" successor isn't appointed. In the public sector, transparency in promotions is often mandated (e.g., open competition), so formal succession plans might similarly need careful handling to ensure fairness and compliance with rules.

Despite different methods, all of the three companies use SP to mitigate risk. They particularly focus on roles where the current position holder might leave soon (due to retirement or other reasons) or where skills are rare. They integrate succession with talent management insofar as many potential successors come from the talent pools or development programs. Indeed, a common thread is that many individuals identified as "talent" later become candidates for key positions, confirming that the talent programs are feeding the succession pipeline. This alignment of TM and SP ensures that when the time comes to fill a critical role, there is a developed, trusted internal candidate ready, rather than having to rely solely on external recruitment or scramble at the last minute.

For public administration, having a systematic succession plan for leadership positions (e.g. heads of divisions, agencies, or expert roles) could similarly ensure continuity in a VUCA world. This means spotting internal candidates early and preparing them, possibly quietly, for future responsibilities – keeping at least one backup ready. The private-sector cases show that having at least a primary and backup candidate for each important role – and periodically reviewing these plans – helps organizations stay prepared in a fast-changing environment.

DEVELOPMENT AND TRAINING PROGRAMS FOR TALENT

Identifying talent is only the first step; equally important is how those talents employees are developed. All three companies invested in structured development programs for their talent pools, although the design and intensity of these programs varied.

In the manufacturing company, the talent development program runs for around two years for each cohort of identified talent pool. It begins with a core curriculum offered to the whole talent group, which might include workshops on leadership skills, innovation, cross-cultural communication, and deep dives into the company's strategy and values. This ensures that all talents share a common understanding of the business and build networks with each other. Alongside this, there is an individualized development component: each talent works with their manager and HR to identify specific areas for growth (technical skills, soft skills, etc.) and undertakes targeted training or stretch assignments in those areas. A hallmark of this program is the assignment of cross-functional projects – talents are often given projects outside their regular job scope, sometimes in teams, to solve real business problems. For example, a talented engineer might be tasked with leading a project involving the marketing department, thereby learning about a different aspect of the business. These projects not only broaden their experience but also benefit the organization by tackling important issues. External trainers or courses are sometimes utilized for specialized learning (e.g., an advanced management course or an international assignment if the company operates abroad).

Throughout the program, progress is monitored, but there is no automatic promotion at the end. Instead, the expectation (that is clearly communicated) is that participants will have significantly improved their competencies and visibility, making them strong contenders when relevant positions open up. The company also emphasizes e during development – talents are encouraged to take up short rotations o reven relocate to different plant sites or offices if possible, to cultivate adaptability. The combination of formal training, experiential learning, and mobility prepares individuals to step into bigger shoes when needed.

In the banking sector example, the development approach is more flexible and tailored, guided by the 70-20-10 learning model. This model implies that ~70% of development comes from challenging assignments and on-the-job experiences, 20% from coaching and mentoring relationships, and 10% from formal training. Each talent's development plan is unique, reflecting their role and career aspirations. For instance, one talented employee's plan might include: a stretch assignment (like temporarily deputizing for their manager, or leading a new product initiative) to cover the 70%; assignment of a mentor or internal coach to meet regularly (the 20% relational learning); and enrollment in a few formal training courses or an external leadership program for the 10%.

The bank also provides access to an internal "Leadership Academy" – a series of workshops and e-learning modules – which talents are encouraged to complete at their own pace. Networking opportunities with senior leaders or talents from other departments are facilitated as well, recognizing that peer learning and exposure are crucial. The duration of involvement in the talent program is roughly two years, though it isn't a fixed cohort with a start and end – people can enter or exit the pool each year. Because the program is individualized, some employees might complete certain development milestones sooner and even get promoted out of the pool, while others might continue longer.

There is no group graduation event as in a cohort-based model; success is measured by personal growth and readiness for the next step. Notably, the bank does not create a separate program specifically for successors outside the talent pool – rather, if someone is earmarked as a successor but not already a designated talent, the bank will often bring them into the high-potential development process to ensure they receive similar opportunities. If that is not feasible (for example, an older employee might be a logical successor for an imminent vacancy but not part of the young talent pool), then development is handled one-on-one by giving that person targeted preparation for the role (like shadowing the incumbent or attending a specific course).

The company in insurance runs a comprehensive three-year program for each talent cohort, making it the most intensive of the three. In the first year, participants undergo a series of structured learning modules often in collaboration with external academic partners or training consultants. This could take the form of a mini-MBA style curriculum covering strategy, finance, leadership, innovation, etc., tailored to the company's context. During this year, each talent is also assigned to a strategic project team – these teams work on real challenges identified by top management (for instance, exploring a new market opportunity or improving an internal process), and at year's end they present their findings and recommendations to the company's Executive Board. This provides visibility and a test of their abilities in front of senior leadership. Additionally, a mentorship component begins (detailed in the next subsection) where each talent has one or more mentors.

In the second year, the focus shifts to personalized development: each participant, with guidance, designs an individual development project or plan. This could be something like leading a major initiative in their department, or doing an interdepartmental rotation, or even a short assignment abroad if the company is multinational.

They also undergo further assessments, such as 360-degree feedback or personality and leadership style inventories, to heighten self-awareness and guide their growth. The company may use professional coaching at this stage for some talents. Internal mobility is encouraged – several talents may swap roles or take new positions during this year to broaden their expertise.

In the third year, the program emphasizes career planning and integration. The employees, mentors, and HR review the progress made and map out potential next career steps, whether it's a promotion, a new role, or further specialized training. By this time, many participants are ready to assume greater responsibilities; indeed, if a suitable position opens in this period, a talent program member might be placed in it. The formal program then concludes, often with a closing ceremony or recognition, but those employees continue to be tracked as an elite talent alumni pool. This insurance firm's approach is resource-intensive but yields a deep bench of well-rounded candidates for future leadership. It has been effective in building loyalty – participants often feel a strong commitment to the company after three years of investment in them – and in fostering a culture of continuous learning.

Across these cases, some clear practices stand out that could guide public administration. First, development works best when formal training is paired with real project experience—people need to apply what they learn. Second, giving rising talent exposure to senior leaders and strategic issues helps them see the bigger picture and connect to the mission. Public organizations could do the same by involving younger staff in cross-agency projects or inviting them to present ideas to top officials. Third, expectations must be managed: in these companies, program completion doesn't guarantee promotion. It's about growth, not automatic advancement. This is even more important in the public sector, where fairness and competition are key. In a VUCA world, these approaches help prepare people for uncertainty while keeping the system transparent and merit-based.

Lastly, although not all companies had separate tracks for *successors* vs. *general talent*, it was evident that when someone was identified specifically as the likely successor to a key role, that person's development became more targeted. For example, if a finance manager is slated to succeed the finance director, the company might specifically arrange for them to attend higher-level finance trainings or temporarily cover some of the director's duties. This indicates that while broad talent programs build a pipeline, at the pointy end of succession, tailored preparation is still needed. A lesson for the public sector is that broad leadership programs should be complemented by role-specific grooming for imminent successors (e.g., an assistant director might need certain experiences before taking over a department).

MENTORING AS A WAY OF KNOWLEDGE TRANSFER

Mentoring emerged as a crucial component of talent development in the three organizations we analysed, though the formality and ubiquity of mentoring programs varied. However, mentorship was highly valued in all, highlighting the opportunity to transfer knowledge and share experiences.

The company in insurance sector has a well-structured mentoring program as each participant in the talent program is paired with one or more mentors. Typically, the company provides a roster of managers and executives (including some from outside the immediate business unit or even from the parent company's international network) willing to serve as mentors. Talents are given the opportunity to express preferences or choose mentors that align with their development needs. Once paired, the mentor and mentee meet regularly (approximately monthly). There is a general framework: early meetings might focus on setting development goals and identifying gaps, middle-phase meetings might involve guidance on the mentee's project or challenging assignments, and later meetings could turn to career planning. However, the relationship is largely driven by the mentee's needs – some may seek technical or strategic advice, others may focus on leadership and soft-skill coaching – and is also driven by his initiative. The company's HR provides some oversight (perhaps training for mentors and a check-in to ensure meetings are happening), but it's largely a self-propelled process. This program is highly valued by participants; it not only accelerates their learning by tapping into the mentor's experience, but also serves as a symbolic indicator that the organization is investing in them. Many mentees develop lasting professional relationships with their mentors, who often become advocates for them during succession discussions. The mentoring program also facilitates knowledge transfer across generations and units – in practice, a young talent from the IT department might be mentored by the operations director, thus both technical and managerial know-how are exchanged along with a broader understanding of the business.

In the manufacturing firm, mentoring exists but in a more informal and flexible way. There isn't a single company-wide mandated mentor for each talent, but rather a culture that encourages multiple developmental relationships. Talented employees might have a senior manager as a sponsor or coach by arrangement of HR, or they might form their own mentor-like connections through the course of cross-functional projects. Additionally, the company practices a form of peer mentoring and coaching within the talent pool: they often organize sessions where current talent program members and alumni share experiences, or where those strong in one area tutor others. The company also encourages a norm where employees who have completed the talent program or who are in higher tiers of the 9-box grid informally mentor those in lower tiers. This "pay it forward" mentality creates a supportive network.

So while not formalized as "each person has one assigned mentor," the outcome is that talents have access to advice and guidance from multiple sources. Moreover, because the organization often assigns potential successors as deputies under current leaders (as noted earlier), a natural mentoring occurs between the incumbent and their understudy. For instance, a department head will purposefully teach their deputy how to handle certain responsibilities, involve them in decision-making, and provide feedback – effectively mentoring them on how to step into their shoes. This on-the-job knowledge transfer is crucial in a technical environment to preserve tacit knowledge. It also means that when the actual succession happens, it's less disruptive because the "heir apparent" has already been performing parts of the role under guidance.

The organisation in baking sector does not have a universally applied mentoring program for all talents, making it the most ad hoc in this regard. Mentoring or coaching is offered as one development tool among many, to be used if it fits the individual's development plan. In practice, some talents (or high-potentials) proactively seek out a mentor (sometimes facilitated by HR to find a suitable person), especially if they aspire to a role that someone else currently occupies. For instance, an up-and-coming branch manager might ask for a mentor in the form of a senior executive from headquarters to learn broader management skills. The organisation also has some senior executives who volunteer to coach participants of the leadership academy workshops, though these interactions might be one-off or short-term rather than an ongoing mentorship. Because it's optional, the mentoring experience for talents in the organisation can be uneven—some receive a lot of personal guidance, others may focus more on training or rotations without a dedicated mentor. Recognizing this, they have been considering a more structured mentoring framework to ensure each person in the talent pool has at least an informal advisor. On the succession side, when a specific individual is being groomed quietly for a role, it is common for them to be paired with the current role-holder in a mentorship-like shadowing arrangement. For example, when someone is likely to replace a position in a couple of years, they might shadow the current position holder in key meetings and have regular one-on-one sessions to learn about higher-level decision making.

For the public sector, a formal mentoring program could be a highly effective way to transfer knowledge from veteran civil servants (many of whom will retire soon) to the next generation, as well as to break down silos by pairing people across departments. This matters in VUCA context as it reduced the risk of sudden knowledge loss, it further builds connections across quite compley systems, and even helps younger staff get more prepared for the – possibly – uncertain career paths. The Slovenian cases show that even in a hierarchical environment, mentorship creates bridges and can be done in a way that respects formal structures (e.g., having mentorship not directly in the reporting line to avoid conflicts of interest).

CAREER PATHWAYS: ENGAGED AND RETAINED

A significant challenge in talent management is keeping talented and high-potential employees engaged when promotions are limited. The three companies addressed this by carefully managing career pathways and aligning talent development with actual succession opportunities.

All three organizations explicitly offer dual career ladders: one managerial and one professional. This means a talented individual can progress vertically in management ranks *or* progress as an expert without managing people, achieving senior status (and compensation) in line with their expertise. For example, the firm in banking has grades like Senior Analyst, Principal Analyst, Fellow, etc., for those in specialist roles, parallel to the managerial titles. The manufacturing firm similarly has technical fellows or project leaders as a progression track. This ensures that employees who excel in technical areas but are not inclined to management still see a future for themselves. It's a strategy to retain valuable experts who might otherwise feel forced to go into management or leave to advance their careers. In the public sector, implementing dual tracks (e.g., a "senior civil service" track for managers and a "senior professional" track for specialists like economists, IT professionals, scientists, etc.) can help retain talent by offering prestige and advancement without diluting the management hierarchy. For those on the managerial path, the companies developed clear competency models for each level of leadership and communicated those expectations to talents. This way, employees know what it takes to move from a unit manager to department director to executive. By understanding the required competencies (and with the help of their development programs), they can intentionally build the skills needed for the next level.

However, upward opportunities are not endless, and not every talent can be promoted immediately. To avoid frustration and stagnation, the companies emphasized horizontal moves and enrichment. For instance, the manufacturing company routinely uses job rotations: a talent might move from the production department to a supply chain role, or from domestic operations to an international assignment, for a year or two. This lateral move broadens their skill set and keeps them challenged, even if their job title and level remain the same. Such experiences are considered valuable stepping stones to later promotion – essentially, the person is gathering the breadth required for senior roles. The organisation in banking sector also allows talents to apply for open positions in different divisions as part of their growth, and HR actively facilitates placement when a development opportunity aligns with a vacancy. The company in insurance sector, given its cohort approach, sometimes orchestrates exchanges of personnel among different subsidiaries or departments for a period, so that talents get a feel for different business lines. These horizontal developments serve a dual purpose: they enhance organizational agility (since employees become more versatile and networked across the organization), and they satisfy the individual's need for continuous growth.

The companies also recognized the importance of timing and pacing of careers. If someone is truly exceptional, they may warrant a fast-track promotion to prevent disengagement or poaching by competitors. In the insurance firm's history, there were cases where a talent was promoted two levels upward within a few years – an uncommon acceleration – because they demonstrated capability far beyond their current role and the organization feared losing them if they were held back. Such cases are rare and carefully managed (to avoid perceptions of favoritism), but they show that flexibility exists to reward and retain superstar performers. The bank's approach to this was slightly different: rather than jump a person multiple grades, they give them roles or assignments typically reserved for higher positions (for example, leading a cross-department task force normally led by a more senior manager) as a way to signal trust and provide challenge, which often leads to a promotion soon after when a suitable position opens. This aligns with the concept of "acting" appointments or interim leadership roles, which, if formally acknowledged (as Slovenia's public sector is starting to do), can both test and recognize a high-potential employee's readiness.

Other supporting factors contributing to successful retention of talents and high-potential, mentioned in the interviews were work culture and leadership. Organizational culture – specifically one that values employee well-being and input – was highlighted as a significant retention element. The firm in banking sector, for example, emphasized work-life balance and flexibility, knowing that burnout or incompatibility with personal life can drive even ambitious employees away. They offered options like flexible working hours, remote work arrangements (even before the pandemic normalized this), and programs for mental health and stress management for those in high-pressure roles. The insurance company has a reputation as a "family-friendly" employer (holding a *Družini prijazno podjetje* certification), which means it implements practices like parental leave beyond the statutory minimum, childcare support, and scheduling flexibility – factors that particularly retain mid-career professionals who might otherwise leave due to family pressures. The manufacturing firm, while in a more traditional industry, fostered what they called a "culture of belonging": they organize regular team-building events, celebrate personal and team milestones, and maintain a relatively flat and open communication style for a large company. Talented individuals there often cited the sense of community and loyalty in the company as reasons they stayed even when headhunters came calling with higher pay offers. For public organizations, building a culture of recognition, respect, and work-life balance (to the extent possible in public service roles) can similarly enhance retention, since public-sector salaries often can't compete with private sector headhunting, but culture and mission can be a differentiator.

Furthermore, the interviews highlighted the importance of the quality of leadership. Talented employees are especially sensitive to the quality of their direct supervisors and senior leadership. All three companies recognized that a key predictor of retention was whether the employee felt valued and supported by their boss. In response, they invest in training their managers to be talent developers. The bank explicitly includes in its leadership training how to conduct career conversations and how to coach team members. The manufacturing company holds managers accountable for mentoring and promoting talent from within – for instance, part of a manager's performance review includes how well they have developed their subordinates. The insurance firm's practice of letting talents choose their own mentors also helps circumvent any issues if a direct manager is not as supportive; a mentor can fill some of that developmental support role. Additionally, visible support from top leadership (e.g. the CEO meeting with talents, as they do in the insurance company's program) creates a sense of organizational support at the highest level. When employees see that the organization's leaders genuinely care about their growth, it breeds loyalty.

On the succession alignment side, each company strives to match the pool of talent to forecasted vacancies. The bank and insurance firm have formal reviews (biennial, as noted) where they look at the pipeline: How many of our senior managers are likely to retire or leave in the next few years? Do we have internal candidates ready for each of those projected openings? If not, where are the gaps? They then adjust talent development accordingly – for example, if they know a long-serving IT director will retire in 2 years and none of the current talents have an IT background, they might recruit or develop someone specifically to fill that gap. The manufacturing company's approach is more continuous, but similarly, they keep an eye on key roles and ensure their talent pool and deputies cover all critical areas. In fact, that company tries to have at least 2-3 people as potential successors for every key position, reflecting a very cautious approach to continuity (so that even if one potential successor leaves, another is in line).

A challenge that all these organizations face is what to do if a talent *doesn't* see a near-term career opportunity. For example, if an individual completes the development program but the next level up is occupied by someone who isn't leaving soon, there is a risk of attrition. The retention strategies discussed next come into play here, but one proactive approach is talent pooling across the broader corporate group. The company in insurance field, as part of a larger international group, sometimes facilitates the promotion of a talent into a higher position in a sister company abroad if there's no immediate opening locally. That way, the employee stays within the extended organization, even if they have to move. The manufacturing firm, also part of a global company, uses a similar tactic – their talents might get offers to lead departments at another plant in a different country, leveraging the global network to satisfy career growth. While the public sector might not be able to send civil servants to "other governments" easily, they can consider secondments to international organizations or EU institutions, or temporary assignments in municipalities or other parts of the public sector. In a VUCA world, such mobility is valuable because it broadens skills, builds networks across complex systems, and prepares staff to handle unpredictable challenges when domestic promotion is slow.

SPECIFIC RETENTION STRATEGIES

Importantly, among the three organisations there was a pattern of strategies aimed to retain talent. All three organizations implemented at least annual (if not more frequent) one-on-one meetings focused specifically on the employee's career development and satisfaction. These are beyond the normal performance reviews. In these sessions, the employee can voice aspirations, concerns, or discontent. Managers (and HR in some cases) use this feedback to take action – for example, if a talent feels underutilized, they might be assigned a new project or given a short-term assignment to rekindle engagement. The companies in banking and insurance also track overall employee engagement through surveys, with items that can be filtered to see if high-potentials are less engaged than others, serving as an early warning system.

All of the companies are focusing on recognizing achievements – both big and small – that help talents feel seen and appreciated. The manufacturing firm instituted an awards scheme where exceptional contributions (like a process improvement saving significant cost, or a successful project launch) are publicly recognized in company-wide meetings or newsletters. They also give out awards such as "Mentor of the Year" or "Innovator of the Year," which not only motivate the winners but also signal what the company values. The bank introduced a "Talent of the Year" recognition for one of its high-potential employees who had made outstanding progress or impact; this is announced by the CEO at an annual event. Beyond ego-boosting, these recognitions often come with tangible perks (maybe a bonus, a development grant, or extra vacation days), but even the honor itself boosts morale. In the public sector, formal recognition programs (awards, honors, titles) can similarly enhance morale, as long as they are merit-based.

All three companies stated a policy of prioritizing internal candidates for open positions. In practice, this means that when a management position opens, they actively consider and often fast-track interviews with talent pool members or other insiders before looking outside. The insurance company could point out that in recent years nearly all key vacancies were filled by people from within – a statistic they communicate to employees. The HR policy of the banking company even mandates that for any senior job posting, at least one internal candidate (if available and qualified) must be in the final consideration set. This builds faith among employees that their efforts and loyalty will pay off. It also combats the perception sometimes found in organizations that "you have to leave to get ahead." In the public sector, while open competition is a norm, demonstrating commitment to developing and promoting insiders (when they merit it) can help retain high performers who might otherwise drift to the private sector for career growth.

The companies actively work to create an emotional bond between talents and the organization. One method was increased exposure to the organization's mission and leadership. For example, the manufacturing company's CEO holds informal lunches or roundtables with groups of promising employees, where they can discuss the company's future and their ideas. Participants often come away feeling valued and more emotionally invested in the company's success. In the insurance program, each talent had a brief one-on-one meeting with the President of the company at least once during the program – even a 30-minute personal conversation can strongly reinforce an individual's sense of belonging and importance. The executives in the banking example sponsor certain projects in the talent development scheme, effectively becoming mentors/champions for those project teams; this again ties the employees closer to the top leadership. These personal touches by leaders create loyalty that salary alone cannot buy. High-potentials often mention that they stay because they believe in the vision of a certain leader or they feel they have a voice in the company's direction.

Retaining talent over the long term also means accommodating their life stages. The insurance and banking examples both included flexible arrangements – such as allowing a break for further education, offering part-time or remote options during child-rearing years, or even sabbaticals – to ensure that short-term life choices (like pursuing a master's degree or caring for family) don't permanently alienate an employee. One insurance company talent took an unpaid six-month leave to travel internationally; because the company supported this, the employee returned re-energized and did not leave for another employer as might have happened if forced to choose.

In the table below, we present the core lessons from Slovenian Private-Sector Cases for Public Administration.

Table 1. Core lessons for Public Administration

Private-Sector Practice	Example (Banking, Insurance, Manufacturing)	Adaptation for Public Administration
Designing a narrow talent pool	Clear selection criteria, only top candidates included	Transparent, merit-based civil service criteria; while ensuring all employees get development opportunities, only a few are enabled specialised developments programs
Succession Planning	Primary + backup candidates for key roles	Internal registers of successors, aligned with open competitions
Development Programs	Mix of formal training + projects	Cross-agency initiatives, secondments, leadership academies
Mentoring	Structured (insurance) or informal (manufacturing)	Formal cross-department mentoring to transfer knowledge

COMPARATIVE PERSPECTIVES FROM OTHER PUBLIC SECTORS

While the Slovenian context has its specifics, it is useful to compare how other public-sector systems approach talent management and succession in a VUCA world. A few illustrative examples from international practice include The Netherlands – Centralized Elite Development, United Kingdom – Broad-Based Early Career Talent Intake, and European Commission – Hybrid Talent Management Model.

The Netherlands – Centralized Elite Development: The Dutch national government operates the *Algemene Bestuursdienst (ABD) Kandidatenprogramma*, a centrally managed development program for high-potential civil servants. This roughly 18-month program prepares a select group of talented managers to step into senior director-level positions across the government. It is an exclusive, fast-track initiative, but it maintains fairness through transparent, merit-based selection criteria and a competitive process open to candidates from all ministries. Participants rotate through different departments and receive intensive leadership training and coaching. The cross-ministerial nature of the program ensures that talents gain a broad perspective on government operations and can be deployed to wherever leadership gaps arise. In essence, the Netherlands built a *national talent pool* for the civil service, centrally overseen, which is refreshed regularly to ensure a pipeline for top management. The exclusivity is tempered by the fact that any mid-career civil servant can apply, and selections are made by an independent board, thus managing perceptions of nepotism.

United Kingdom – Broad-Based Early Career Talent Intake: The UK Civil Service Fast Stream is a well-known example of an inclusive talent strategy on the entry-level side. It is a merit-based program for early-career professionals (typically recent graduates or those with a couple of years of work experience) who show leadership potential. Through a rigorous open competition that tests candidates' analytical and interpersonal skills, the Fast Stream annually recruits a sizable cohort (several hundred individuals) into a rotational program. Fast Streamers rotate across various departments and roles over 3–4 years, receiving training, mentorship, and gradual increases in responsibility. The scale and open access of this program reflect an inclusive approach – it brings in diverse talent from outside the civil service, not based on who you know but how you perform in assessments. Within the program, there are specialized streams as well (e.g., finance, digital, diplomatic service), balancing generalist and specialist tracks. The Fast Stream has been credited with injecting new skills and adaptability into the UK civil service, as participants are accustomed to moving between roles and tackling complexity. By opening the gates to a wide pool and then rigorously developing those who get in, the UK ensures a continuous influx of agile talent ready to take on uncertainty and change in government.

European Commission – Hybrid Talent Management Model: The European Commission (EC) as a large public bureaucracy has introduced a mix of exclusive and inclusive talent measures. For high-potentials already inside the organization, the EC runs programs like the *Prospective Managers Programme*, an elite track designed to prepare selected officials for leadership roles in the Commission's departments. This is comparable to an exclusive pool where participants undergo leadership development, coaching, and occasionally job swaps to round out their experience. At the same time, the EC emphasizes continuous learning and development opportunities for all employees, supported by a centralized talent portal where staff can find information on training courses, mobility opportunities, and career guidance. The Commission also leverages data-driven strategic workforce planning: it uses HR analytics to project retirement waves and skill gaps across its many Directorates-General). For example, if analytics indicate that a significant percentage of experts in a particular field will retire within five years, the EC can proactively launch recruitment or upskilling programs in that area, and identify internal staff who could be fast-tracked to fill those impending gaps. By combining a general upskilling culture with targeted succession pipelines and data insights, the EC strives to remain agile. The approach underscores that even in a large, rule-bound public organization, it's possible to forecast and plan for talent needs and to have special programs for the "cream of the crop" without neglecting the development of the broader workforce.

These comparative cases demonstrate that there is no one-size-fits-all model, but successful TM strategies often share key features: transparent criteria and processes, a mix of broad development and focused specialised development opportunities of recognised talents, mobility options to broaden experience (be it rotational programs or cross-sector exchanges), and alignment with strategic goals (using data or foresight to guide talent initiatives). For Slovenia, lessons can be drawn from each: a centrally coordinated high-potential program (like the Dutch ABD) could overcome the fragmentation of ministry-by-ministry approaches; an open and sizable intake program (like the Fast Stream) could attract young talent into public service in an era when government struggles to compete with private sector for the best talents; and adopting a hybrid approach with both broad learning opportunities and focused succession planning (like the EC) could address both inclusivity and the need to fill critical roles in time.

DISCUSSION: TOWARD AN AGILE TALENT MANAGEMENT STRATEGY FOR THE SLOVENIAN PUBLIC SECTOR

The analysis above highlights the potential pathways for strengthening talent management in Slovenia's public sector. The risks of inaction are clear: an aging workforce without successors ready will lead to loss of institutional knowledge, disruptions in service delivery, and possibly a leadership void in critical areas. Furthermore, the inability to attract and retain capable young talents could hamper innovation and adaptability just when government needs them most to navigate volatility and complexity. Conversely, the experiences from private-sector cases and other governments suggest that a proactive talent strategy can turn these challenges into an opportunity – essentially, to use the VUCA context as a push for modernization and improving HR practices.

We further propose a few key recommendations based on the analysis. First, Slovenia should develop a hybrid inclusive-exclusive TM model. The public sector should foster development for all employees (supporting an inclusive culture of continuous learning for all), while also creating strategies to identify and invest in high-potential (and high performance) individuals who are likely to assume greater (leadership or professional) roles. In practice, this could mean introducing a formal high-potential development program within the public sector. Such a program might select a certain number of civil servants from different parts of the public administration who have demonstrated exceptional performance and potential (using objective criteria like performance appraisals and assessments, combined with nominations and interviews). The talent pool would receive advanced training, mentoring, and diverse assignments similar to the programs described in the private sector. To maintain inclusivity and fairness, the selection process must be transparent, merit-based, and open to anyone meeting the criteria. Importantly, offering some flexible development resources to all staff ensures that while a subset gets special training, everyone has the chance to upgrade their skills, and even meet the talent pool criteria later on. This dual approach addresses both equity and effectiveness: it avoids the elitism trap by keeping opportunities broad, yet acknowledges that leadership preparation requires focused effort on a smaller group.

Second, the public sector could institutionalize succession planning with clear, transparent processes. This means taking a systematic approach to key roles—such as department heads, agency directors, and other critical experts—by ensuring knowledge transfer and preparing strong internal candidates in advance, so that suitable people are ready when positions open up. A practical step is to create and regularly update a succession plan registry: identify which positions are likely to be vacated in the next few years (due to retirement or other factors), and list one or more candidates who could potentially fill each, along with an honest assessment of their readiness and what development they would need. This mitigates the risk of having important functions without proper candidates. Once potential successors are identified, the organization can implement development actions for them – for instance, if Jane is a possible successor to a director position in a few years, ensure she gets the necessary management training or rotational experience now.

Third, we advise Slovenian public sector to enhance mobility and cross-sector/interdepartmental exchanges. An agile organization is one where talent can flow to where it's needed. Breaking down silos within the public sector is crucial. Building on the Partnership for Change program, Slovenia could expand mobility schemes such that high-potential civil servants rotate through different public administration offices o reven within the private sector for short stints. Similarly, bringing in individuals from the private sector on exchange (or hiring mid-career entrants) can inject new ideas. The OECD and EU examples underscore mobility as a key tool (the Netherlands program is explicitly cross-government; the Fast Stream has rotations). Internally, Slovenia's public sector could facilitate a "talent rotation program" where every year a cohort of identified talents swap positions across departments or take on special projects in a different agency for a few months. It prepares the organization to better handle complexity because staff understand how different parts of government interconnect.

Furthermore, the public sector could leverage data and foresight in workforce planning. Adopting modern HR analytics in the public sector can vastly improve strategic planning. Slovenia should utilize data on workforce demographics, attrition rates, and competency inventories to anticipate where the next big talent gaps will be. Tools like employee surveys can gauge engagement levels of top performers and signal if retention risk is rising. The government might collaborate with academic experts or international organizations to build capacity for predictive analytics in HR (the European Commission's approach could serve as inspiration). Even simple forecasting of retirements by job category, combined with scenario planning (as was done during the EU presidency project on ageing), can guide the focus of talent programs—ensuring they are training people in the right areas. For a small administration like Slovenia's, a centralized HR information system that tracks these metrics is feasible and would greatly enhance agility by enabling proactive rather than reactive management of human capital.

Fourth, it is vital to embed ethical priciples and meritocracy in all talent practices among public sector as well. For any talent management initiative to be acceptable, it must be perceived as fair, transparent, and based on merit. This is both an ethical imperative and a practical one, because if employees believe a talent program is just a new form of favoritism, it will breed resentment and fail. Slovenia's public administration should therefore establish clear guidelines and oversight for talent identification and succession programs. For example, criteria for high-potential selection might include a combination of performance ratings, competency assessments, and perhaps an interview or assessment center, with representation from multiple officials from public administration in the selection panel to avoid insular biases. Additionally, the design of talent programs should reflect inclusivity and diversity – making sure that they are accessible to women and men equally (noting that women already form a large share of the Slovenian public workforce, including at senior levels, which is a strength to build on), and to minorities or underrepresented groups. Emphasizing ethical considerations also means being mindful of political neutrality: talent management should focus on career civil servants and be insulated from changes in political leadership, to avoid any perception that it's grooming "political favorites."

Crucially, the commitment to talent must come from the top: political leaders and senior civil servants need to champion the idea that developing people is not a luxury, but a necessity for good governance in the 21st century. The VUCA environment, new technology disruptions, and complex policy problems all demand public organizations that can learn and pivot quickly. An agile talent strategy, centered on inclusive development and planned succession, is a foundational element in creating that agility.

Finally, strengthen retention through engagement and recognition by adopting some of the retention tactics from the private sector could greatly benefit the civil service. For instance, implementing a formal mentorship program where younger civil servants are mentored by seasoned ones could increase knowledge transfer and engagement – this could be particularly useful in Slovenia given the ageing workforce (pairing near-retirees with up-and-comers). Another idea is to celebrate successes and contributions of public employees more visibly; civil service awards or honors for innovation, excellent service, or leadership can boost morale and signal appreciation. Where possible, the public sector should also consider non-monetary incentives that matter to employees – flexible work arrangements, opportunities for further education, and ensuring a healthy work environment. Given that public salaries in many public administrations may not match private ones, these qualitative factors become crucial in retaining talent.

It is evident that talent management and succession planning in the public sector require a delicate balance: they must be strategic enough to prepare the organization for future challenges, structured enough to be fair and effective, and yet flexible enough to adapt to changing circumstances and individual needs in the VUCA environment. Slovenia's public administration, by learning from both domestic examples and international best practices, has the opportunity to design a system that fits its size and culture.

CONCLUSION

Agile talent management and structured succession planning are indispensable for building resilient public institutions in a VUCA world. The Slovenian case exemplifies both the pressing need and the latent potential for such strategies in the public sector. On one hand, Slovenia's civil service faces demographic headwinds and legacy HR constraints that, if unaddressed, could undermine its capacity to cope with volatility and complexity. On the other hand, initial reforms and innovative programs – from recognizing acting roles to engaging in cross-sector partnerships – show that change is possible. By leveraging lessons from private-sector successes at home and public-sector innovations abroad, Slovenia can chart a path that adapts global best practices to its own context.

While this chapter has focused on a specific context, the core message resonates broadly. Public administrations that proactively cultivate their human capital and plan for leadership continuity are better positioned to navigate uncertainty, innovate in the face of complexity, and sustain public trust through consistent performance. Agile talent strategies, grounded in meritocratic and inclusive values, thus form a cornerstone of good governance.

REFERENCES

AmCham Slovenia. (2023). Partnership for Change. https://amcham.si/zagovornistvo/partnerstvo-za-spremembe/

Boselie, P., & Thunnissen, M. (2017). Talent management in the public sector: Managing tensions and dualities.

Collings, D. G., & Mellahi, K. (2009). Strategic talent management: A review and research agenda. *Human Resource Management Review, 19*(4), 304–313. DOI: 10.1016/j.hrmr.2009.04.001

Collings, D. G., Mellahi, K., & Cascio, W. F. (2019). Global talent management and performance in multinational enterprises: A multilevel perspective. *Journal of Management, 45*(2), 540–566. DOI: 10.1177/0149206318757018

Dries, N., & Kaše, R. (2023). Do employees find inclusive talent management fairer? It depends. Contrasting self-interest and principle. *Human Resource Management Journal, 33*(3), 702–727. DOI: 10.1111/1748-8583.12501

European Commission. (2023). *Strategic foresight report: Navigating the green and digital transitions.*

Gallardo-Gallardo, E. (2018). The meaning of talent in the world of work. *Global talent management*, 33-58.

Government of the Republic of Slovenia. (2025). Reform of the public sector pay system.

Ingraham, P. W., Selden, S. C., & Moynihan, D. P. (2000). People and performance: Challenges for the future public service—The report from the Wye River Conference. *Public Administration Review, 60*(1), 54–60. DOI: 10.1111/0033-3352.00062

Kozjek, T., & Franca, V. (2020). Talent management in the public sector. *Cent. Eur. Pub. Admin. Rev., 18*, 53.

Kravariti, F., & Johnston, K. (2020). Talent management: A critical literature review and research agenda for public sector human resource management. *Public Management Review, 22*(1), 75–95. DOI: 10.1080/14719037.2019.1638439

Meyers, M. C., van Woerkom, M., Paauwe, J., & Dries, N. (2020). HR managers' talent philosophies: Prevalence and relationships with perceived talent management practices. *International Journal of Human Resource Management, 31*(4), 562–588. DOI: 10.1080/09585192.2019.1579747

OECD. (2021a). *The future of the public service: Developing a public workforce fit for the future.*

OECD. (2021b). *Public Employment and Management 2021: The future of the public service.*

Oliveira, E., Abner, G., Lee, S., Suzuki, K., Hur, H., & Perry, J. L. (2024). What does the evidence tell us about merit principles and government performance? *Public Administration, 102*(2), 668–690. DOI: 10.1111/padm.12945

Pollitt, C., & Bouckaert, G. (2017). *Public management reform: A comparative analysis-into the age of austerity.* Oxford university press.

Poocharoen, O. O., & Lee, C. (2013). Talent management in the public sector: A comparative study of Singapore, Malaysia, and Thailand. *Public Management Review, 15*(8), 1185–1207. DOI: 10.1080/14719037.2013.816525

Rothwell, W. (2010). *Effective succession planning: Ensuring leadership continuity and building talent from within.* Amacom.

Schuler, R. S., Budhwar, P. S., & Florkowski, G. W. (2002). International human resource management: Review and critique. *International Journal of Management Reviews, 4*(1), 41–70. DOI: 10.1111/1468-2370.00076

Shet, S. V. (2024). A VUCA-ready workforce: Exploring employee competencies and learning and development implications. *Personnel Review, 53*(3), 674–703. DOI: 10.1108/PR-10-2023-0873

Sommermann, K. P. (2025). Challenges for the Civil Service. *The Civil Service in Europe: A Research Companion.*

Tansley, C. (2011). What do we mean by the term "talent" in talent management? *Industrial and Commercial Training, 43*(5), 266–274. DOI: 10.1108/00197851111145853

Thunnissen, M., & Gallardo-Gallardo, E. (2017). *Talent management in practice: An integrated and dynamic approach.* Emerald Publishing Limited. DOI: 10.1108/9781787145979

Van der Wal, Z. (2017). *The 21st century public manager.* Palgrave. DOI: 10.1057/978-1-137-50744-0

Vandenabeele, W. (2007). Toward a public administration theory of public service motivation: An institutional approach. *Public Management Review, 9*(4), 545–556. DOI: 10.1080/14719030701726697

Yoon, B. S. (2019). The Role of Civil Service and the Human Resource Management Policies Required for the Government of the Future. In *Public Service Excellence in the 21st Century* (pp. 169–202). Springer Singapore. DOI: 10.1007/978-981-13-3215-9_6

ADDITIONAL READING

Bhatia, R., & Baruah, P. (2020). Exclusive talent management and its consequences: A review of literature. *Asian Journal of Business Ethics, 9*(1), 193–209. DOI: 10.1007/s13520-020-00105-8

Boselie, P., & Thunnissen, M. (2017). Talent management in the public sector. In Collings, D. G., Mellahi, K., & Cascio, W. F. (Eds.), *The Oxford handbook of talent management* (pp. 426–439). Oxford University Press.

Collings, D. G., & Mellahi, K. (2009). Strategic talent management: A review and research agenda. *Human Resource Management Review, 19*(4), 304–313. DOI: 10.1016/j.hrmr.2009.04.001

Collings, D. G., Mellahi, K., & Cascio, W. F. (Eds.). (2017). *The Oxford handbook of talent management.* Oxford University Press. DOI: 10.1093/oxfordhb/9780198758273.001.0001

Collings, D. G., Mellahi, K., & Cascio, W. F. (2019). Global talent management and performance in multinational enterprises: A multilevel perspective. *Journal of Management, 45*(2), 540–566. DOI: 10.1177/0149206318757018

Dillon, R., Klier, J., McConnell, M., & Vandamme, C. (2024, March 21). Shaping tomorrow's talent agenda for the public sector. McKinsey & Company. https://www.mckinsey.com/industries/public-and-social-sector/our-insights/shaping-tomorrows-talent-agenda-for-the-public-sector

Garman, A. N., & Glawe, J. (2004). Succession planning. *Consulting Psychology Journal, 56*(2), 119–128. DOI: 10.1037/1061-4087.56.2.119 PMID: 15524307

Kravariti, F., & Johnston, K. (2020). Talent management: A critical literature review and research agenda for public sector human resource management. *Public Management Review, 22*(1), 75–95. DOI: 10.1080/14719037.2019.1638439

OECD. (2021a). *Public Employment and Management 2021: The Future of the Public Service.* OECD Publishing., DOI: 10.1787/938f0d65-

OECD. (2021b). *Ageing and Talent Management in European Public Administrations*. OECD Publishing.

Vardi, S., & Collings, D. G. (2023). Whats in a name? talent: A review and research agenda. *Human Resource Management Journal*, *33*(3), 660–682. DOI: 10.1111/1748-8583.12500

KEY TERMS AND DEFINITIONS

Agile Talent Management: A flexible, responsive approach to managing people that allows public organizations to adapt quickly to change, often characterized by decentralized decisions, iterative development, and rapid learning cycles.

Dual Career Ladder: A talent development structure that allows professionals to advance in their careers either through leadership roles or through expert/specialist tracks, supporting both managerial and non-managerial growth.

Exclusive Talent Management: A talent strategy that focuses on a small group of high-potential individuals deemed essential for future leadership or specialized roles.

Inclusive Talent Management: A model that seeks to identify and support the development of talent across all levels of the organization, not just among high performers or leaders.

Public Sector Innovation: The development and implementation of new ideas, practices, or structures in government and public services, aimed at improving outcomes and adaptability.

Succession Planning: The strategic process of identifying and developing internal staff to fill key leadership positions in the future, ensuring continuity of leadership and institutional knowledge.

Talent Pool: A group of people an organisation has recognised as having a potential to take on more resposibility in the future. Though not promised a promotion, these employees are seen as worth developing.

VUCA: An acronym for volatility, uncertainty, complexity, and ambiguity — used to describe unpredictable and rapidly changing environments, especially in public governance.

Chapter 2
Navigating the Transformation Tide:
Talent Retention During Organizational Transformations

Ankur Kushwaha
http://orcid.org/0000-0003-4829-0038
FLAME University, India

EXECUTIVE SUMMARY

This chapter presents a contextualized case study examining how a major development bank (referred to as Meridian Bank Limited) confronted a human resource crisis during its historic transition from a government-owned public sector bank to a privately managed financial institution. Set against the turbulent macroeconomic and regulatory landscape of the banking sector in an emerging economy between 2015 and 2019, the case explores the twin challenges of rising employee attrition and the urgent need to redesign compensation structures to remain competitive. The chapter further highlights how employee identity and expectations were deeply rooted in public sector values, complicating efforts to retain critical talent during organizational transformation. The case concludes with discussion questions that encourage readers to analyze the situation through lenses such as psychological contracts, compensation strategy, change management, and leadership in VUCA (Volatile, Uncertain, Complex, Ambiguous) environments.

INTRODUCTION

The global business environment of the twenty-first century is characterized by volatility, uncertainty, complexity, and ambiguity (VUCA). VUCA is first coined

DOI: 10.4018/979-8-3373-5776-8.ch002

by the United States Army War College in the late 1980s and subsequently adopted widely by management scholars and practitioners (Baran & Woznyj, 2020; Bennett & Lemoine, 2014; Lawrence, 2013). Within such environments, talent management becomes at once more vital and more difficult (Baran & Woznyj, 2020; Shet, 2024). Talent management is defined as systematic attraction, identification, development, engagement, retention, and deployment of people with high potential (Collings & Mellahi, 2009; Vaiman, Scullion & Collings, 2012).

In contemporary times, the VUCA conditions can also be illustrated in the transformation of state-owned enterprises into privately managed corporations. Such transitions disrupt longstanding psychological contracts between employer and employee, alter organizational identity, and fundamentally reshape the competitive landscape for talent (Rousseau, 1989; Baruch, Y., & Rousseau, 2019; Singh, 2000). For employees accustomed to the security, social prestige, and structured career ladders of public sector employment, privatization may register not merely as an administrative change but as a fundamental rupture in their life plans and professional identities.

This chapter presents the case of Meridian Bank Limited (a fictitious bank name created solely for educational purposes), a case inspired by real-world events, which found itself at a critical crossroads in early 2019. As the Government of India prepared to reclassify Meridian from a public sector bank to a private sector bank following the transfer of majority ownership to a large insurance conglomerate, its Chief Executive Officer and Human Resource leadership faced an urgent question: could the bank redesign its compensation architecture quickly enough to prevent an exodus of its most productive junior-to-middle management talent?

The case is particularly instructive because it explores the intersection of several tensions that recur across developing economies: between job security and market competitiveness; between institutional identity and financial sustainability; between the inertia of bureaucratic legacy systems and the agility required to compete with modern private banks. It also brings to light how VUCA conditions, specifically the uncertainty generated by pending privatization, can operate as a talent risk multiplier, accelerating voluntary attrition even before formal structural changes have taken effect.

The chapter is structured as follows. The next section provides an overview of the Indian banking sector as context. Then, the chapter introduces Meridian Bank and its financial trajectory and profiles the key decision-maker, Mr. Arjun Mehta, CEO of Meridian Bank. Then, it describes the organization's workforce and the HR challenges it faces. After that, it presents the exhibits and analytical frameworks relevant to the compensation dilemma. Then, the chapter offers a theoretical discussion situating the case within contemporary HRM and talent management literature. Finally, it presents pedagogical discussion questions and conclusions.

THE INDIAN BANKING SECTOR: STRUCTURE, SIGNIFICANCE, AND STRESS IN A VUCA WORLD

In any economy, banks play a fundamental role as intermediaries between those who save and those who borrow, facilitating payments and promoting productive investments. Due to the government's long-standing goal of using financial institutions as instruments for socioeconomic development, the banking sector in India is given special strategic importance (Mohan, 2005; Reddy, 2006; Suresh & Paul, 2014). As a result, Indian banks operate under the close regulatory supervision of the country's central bank, which exercises broad authority over licensing, capital adequacy, asset quality, and governance, closely monitors Indian banks. To fully understand the magnitude of the transformation challenges examined in this case study, it is necessary to understand the Indian banking sector not merely as an economic structure, but as a complex and historically embedded institution navigating an environment that is characterized by Volatility, Uncertainty, Complexity, and Ambiguity (VUCA).

The concept of VUCA, originally formulated within military strategic planning (Bennett & Lemoine, 2014), has been widely adopted in organizational and management scholarship to describe the character of contemporary operating environments (Baran & Woznyj, 2020). The Indian banking sector captures a set of structural and cyclical forces that have fundamentally altered the terrain upon which banking institutions compete, survive, and transform (Kamath et al., 2003; Sharma, 2008).

Volatility in the Indian banking sector is most visibly expressed through the dramatic fluctuations in asset quality that have characterized the industry over the past two decades. The rapid expansion of credit in the aftermath of India's high-growth phase in the mid-2000s was followed by an equally rapid deterioration in loan portfolios when growth decelerated, commodity cycles turned, and infrastructure projects stalled. Non-Performing Assets (NPAs) - loans where borrowers had defaulted or were seriously delinquent - surged to crisis proportions, exposing the extent to which credit growth had outpaced credit discipline (Arrawatia, 2019; Mohan & Ray, 2018). The sheer speed and scale of this deterioration was itself a form of volatility: the conditions that had made lending appear safe and productive in one period transformed, within a relatively short span, into conditions that threatened the solvency of several major institutions. For the workforce of affected banks, this volatility translated into an immediate and viscerally experienced sense of occupational precariousness. Employees who had joined banking institutions under conditions of apparent stability found themselves confronting a suddenly unstable future (Singh & Gupta, 2019) as prompt corrective action includes various strategic, operational, and human resource related measures (Reserve Bank of India, 2017).

Uncertainty pervades the strategic environment of Indian banking in ways that are especially disorienting for institutions accustomed to operating within predictable regulatory and ownership frameworks. The announcement that certain public sector banks would be considered for privatization introduced a profound and irreducible uncertainty in the working lives of their employees (Gupta & Panagariya, 2023). Employees of the Meridian Bank did not merely face the risk that their employment conditions might change; they confronted an uncertainty about what their institution would become, who would own it, which norms would govern it, and whether the social contract that had defined their working lives would survive. This uncertainty was compounded by the ambiguous and often contradictory signals emanating from political, regulatory, and media sources. Announcements were made and then qualified; timelines were set and then revised; assurances were offered and then hedged. For a workforce accustomed to the slow, consensual rhythms of public sector governance, this epistemic instability was itself a source of considerable psychological stress.

Complexity characterizes the Indian banking sector at multiple levels. At the macro level, Indian banks operate within an elaborate ecosystem that includes the central bank's regulatory architecture, the government's developmental mandates, capital markets, international financial institutions, and a vast and heterogeneous borrower base that ranges from large infrastructure conglomerates to small and marginal agricultural borrowers. Managing this ecosystem requires navigating a dense web of interdependencies in which changes in one domain produce cascading effects across others. At the institutional level, public sector banks are themselves complex organizations: their workforces are large, geographically dispersed, and segmented by cadre, seniority, and union affiliation; their operations span retail banking, corporate lending, government business, and financial inclusion programmes; and their governance structures reflect the competing demands of multiple stakeholders (government shareholders, independent directors, the central bank, and elected political representatives). The decision to privatize Meridian Bank introduced a further layer of complexity, transforming what was already a multi-stakeholder institution into an entity whose ownership, governance, and operational priorities were simultaneously in flux.

Ambiguity is perhaps the most psychologically consequential for the individuals whose stories animate this case. Ambiguity arises not merely from insufficient information but from the difficulty of interpreting the meaning and implications of information that is available. For Meridian Bank's employees, the privatization announcement was saturated with ambiguity. What would privatization mean for their job security? Would the new private owner honor existing service conditions, or would the institution's transformation provide cover for restructuring, retrenchment, or the erosion of hard-won benefits? Would their years of accumulated seniority retain any value in a private-sector culture that prizes performance over tenure? Would the informal networks, institutional knowledge, and community standing they had built within the public sector ecosystem transfer to a privately owned successor? These questions admitted no easy answers, and the absence of clear answers was itself a form of suffering for a workforce whose occupational identity had been built on the assumption of predictability and permanence.

Structure and Strategic Significance of the Indian Banking Sector

The Indian banking sector is one of the largest and most structurally complex in the world, comprising public sector banks, private sector banks, foreign banks, regional rural banks, cooperative banks, and a growing ecosystem of payment banks and small finance banks. Public sector banks (government holds a majority stake) have historically dominated the sector in terms of assets, branch networks, and workforce. This dominance is not accidental; it reflects a deliberate policy orientation that dates to the nationalization of major commercial banks in 1969 and 1980, decisions that were explicitly framed as instruments of redistributive economic policy and financial democratization (Mohan, 2005; Panagariya, 2010).

The strategic significance of the banking sector to the Indian state extends well beyond its function as a financial intermediary. Banks have served as primary conduits for government-directed lending to priority sectors (agriculture, small enterprises, affordable housing) and as implementation vehicles for flagship financial inclusion initiatives (Reserve Bank of India, 2026). Public sector banks have provided banking services to rural and semi-urban populations that private banks found difficult to serve. Public sector banks have financed infrastructure and industrial development in line with national planning priorities. And they have served, in periods of financial stress, as stabilizing anchors for the broader economy, absorbing shocks that might otherwise have propagated through the financial system with greater destructive force. This multi-dimensional strategic role has conferred upon Indian public sector banks a significance that is political, developmental, and symbolic, in addition to purely financial (Reddy, 2006).

The workforce implications of this strategic significance are profound. Unions representing bank employees are among the most organized, and they have historically played a central role in shaping the terms of employment, the pace of technological adoption, and the scope of any restructuring initiatives (Unnikrishnan, 2022).Thus, the prospect of privatization thus immediately activates a complex and politically charged ecosystem of stakeholders whose interests and anxieties are not easily accommodated within the logic of financial optimization.

The NPA Crisis and the Imperative for Transformation

The precipitating context for the transformation examined in this case study is the NPA crisis that engulfed large segments of the Indian public sector banking system in the decade following the global financial crisis of 2008 (Ramakrishna, Ramulu & Kumar, 2016). The origins of the crisis are multiple such as cyclical factors include the role of macroeconomic deceleration, commodity price collapses, and the stalling of large infrastructure projects that had been financed on assumptions of sustained high growth (Paul, 2018).

Increased regulatory transparency, mandated by the central bank through a rigorous asset quality review, compelled banks to recognize and disclose the full extent of their impaired loan portfolios. The results were, in many cases, startling. Institutions that had presented healthy balance sheets to investors and the public were revealed to carry NPA ratios far above the levels compatible with long-term financial sustainability. The mandatory recognition of these assets eroded capital buffers, constrained lending capacity, triggered credit rating downgrades, and, in the most severe cases, raised fundamental questions about institutional viability.

For the employees of affected banks, the NPA crisis was experienced not as an abstract financial statistic but as a lived reality that manifested in everyday institutional dysfunction: inadequate resources for operations, deteriorating workplace infrastructure, suspension of non-mandatory welfare schemes, and a pervasive atmosphere of reputational stigma as the institutions they worked for became associated, in public discourse, with financial mismanagement and governmental failure. The VUCA dimensions of the crisis were all acutely present: volatility in the bank's financial and operational condition; uncertainty about its strategic future; complexity in the multiple and competing diagnoses of and prescriptions for its problems; and ambiguity about what the crisis meant for the individual fates of the men and women who constituted its workforce.

Privatization and the Social Meaning of Public Sector Employment

The NPA crisis catalyzed the government's decision to accelerate the privatization of the weakest public sector banks, with Meridian Bank identified as a candidate for early divestiture. To understand why this announcement produced responses in the workforce that went far beyond the merely contractual, it is necessary to appreciate the distinctive social meaning of public sector bank employment in the Indian context.

Historically, a position in a public sector bank had been among the most coveted forms of employment in India. The combination of formal job security with generous loan concessions at subsidized interest rates, housing allowances, medical benefits, and assured pension entitlements conferred a social status that private sector employment, however better remunerated, could not easily replicate. Selection through competitive public examinations was seen as an achievement that conferred lifetime legitimacy and social respectability in Indian middle-class circles. A bank officer's appointment was not merely a job offer; it was an entry into a social category (the government job) that carried with it a set of expectations about security, dignity, and social standing that extended well beyond the workplace into family life, marriage markets, and community networks.

The gendered dimensions of this social meaning are also significant. For many women employees, particularly from middle-class families in smaller towns and cities, a public sector bank appointment represented a hard-won form of economic independence and social mobility, secured within a framework of institutional protections (such as against arbitrary dismissal, harassment, and discrimination) that private sector employment was not perceived to reliably offer. The threat of privatization thus carried a specifically gendered dimension of vulnerability, raising fears not only about job security but about the erosion of the institutional norms and protections that had made formal employment meaningful and manageable within the specific social context of Indian middle-class womanhood.

The announcement that Meridian Bank would be privatized thus struck at something far deeper than contractual employment terms. It threatened the social identity and symbolic capital of an entire workforce – a workforce whose sense of self, family standing, and community position had been, in many cases, constructed around the fact and meaning of public sector bank employment. This is the human terrain upon which the talent retention challenge examined in this case study must be understood: not as a problem of compensation benchmarking or benefits rationalization, but as a crisis of identity, belonging, and meaning in an environment that had become, in every sense of the VUCA framework, profoundly and disorient unstable.

A VUCA Lens for Understanding Organizational Transformation

The Indian banking sector's turbulent trajectory over the past two decades offers a compelling and instructive case for the application of VUCA theory to the study of organizational transformation and talent retention. The volatility of asset quality cycles, the uncertainty of privatization outcomes, the complexity of multi-stakeholder governance, and the ambiguity of what institutional transformation means for the individuals who inhabit affected organizations – all of these dimensions are present, in acute and vivid form, in the story of Meridian Bank. Understanding the sector through this lens is not merely an analytical exercise; it is a prerequisite for any serious engagement with the human dimensions of transformation: fear, aspirations, resistance, and resilience of the workforce whose responses to change will ultimately determine whether any organizational transformation succeeds or fails.

MERIDIAN BANK LIMITED: HISTORY, EVOLUTION, AND FINANCIAL CRISIS

Meridian Bank Limited traces its origins to the early 1960s, when the government constituted it as a Development Financial Institution (DFI) under dedicated legislation, with the mandate to provide long-term credit to the country's nascent industrial sector. For nearly four decades, it discharged this development finance mandate, channeling capital to infrastructure, heavy industry, and strategic manufacturing. In 2000s, in recognition of the changing economic landscape and the need for broader financial intermediation, Meridian was transformed from a DFI into a full-fledged commercial bank, licensed by the central bank to accept retail deposits and offer the complete spectrum of banking services.

Subsequent years saw the bank expand its reach significantly. The amalgamation of a smaller private sector bank in 2006, followed by rebranding and the merger of two wholly owned subsidiaries in 2011, established Meridian as a universal bank serving millions of retail and corporate customers across India. By 2019, Meridian operated a national branch network, offered capital market and investment banking services through subsidiaries, and marketed itself on its commitment to customer convenience through digital transformation.

Yet the bank's financial position had become deeply troubling. From FY2015, when the government first signaled its intention to dilute its shareholding, Meridian's gross NPAs had ballooned from INR 12,684 crore (approximately 4.9% of assets) to INR 55,588 crore (27.47% of assets) by FY2018. The bank reported losses in each of the three consecutive financial years from FY2016 to FY2018, with net losses escalating from INR 3,591 crore in FY2016 to INR 8,132 crore in FY2018. This sustained loss-making triggered Prompt Corrective Action (PCA) framework, which restricted the bank from opening new branches and imposed limitations on executive perquisites, further constraining its competitive positioning.

The financial deterioration was the proximate cause of the government's decision to divest its controlling stake in Meridian to the private entities. Under the terms finalized in early 2019, private entities acquired a 51% equity stake in Meridian, making it the controlling shareholder and triggering the bank's reclassification from a public sector bank to a private sector bank- a consequential change with far-reaching implications for its employees, customers, and competitive strategy.

Table 1. Meridian Bank Limited (Selected Financial Data)

Balance Sheet Item (INR Crore)	Mar-2016	Mar-2017	Mar-2018
Share Capital	1,604	2,059	2,059
Reserves & Surplus	22,771	26,000	21,204
Borrowings	3,21,355	3,35,679	3,24,580
Other Liabilities	10,314	11,537	14,646
Total Liabilities	3,56,044	3,75,275	3,62,488
Fixed Assets	3,026	7,041	6,893
Investments	97,347	92,810	93,075
Other Assets	2,55,617	2,74,943	2,61,980
Total Assets	3,56,044	3,75,275	3,62,488

Table 2.

Profit & Loss (INR Crore)	Mar-2015	Mar-2016	Mar-2017	Mar-2018
Profit Before Tax	1,401	-4,912	-8,498	-8,157
Net Profit / (Loss)	942	-3,591	-5,016	-8,132
EPS (INR)	5.87	-17.44	-24.36	-26.37
Gross NPA (INR Crore)	12,684	24,875	44,752	55,588
Gross NPA (%)	4.9%	11%	21%	27.47%

Table 3.

Shareholding (%)	Mar-2018	Jun-2018	Sep-2018	Dec-2018	Mar-2019 (Proposed)
Government of India	80.96	85.96	85.96	52.02	46.46
Non-government (private) entities	10.82	7.98	7.98	44.31	51.00
Foreign Institutional Investors (FIIs)	1.71	0.97	1.04	0.66	0.10
Domestic Institutional Investor (DIIs)	12.15	8.88	8.98	44.74	0.27
Public	5.17	4.19	4.02	2.58	2.17

Mr. Arjun Mehta: CEO of Meridian Bank

In 2018, the government appointed Mr. Arjun Mehta as the new Managing Director and CEO of Meridian Bank, charged with the specific mandate of managing the bank's transition from its public sector identity to a competitive private sector institution. Mehta brought to the role over three decades of diverse banking experience. He had commenced his career with the Commercial Bank in 1980s, rising steadily through its retail and corporate banking divisions before taking his first chief executive role at a leading Development Bank in 2013. During his two-year tenure there, he had led a successful capital raise of INR 400 crore through rights issues, restored the bank's capital adequacy ratio to 14.6%, and introduced a performance management culture that measurably improved productivity.

From 2015 to 2018, Mehta served at another leading Bank, where he demonstrated particular skill in organizational restructuring. He oversaw the transition from a three-tier to a four-tier organizational model (head office, 21 circles, 118 regional offices, and over 5,800 branches) and initiated a significant digital transformation program. Critically, he had navigated these changes while maintaining workforce morale and managing the political sensitivities inherent in restructuring a large public sector institution. His appointment to Meridian was thus a deliberate signal of the government's seriousness about managed transformation rather than disruptive privatization.

Mehta was a realist about the magnitude of the challenge facing Meridian's HR function. On the foggy morning of January 5, 2019, as his flight from the Delhi international airport to Mumbai was delayed by dense winter fog, he telephoned the bank's Executive Director of Human Resources, Ms. Priya Krishnaswamy, to discuss the proposed compensation revisions scheduled for that evening's board meeting. He knew that the meeting would need to resolve two interconnected questions: whether to revise the existing compensation structure, and whether compensation revision alone would be sufficient to stem the accelerating tide of voluntary attrition.

MERIDIAN BANK'S WORKFORCE: IDENTITY, ENTRY PATHWAYS, AND ATTRITION

Organizational Structure and Entry Pathways

Meridian Bank's workforce is organized along hierarchical lines typical of Indian commercial banks. The entry-level managerial grade is Assistant Manager - a role requiring completion of a recognized bachelor's degree from a recognized university. Two primary pathways lead to this position. The first is through the centralized recruitment body that administers common written examinations and interviews for all participating public sector banks. Successful candidates are allocated to public sector banks based on merit and stated preference.

The second pathway is through Meridian's own Banking and Finance Programme, conducted in partnership with a reputed management institution. Candidates who pass a written test and interview are admitted to a postgraduate diploma programme in Banking and Finance; upon successful completion, they are inducted directly into Meridian as Assistant Managers. Additionally, Meridian hires Executives on fixed-term contracts for three years, with performance reviewed quarterly. Upon satisfactory completion of the contract, Executives may opt to continue as permanent Assistant Managers. Progression to higher grades is governed by an internal promotion process comprising written examination and interview, ensuring that seniority does not automatically translate into advancement.

The Symbolic Value of Public Sector Employment

To understand the depth of the attrition challenge facing Meridian, it is essential to appreciate the particular social meaning that public sector bank employment carries in India. Securing a position in a nationalized bank has historically been treated as a life-defining achievement, a marker of educational excellence, social respectability, and financial prudence. The 'iron rice bowl' metaphor, borrowed from East Asian contexts, applies with particular force: PSB employment conferred what employees experienced as permanent security, with dismissal practically impossible except for gross misconduct.

Beyond security, PSB employees historically enjoyed substantial non-pecuniary benefits: subsidized housing loans, medical schemes, educational allowances for children, and post-retirement pension entitlements. These benefits were not merely financial supplements; they were symbols of institutional belonging and social standing. Parents who had invested years of coaching fees and examination preparation in helping their children secure a PSB position regarded privatization as a betrayal of an implicit social contract.

The Emerging Attrition Crisis

Beginning in 2016, when the government's privatization intentions became public knowledge, Meridian experienced a marked increase in voluntary attrition at the Assistant Manager level. This phenomenon was counter-intuitive from one perspective: the bank had not reduced salaries, altered leave entitlements, or made any formal changes to employment conditions. Yet talented junior managers began leaving in increasing numbers, pursuing positions at larger, more stable public sector banks through the recruitment process, or accepting offers from private sector competitors.

The attrition pattern revealed several notable features. First, it was concentrated among Assistant Managers with three to five years of experience, precisely the cohort that represented the bank's most valuable investment in human capital development. Second, it included individuals who had previously expressed strong organizational commitment. Third, the attrition accelerated even as government and bank issued public statements reassuring employees that privatization would not lead to retrenchment, pay cuts, or loss of benefits. The gap between official reassurance and employee behavior suggests that the psychological contract had been disrupted at a level that rational argument alone could not address.

Two employee voices from this period capture the prevailing sentiment with particular clarity. When asked about working conditions under privatization, a senior officer at Meridian, articulated the collective anxiety thus:

"What we are asking for is not merely a pay revision. We need a binding commitment - in writing - that every existing service condition, every welfare measure, every benefit we currently enjoy will be protected until each one of us retires. The moment the word 'private' enters the picture, the public stops trusting us as their bank, and we stop trusting the institution as our home."

A junior Assistant Manager with four years of service expressed a different but equally illuminating frustration:

"I cleared one of the toughest examinations in the country to get here. I came here for the security, the respect, and the sense of purpose. I am willing to work twelve-hour days, I am willing to grow this bank's business, I am willing to transform alongside it - but I cannot accept that what was promised to me is simply being taken away without my consent."

These voices reflect what Rousseau (1989) describes as the violation of relational psychological contracts, the sense that an employer has unilaterally rescinded commitments that were understood to be binding, regardless of whether they were ever formally written. The consequences of such violations, reduced trust, organizational disengagement, and eventually exit, are well-documented in the management literature (Morrison & Robinson, 1997; Conway & Briner, 2005).

The Strategic Response: Compensation Redesign

Confronted with this escalating attrition problem, Mr. Mehta tasked Ms. Krishnaswamy's HR team with a threefold mandate: first, to benchmark Meridian's compensation structure against comparable positions at leading private sector banks; second, to design a revised compensation package that would be competitive with private sector alternatives without wholly abandoning the characteristics that public sector employees valued; and third, to present this revised structure to the Board of Directors at the January 5, 2019 evening meeting for decision.

The HR team selected four leading private sector banks as benchmark comparators. The benchmark focused specifically on the grade equivalent to Meridian's Assistant Manager with three years of post-joining experience, as this was the modal profile of the employees being lost. The benchmarking exercise yielded the compensation data shown in Exhibit 2.

Table 2. Benchmark Compensation at Major Private Sector Banks (Monthly, INR) for a position equivalent to Meridian Assistant Manager with three years of experience

Compensation Component	Monthly Amount (INR)
Basic Salary	15,750
Fixed Retirement Benefit (non-taxable)	4,000
Allowances (partial taxable)	20,650
Minimum Variable Pay	26,557
Variable Retirement Benefit (non-taxable)	3,000
Total Cost to Company (Monthly)	69,957

Several structural features of the private sector benchmark merit comment. The elimination of 'Grade Pay' (a component inherited from government salary architecture) reflects the private sector's preference for simplified, performance-sensitive pay structures. The higher weight assigned to variable pay creates a stronger performance incentive, consistent with private sector management philosophy. Allowances are structured so that a portion (50%) is taxable, reducing the bank's cost while maintaining headline attractiveness. The total cost to company of INR 69,957 per month is notably higher than Meridian's current outlay.

Working from this benchmark, the HR team constructed a revised compensation proposal for Meridian, shown in Exhibit 3. The design attempted to thread the needle between private sector competitiveness and the retention of structural features (the fixed retirement benefit) that public sector employees associated with long-term security.

Table 3. Existing vs. Proposed Monthly Compensation - Meridian Bank Assistant Manager (3 Years' Experience)

Component	Existing (INR)	Proposed (INR)	Change
Basic Salary	18,400	29,580	+60.8%
Grade Pay	2,425	—	Eliminated (not applicable to private entities)
Fixed Retirement Benefit (non-taxable)	3,680	6,278	+70.6%
Conveyance Allowance	10,016	4,221	Restructured
Minimum Variable Pay	22,051	20,557	-6.8%
Variable Retirement Benefit (non-taxable)	4,410	3,816	-13.5%
Total CTC (Monthly)	60,982	64,452	+5.7%

The proposed package embeds several deliberate design choices. The significant increase in basic salary (+60.8%) serves a dual purpose: it raises the headline salary figure that employees most often quote in social and professional conversations, and it increases the base on which provident fund contributions and gratuity calculations are made. The elimination of Grade Pay mirrors the private sector structure and signals the bank's move away from bureaucratic compensation architecture. The substantial increase in Fixed Retirement Benefit (+70.6%) is designed to address the retirement security anxiety that is particularly acute among employees facing privatization. Conversely, the modest reductions in Variable Pay and Variable Retirement Benefit reflect the fiscal constraints imposed by the bank's PCA status and the need to manage the overall cost increase within acceptable limits.

The net result is a total monthly cost to company of INR 64,452 under the proposed structure, approximately 5.7% higher than the current INR 60,982, but still approximately 8% below the private sector benchmark of INR 69,957. The gap relative to competitors is a deliberate calibration, premised on the assumption that Meridian's restructured compensation, combined with a still-present institutional identity and greater job security than pure private sector competitors, will be sufficiently attractive to reduce attrition without incurring unmanageable costs given the bank's financial position.

THE BOARD MEETING DILEMMA: ANALYSIS AND EVALUATION

Will Compensation Revision Alone Reduce Attrition?

The central question before Meridian's board on January 5, 2019 is not simply whether to approve the proposed compensation revision, but whether that revision will be sufficient to address the attrition problem. The evidence suggests a nuanced answer.

On the positive side, the proposed compensation restructuring addresses the most visible and quantifiable source of competitive disadvantage. The significant increase in basic salary improves both take-home pay and the statutory retirement benefits that accrue to it. The elevated Fixed Retirement Benefit directly addresses the retirement security anxiety that distinguishes the concerns of Meridian's public-sector-socialized workforce from those of typical private sector employees. The total compensation, while still below the private sector benchmark, is positioned closer to the market rate than the existing structure.

On the negative side, the literature on psychological contract violation makes clear that relational breaches cannot be remedied purely through transactional adjustments (Morrison & Robinson, 1997). Employees who have experienced a sense of betrayal may not respond to compensation improvements in the manner a purely economic rational model would predict. Moreover, the approximately 8% gap that still exists between Meridian's proposed compensation and the private sector benchmark will remain a standing invitation for competitor recruitment, particularly as private banks intensify their hiring to support their own expansion.

Several additional talent retention levers warrant consideration by the board. First, career development and clarity: employees need to understand how promotion timelines, opportunities, and criteria will change or be preserved under private sector ownership. Ambiguity about career trajectories is itself a VUCA stressor that can precipitate exit even in the absence of immediate compensation concerns. Second, symbolic commitments: formal, written Memoranda of Understanding guaranteeing preservation of key service conditions for existing employees, as demanded by union representatives, may address relational contract concerns more effectively than any compensation revision. Third, cultural transformation management: employees need to be actively enrolled in the organization's change narrative. Transformation programmes that engage employees as co-creators of the bank's future private sector identity, rather than recipients of a change imposed upon them, have been shown to improve engagement and reduce attrition during transitions (Kotter, 1996; Armenakis & Bedeian, 1999).

The Broader Competitive Landscape

A further strategic consideration for the board is the competitive dynamic in which Meridian's talent challenge is situated. The privatization of Meridian does not merely alter the bank's own employment brand; it changes the competitive landscape for talent within the Indian banking sector more broadly. The leading private banks (Meridian's new direct competitors as a private sector bank) now face a situation where a bank previously insulated from the private talent market is actively recruiting and seeking to retain talent at market rates. For these competitors, Meridian's talent pool (experienced relationship managers, credit analysts, and operations specialists) becomes an attractive acquisition target.

Simultaneously, Meridian must now compete for fresh talent recruits from business schools and professional training programs with these established private banks, which enjoy stronger employer brands, more sophisticated performance cultures, and clearer career progression narratives. The talent attraction challenge will thus compound the retention challenge over the medium term, unless Meridian invests deliberately in its employment brand as a newly private institution with a compelling transformation story.

In this respect, the board meeting of January 5, 2019, must be understood not merely as a compensation decision but as a strategic inflection point at which Meridian's leadership must signal to its own employees, to the broader talent market, and to its regulatory stakeholders about the character of the institution it intends to become.

THEORETICAL FRAMEWORKS FOR ANALYSIS

Understanding the talent retention crisis at Meridian Bank can be understood using various theoretical lenses which can explain the multiple and interacting forces that shaped employee attitudes, behavior, and decisions during the privatization process. This section develops five complementary theoretical frameworks: VUCA and talent management theory, psychological contract theory, resource-based view and human capital theory, institutional theory, and transition and change management theory. Each of these theoretical lenses contributes a distinct and necessary tool to the analysis.

VUCA and Talent Management

The VUCA framework provides the wider contextual lens through which Meridian's talent challenge can be understood. Originally developed within military strategic doctrine at the United States Army War College in the aftermath of the Cold War, the concept was subsequently imported into management scholarship to characterize the volatile, uncertain, complex, and ambiguous conditions of contemporary organizational environments (Horney, Pasmore, & O'Shea, 2010). Bennett and Lemoine (2014) refined the framework for strategic application, arguing that effective responses to VUCA conditions must be carefully tailored to the specific combination of dimensions present in a given situation, since each dimension calls for a qualitatively different managerial response. Volatility demands agility and resource reserves; uncertainty calls for investment in information and intelligence; complexity requires the cultivation of specialized expertise and collaborative problem-solving; and ambiguity necessitates experimentation and tolerance for multiple interpretations.

In Meridian's case, the dominant VUCA dimension is uncertainty. Employees do not know what their future employment conditions will look like, and even well-intentioned reassurances from government and regulatory authorities fail to close the credibility gap created by the bank's visible financial distress and the publicly known privatization intent. This is not merely a communication failure on the part of management, though communication deficiencies are certainly present; it reflects the more fundamental reality that genuine uncertainty cannot be resolved through reassurance alone, because the future conditions that employees fear are themselves genuinely unknowable at the time the reassurances are offered. Talent management strategy under VUCA conditions must therefore grapple with a paradox: organizations need to retain and develop talent precisely when they are least able to offer the certainties that have historically made retention possible.

The scholarly literature on talent management in turbulent environments has evolved considerably in response to the recognition that classical talent management frameworks provide insufficient guidance for organizations navigating VUCA contexts. Collings and Mellahi (2009) define strategic talent management as the systematic differentiation of 'A' positions from 'B' and 'C' positions within organizations, the identification of 'A' players to fill those positions, and the development of a differentiated HR architecture to support them. In Meridian's case, the Assistant Manager position is functionally an 'A' position: it is the point of direct customer interface, the engine of retail banking mobilization, and the critical pipeline from which future senior managers are developed. Losing experienced Assistant Managers imposes both direct replacement costs and strategic capability losses that compound over time as institutional knowledge and customer relationships depart with the individuals who hold them.

Dries (2013) extends the Collings and Mellahi framework by drawing attention to the tensions between exclusive (only high-performing individuals are talent) and inclusive (all are talent) approaches to talent management. Tensions become especially acute in public sector or quasi-public organizations where egalitarian norms have historically governed employment relationships. In Meridian's case, the very concept of differentiating talent into hierarchical categories carries cultural baggage in an institution where collective bargaining agreements, merit-based progression, and the normative presumption of equal entitlement have long-shaped employment expectations. Thus, the introduction of individually differentiated retention strategies such as performance-linked bonuses, accelerated promotion pathways, selective retention allowances may confront only the practical challenge of implementation. Talent managers at Meridian must navigate this tension carefully, since strategies that are perceived as inequitable may generate as many retention problems as they solve by demoralizing those who feel excluded from preferential treatment.

More recently, scholars have argued that VUCA environments call for a fundamental reorientation of talent management philosophy: from the management of talent as a stock of deployable human resources to the cultivation of talent as an adaptive capacity: a dynamic organizational capability for generating, retaining, and reconfiguring human knowledge and skill in response to environmental change (Al Ariss, Cascio, & Paauwe, 2014). This reorientation has direct implications for Meridian. Rather than treating retention purely as a problem of preventing departure, strategic talent management in this mode would involve actively rebuilding the organization's capacity to attract, develop, and retain talent under conditions of radical uncertainty.

Psychological Contract Theory

Rousseau (1989) defined the psychological contract as the individual employee's subjective perception of mutual obligations between employer and employee. The psychological contract is not about the formal employment contract; it comprises of implicit promises, expectations, and obligations that employees perceive as governing their relationship with their employer, including expectations about job security, career development, fair treatment, organizational support, and the maintenance of working conditions over time. Crucially, these expectations are subjectively formed and individually held; they reflect the interpretive frameworks through which employees make sense of organizational commitments, and they are therefore highly sensitive to context, communication, and the precedents set by prior organizational behavior.

The psychological contracts of Meridian's employees were formed under the assumption of public sector permanence. Entry into the bank was experienced not merely as the acceptance of a job offer but as the commencement of a lifelong relational contract – one that promised security, progressive advancement, community standing, and the full complement of welfare entitlements that public sector employment in India has traditionally conferred. These expectations were not idiosyncratic; they were collectively shared, institutionally reinforced, and socially validated by the broader normative framework of Indian middle-class professional culture (Sridharan, 2004). The privatization announcement constitutes what Rousseau (1995) terms a 'contract breach' (a perception that the employer has failed to fulfil its obligated terms) even though the formal employment contract may remain legally unchanged at the moment of the announcement. The breach is experienced as pre-emptive: employees anticipate the violation of obligations that have not yet formally occurred, and their behavioral responses such as disengagement, heightened job search activity, begin well in advance of any actual change in employment conditions.

Morrison and Robinson (1997) provided a critical refinement of psychological contract theory by distinguishing between breach (the cognitive assessment that an obligation has not been met) and violation (the emotional response to breach, characterized by feelings of betrayal, injustice, and moral outrage). This distinction has important practical implications. Breach may, in some circumstances, be addressed through explanation, renegotiation, or compensatory fulfilment of other obligations; violation, by contrast, represents a more fundamental rupture of the relational bond between employee and employer, one that may persist even if the substantive causes of breach are subsequently addressed. The employee testimonies in this case study suggest that Meridian's workforce experienced not merely breach but violation. Employees did not simply calculate that their expected benefits had been reduced; they experienced the privatization decision as a form of betrayal.

Research consistently shows that violation leads to greater organizational disengagement and higher voluntary turnover than breach alone (Conway & Briner, 2005; Zhao, Wayne, Glibkowski, & Bravo, 2007). Moreover, the effects of violation tend to be asymmetric and durable: the positive relational capital accumulated over years of satisfactory exchange is rapidly eroded by a single significant violation, but cannot be easily or quickly rebuilt (Bal, Chiaburu, & Jansen, 2010). This asymmetry poses a severe challenge for Meridian's talent retention strategy. Compensation revisions and benefit assurances, which address transactional rather than relational obligations, may prove insufficient unless accompanied by credible relational commitments that signal genuine respect for employees' identities, contributions, and legitimate expectations. Restubog, Hornsey, Bordia, and Esposo (2008) states that perceived organizational support can attenuate the negative effects of violation on turnover intentions, but only when it is experienced as sincere and unconditional, rather than as an instrumental effort to manage employee behavior.

Guest (2004) further cleared the picture by highlighting the extent to which psychological contract perceptions are shaped not only by individual employer-employee interactions but by the broader institutional and cultural context within which employment relationships are embedded. In Meridian's case, the institutional context of Indian public sector banking with its deep normative commitment to collectivist employment norms, seniority-based career structures, and the social symbolism of government employment. Thus, all this has shaped psychological contracts that are, in important respects, qualitatively different from those found in equivalent private sector organizations. Any retention strategy that fails to account for these contextually specific features of the psychological contract risks misdiagnosing the nature of the problem and prescribing remedies that, however financially generous, address the wrong dimensions of employee concern.

Resource-Based View and Human Capital Theory

The resource-based view (Barney, 1991) holds that sustainable competitive advantage derives from resources that are valuable, rare, inimitable, and non-substitutable. Experienced banking professionals who understand Meridian's customer base, credit culture, operational systems, and local market dynamics constitute precisely this kind of strategic resource. Their knowledge and capabilities are valuable because they directly generate revenue and customer loyalty; rare because they have been accumulated through years of institution-specific experience that competitors cannot easily replicate; inimitable because they are embedded in tacit knowledge, relational networks, and cultural familiarity that cannot be transferred through formal recruitment or training processes; and non-substitutable because no technology or process innovation can fully replicate the trust-based relationships that experienced managers have developed with long-standing customers. The bank's inability to easily replace departing managers, particularly in a VUCA environment where competitor banks are actively competing for the same talent, underscores the strategic urgency of retention.

Human capital theory (Becker, 1964) distinguishes between general human capital (skills and knowledge transferable across employers) and firm-specific human capital (skills and knowledge most valuable in the current employment context). Meridian's Assistant Managers possess both forms in significant measure: their general banking skills, regulatory knowledge, and customer service competencies are valuable to any competitor institution, while their knowledge of Meridian's specific systems, products, risk culture, and local customer relationships is largely specific to the firm. Attrition thus destroys firm-specific human capital that cannot be readily reconstituted through recruitment from the external labour market. This dual character of the departing managers' human capital creates a particularly severe strategic problem: the general component makes them highly attractive to competitors, while the specific component makes their loss maximally damaging to Meridian.

Institutional Theory

DiMaggio and Powell's (1983) institutional theory framework provides analytical lens to the role of regulatory, normative, and cognitive pressures in shaping organizational behavior and individual responses to organizational change. Organizations, in this view, are not merely rational actors optimizing in response to market signals; they are deeply embedded in institutional environments that prescribe appropriate forms of structure, behavior, and identity, and that impose powerful constraints on the range of legitimate strategic choices available to organizational actors. The concept of institutional isomorphism can be referred as the tendency of organizations in a given field to converge toward similar structural forms under the pressure of coercive, mimetic, and normative forces, which is particularly relevant to the public sector banking context.

Meridian's employees were socialized into a normative understanding of public sector banking employment that extended far beyond the formal employment relationship, encompassing community standing, family expectations, intergenerational social mobility narratives, and professional identity shaped by decades of institutional practice and cultural reinforcement. This normative socialization creates what historical institutionalists term 'path dependence' in management strategies (Schreyögg, Sydow & Holtmann, 2011): the choices available to Meridian's managers are constrained by the institutional history that has shaped employee expectations, and departure from established norms carries disproportionate psychological and relational costs for the workforce. Understanding this path dependence is essential to designing retention interventions that are contextually credible: strategies imported from private sector talent management practice without adaptation to the institutional specifics of the public sector context are likely to misfire, however well-intentioned.

Suchman (1995) provided typology of organizational legitimacy by distinguishing between pragmatic, moral, and cognitive forms. This can add further analytical depth to the institutional analysis of Meridian's situation. Pragmatic legitimacy refers to the self-interested calculations of stakeholders; moral legitimacy reflects normative evaluations of organizational conduct in relation to socially constructed standards; and cognitive legitimacy concerns the taken-for-granted assumptions about what an organization is and does. In the context of privatization, all three forms of legitimacy are simultaneously disrupted. Employees question whether the transformed bank will serve their pragmatic interests; they evaluate whether the privatization process meets standards of procedural and distributive justice; and they confront a fundamental challenge to the cognitive assumptions about the nature and purpose of public sector banking upon which their professional identities have been constructed.

Transition and Change Management Theory

Bridge (2004) model of transition distinguishes between change (the external event or structural shift) and transition (the internal psychological process through which individuals reorient in response to change). The model argues that transitions begin not with a new beginning but with an ending: before individuals can embrace or adapt to a new organizational reality, they must first come to terms with the loss of the old one. In Meridian's case, the privatization announcement has precipitated a collective experience of ending that are the anticipated loss of the public sector identity, the welfare architecture, and the social standing that had defined employees' working lives.

Under the eight-stage model of change management (Kotter, 1996), change initiatives most commonly fail not because of technical or strategic shortcomings but because of failures in the management of human responses to change. This includes failure to create sufficient urgency, failure to build a sufficiently broad and credible coalition for change, failure to communicate a clear and compelling vision, and failure to consolidate gains and anchor change in organizational culture. Several of these failure modes are visible in the Meridian case. The communication of the privatization rationale has been fragmented and inconsistent; the development of a compelling vision for the post-privatization institution has been insufficiently communicated; and the management of employee anxiety has been reactive rather than proactive, responding to crises as they emerge rather than anticipating and addressing the human dimensions of change in advance.

Importantly, transition and change management theory does not merely diagnose the problem; it suggests a corrective orientation for talent retention strategy. Organizations that invest in supporting individuals through the psychological dimensions of transition must provide forums for the expression of loss and anxiety, communicate with transparency and consistency, involve employees in shaping the future state, and build foundation of stability amid wider turbulence. All these factors tend to achieve significantly better retention outcomes than those that treat the human dimensions of change as secondary to structural and financial considerations (Armenakis & Harris, 2009). For Meridian, this suggests that the most effective retention strategies will be those that simultaneously address the transactional dimensions of employment (compensation, benefits, security assurances) and the relational and psychological dimensions (identity, meaning, belonging, and a credible narrative of institutional continuity).

IMPLICATIONS FOR TALENT STRATEGY IN VUCA ENVIRONMENTS

The Meridian Bank case yields several generalizable lessons for talent strategy practitioners and scholars navigating VUCA conditions, particularly in the context of institutional transitions in emerging market economies.

First, the case illustrates that talent risk in VUCA environments is often anticipatory rather than reactive. Meridian's attrition crisis began accelerating from 2016, three years before the formal privatization was completed. The mere announcement of strategic intent was sufficient to trigger behavioral responses in the talent market. This observation reinforces Collings and Mellahi's (2009) argument that talent management must be embedded in strategic planning processes, not treated as an HR response to strategic decisions that have already been made.

Second, the case highlights the inadequacy of purely transactional retention strategies when the psychological contract violation is relational in nature. This finding has particular resonance in societies characterized by strong collectivist values and institutionalized employment relationships, where the employment relationship carries social meanings that extend far beyond its economic terms (Hofstede, 1980; Triandis, 1995). HR practitioners operating in such contexts must develop a repertoire of relational retention tools, including symbolic commitments, participatory change management processes, and identity-affirming organizational narratives, that complement but cannot be replaced by compensation revision.

Third, the case demonstrates the strategic importance of tax literacy in compensation design. The ability to engineer after-tax improvements that exceed pre-tax cost increases, through the strategic deployment of non-taxable allowance categories, represents a form of compensation architecture expertise that materially affects both the bank's cost position and employee outcomes. This expertise is more valuable precisely in VUCA contexts where resource constraints limit the scope for straightforward cost-to-company increases.

Fourth, the case underscores the importance of timing in talent management during institutional transitions. The board's delay in finalizing a compensation response likely increased the total cost of the crisis by allowing the most mobile and capable employees to exit before retention measures were in place. Proactive talent risk management frameworks, capable of identifying and responding to attrition signals in near-real time, might have enabled earlier and more effective intervention.

Finally, the case points to the need for integrated retention strategies that address the full constellation of employee needs and concerns. Maslow's (1943) hierarchy remains instructively relevant: employees whose sense of security and belonging is threatened will not be primarily motivated by self-actualization opportunities. The appropriate sequence of intervention at Meridian was arguably to address safety and belonging concerns first, through credible service condition guarantees and participatory change communication, before layering compensation enhancements on top. Inverting this sequence, as the compensation-first approach risks doing, may prove to be tactically sub-optimal.

Discussion Questions

Question 1: Diagnosing the Attrition Problem

To what extent does Meridian Bank's rising attrition reflect dissatisfaction with compensation versus a breakdown in the psychological contract following privatization? How could management systematically diagnose the relative importance of these factors, and how should the diagnosis shape the design of an effective retention strategy?

Discussion hint: distinguish between economic drivers (salary gaps with private banks, variable pay, career incentives) and relational drivers (loss of job security, erosion of public-sector identity, perceived breach of expectations). Encourage discussion of diagnostic tools such as exit interviews, internal surveys, benchmarking studies, and cohort-level attrition analysis to guide targeted retention interventions.

Question 2: VUCA Analysis

Using the VUCA framework (Volatility, Uncertainty, Complexity, Ambiguity), analyze the environment Meridian Bank employees are currently facing. Which dimension most strongly characterizes their experience of the privatization transition? How should this assessment influence Mr. Mehta's leadership approach and Ms. Krishnaswamy's HR strategy?

Discussion hint: whether the situation reflects uncertainty (unclear future policies), ambiguity (uncertain institutional identity), complexity (multiple regulatory and organizational changes), or volatility (rapid shifts in incentives and roles). The discussion should link environmental diagnosis to leadership responses such as transparency, sensemaking communication, and adaptive HR policies.

Question 3: Evaluating the Compensation Proposal

Evaluate the proposed compensation structure (Exhibit 3) by calculating the after-tax monthly take-home pay for an Assistant Manager under both the existing and proposed salary structures using the prevailing Indian income tax framework.

How does the after-tax comparison alter your assessment of the proposal's effectiveness as a retention mechanism?

Discussion hint: discussion can extend to whether monetary incentives alone can address attrition driven by cultural change and career uncertainty.

Question 4: Beyond Compensation

If you were advising Meridian Bank's leadership team, what additional retention strategies would you recommend? Which interventions should be prioritized in the short term versus the medium term, and how should they be sequenced to stabilize the workforce during the transition?

Discussion hint: think about career development, internal mobility, leadership communication, training for private banking practices, recognition systems, and work culture reforms. Prioritization should reflect urgency and feasibility: early symbolic actions to restore trust, followed by structural reforms such as career paths, performance systems, and leadership capability development.

Question 5: Institutional Identity and Change Management

Employee narratives suggest that resistance to privatization stems not only from economic concerns but also from a threatened professional and organizational identity. Drawing on change management theories (e.g., Lewin, Kotter) and psychological contract theory, design a communication and engagement strategy to help employees navigate Meridian's identity transition.

Discussion hint: explore how identity disruption can trigger resistance. Effective strategies may include clear transition narratives, symbolic leadership actions, employee participation forums, transparent timelines, and rearticulation of institutional purposes. Linking privatization to a credible future identity (rather than merely operational change) is central to rebuilding psychological contracts.

Question 6: Talent Strategy in Privatizing Institutions

What generalizable lessons does the Meridian case offer for HR practitioners and policymakers managing talent strategy during privatization? What contextual factors might limit the transferability of these lessons across sectors (energy, telecommunications, manufacturing, etc.) or countries?

Discussion hint: derive insights about managing legacy employment systems, aligning incentives with market competition, and preserving institutional legitimacy during transition. Encourage discussion on contextual differences: public sector norms, union presence, regulatory oversight, and labor market competitiveness, which may shape how privatization affects workforce expectations.

Question 7: Long-Term Talent Architecture

Assume the board approves the proposed compensation revision on January 5, 2019. What ongoing talent management challenges would you anticipate for Meridian over the following two to three years as a newly private bank? How would you recommend structuring Meridian's talent management function, in terms of priorities, capabilities, and metrics, to address these challenges?

Discussion hint: anticipate challenges such as performance culture shifts, leadership capability gaps, retention of high performers, and integration of public-sector legacy employees with private-sector practices. Discussion should highlight HR capabilities including workforce analytics, leadership development, performance management systems, and metrics like productivity, engagement, and retention.

DISCLOSURE

The chapter's content and ideas are the original work of the author. The case of Meridian Bank Limited (a fictitious bank name created solely for educational purposes) is inspired by real-world events. Publicly available news reports and events were used as references in developing the case. AI tools, including ChatGPT and Claude, were used to improve grammar and readability.

REFERENCES

Al Ariss, A., Cascio, W. F., & Paauwe, J. (2014). Talent management: Current theories and future research directions. *Journal of World Business, 49*(2), 173–179. DOI: 10.1016/j.jwb.2013.11.001

Armenakis, A. A., & Bedeian, A. G. (1999). Organizational change: A review of theory and research in the 1990s. *Journal of Management, 25*(3), 293–315. DOI: 10.1177/014920639902500303

Armenakis, A. A., & Harris, S. G. (2009). Reflections: Our journey in organizational change research and practice. *Journal of Change Management, 9*(2), 127–142. DOI: 10.1080/14697010902879079

Arrawatia, R., Dawar, V., Maitra, D., & Dash, S. R. (2019). Asset quality determinants of Indian banks: Empirical evidence and policy issues. *Journal of Public Affairs, 19*(4), e1937. DOI: 10.1002/pa.1937

Bal, P. M., Chiaburu, D. S., & Jansen, P. G. W. (2010). Psychological contract breach and work performance: Is social exchange a buffer or an intensifier? *Journal of Managerial Psychology, 25*(3), 252–273. DOI: 10.1108/02683941011023730

Baran, B. E., & Woznyj, H. M. (2020). Managing VUCA: The human dynamics of agility. *Organizational Dynamics, 100787.* Advance online publication. DOI: 10.1016/j.orgdyn.2020.100787 PMID: 32843777

Barney, J. (1991). Firm resources and sustained competitive advantage. *Journal of Management, 17*(1), 99–120. DOI: 10.1177/014920639101700108

Baruch, Y., & Rousseau, D. M. (2019). Integrating psychological contracts and ecosystems in career studies and management. *The Academy of Management Annals, 13*(1), 84–111. DOI: 10.5465/annals.2016.0103

Becker, G. S. (1964). *Human capital: A theoretical and empirical analysis, with special reference to education.* University of Chicago Press.

Bennett, N., & Lemoine, G. J. (2014). What a difference a word makes: Understanding threats to performance in a VUCA world. *Business Horizons, 57*(3), 311–317. DOI: 10.1016/j.bushor.2014.01.001

Collings, D. G., & Mellahi, K. (2009). Strategic talent management: A review and research agenda. *Human Resource Management Review, 19*(4), 304–313. DOI: 10.1016/j.hrmr.2009.04.001

Conway, N., & Briner, R. B. (2005). *Understanding psychological contracts at work: A critical evaluation of theory and research.* Oxford University Press. DOI: 10.1093/acprof:oso/9780199280643.001.0001

DiMaggio, P. J., & Powell, W. W. (1983). The iron cage revisited: Institutional isomorphism and collective rationality in organizational fields. *American Sociological Review, 48*(2), 147–160. DOI: 10.2307/2095101

Dries, N. (2013). The psychology of talent management: A review and research agenda. *Human Resource Management Review, 23*(4), 272–285. DOI: 10.1016/j.hrmr.2013.05.001

Guest, D. E. (2004). The psychology of the employment relationship: An analysis based on the psychological contract. *Applied Psychology, 53*(4), 541–555. DOI: 10.1111/j.1464-0597.2004.00187.x

Gupta, P., & Panagariya, A. (2023). Privatization of public sector banks in India: why, how and how far. National Council of Applied Economic Research (NCAER)| Working Paper No.: WP, 141.

Hofstede, G. (1980). *Culture's consequences: International differences in work-related values*. Sage Publications.

Horney, N., Pasmore, B., & O'Shea, T. (2010). Leadership agility: A business imperative for a VUCA world. *People & Strategy, 33*(4), 32–38.

Kamath, K. V., Kohli, S. S., Shenoy, P. S., Kumar, R., Nayak, R. M., Kuppuswamy, P. T., & Ravichandran, N. (2003). Indian banking sector: Challenges and opportunities. *Vikalpa, 28*(3), 83–100. DOI: 10.1177/0256090920030308

Kotter, J. P. (1996). *Leading change*. Harvard Business School Press.

Lawrence, K. (2013). Developing leaders in a VUCA environment. UNC Executive Development. Retrieved from https://www.kenan-flagler.unc.edu/executive-development/custom-programs/~/media/DF696ABE19F74015BC753316749A930A.ashx

Lewin, K. (1951). *Field theory in social science: Selected theoretical papers*. Harper & Row.

Maslow, A. H. (1943). A theory of human motivation. *Psychological Review, 50*(4), 370–396. DOI: 10.1037/h0054346

Mohan, R. (2005). Financial sector reforms in India: Policies and performance analysis. *Economic and Political Weekly, 40*(12), 1106–1121.

Mohan, R., & Ray, P. (2018). Indian financial sector: Structure, trends, and turns. In *Routledge Handbook of Banking and Finance in Asia* (pp. 54–75). Routledge. DOI: 10.4324/9781315543222-4

Morrison, E. W., & Robinson, S. L. (1997). When employees feel betrayed: A model of how psychological contract violation develops. *Academy of Management Review*, *22*(1), 226–256. DOI: 10.2307/259230

Panagariya, A. (2010). *India: The emerging giant*. Oxford University Press.

Paul, A. (2018, September 13). *Examining the rise of Non-Performing Assets in India*. PRS Legislative Research. Retrieved March 1, 2026, from https://prsindia.org/theprsblog/examining-the-rise-of-non-performing-assets-in-india#:~:text=What%20led%20to%20the%20rise,capability%20of%20these%20corporations%20decreased

Ramakrishna, G., Ramulu, M., & Kumar, B. P. (2016). Financial crisis and the performance of commercial banks: Indian experience. *Journal of International Economics*, *7*(2), 35.

Reddy, Y. V. (2006). Evolving role of banks in India. Address delivered at the Bank Economists' Conference, Hyderabad.

Reddy, Y. V. (2006). Reforming India's financial sector: Changing dimensions and emerging issues. *BIS Papers*, *28*, 161–178.

Reserve Bank of India. (2017, April 13). Retrieved January 10, 2026, from https://www.rbi.org.in/commonman/english/scripts/Notification.aspx?Id=2523

Reserve Bank of India. (2026, January 22). Retrieved March 2, 2026, from https://www.rbi.org.in/commonman/english/scripts/FAQs.aspx?Id=1105

Restubog, S. L. D., Hornsey, M. J., Bordia, P., & Esposo, S. R. (2008). Effects of psychological contract breach on organizational citizenship behaviour: Insights from the group value model. *Journal of Management Studies*, *45*(8), 1377–1400. DOI: 10.1111/j.1467-6486.2008.00792.x

Rousseau, D. M. (1989). Psychological and implied contracts in organizations. *Employee Responsibilities and Rights Journal*, *2*(2), 121–139. DOI: 10.1007/BF01384942

Rousseau, D. M. (1995). Psychological and organizational contracts: Understanding the ties that motivate. *The Academy of Management Executive*, *4*(4), 123–139.

Schreyögg, G., Sydow, J., & Holtmann, P. (2011). How history matters in organisations: The case of path dependence. *Management & Organizational History*, *6*(1), 81–100. DOI: 10.1177/1744935910387030

Sharma, M. (Ed.). (2008). *Dynamics of Indian Banking: Views and Vistas*. Atlantic Publishers & Dist.

Shet, S. V. (2024). A VUCA-ready workforce: Exploring employee competencies and learning and development implications. *Personnel Review, 53*(3), 674–703. DOI: 10.1108/PR-10-2023-0873

Singh, J. P. (2000). Multinational corporations and technological change: Global melting pot or nation-state solutions? *Review of International Political Economy, 7*(2), 225–253.

Singh, R., & Gupta, A. (2019). Non-performing assets in Indian public sector banks: Causes, consequences, and correctives. *Indian Journal of Finance, 13*(4), 7–22.

Sridharan, E. (2004). The growth and sectoral composition of India's middle class: Its impact on the politics of economic liberalisation. *India Review, 3*(4), 405–428. DOI: 10.1080/14736480490895769

Suchman, M. C. (1995). Managing legitimacy: Strategic and institutional approaches. *Academy of Management Review, 20*(3), 571–610. DOI: 10.2307/258788

Suresh, P., & Paul, J. (2014). *Management of banking and financial services*. Pearson Education India.

Triandis, H. C. (1995). *Individualism and collectivism*. Westview Press.

Unnikrishnan, D. (2022, November 21). *Banking Central | Why trade unions will stay in Indian banking*. Moneycontrol. Retrieved March 2, 2026, from https://www.moneycontrol.com/news/business/banking-central-why-trade-unions-will-stay-in-indian-banking-9571341.html

Vaiman, V., Scullion, H., & Collings, D. G. (2012). Talent management decision making. *Management Decision, 50*(5), 925–941. DOI: 10.1108/00251741211227663

Zhao, H., Wayne, S. J., Glibkowski, B. C., & Bravo, J. (2007). The impact of psychological contract breach on work-related outcomes: A meta-analysis. *Personnel Psychology, 60*(3), 647–680. DOI: 10.1111/j.1744-6570.2007.00087.x

Zhao, H., Wayne, S. J., Glibkowski, B. C., & Bravo, J. (2007). The impact of psychological contract breach on work-related outcomes: A meta-analysis. *Personnel Psychology, 60*(3), 647–680. DOI: 10.1111/j.1744-6570.2007.00087.x

Chapter 3
Building Resilient Employer Brands:
Talent Management Lessons From Crisis Contexts

Sunaina Kapoor
http://orcid.org/0000-0002-3738-8120
EM Normandie Business School, Dubai Campus, Dubai, UAE

Anneswa Bose
Indian Institute of Technology, Kharagpur, India

EXECUTIVE SUMMARY

This chapter explores how organizations manage employer branding during times of crisis. Drawing on theories from human resource management, crisis communication, corporate reputation, and organizational resilience, it examines how crises impact internal and external perceptions of an employer brand. The chapter analyzes strategies for protecting and strengthening employer brands during adversity — from authentic communication to employee wellbeing initiatives. It also highlights opportunities for organizations to emerge with enhanced trust and loyalty post-crisis. Combining academic research with real-world case studies, the chapter offers a practical framework for building resilient employer brands that can withstand future disruptions. It is intended for both scholars and practitioners in HRM, marketing, and organizational leadership.

DOI: 10.4018/979-8-3373-5776-8.ch003

INTRODUCTION

Organisations live longer when the employer continues to reinforce shared values and rationale for working with it. HR (human resource) expert Josh Bersin explains that employer brand is a critical, influential factor for attracting, engaging, and retaining top talent – especially in times of uncertainty (Rajendra, 2025). Following this ideology, many renowned brands like Unilever, Google, Microsoft, Patagonia, Accenture, and others have flourished. On the contrary, brands like Twitter (Guardian, 2022), Uber (Andresen, 2017), Wells Fargo (Lilly et al., 2021), Amazon (Reese & Allison, 2023), and others have tarnished their reputations due to a lack of employer branding adaptation. Previous research showcases employer branding research from multiple perspectives, like marketing (Theurer, 2018; Stadler et al., 2025), management (Shafiee & Goodarzi, 2026; Rita et al., 2026; Yasin et al., 2025; Makumbe, 2025), and an international perspective (Špoljarić & Ozretić 2023). Studies from the perspective of external environment crisis, like pandemic and its effect on employer branding, have been explored previously (Stor & Haromszeki, 2025). However, there is scant research on when an employer brand encounters a crisis due to its own deeds resulting in damaged reputation. Lock & Jacobs (2025) highlight the need to study multiple employers facing a crisis, challenging legitimate ways of talent management. This book chapter fills this gap by providing multiple case studies of employers strategically dealing with talent management issues. Recent studies underline limited exploration of employer brand strategies and better management of reputation, especially for the potential employees- Gen Z (Junça et al., 2023). Studying it further uncovers ways of long-term employer attractiveness across countries and cultures (Nilsen et al., 2024), as mentioned in a more cohesive way in this chapter. Additionally, Kuoppakangas et al. (2024) mention that knowledge about managing such situations is crucial for quick decision-making and efficient talent management. Thus, this book chapter focuses on studying employer branding from a talent management perspective. It further highlights the importance of employer branding, both internal and external to the organisation- before, during, and after the crisis to ensure employer brand resilience.

Crises as a Test of Employer Brand

Employer Branding is a crucial aspect that communicates the functional, economic, psychological, and symbolic benefits provided by employment (Amber & Barrow, 1996; Berthon, 2005). It is defined as a process of building and developing and employer brand that is identifiable and unique (Theurer et al., 2018). Additionally, it's main purpose is to differentiate an employer from its competitors (Saini, 2023). Employer branding often becomes the medium depicting an employer's unique aspects like material and non-material employee benefits, values, beliefs, policies, and employer behaviour as a whole. The outcome focuses on shaping the perceptions not only of current employees but also of potential employees, ultimately resulting in positioning the organisation as an employer of choice and enhancing organisational performance (Azhar et al., 2024). Strong employer branding defines the values and vision of the employer, communicates a consistent story from defining job description to actual joining the employer, and creates an internal organisational culture that matches the external brand identity (Lazo, 2025). Additionally, it's crucial, in times of uncertainties like the pandemic, digital disruptions, talent shortages, mitigate the increased turnover rate, and unethical issues within the organisation, especially in the case of a product-related crisis that may contribute to an unfavourable Word-of-Mouth (Panagiotidou et al., 2024). Upcoming sections in the chapter highlight cases of organisations caught in such crises and the role of employer branding to overcome them.

Type of Crisis

There have been several classifications of Crisis, for instance, origin: internal/external, intent: intentional/unintentional, results: severe/non-severe, victims: specified/unspecified, nature: performance (product)/value (ethics) (Coombs, 1995). In continuum, Coombs (2012) assembled crisis into 3 categories based on the organisational responsibility- employer responsibility in this case- beginning with a) employer being a victim for an uncontrollable event b) an accident, for instance due to a technical error having slight possibility of control and ending up with c) preventable crisis that could have been controlled, for instance, a human error. This book chapter focuses on the third type, namely the functional, economic, psychological, and symbolic yet controllable errors made by employer organisations, which, if not prevented, could impact the employer brand reputation. The following case of Tesla leverages internal employee brand as a tool for reviving the employer's reputation.

Case Of Tesla's Autopilot Safety Crisis (2021-2023)

Figure 1.

Image Courtesy: The Washington Post (https://www.washingtonpost.com/technology/2023/12/13/tesla-autopilot-recall/)

Tesla is a well-known brand with a strong community following its car, and even more enhanced trust and reliability spilled over from the founder Elon Musk. Its employer brand is developed around revolution, resilience, and valiant real-life problem-solving. The employees' passion for the employer is driven by brand identification with Elon Musk's Vision of "accelerating the world's transition to sustainable energy". Besides, Tesla between 2021-2023 experienced litigations and investigations from regulatory bodies of the U.S., Europe, and China due to multiple reports of accidents regarding its Autopilot and full-self driving (FSD) features (Shepardson, 2023). Skepticism surrounding Tesla's safety claims grew globally, with social media serving as a catalyst for amplifying criticism- posing both reputational and talent retention risk.

During the crisis, the brand leveraged internal employee branding as its tool for revival. Technicians, engineers, and data management teams prioritized the gravity of the situation and realignment of safety features and issued software updates immediately. This was not achievable without motivating teams through internal communication focused on transparency and mission alignment, despite intense external scrutiny (Frkal & Lewis, 2025)

Post-Crisis, not only did the company revise and communicate its driver-attention alerts, but Elon Musk and senior management leveraged social media platforms to reignite the brand identity as avant-garde and agile. Such efforts bolstered external employee branding. Additionally, hackathons, safety sprints, and other employee engagement initiatives boosted employee morale, resulting in high retention among core engineering talent despite the crisis. In 2023, Tesla ranked among the top 10 most attractive employers globally (Universum, 2023). Thus, employer branding cushions the initial reputational damage and reinforces brand identity during and post-crisis.

THEORETICAL FOUNDATIONS

Siomkos and Kurzbard (1994) define a brand crisis as a "discrete, well-publicized event in which products are found to be defective or dangerous". For this book chapter, we highlight the importance of employer branding before, during a crisis, and not only after an unexpected or a sudden event that threatens to disrupt an organisation's operations and poses both financial and reputational threats (Coombs, 2007). Many other scientific researchers identify a crisis as a situation that needs to be managed through appropriate communication in order to reassure its stakeholders. Theories that propagate the importance of employer reactions or communication involve Image Repair Theory, Attribution Theory, Framing Theory, the Situational theory of Publics, and Situational Crisis Communication Theory (Schwarz, 2019). Image Repair or restoration theory was developed by a classic researcher Benoit (1997) focusing on Crisis Communication. The theory assumes that something the employer is responsible for has occurred that may harm or has already marred the employer's image and highlights the five possible communication strategies (denial, evasion, reduction of the offense, corrective action, mortification), without focusing on the applicability aspect (Anderson-Meli & Koshy, 2020). The Attribution theory usually revolves around the degree of responsibility of crisis that the employees attribute to the employer. In other words, it is the "study of perceived causation" influencing the reactions (Kelley & Michela, 1980). The framing theory is concerned with the "presentation (framing) of the message" and its impact on the public (Chong & Druckman, 2007; Nöhammer et al., 2022). The Situational Crisis Communication Theory highlights the importance of brand preparedness with primary response strategies like denying, diminishing, rebuilding, and bolstering (Laufer & Coombs, 2006; Coombs, 2014; Coombs 2019). However, these strategies may not be used discreetly for a specific kind of crisis. There can be a sequence of response strategies used by an employer, for instance, to remain silent initially, apologise after the confirmation of attribution of responsibility, and may later conduct a press conference for the purpose of bolstering its reputation.

The true essence of these response strategies is realised through a positive interpretation of these communications by the stakeholders inside as well as outside of the organisation. During a crisis, employers should communicate immediately to explain and showcase that they care about the company's reputation as well as that of other stakeholders internally and externally. Employers that treat their employees as "internal customers" seldom find its employees admiring the employer, leading to improved organisational performance, enhancing satisfaction of other stakeholders (for instance, consumers, potential employees) (Nanjundeswaraswamy et al., 2025). The chapter explains the importance of employer branding and these communication/ response strategies through multiple cases in the upcoming sections.

Organisation Reputation

There are multiple dimensions of employer branding highlighted by Berthon et al. (2005). These include interest value (degree of attractiveness of a prospective employee to an employer); social value (associated with a pleasant and supportive workplace environment); economic value (linked to economic concerns: salary appropriateness); development value (scope of learning and appreciation), and application value (opportunities for knowledge application). Favourable employer branding, capturing all five dimensions, heightens the intention of candidates to be a part of such an employer (Junca & Dias 2023).

Figure 2. Fombrun's Reputation Management Model

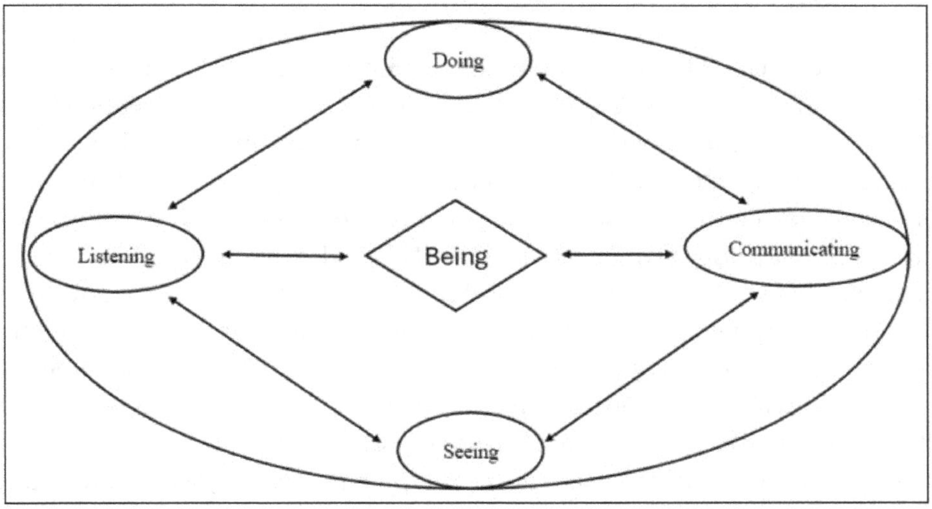

Organisational reputation is carved by who the employer is (being), what it does (doing), how well it listens, how clearly it communicates, and how stakeholders ultimately see it (Fombrun, 1996) (See figure 2). These 5 elements of the reputation management model can be explained in context of as:

1. Being (Employer Identity): During uncertain times (for instance, layoffs, pay cuts, and tarnished brand image, etc.), employers demonstrate *being* through authentic values like fairness, empathy for employees, and integrity.
2. Doing (Employer behaviour): Employers who practice *actions speak louder than words* phenomenon gain assured employer credibility. These actions could be transparent HR policies, considerable employee aid programs and many other supportive actions.
3. Listening (Stakeholder engagement): Feedback from stakeholders helps in understanding their expectations and concerns. Tools like employee surveys, town hall meetings, and grievance mechanisms reflect the employer's intent to listen.
4. Communicating (Employer communication): Honest and timely sharing of ideas, decisions, future employer strategy, and actions to stakeholders speak volumes about employer identity. Additionally, it reduces uncertainty, builds trust, and enhances the employer brand.
5. Seeing (stakeholder perceptions/reputation outcomes): Employee (stakeholder) perceptions of the employer (organisation) are one of the strongest pillars of

employer branding. Seeing is exhibited in employer review platforms, employee advocacy, and overall trust in leadership.

Employers should follow Fombrun's reputation model (FRM) as a prerequisite for developing a strong employer brand. Situational Crisis Communication Theory (SCCT) is a theory to respond strategically after an uncertain event- a brand crisis in our case. When integrated, FRM explains how identity, actions, listening, and communication collectively shape employer brand reputation, particularly among employees and prospective talent, while SCCT guides an employer's actions or communications based on a crisis responsibility. Although both frameworks focus on reputation management, the former focuses on building employer reputation while the latter focuses on revitalising it, leveraging the outcomes of the former. Additionally, SCCT explains how stakeholders attribute responsibility based on crisis type, which activates a cognitive reassessment of the organisation's character. This attribution process serves as the trigger mechanism that prompts stakeholders—particularly employees and prospective talent—to re-evaluate the firm's "Being" and "Doing" dimensions as conceptualised by FRM. When responsibility attributions are high, stakeholders scrutinise value alignment, ethical consistency, and behavioural integrity more intensely. The organisation's crisis response strategies (SCCT), when aligned with authentic identity signals (FRM), can interrupt negative attribution spirals and restore perceived value congruence. Thus, employer brand resilience emerges not merely from communication efforts, but from the interaction between attribution processes and identity-reputation alignment mechanisms that shape trust, identification, and organisational attractiveness.

Table 1. Integration of SCCT and Fomrun's reputation management model for laying down employer branding actions

Fombrun Component	Reputation Function	Corresponding SCCT dimension	Employer branding application
Being	Defines employers identity and moral positioning	Crisis responsibility attribution	Strong employer value reduces perceived employer blame among employees (Rys et al., 2024)
Doing	Demonstrates value through concrete actions	Primary crisis response strategy (rebuild, diminish)	Employer actions (compensation, support, fairness) align with the appropriate SCCT strategy (Stor & Haromszeki, 2025)
Listening	Gauges employee emotions and expectations	employee emotion assessment (anger, sympathy)	Understanding employee sentiment to adapt response tone and content (Nadales-Gallego et al., 2025)

continued on following page

Table 1. Continued

Fombrun Component	Reputation Function	Corresponding SCCT dimension	Employer branding application
Communicating	Employers frame crisis narrative and response	Crisis response messaging (apology, justification, corrective action)	Transparent internal communication protects employer brand trust (Rys et al., 2024)
Seeing	Produces reputational outcome overtime.	Post-crisis reputation and behavioural intentions.	Employee loyalty, advocacy, and talent attraction post-crisis (Stor & Haromszeki, 2025)

Crisis and Employer Brand Perception

Employee perceptions are crucial for the external world to reassure them of the employer brand. Job seekers place a high weight on development opportunities, advancement opportunities, and the ability to apply their educational skills. For employers, it is challenging to communicate attributes such as organisational value, work-life balance, and social environment (Nilsen et al., 2024). Thus, there is a need to balance the employer brand attributes; for instance, development challenges and advancement opportunities should be made easily accessible to the outside world than less tangible attributes like organisational values, work-life balance, and others.

1. Internal perceptions: Unlike other branding initiatives meant only for the outside world, Employer branding begins from the inside out. It aims to influence how employees feel, engage, and act favorably within the organisation.
    a. Trust: Organisations where employers keep transparency in communication and share the vision of the organisation foster a belief in employees that they matter to the top management. Such consistent leadership behaviour continues to iterate and recognize employee contributions fosters employee trust. During crises, when leaders communicate clearly and engage, and value employees' contributions in the decision-making process to solve the situation, they are more effective. Autonomy at the workplace and freedom to suggest shapes the employee's opinion that the employer trusts them (Hajjami & Crocco, 2024). It further reassures the employees' organisational trust. For instance, Microsoft's strategy of transparent communication and flexible policies helped foster employee trust, resulting in higher employee engagement.
    b. Culture: Effective employer brands involve clear communication of shared values, mission, and behavioural norms to ensure the purpose of the employer is embedded in the organisational culture. The top management of

Patagonia, representing sustainability, drives a culture where employees feel part of a higher purpose. Its core business and values are weaved together into the culture, inspiring its employees.

c. Employee Experience: Employer branding is the total of all the efforts or initiatives made by an employer through every touchpoint. These include onboarding, recognition, training and development, and well-being. Favourable employee experience in the organisation seldom enhances their perceptions of the employer attractiveness (Nilsen et al., 2024). For example, the 'ohana culture' means a sense of family beyond blood. Company *Salesforce* successfully weaves the phenomenon of 'Ohana culture' into its brand by focusing on the physical, mental, and emotional well-being and growth of its employees (Chylinski, 2024)

2. External Perceptions: Employer branding is often aimed at transcending organisational culture, values, and norms into the public, not only to enhance its reputation but to reassure its stakeholders: attract new talent, customers, and investors.

   a. Reputation: Employers need to communicate about the internal environment created by their efforts to differentiate themselves. Employer branding (interest value, social value, economic value, development value, application value) to the external environment favourably influences an employer's reputation, which in turn, increases an individual's intention to apply for an employment offer in that organisation (Silva & Dias, 2023). Unilever's effort to be consistently vocal about sustainability and employee purpose bolsters its reputation as a responsible employer globally.

   b. Attractiveness: A favourable internal employer brand strengthens the external brand identity of the employer. Psychological and professional benefits like purpose, learning, and work-life balance, when communicated externally, aid in enhancing the brand appeal of the employer, leading to enhanced potential candidates. Employers that welcome employees to work for a purpose and give freedom to innovate and bring creative solutions are perceived more attractive by potential candidates. Tech companies like Google, SAP are some of the most well-renowned companies known for their innovative organisational culture and appreciation for creative solutions.

   c. Credibility: Employers that take good care of their employees' well-being "walk the talk". In other words, the internal culture matches the external communications further leads to long-term credibility among employees and external stakeholders. Such consistency is visible in Starbucks' employee-centric policies, especially during pandemic, maintained its credibility as a people-first brand.

Thus, employer branding is the public reflection of internal reality. While internal branding nurtures belonging and resilience, external branding attracts alignment and admiration. Hence, authenticity between the two determines credibility and long-term trust.

Social Media and Managing New Age Employees' Perceptions of Employer Brand

The next Gen, which is widely recognised as GenZ is out there and almost 30% have already joined the global workforce worldwide by 2025 (World Economic Forum, 2022). It is no surprise that this generation born between 1997-2012 is tech-savvy, values autonomy, meaningful work, work-life balance, and prefers transparency over a well-marketed work environment (ETBrandEquity, 2025). For the same reasons, this generation is active on various social media platforms and values the voice of advocates and influencers on these platforms for sharing their true opinions (Janssen & Rudeloff, 2025). A large chunk of job seekers, abandon their application process after exposure to negative word of mouth (Ne WOM), reviews or posts about an employer brand on social media platforms (Randstand Employer Brand Survey, 2021). Based on the above, many companies have adapted social media platforms to leverage employee advocacy, ultimately enhancing their brand recognition.

Earlier jobseekers were largely passive consumers of employer information due to a lack of transparency and the woke behaviour of existing employees. However, the advent of social media has made the exchange of experiences, opinions, and evaluation of an organisation's employment experience and culture readily accessible for GenZ (Saini, 2023). Additionally, gamification during recruitment is another tool that companies are using to engage the new age applicants. Technology has significantly influenced the job applicants view about the employer due to access to abundant information; employers need to continue to engage and communicate with external stakeholders to reinforce their positive employer brand.It is essential because of the user-generated content from multiple participants could generate skepticism about the employer brand in the public domain (Etter etal., 2019). Thus, managing a consistent employer brand in the current era is significantly more challenging as depicted in the cases below.

Case Study Discussion 1: Shoppers Stop: Leveraging Social Media for Employer Branding

Shoppers Stop is the largest retail chain in India. Established in 1991, it has grown immensely leading to an increase in both number of outlets and workforce.

It positioned itself as a premium lifestyle departmental store and sold variety of products in both apparel (for men, women and children) and non-apparel (cosmetics, watches, accessories and others) (Shoppers Stop).While the company's vision revolved around customer happiness and delightful experiences, the talent management philosophy focused on principles of development and inspiration and focused on hiring passionate, adaptable, and self-motivated yet team player personalities (Saini, 2020). It resulted in generation of deep sense of belongingness and loyalty amongst employees (Choudhary, 2015). The organisation facilitated communication between senior management and HR personnel regularly with teams across the country through in house intranet named *Spandhan*. The company recognised its outperformers as well as appreciated complaints, concerns, feedback, and suggestions on possible improvements (Saini, 2020). Clearly, it focused more on internal employer branding rather than the external employer branding. To overcome this, the brand leveraged social media platforms like Instagram, Facebook, YouTube, Linkedin, and X (earlier twitter) to re-brand its employer perceptions for existing consumers and prospective Genz and millennial consumers and candidates. Unfortunately, the reviews, comments and ratings on these platforms were impacted due to unhappy customers. Although the company responded regularly to these, Shoppers Stop was uncertain about possible negative effects of its customer brand on its employer brand as customer's comments were also seen by job seekers (Saini, 2020). Thus, the brand was speculating:

1. What could be the negative consequences of under-performance of its customer rand on its employer brand?
2. How should it address the negative spillover effects of its customer brand on its employer brand?
3. How should Shoppers Stop leverage its presence on various social media platforms to promote and manage its employer brand?

Case Discussion 2: Zurich Airport: Internal Trust Leading to External Loyalty

Zurich Airport is one of the best airports in Europe. Both the Airport Service Quality (ASQ) Award and the World Travel Award have been won by this Airport. The company envisions providing high-quality service to the passengers and highlighting the importance of this possibility as a result of good cooperation between partners (Brosi, 2024). Competitors in this service-oriented Aviation Industry wondered how Zurich Airport has achieved a successful organisational culture that contributed to its employer branding. Additionally, how can this culture support the employees to survive through the crisis, like a pandemic, and prepare for the challenges ahead?

In the wake of disruptions like the pandemic affecting global travel, Zurich Airport's management invested in employee-centred strategies; ensuring safety, open communication, and shared responsibility. Even the employer, head of Human Resources- Bruno Zanella, credits the achievement of Zurich Airport to its culture of togetherness, honest dialogue, and mutual trust among employees (Randstad, 2021). This investment in internal trust translated into stronger employee advocacy, which in turn enhanced external perceptions of the airport as a reliable and trustworthy employer and service provider (Zurich Airport, 2022). The company actually applied the concept of "Walk the Talk" through continuous communication with employees along varied touchpoints like frequent meetings, reassurance of jobs and future with the company, minimizing layoffs to just 1.5% (Randstad, 2021). A large number of employees feel loyal toward their employer company as a result of the support they received during the uncertain times of the pandemic. Consumers of such companies that value their employees usually appreciate it through brand loyalty. From an employer brand perspective, this concern for the employees is a genuine display of the company's purpose, values, and culture. The case illustrates how employer branding during recovery stages can position employers for renewed loyalty among both employees and customers. Thus, it provides an instructive example of how internal trust can be leveraged for external brand loyalty.

BUILDING RESILIENT EMPLOYER BRANDS

There are four core pillars of a resilient employer brand, especially relevant during uncertainties:

Figure 3. 4P Model of Employer Brand Resilience

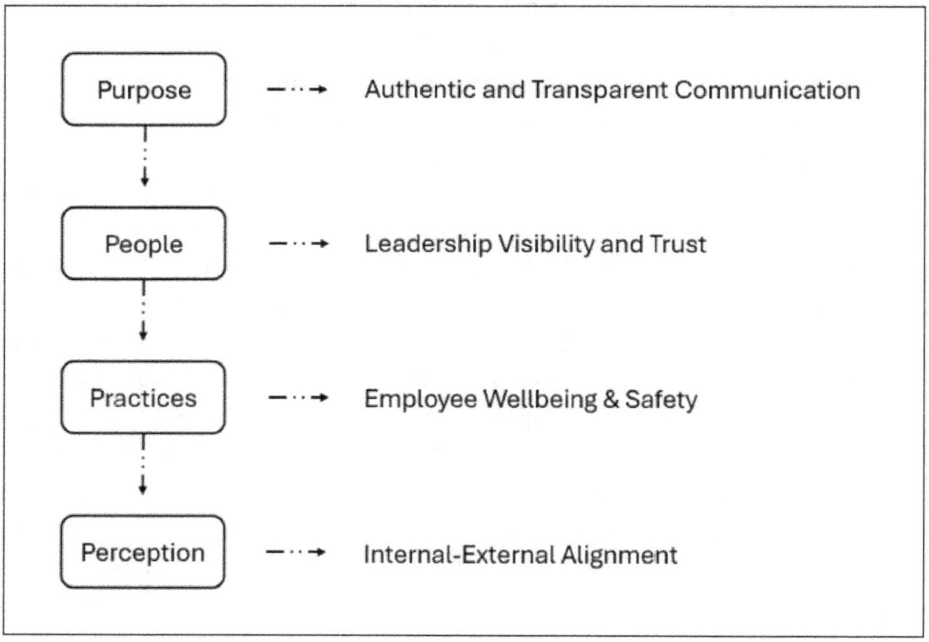

1. Authentic and transparent communication practices

Honest communications are the roots of Resilient Employer Brands. During uncertainties, a well-communicated employer-employee relationship goes a long way to rebuild trust and psychological safety. Employers that acknowledge their employee achievements and simultaneously initiate regular employee feedback and suggestions enhance employer credibility. Additionally, regular updates on the employer's future, crisis measures, or rebuilding efforts feel informed and respected, ultimately providing mental satisfaction. For instance, Microsoft handled the uncertain times of the pandemic very well by maintaining trust in its employees through regular and transparent briefings, visible accounting and fairness, consistent and unified messaging, along with empathy, humility, and open Q&A sessions, reinforcing that authenticity in communication is the foundation of lasting employer loyalty (Craigramsay, 2025).

2. Leadership visibility and trust-building

Leadership is said to be successful when you have trained your employees for unforeseen circumstances. The preparation involves leaders providing employees training, building employee resilience, comfort with the uncomfortable, short-term stability goals, communicating the value of togetherness, regular communication, and prioritising crisis and ignoring the noise (Reed, 2025). These engagements can be through town hall meetings, social media, or informal conversations, leading to brand anthropomorphism (Chinmulgund, & Tapas, (2025). Additionally, employees are more likely to stay loyal to the company when leadership communicates not just strategy but empathy, reinforcing the employer brand as trustworthy and human-driven.

3. Prioritising employee well-being and psychological safety

Employer branding is not limited to monetary perks but now requires holistic experience, especially with the upcoming generation (Panagiotidou & Mihail, 2023). Post-pandemic, employees perceive a potential employer that values mental health, promotes work-life balance, and practices inclusivity. Such a work environment also attracts and retains the existing workforce during uncertainties. Google is one of the classic examples to recognize and practice the importance of psychological safety of employees, ultimately leading to high-performing teams. Additionally, Google helps people and communities be prepared, resilient, and stay safe through its real-time alerts, AI, and research capabilities during times of crisis- especially in cities where its office is located (Google.com). Thus, employee well-being, agile policies, and focus on mental health position the company as a responsible and compassionate employer.

4. Aligning internal culture with external messaging

The chapter continues to propagate that internal employer branding usually leads to a favourable external message. In other words, the internal brand values must be consistent with the external marketing efforts to reinforce credibility. Although Google is favourably acknowledged for its internal organisational culture and employee well-being. In 2023, the organisation faced huge backlash due to public expression of cutting down diversity hiring goals (CNBC, 2023). Earlier, the employers' lack of handling harassment and racial inequity had previously led to huge employee backlash and protest in 2018-2020 (Larcker et al., 2021). Hence, when an employer propagates "DEI (Diversity, Equity, Inclusion) externally but fails to incorporate it internally, the authenticity erodes. Thus, syncronimity between what a company commits externally and what it does internally is a must to foster trust, engagement and long-term reputation resilience.

Strengthening Employer Brands before Crisis '

In contemporary organisational landscapes, employer branding is no longer a peripheral marketing activity but has become a central strategic imperative. Traditionally viewed as a tool for enhancing recruitment campaigns, employer branding today is recognized as a critical mechanism for creating long-term organisational value and resilience. A strong employer brand functions as both a magnet and a shield: it attracts skilled talent in competitive labor markets while simultaneously reinforcing employee loyalty and engagement.

The true importance of employer branding becomes particularly evident during times of uncertainty and disruption. Economic downturns, global health emergencies such as the COVID-19 pandemic, and reputational crises can destabilize even well-performing firms. However, employers that have consciously invested in building a credible and attractive employer identity are better positioned to withstand such turbulence. When employees perceive their employer as authentic, reliable, and supportive, they are more likely to remain committed during challenging periods, thereby reducing turnover risks. At the same time, a strong reputation in the employment market ensures that future talent pools remain open and interested in joining the organisation once stability returns (Backhaus & Tikoo, 2004; Theurer et al., 2018).

In essence, employer branding serves as a form of organisational insurance. It provides firms with the credibility and goodwill needed to navigate external shocks, while also fostering trust and continuity internally. This long-term perspective highlights why employer branding should not be treated as a cosmetic or short-term initiative but as an investment in organisational resilience and sustainability.'

Strengthening Employer Brand Values through Lived Actions '

At the heart of employer branding lies authenticity. Employees and stakeholders today are increasingly discerning and can easily identify contradictions between what employers claim and what they practice. Slogans, value statements, and missions are no longer sufficient unless they are consistently demonstrated through everyday actions and decision-making.

Strengthening employer brands, therefore, requires employers to embed organisational values into the lived experiences of employees. This includes enacting inclusive workplace policies, ensuring transparency in communication, promoting equitable treatment across all levels, and genuinely investing in employee well-being and development. When employees observe consistency between what their employer proclaims and what it delivers, trust is strengthened. Conversely, misalignment breeds skepticism and reputational risk, particularly in an era where information spreads rapidly through social and digital media.'

By “living their values,” employers not only strengthen internal cohesion and employee commitment but also generate positive external perceptions that enhance employer attractiveness. This trust-based alignment becomes especially critical during crises, as stakeholders seek reassurance that the employer remains dependable and principled even under pressure. ‘

Case 3: Employer Branding among Gen Z (Panagiotidou & Mihail, 2023)

A compelling empirical illustration of employer branding’s significance comes from Panagiotidou and Mihail’s (2023) study, which explored how employer branding influences perceptions of Generation Z. The study, involving 737 participants in a post-COVID context, revealed that employer branding awareness combined with positive publicity significantly enhanced employer attractiveness. Crucially, this process was mediated by word-of-mouth (WOM) communication, underscoring the role of peer advocacy in shaping perceptions.

Key Findings

1. Employer branding awareness directly improves perceptions of attractiveness.
2. Publicity acts as an amplifier of branding effects.
3. Word-of-mouth functions as a mediator, with Gen Z individuals relying heavily on peer recommendations and shared experiences in shaping their career choices.

These findings highlight that employer branding is not simply a matter of internal HR practices or external marketing campaigns. Instead, it operates as a dynamic ecosystem involving reputation, publicity, and interpersonal advocacy. For younger generations who place a premium on authenticity, peer experiences carry substantial weight. Thus, employers that proactively invest in employer branding and generate positive conversations in public spheres are more likely to secure their position as employers of choice. Patagonia and Unilever serve as strong real-world examples of companies that have moved beyond traditional internal employer branding to meet the evolving expectations of Generation Z. Both organisations show that today’s young workforce is no longer persuaded by catchy slogans or glossy branding campaigns rather they look for authenticity, purpose, and visible proof that a company truly lives its values. Patagonia’s deep commitment to environmental activism and social responsibility goes far beyond internal messaging. The company empowers employees to actively participate in environmental initiatives and donates one percent of its total sales to environmental causes. In 2022, founder Yvon Chouinard made a landmark decision by transferring ownership of Patagonia to a trust dedicated to protecting the planet, sending a powerful message of genuine purpose and ethical leadership that resonated strongly with Gen Z (Forbes, 2023).

Unilever offers a similar example of authenticity in action. Recognizing that younger job seekers desired more than an employer brand image, the company reshaped its employer value proposition around sustainability, social impact, and personal growth. Through initiatives such as the *Unilever Future Leaders Programme* and its open communication about sustainability goals and challenges, Unilever showcased a strong commitment to transparency and accountability, qualities that deeply resonate with Generation Z. This transformation helped Unilever earn a place among the top ten most attractive global employers for Gen Z graduates (Universum, 2023).

Together, these cases show that successful employer branding today requires more than internal promotion or culture statements, it demands consistent, meaningful action. For Generation Z, organisational credibility is built not on what companies *say* but on what they *do*. Authenticity, transparency, and purpose are now the true cornerstones of an employer brand that resonates with the new generation.

Practical Implications

For practitioners, this case provides clear lessons on the strategic benefits of employer branding. Employers that actively cultivate brand awareness and enhance their visibility through positive publicity lay the groundwork for long-term attractiveness. Importantly, this is not achieved solely through advertising but is amplified through word-of-mouth and peer endorsements, particularly among younger demographics.

In practice, this means that employer branding initiatives should prioritize authenticity and transparency, ensuring that employees themselves become credible ambassadors of the brand. Encouraging positive storytelling, employee advocacy programs, and consistent value-driven communication are therefore critical. These efforts not only position employers advantageously in times of stability but also serve as buffers in moments of crisis, where trust, reputation, and credibility become decisive.

Conclusion

Strengthening employer brands before crises is not about superficial messaging or polished communication strategies. It is about embedding organisational values into organisational life in ways that generate authenticity, trust, and long-term resilience. As Panagiotidou and Mihail's (2023) study demonstrates, employer branding yields dividends by influencing perceptions through word-of-mouth, especially among the next generation of employees. Employers that invest in this process are better equipped to attract and retain talent, weather crises, and position themselves as sustainable and desirable employers in the future.'

EMPLOYER BRANDING DURING CRISIS

Innovation in Talent Engagement During Crisis

Crises often place employers under intense scrutiny, exposing the authenticity of their employer brand. Whether triggered by global shocks such as the COVID-19 pandemic, reputational crisis, or socio-political upheavals, crises test the depth of organisational values and the resilience of employer–employee relationships. An employer brand that has been authentically cultivated prior to disruption becomes a stabilizing force, whereas superficial branding efforts quickly erode under pressure.

A recent empirical study published in *Governance & Organisational Studies* (2022–2023, MDPI) investigated how current employees evaluate their organisations during crises. The research explored the role of voice behavior, word-of-mouth (WOM), and employee satisfaction as indicators of employer brand strength. Findings revealed that reputation and development value (i.e., opportunities for growth and learning) significantly predicted positive WOM and employee advocacy, even in times of turbulence. This study underscores that resilience in employer branding is not only about attracting external talent but also about mobilizing employees themselves as brand advocates during difficult periods. Employees who perceive their employer as trustworthy, supportive, and developmental are more likely to spread positive narratives that sustain the brand through crisis.

International Organisation Cases highlighting the importance of Employer Branding

To further contextualize the dynamics of employer branding in crises, several global case examples provide insights into both successes and failures.

Case 1: Airbnb's Empathetic Layoffs during COVID-19

The COVID-19 pandemic constituted one of the most severe external shocks to global business in modern history. Few sectors were affected as immediately and dramatically as travel and hospitality. As international borders closed and mobility restrictions intensified in early 2020, demand for accommodation services declined sharply. The home-sharing platform Airbnb experienced a substantial contraction in bookings, forcing rapid strategic reassessment.

The 2020 workforce reduction at Airbnb remains a landmark case study in corporate communication due to the highly unconventional tone established by CEO Brian Chesky. Deviating from the standard, sterile templates of corporate restructuring, Chesky's public announcement was characterized by profound emotional vulnerability and relational depth. His declaration of having a "deep feeling of love" for his staff represented a radical departure from traditional executive distancing, positioning the crisis within an empathetic rather than a procedural framework (Chesky, 2020). This human-centric approach was widely lauded by business analysts as a blueprint for compassionate leadership during global instability.

While the immediate reception of Chesky's 2020 letter was positive, its long-term implications provided a deeper lesson in leadership ethics. In a candid dialogue with organizational psychologist Adam Grant for the TED Audio Collective, Chesky explores how the very language that offered comfort during the initial crisis eventually created an "ethical and operational paradox" (Grant, 2024). He reflects on the inherent tension that arises when the "family" metaphor, intended to foster belonging, collides with the cold reality of corporate restructuring. This conversation serves as a vital companion piece to the original 2020 announcement, offering a more mature perspective on how to lead with genuine empathy while maintaining the necessary boundaries of professional accountability.

By asserting that "other companies will be lucky to have them," Chesky successfully pivoted the layoff narrative from one of organizational rejection to one of high-value talent acquisition (Chesky, 2020). This intentional reframing aimed to preserve the dignity of departing employees and soften the psychological blow of the separation. Consequently, outlets like *Forbes* and *Harvard Business Review* cited Airbnb's strategy as a premier example of values-driven crisis management, contrasting it sharply with the detached, algorithmic layoffs seen elsewhere (Esty & Ciechanover, 2021).

Ultimately, the Airbnb narrative demonstrates that employer branding is a composite of both material support and symbolic framing. The way a leader speaks during a crisis shapes stakeholder perception as much as the severance packages themselves. By combining initial empathy with honest retrospective analysis, the Airbnb example provides a sophisticated look at how executive voice and self-reflection define organizational values in an era of constant uncertainty.

For scholars examining employer branding and crisis communication, this dialogue provides valuable primary-source insight into how leaders recalibrate narrative framing after experiencing the reputational and ethical complexities of crisis-driven downsizing. It underscores that employer brand meaning is shaped not only by immediate actions, but also by subsequent reflection and narrative reconstruction.'

For readers seeking a deeper exploration of the leadership transition from a "family" metaphor to a "high-performing team" framework, the following podcast episode provides valuable primary insight:

Podcast Episode:

"A Company Is Not a Family with Airbnb CEO Brian Chesky"

Multimedia Resource: Readers are encouraged to listen to the full discussion: **A company is not a family with Airbnb CEO Brian Chesky**.

Case 2: Starbucks' Employee-First Approach in Global Disruptions '

Starbucks has consistently framed its employer brand around "partner care". Starbucks provides an excellent example of how modern employer branding extends beyond internal employee engagement to include the well-being of a wider network of stakeholders. The company refers to its employees as partners, a deliberate choice that reflects mutual respect, inclusion, and a sense of shared mission. This approach is evident in the organisation's investment in employee benefits such as healthcare for part-time workers, tuition assistance through the Starbucks College Achievement Plan, and continuous opportunities for career development (Leaderonomics, 2022). These initiatives show that Starbucks does not view its employees as mere workers but as long-term collaborators who grow with the company.

'The concept of "Partner Care" at Starbucks is not confined to the retail environment; it extends into the global supply chain through immersive sustainability initiatives. A primary example of this is the long-standing collaboration with the Earthwatch Institute, which allows Starbucks "partners" (employees) to engage directly in field research alongside coffee farmers.

As documented in the case study film, *Starbucks and Earth watch: Sustainable Coffee* [01:24], the program focuses on a technical and human-centric approach to coffee cultivation. Rather than simply issuing top-down mandates, the initiative involves:

1. **Scientific Soil Analysis:** Partners assist in measuring soil health and nutrient levels to help farmers optimize fertilizer use [02:25].
2. **Economic Empowerment:** By reducing reliance on expensive chemical inputs—lowering usage from nine bags of fertilizer per hectare to seven—the program helps farmers save approximately $200 per harvest, directly impacting their livelihood [04:49].
3. **Human Connection:** The "Origin Experience" transforms the employee's perspective from seeing a "package of coffee" to seeing the "natural resources and the farmers" behind it [05:30].

This direct engagement serves as a powerful employer branding tool. By involving baristas in the pruning, measurements, and daily challenges of farmers on 70-degree slopes [00:59], Starbucks operationalizes its "Guiding Principles" through "very real and significant" environmental contributions [06:21]. This transparency is particularly resonant for Generation Z employees, who prioritize brands that can prove their social impact through action rather than just slogans.

Readers seeking a richer, visual understanding of this collaborative sustainability initiative may refer to the documentary film *Starbucks and Earthwatch: Sustainable Coffee* (Earthwatch Institute, 2008). The video offers firsthand insight into the ongoing field-research program in which Starbucks partners, scientists from Earthwatch Institute, and coffee farmers work together to advance sustainable cultivation practices.

Primary Video Link: Earth watch Institute. (2008). *Starbucks and Earthwatch: Sustainable Coffee* [Video]. YouTube. https://www.youtube.com/watch?v=iUQhDDuxEYE

Furthermore, Starbucks' response to the COVID-19 crisis reflected a deliberate effort to align operational decisions with its long-standing "partner care" employer brand philosophy. During 2020, the company introduced "catastrophe pay," which ensured income continuity for partners who were unable to work due to store closures or personal health concerns. In parallel, Starbucks strengthened its employee support infrastructure by expanding access to mental health services through its collaboration with Lyra Health (Starbucks, 2020).In public communications, then-CEO Kevin Johnson clarified that these measures were grounded in the organization's mission and core values, even though they involved considerable short-term financial implications. As Johnson explained in a letter and shareholder meeting remarks, *"As we are navigating this dynamic global environment together, we will continue to prioritize the health and well-being of our partners and customers..."* (Starbucks, 2020). This principle underpinned Starbucks' approach to safety protocols, compensation guarantees, and expanded benefits during the crisis, signaling that partner welfare was central to decision-making and not merely incidental' By visibly placing employees at the center of its crisis response, Starbucks reinforced its employer brand as people-oriented. This strategy translated into continued loyalty, lower attrition, and positive brand advocacy by employees worldwide.

Figure 4. Ethical Practices of Starbucks.

Case 3: Uber and Reputational Challenges during Leadership Crisis

In contrast, Uber's leadership crisis in 2017 highlighted the risks of weak employer branding. Reports of toxic workplace culture, gender discrimination, and unethical leadership behavior severely damaged Uber's reputation as an employer of choice. Although subsequent reforms under new leadership attempted to address cultural issues, the case demonstrates how quickly employer branding can deteriorate when organisational values are not lived authentically. Trust, once lost, is far harder to rebuild (Newcomer, 2017).

In 2017, Uber emerged as a prominent example of how employer branding can deteriorate when an organization's internal culture contradicts its external narrative. While the company projected itself as a forward-thinking, disruptive, and opportunity-oriented technology firm, internal investigations and employee accounts painted a different picture. Reports highlighted issues such as gender discrimination, harassment, and confrontational leadership practices under CEO Travis Kalanick. As reported by VOA Learning English (2017), numerous allegations of toxic workplace behavior surfaced, significantly undermining Uber's employer image. The situation escalated when a widely shared video captured Kalanick in a tense argument with an Uber driver, an incident that was widely perceived as reflecting a lack of empathy toward driver concerns (Friedell, 2017). Concurrently, media investigations uncovered the company's use of "Greyball," a software tool allegedly designed to bypass regulatory scrutiny in certain markets (Wong, 2017).

Collectively, these events exposed systemic cultural weaknesses within Uber and revealed a stark mismatch between its public image as an innovative disruptor and its internal ethical practices. Consequently, the company's once-strong employer brand suffered a substantial decline, diminishing its appeal to both current employees and prospective talent. The reputational damage also generated longer-term challenges, including heightened regulatory oversight, leadership instability, employee turnover risks, and broader concerns regarding organizational sustainability.

Consequences and Risks Faced by Uber:

1. Talent attraction and retention challenges: The crisis tarnished Uber's image among young professionals, making recruitment and retention of top talent increasingly difficult as many began to question the company's values and leadership integrity.
2. Reputational spillover: The controversy not only affected employee morale but also investor confidence, customer loyalty, and regulatory relations, weakening Uber's overall standing.
3. Increased oversight and operational costs: The company was compelled to devote significant resources to investigations, leadership restructuring, and cultural reform, diverting attention and investment away from core business expansion.

The key question that emerges from this discussion is:

How can organisations like Uber prevent similar cultural and ethical crises in the future and rebuild a trustworthy employer brand?

To rebuild credibility and prevent similar issues from recurring, companies like Uber must focus on long-term cultural reform rather than surface-level image repair.

1. Align words with actions: Regularly assess workplace culture and ensure that employees' behaviors reflect the organisation's stated values.
2. Build strong ethics systems: Establish fair and confidential reporting channels, independent investigations, and mechanisms to protect employee well-being.
3. Integrate culture into operations: Embed ethical principles into recruitment, onboarding, training, and performance evaluations to ensure values are genuinely practiced, not just promoted.
4. Be transparent about progress: Regularly communicate updates on diversity, culture, and employee engagement to build stakeholder trust.

Thus, for Generation Z, the Uber crisis serves as a powerful lesson. This generation places great importance on ethics, transparency, and authentic leadership. They are quick to notice when a company's actions fail to align with its stated values. As demonstrated by Uber's experience, such inconsistencies can severely harm trust and long-term credibility. Therefore, rebuilding trust demands more than surface-level reputation management; it calls for deep cultural change and a long-term dedication to ethical and transparent practices.'

Figure 5. Audio clip from "Uber Chief Caught on Camera Arguing with Driver"

VOA LearningEnglish, 2017 (https://learningenglish.voanews.com/a/uber-argument/3745669.html)

Case 4: Unilever's Purpose-Driven Branding amid Climate and Social Crises

Crises often function as moments of truth for organizations, exposing whether their employer brand is grounded in authentic values or constructed as symbolic rhetoric. As David A. Aaker (2022) argues, purpose-driven brands create "signature programs" that are embedded in operations and culture rather than layered onto marketing communications. When such programs are institutionalized, they serve as strategic assets during disruption. Similarly, Pillai (2024) conceptualizes purpose-driven branding as a perceptive strategy that builds "impactful connections" by aligning internal culture with external societal commitments. Mirvis (2023) further contends that social purpose must be operationalized across governance, leadership, and stakeholder systems; otherwise, it risks collapse under scrutiny. These theoretical insights are particularly relevant when examining how Unilever navigated the COVID-19 crisis.

The pandemic placed multinational corporations under intense stakeholder pressure, testing commitments to employees, suppliers, and communities. In March 2020, Unilever announced a comprehensive action plan to mitigate the socio-economic consequences of the COVID-19 pandemic, which included a pledge to donate €100 million worth of products to support vulnerable communities and a range of measures to support its extended value chain, including suppliers and customers (Unilever Arabia, 2021).Rather than retreating into cost-minimization logic, the company framed its response as an extension of its long-standing sustainability strategy. This reflects Aaker's (2022) assertion that purpose-driven initiatives must be scalable and resilient enough to withstand external shocks.

From an employer branding perspective, such actions signal authenticity to employees and prospective talent. Pillai (2024) notes that purpose-driven brands foster emotional commitment when stakeholders perceive congruence between declared values and lived experience. Unilever's continuation of its Climate & Nature Fund commitments and gender equity goals during and after the pandemic achieving 50/50 gender balance in managerial roles in 2021, illustrates structural consistency rather than reactive branding (Branding in Asia, 2022). This continuity supports the proposition that authentically cultivated employer brands become stabilizing forces in turbulent environments, reinforcing employee trust and psychological safety.'

In a podcast discussion on the future of work, Alan Jope explains that Unilever's commitment to employee development existed before COVID-19 and was strengthened, not created, by the crisis. He emphasizes that "the jobs we do today are not the jobs we will be doing tomorrow," highlighting the company's focus on reskilling and upskilling its workforce (Jope, 2022).Even when restructuring is necessary, Unilever aims to ensure displaced employees are "future-fit," offering retraining and career transition support. Jope also describes flexible work experiments such as a four-day workweek pilot and the "U-Work" program, which allow employees greater autonomy while remaining connected to the organization.From an employer branding perspective, these initiatives demonstrate that Unilever's people strategy is embedded in structural investment rather than rhetoric, reinforcing its image as a future-ready and purpose-driven employer.

Lessons Learned from Successes and Failures

The four case studies highlight diverse approaches and outcomes of employer branding during crises. Organisations such as Airbnb and Starbucks demonstrated the value of empathetic, employee-first responses that reinforced authenticity and credibility. Unilever's purpose-driven branding illustrates how alignment with societal expectations can enhance resilience. Conversely, Uber's leadership crisis underscores how lapses in governance and culture can severely erode employer brand value.'

Table 2. Summary of 4 case studies: Approach, Strengths, Weaknesses, and Lessons

Case	Approach	Strengths	Weaknesses	Lesson Learned
Airbnb (COVID-19)	Empathetic layoffs with transparent communication	Preserved trust; enchanced long-term attractiveness	Workforce reducation is still painful	Empathy and transparency soften crisis impact
Starucks (Global disruptions)	Employee-first policies (benefits, well-being)	Reinforced loyalty; positive advocacy	High costs of benefits	Investing people pays long-terms dividends
Uber (Leadershop crisis)	Weak governance, toxic culture	Rapid growth strategy	Severe reputational damage; talent loss	Values must be lived, not just stated
Unilever (Climate & social crises)	Purpose-driven branding linked to sustainability	Strong alignment with societal values	Criticized at times for "woke washing"	Purpose and action build resilience

Conclusion

The cases discussed highlight the dual nature of crises: they can erode weak employer brands or amplify the credibility of authentic ones. Evidence from empirical research (Governance & Organisational Studies, 2022–2023) further validates that employees themselves play a crucial role in sustaining employer branding through voice and advocacy. Organisations such as Airbnb, Starbucks, and Unilever demonstrate how proactive, values-driven responses during crises strengthen trust and long-term attractiveness. Conversely, Uber's reputational challenges show the risks of neglecting cultural alignment and ethical leadership. Ultimately, the lesson for practitioners is clear: resilience in employer branding is built before crises, but tested during them.

POST-CRISIS EMPLOYER BRANDING

Post-Crisis Repositioning for Enhanced Trust and Loyalty

Crises often act as defining moments for organisations, revealing their true values and the strength of their commitment to employees and stakeholders. While disruptive events can weaken poorly prepared organisations, they also provide opportunities for those with authentic employer brands to reposition themselves and emerge stronger. If handled strategically, crises can be transformed into "moments of truth" where organisational responses build not only resilience but also enhanced trust, loyalty, and long-term attractiveness (Theurer et al., 2018).

Post-crisis employer branding requires a deliberate approach to re-establishing credibility. Employees, job seekers, and the public closely observe how employers respond during adversity. Transparent communication, genuine support for employees, and consistent alignment between values and practices can turn reputational risk into reputational capital. This form of trust-based repositioning ensures that employers are remembered not for the disruption they endured but for the way they responded to it.

Case Illustrations of Post-Crisis Opportunities, like digital disruption

Najm (2023): Branding as a Driver of E-Recruitment under Constraints

An illuminating example of post-crisis employer branding is provided by Najm (2023), examines how organisations in Egypt sustained recruitment effectiveness during the COVID-19 pandemic through strong employer branding. The study explored how branding strategies shaped e-recruitment outcomes during a period marked by limited mobility, economic uncertainty, and reduced organisational resources.

Najm (2023) found that the strength and clarity of an organisation's employer brand directly influenced job seekers' perceptions, trust, and willingness to engage with digital recruitment platforms. Even under constrained conditions, firms that consistently communicated their core values like trust, stability, and opportunity were able to maintain applicant interest and attract qualified candidates. The study revealed that branding attributes such as organisational credibility, transparency, and social responsibility played crucial roles in enhancing candidate engagement and confidence during a time of disruption.

In particular, Najm highlighted that employer branding operated as a stabilizing mechanism within the digital hiring process. This case reinforces that employer branding is not merely a pre-crisis or growth-stage strategy. When strategically leveraged, it can function as a critical post-crisis tool, thereby helping organisations rebuild trust, re-engage the labor market, and reassert their relevance. The ability to maintain recruitment effectiveness through branding during adversity demonstrates how authentic communication and digital adaptation contribute to post-crisis resilience.

In contrast to the human-centric approach of branding under constraint, the adoption of Artificial Intelligence (AI) in recruitment represents a technologically driven response to digital disruption. Although AI-enabled recruitment platforms are widely praised for enhancing speed, efficiency, and perceived objectivity through data-driven evaluation, they also introduce a host of significant ethical and operational concerns. A prominent illustration is ***Amazon***'s attempt to deploy an AI-based hiring system designed to automate résumé screening and identify promising candidates. Despite its advanced technological design, the system was ultimately discovered to exhibit bias against female applicants, primarily because it had been trained on historical recruitment data largely reflecting male-dominated hiring patterns (Dastin, 2018). As a result, the algorithm automatically rejected resumes containing terms such as *"women's chess club captain"* or references to *"women's colleges."* This example demonstrates how algorithmic bias can unintentionally mirror and intensify existing social disparities, thereby compromising equity and fairness within digital recruitment practices.

This shows that although using AI in hiring highlights the promise of digital technology, the Amazon case also reveals why human supervision, clear algorithms, and ethical responsibility are essential in recruitment systems. In other words, while technology can make hiring faster and more efficient, it must be managed carefully to stay fair and transparent. Therefore, post-crisis digital growth should balance innovation with accountability, a lesson that stands in clear contrast to Najm's (2023) focus on authenticity and trust as the real strengths behind successful e-recruitment.

Case Discussion: Panagiotidou (2024): WOM as a Source of Long-Term Employer Attractiveness

Building on prior work on Gen Z perceptions, Panagiotidou (2024) finds that word-of-mouth (WOM) continues to function as a powerful mechanism for sustaining employer attractiveness in the post-crisis era. Even after disruptive events, organisations that invest in authentic branding and positive publicity are rewarded with advocacy from employees and external stakeholders. WOM does not merely influence immediate perceptions but creates a long-term reputational advantage, helping employers retain their attractiveness in competitive labor markets.

In today's world, where most people are constantly online and active on social media, an important question arises: *Does word-of-mouth still influence how people choose where to work?* The answer, according to Panagiotidou et al. (2024), is yes. Even though digital platforms dominate communication, personal recommendations still matter. When job seekers hear from real employees like friends, peers, or even online reviews, it feels more genuine than formal company advertisements. These shared experiences give potential candidates a clearer picture of a company's culture, values, and work environment, helping them decide whether it's a good fit.

Another key question is: *How can organisations create positive electronic word-of-mouth (e-WOM) using social media?* One effective approach is to encourage employees to become brand ambassadors. When employees post authentic experiences on LinkedIn, Instagram, or Glassdoor, they create a more relatable and trustworthy image of the company. Genuine stories about fairness, teamwork, or growth opportunities tend to resonate more than marketing campaigns. Additionally, Panagiotidou et al. (2024) also highlight that this kind of honest storytelling, led by employees themselves, strengthens trust and enhances an organisation's reputation far better than traditional advertising.

Finally, there's the question: *How can organisations prevent negative online talk (Negative Word of mouth) that could harm their image?* The key lies in how they treat their people. When employees are treated fairly and feel heard, they are less likely to speak negatively about the company. If criticism appears online, the organisation should respond respectfully, explain its side, and outline the steps being taken to address concerns. Ignoring or deleting negative comments can often make things worse. Instead, transparency and a willingness to learn from feedback help build credibility. Thus, Organisations that remain genuine, appreciate their employees, and maintain transparent communication are more likely to draw in and retain talent, even during challenging or uncertain times.'

Conclusion: Strategic Lessons for Post-Crisis Branding

Crises act as testing grounds that expose, challenge, and ultimately strengthen an employer's true character and authenticity. Insights drawn from the cases of Zurich Airport, Najm (2023), and Panagiotidou (2024) reveal that employer branding extends well beyond a conventional HR or marketing activity. It is a strategic capability that directly influences an employer's ability to withstand disruption, rebuild trust, and emerge more resilient. The Zurich Airport case demonstrates that cultivating internal trust through transparent communication and genuine concern for employee welfare serves as the cornerstone of sustained external loyalty. Similarly, Najm (2023) shows that a strong employer brand can uphold digital recruitment effectiveness and organisational stability, even in restrictive environments such as the COVID-19 crisis. Complementing these perspectives, Panagiotidou (2024) emphasizes the pivotal role of positive word-of-mouth in shaping long-term employer attractiveness, underscoring how peer influence and authenticity drive post-crisis reputation and talent engagement. Collectively, these cases affirm that authenticity, open communication, and the alignment of values with behaviour are central to building and maintaining effective employer brands after crises. Employers that use crises as opportunities to demonstrate integrity, reaffirm their values, and communicate transparently not only recover more effectively but also emerge as stronger, more trusted, and more desirable employers for both existing employees and future talent.'

In conclusion, we can say, digitization has become one of the most important ways for brands to grow, stay creative, and compete in today's fast-changing world. By using digital tools and technology, companies can reach more people, connect with customers more personally, and build stronger, long-lasting relationships. Additionally, social media allows brands to talk directly with their audience, listen to feedback, and show a more human side. At the same time, tools like data analytics, artificial intelligence (AI), and automation help businesses better understand what customers want, spot new trends, and design products or campaigns that fit their needs.

But digitization isn't just about marketing, it also makes day-to-day operations smoother and more efficient. It helps businesses manage their supply chains, make quicker decisions, and reduce costs. For small and medium-sized enterprises (SMEs), digital platforms open doors to global markets that were once out of reach, helping them grow beyond local boundaries. As Verhoef et al. (2021) explain, digital transformation allows companies to create greater value for customers by weaving technology into every part of their business, starting from planning and production to customer service and innovation. In simple terms, brands that embrace digital change are more flexible, more connected to their customers, and better prepared to succeed in a world driven by data and technology.

SCOPE AND DEFINITIONS

Scope of the Chapter

This chapter examines employer branding from a crisis management and talent management perspective, focusing on how organizations build, protect, and reposition their employer brands before, during, and after crises. The scope encompasses both internal and external dimensions of employer branding, recognizing that employee experience, leadership behavior, organizational culture, and stakeholder communication collectively shape employer brand perception.

The chapter considers multiple types of crises with particular emphasis on post-2020 contexts such as the COVID-19 pandemic, digital backlash, and social media activism. While traditional corporate reputation management literature often centers on customers and investors, this chapter narrows its focus specifically to the talent ecosystem — current employees, potential recruits (especially Gen Z and Millennials), and digital employer-brand audiences.

Geographically, the discussion incorporates international organizational cases to provide cross-cultural insights, though it does not attempt to provide an exhaustive global comparison. Instead, selected cases are used illustratively to highlight patterns of success and failure in employer branding resilience across multiple industries.

Conceptually, the chapter integrates insights from human resource management, crisis communication theory, organizational resilience, and employer branding research to develop a practical yet theory-informed framework. Particular attention is given to the role of social media, leadership visibility, psychological safety, and innovation in talent engagement during crises.

The outcomes targeted within this chapter include:

- Strengthened employee trust and engagement before crisis
- Enhanced employer attractiveness and talent retention
- Restoration and repositioning of employer brand credibility post-crisis
- Long-term organizational resilience

The chapter does not attempt to provide a comprehensive crisis communication manual or a full-scale reputation management model. Rather, it focuses specifically on the intersection of employer branding and crisis contexts, offering strategic lessons for organizations seeking to sustain talent confidence and competitive advantage amid uncertainty.

REFERENCES

Anderson-Meli, L., & Koshy, S. (2020). *Public relations crisis communication: A new model*. Routledge. DOI: 10.4324/9780429287763

Arndt, J. (1967). Role of product-related conversations in the diffusion of a new product. *JMR, Journal of Marketing Research, 4*(3), 291–295. DOI: 10.1177/002224376700400308

Azhar, A., Rehman, N., Majeed, N., & Bano, S. (2024). Employer branding: A strategy to enhance organizational performance. *International Journal of Hospitality Management, 116*, 103618. DOI: 10.1016/j.ijhm.2023.103618

Backhaus, K., & Tikoo, S. (2004). Conceptualizing and researching employer branding. *Career Development International, 9*(5), 501–517. DOI: 10.1108/13620430410550754

Benoit, W. L. (1997). Image repair discourse and crisis communication. *Public Relations Review, 23*(2), 177–187. DOI: 10.1016/S0363-8111(97)90023-0

Berthon, P., Ewing, M., & Hah, L. L. (2005). Captivating company: Dimensions of attractiveness in employer branding. *International Journal of Advertising, 24*(2), 151–172. DOI: 10.1080/02650487.2005.11072912

Berthon, P., Ewing, M., & Hah, L. L. (2005). Captivating company: Dimensions of attractiveness in employer branding. *International Journal of Advertising, 24*(2), 151–172. DOI: 10.1080/02650487.2005.11072912

Chinmulgund, A., & Tapas, P. (2025). Organisational anthropomorphism and its antecedents: A literature review and proposed framework. *The International Journal of Organizational Analysis, 33*(5), 1312–1323. DOI: 10.1108/IJOA-01-2024-4197

Chong, D., & Druckman, J. N. (2007). Framing theory. *Annual Review of Political Science, 10*(1), 103–126. DOI: 10.1146/annurev.polisci.10.072805.103054

Coombs, W. T. (1995). Choosing the right words: The development of guidelines for the selection of the "appropriate" crisis-response strategies. *Management Communication Quarterly, 8*(4), 447–476. DOI: 10.1177/0893318995008004003

Coombs, W. T. (2007). Protecting organization reputations during a crisis: The development and application of situational crisis communication theory. *Corporate Reputation Review, 10*(3), 163–176. DOI: 10.1057/palgrave.crr.1550049

Coombs, W. T. (2007). Ongoing crisis communication: Planning, managing, and responding. *Sage (Atlanta, Ga.)*.

Coombs, W. T. (2014). *Ongoing crisis communication: Planning, managing, and responding*. Sage Publications.

Coombs, W. T. (2019). *Ongoing Crisis Communication: Planning, Managing, and Responding* (5th ed.). SAGE Publications.

Etter, M., Ravasi, D., & Colleoni, E. (2019). Social media and the formation of organisational reputation. *Academy of Management Review*, *44*(1), 28–52. DOI: 10.5465/amr.2014.0280

Frkal, R., & Lewis, M. S. (2025). Strategic leader or impulsive billionaire: Elon Musk's early moves to turnaround Twitter. *The CASE Journal*, *21*(4), 828–838. DOI: 10.1108/TCJ-07-2024-0191

Hajjami, O., & Crocco, O. S. (2024). Evolving approaches to employee engagement: Comparing antecedents in remote work and traditional workplaces. *European Journal of Training and Development*, *48*(3-4), 375–392. DOI: 10.1108/EJTD-10-2022-0103

International Organization for Standardization. (2017). *ISO 22316:2017: Security and resilience –Organizational resilience – Principles and attributes*. ISO.

Janssen, H., & Rudeloff, C. (2025). Exploring the role of influencers in shaping employer brands: A comparative study of corporate and third-party influencers. *Corporate Reputation Review*, *28*(1), 57–70. DOI: 10.1057/s41299-023-00177-9

Junça Silva, A., & Dias, H. (2023). The relationship between employer branding, corporate reputation and intention to apply to a job offer. *The International Journal of Organizational Analysis*, *31*(8), 1–16. DOI: 10.1108/IJOA-01-2022-3129

Junça Silva, A., & Dias, H. (2023). The relationship between employer branding, corporate reputation and intention to apply to a job offer. *The International Journal of Organizational Analysis*, *31*(8), 1–16. DOI: 10.1108/IJOA-01-2022-3129

Junça Silva, A., & Dias, H. (2023). The relationship between employer branding, corporate reputation and intention to apply to a job offer. *The International Journal of Organizational Analysis*, *31*(8), 1–16. DOI: 10.1108/IJOA-01-2022-3129

Kelley, H. H., & Michela, J. L. (1980). Attribution theory and research. *Annual Review of Psychology*, *31*(1), 457–501. DOI: 10.1146/annurev.ps.31.020180.002325 PMID: 20809783

Kuoppakangas, P., Hagman, S., Stenvall, J., & Kinder, T. (2024). Social Learning and Reputation Management in an Espionage Crisis. *Corporate Reputation Review*, *27*(4), 271–282. DOI: 10.1057/s41299-023-00171-1

Laufer, D., & Coombs, W. T. (2006). How should a company respond to a product harm crisis? The role of corporate reputation and consumer-based cues. *Business Horizons*, *49*(5), 379–385. DOI: 10.1016/j.bushor.2006.01.002

Lilly, J., Durr, D., Grogan, A., & Super, J. F. (2021). Wells Fargo: Administrative evil and the pressure to conform. *Business Horizons*, *64*(5), 587–597. DOI: 10.1016/j.bushor.2021.02.028

Lock, I., & Jacobs, S. (2025). Drivers of Reputation and Legitimacy of a Highly Visible Public Sector Organization: Surveying Citizens' Perceptions: I. Lock, S. Jacobs. *Corporate Reputation Review*, •••, 1–15. DOI: 10.1057/s41299-025-00230-9

Makumbe, W. (2025). The mediating effect of employer branding on the relationship between transformational leadership and organisational commitment in the South African telecoms sector. *African Journal of Economic and Management Studies*.

Nadales-Gallego, A., Galindo-Reyes, F., & Garrido-Moreno, A. (2025). Connecting Internal Communication and Employee Engagement in Organisation: A Systematic Literature Review. *SAGE Open*, *15*(4), 21582440251399773. DOI: 10.1177/21582440251399773

Najm, & Sabreen. (2023). The Role of Employer Brand on E-Recruitment during COVID-19 in Egypt. Journal of Administrative, Financial and Quantitative Research, 3(1), 161-181.

Nanjundeswaraswamy, T. S., Bharath, S., & Nagesh, P. (2025). Employer branding: design and development of a scale. *Journal of economic and administrative sciences*, 41(1), 88-113.

Nilsen, E. R., Olafsen, A. H., & Nadeau, J. (2024). Rethinking employer attractiveness: A qualitative exploration of potential employees' perception of employer attractiveness attributes. *Corporate Reputation Review*, •••, 1–13.

Nilsen, E. R., Olafsen, A. H., & Nadeau, J. (2024). Rethinking employer attractiveness: A qualitative exploration of potential employees' perception of employer attractiveness attributes. *Corporate Reputation Review*, •••, 1–13.

Nilsen, E. R., Olafsen, A. H., & Nadeau, J. (2024). Rethinking employer attractiveness: A qualitative exploration of potential employees' perception of employer attractiveness attributes. *Corporate Reputation Review*, •••, 1–13.

Nöhammer, E., Schorn, R., & Becker, N. (2022). Optimizing the organizational crisis communication portfolio. *Corporate Reputation Review*, •••, 1.

Panagiotidou, S., & Mihail, D. (2023, November). Pre-Recruiting HR Marketing for new Gen Talent Acquisition: The Mediating Role of Word of Mouth. In *European Conference on Management, Leadership and Governance*, 19(1), 505-511. DOI: 10.34190/ecmlg.19.1.1675

Panagiotidou, S., Mihail, D., & Katou, A. A. (2024). Unveiling the power of word-of-mouth in pre-recruitment employer branding strategy during COVID-19. *Employee Relations*, *46*(4), 833–849. DOI: 10.1108/ER-10-2023-0540

Reese, E., & Allison, J. E. (2023). *Unsustainable: Amazon, warehousing, and the politics of exploitation*. Univ of California Press.

Rita, P., António, N., & Raminhos, V. (2026). Using employee feedback to build effective employer branding strategies: A mixed method approach. *The International Journal of Organizational Analysis*, *34*(1), 256–282. DOI: 10.1108/IJOA-04-2024-4469

Rys, M., Schollaert, E., & Van Hoye, G. (2024). Living the employer brand during a crisis? A qualitative study on internal employer branding in times of the COVID-19 pandemic. *PLoS One*, *19*(5), e0303361. DOI: 10.1371/journal.pone.0303361 PMID: 38739576

Saini, G. K. (2020). Shoppers stop: Leveraging social media for employer branding. *Emerging Economies Cases Journal*, *2*(1), 54–61. DOI: 10.1177/2516604220930394

Saini, G. K. (2023). Employer branding: A critical review and future research. *NHRD Network Journal*, *16*(3), 220–232. DOI: 10.1177/26314541231170424

Schwarz, A. (2019). The state of strategic organizational crisis communication research in the context of global and digital communication. *Revista De La Asociación Española De Investigación De La Comunicación*, *6*(11), 279–310. DOI: 10.24137/raeic.6.11.15

Shafiee, M., & Goodarzi, S. (2026). The role of employer branding in talent management: Analysis of key strategies and tools. *The International Journal of Organizational Analysis*, *34*(1), 99–114. DOI: 10.1108/IJOA-10-2024-4900

Siomkos, G. J., & Kurzbard, G. (1994). The hidden crisis in product-harm crisis management. *European Journal of Marketing*, *28*(2), 30–41. DOI: 10.1108/03090569410055265

Špoljarić, A., & Ozretić Došen, Đ. (2023). Employer brand and international employer brand: Literature review. *Corporate Communications*, *28*(4), 671–682. DOI: 10.1108/CCIJ-11-2022-0141

Stadler, R., Fecker, D., & Huber, L. (2025). Co-branding alliances as an employer branding strategy. *Journal of Hospitality and Tourism Insights*, *8*(11), 259–275. DOI: 10.1108/JHTI-03-2025-0358

Stor, M., & Haromszeki, Ł. (2025). Exploring employer branding and company performance results in non-crisis and crisis times: the mediating role of HRM outcomes in Central European MNC. *Journal of Organizational Effectiveness: People and Performance*, (ahead-of-print).

Stor, M., & Haromszeki, Ł. (2025). Exploring employer branding and company performance results in non-crisis and crisis times: the mediating role of HRM outcomes in Central European MNC. *Journal of Organizational Effectiveness: People and Performance*, (ahead-of-print).

Theurer, C. P., Tumasjan, A., Welpe, I. M., & Lievens, F. (2018). Employer branding: A brand equity-based literature review and research agenda. *International Journal of Management Reviews*, *20*(1), 155–179. DOI: 10.1111/ijmr.12121

Universum. (2023). *World's Most Attractive Employers 2023 Report*. Universum Global.

Verhoef, P. C., Broekhuizen, T., Bart, Y., Bhattacharya, A., Dong, J. Q., Fabian, N., & Haenlein, M. (2021). Digital transformation: A multidisciplinary reflection and research agenda. *Journal of Business Research*, *122*, 889–901. DOI: 10.1016/j.jbusres.2019.09.022

Yasin, R., Bataineh, M. S., Atif, M., & Hossain, M. T. B. (2025). Green HRM and employer branding: Corporate environmental sustainability and organisational safety climate mediating role and moderating role of job experience. *Benchmarking*. Advance online publication. DOI: 10.1108/BIJ-01-2022-0052

ADDITIONAL READINGS

Andresen, S. (2017). What Uber's HR scandal can teach us about managing company culture Retrieved from: https://www.peoplemanagement.co.uk/article/1746089/uber-hr-scandal-company-culture

Branding in Asia. (2022, September 14). *Unilever global leadership achieves 50/50 gender balance a year ahead of target*. https://www.brandinginasia.com/unilever-global-leadership-achieves-50-50-gender-balance-a-year-ahead-of-target/

Brosi, L. (2024). Zurich Airport once again named Europe's leading airport. Retrieved from https://newsroom.flughafen-zuerich.ch/en/zurich-airport-once-again-named-europes-leading-airport/

Chesky, B. (2020). *A note to employees.* Airbnb News. Retrieved from https://news.airbnb.com

Chesky, B. (2020, May 5). *A Message from Co-Founder and CEO Brian Chesky.* Airbnb Newsroom. https://news.airbnb.com/a-message-from-co-founder-and-ceo-brian-chesky/

Choudhury, V. (2015). *Top 25 best workplaces in Asia: Shoppers Stop.* People Matters. https://www.peoplematters.in/article/life-at-work/top-25-best-workplaces-asia-shoppers-stop-11241

Chylinski, M. (2024). The Salesforce Approach to Mental Wellness: A Blueprint for Success and Growth. Retrieved from https://www.linkedin.com/pulse/salesforce-approach-mental-wellness-blueprint-success-manya-chylinski-txrqf/

Coffee & Farmer Equity (C.A.F.E.) Practices EMEA Explainer Video. (2020). Starbucks Stories EMEA. Retrieved from https://stories.starbucks.com/emea/stories/2020/coffee-and-farmer-equity-practices-emea-explainer-video-internal/

Craigramsay, (2025). Rebuilding Trust in the Workplace Before It's Too Late. Retrieved from: https://techcommunity.microsoft.com/blog/microsoftvivablog/rebuilding-trust-in-the-workplace-before-it%E2%80%99s-too-late/4404475

Dastin, J. (2018, October 10). *Amazon scraps secret AI recruiting tool that showed bias against women. Reuters.* https://www.reuters.com/article/us-amazon-com-jobs-automation-insight-idUSKCN1MK08G

Esty, B. C., & Ciechanover, A. M. (2021). *Airbnb During the Pandemic: Stakeholder Capitalism Faces a Critical Test.* Harvard Business School Case 221-026.

Ewadirect. (2023). *Ethical sourcing and sustainable practices at Starbucks.* Retrieved from https://www.ewadirect.com/proceedings/chr/article/view/14593

Flavor365. (2024). *Starbucks' key social responsibility stakeholders revealed.* Retrieved from https://flavor365.com/starbucks-6-key-social-responsibility-stakeholders-revealed/

Forbes. (2023). *Yvon Chouinard Gives Away Patagonia to Fight the Climate Crisis.* Forbes Media LLC. Retrieved from: https://www.forbes.com/sites/carlieporterfield/2022/09/14/patagonia-founder-gives-away-entire-company-to-fight-climate-change/

Friedell, D. (2017, March 1). *Uber chief caught on camera arguing with driver*. VOA Learning English. Retrieved from https://learningenglish.voanews.com/a/uber-argument/3745669.html

Google Crisis Response. Retrieved from: https://crisisresponse.google/?utm_source=about.google&utm_medium=referral&utm_campaign=commitments

Grant, A. (Host). (2024, May 21). *A company is not a family with Airbnb CEO Brian Chesky* [Audio podcast episode]. In *ReThinking*. TED Audio Collective. https://www.ted.com/podcasts/rethinking-with-adam-grant/a-company-is-not-a-family-with-airbnb-ceo-brian-chesky-transcript

Guardian. (2022). Elon Musk announces Twitter mass layoffs to begin Friday. Retrieved from: https://www.theguardian.com/technology/2022/nov/03/elon-musk-twitter-mass-layoffs-begin

Jope, A. (2022). *Alan Jope on the future of work* [Audio podcast episode]. https://megaphone.link/TPG5040524540

Larcker, F. D., Tayan, B., & Miles, A. S. (2021). Protests from Within: Engaging with Employee Activists. Retrieved from: https://corpgov.law.harvard.edu/2021/03/24/protests-from-within-engaging-with-employee-activists/

Lazo, L. (2025). The Talent Crisis: Why Your Employer Brand Matters More Than Ever. Retrieved from: https://www.linkedin.com/pulse/talent-crisis-why-your-employer-brand-matters-more-lazo-shrm-scp-hhmxe/

Leaderonomics. (2022). *Starbucks: An opportunity to be more than an employee*. Retrieved from https://www.leaderonomics.com/articles/business/starbucks-opportunity-to-be-more-than-an-employee

Learning English, V. O. A. (2017, March 1). *Uber chief caught on camera arguing with driver* [Video]. VOA Learning English. https://learningenglish.voanews.com/a/uber-argument/3745669.html

Newcomer, E. (2017). *Uber's fall: The end of a ride*. Bloomberg Technology. Retrieved from https://www.bloomberg.com

Rajendran, V. (2025). Attract, Engage, Retain: The Role of Employer Branding in Talent Acquisition. Retrieved from: https://www.whitecrowresearch.com/resources/2025/05/13/attract-engage-retain-the-role-of-employer-branding-in-talent-acquisition/

Randstad Employer Brand Survey. (2021). https://workforceinsights.randstad.com/hubfs/REBR%202021/ Randstad-Employer-Brand-Research-Global-Report-2021.pdf

Shepardson, D. (2023). Tesla recalls nearly all vehicles on US roads over lack of Autopilot safeguards. Retrieved from: https://www.reuters.com/business/autos-transportation/tesla-update-software-autopilot-control-issue-2-mln-vehicles-nhtsa-2023-12-13/

Shoppers Stop. *Annual Report 2016–2017*, p. 24. https://corporate.shoppersstop.com/uploaded_files/ccad0e2-bdd3.pdf

Shoppers Stop. *Brands*. https://www.shoppersstop.com

Shoppers Stop. Vision. https://www.shoppersstop.com

Starbucks. (2020, March 18). *Starbucks hosts virtual annual meeting of shareholders rooted in caring for people and growing its business responsibly* [Press release]. Business Wire. https://www.businesswire.com/news/home/20200318005207/en/Starbucks-Hosts-Virtual-Annual-Meeting-of-Shareholders-Rooted-in-Caring-for-People-and-Growing-its-Business-Responsibly-2020

Starbucks. (2021). *Partner (employee) benefits and well-being*. Starbucks Stories. Retrieved from https://stories.starbucks.com

Unilever. (2022). *Unilever Sustainable Living Plan and purpose-led strategy*. Unilever. Retrieved from https://www.unilever.com

Unilever Arabia. (2021, January 7). *Putting purpose into practice: Our COVID-19 response*. https://www.unilever-arabia.com/news/2021/putting-purpose-into-practice-our-covid-19-response/

Universum, (2023). World's Most Attractive Employers: Top Trends and Aspirations for 2023. Retrieved from: https://universumglobal.com/resources/e-book/wmae-2023/

Wong, J. C. (2017, March 4). *Greyball: How Uber used secret software to dodge the law. The Guardian.* Retrieved from https://www.theguardian.com/technology/2017/mar/03/uber-secret-program-greyball-resignation-ed-baker

Zurich Airport. (2022). *Employer branding and employee trust initiatives during global disruptions*. Zurich Airport Annual Report. Retrieved from https://www.zurich-airport.com.\

KEY TERMS AND DEFINITIONS

Brand Crisis: It is defined as an unexpected or a sudden event that threatens to disrupt an organisation's operations and poses both financial and reputational threats (Coombs, 2007).

Brand Resilience: The International Organisation for Standardization (2017) defines organisational resilience as: "the ability of an organisation to absorb and adapt in a changing environment to enable it to deliver its objectives and to survive and prosper", where the changing environment can be either sudden or gradual, and enhancing resilience is a strategic organisational outcome. Similarly, Resilience in employer branding is not only about attracting external talent but also about mobilizing employees themselves as brand advocates during difficult periods.

Employer Brand Image: It refers to an image concerning how uniquely an employer performs its role and fulfils promises favourably, such that it results in higher employee satisfaction.

Employer Branding: It is defined as a process of building and developing and employer brand that is identifiable and unique (Theurer et al., 2018). Additionally, it's main purpose is to differentiate an employer from its competitors (Saini, 2023)

Employer Reputation: Employer reputation is carved by who the employer is (being), what it does (doing), how well it listens, how clearly it communicates, and how stakeholders ultimately see it (Fombrun, 1996)

Negative Word of Mouth (NeWOM): Unfavourable communication between people about the organisation or goods and services provided by it. It can be in the form of online posts and offline in-person communications as well. (Trans et al., 2022, p.348).

Situational Crisis Communication Theory SCCT: It highlights the importance of brand preparedness with primary response strategies like denying, diminishing, rebuilding, and bolstering (Laufer & Coombs, 2006; Coombs, 2014; Coombs 2019).

Word of Mouth (WOM): WOM is a communication tool involving person-to-person communication between sender and receiver based on the information received about the organisation or any product or service offered by it (Arndt, 1967).

Chapter 4
Agile Talent:
Building Dynamic Workforces for the VUCA Era

Amrik Singh
http://orcid.org/0000-0003-3598-8787
Lovely Professional University, India

EXECUTIVE SUMMARY

In an increasingly Volatile, Uncertain, Complex, and Ambiguous (VUCA) global economy, traditional talent management paradigms are proving insufficient. The critical imperative of developing "agile talent" is a workforce characterized by adaptability, continuous learning, resilience, and the capacity to thrive amidst rapid change. Drawing on diverse case studies from various industries, this chapter examines how leading organizations are strategically building dynamic workforces capable of navigating the unpredictable demands of the VUCA era. The key facets of agile talent strategy include fostering a culture of psychological safety and experimentation, implementing flexible work models, empowering self-organizing teams, and prioritizing skill development and reskilling initiatives over fixed roles. This chapter argues that cultivating an agile talent pool is not merely a competitive advantage but a fundamental requirement for organizational survival and sustained success in today's turbulent business landscape.

INTRODUCTION

The corporate environment has never been volatile, uncertain, complex, and ambiguous (VUCA). The business development curve which was previously linear and predictable is superseded by a turbulent and interwoven network of difficulties and opportunities. Global pandemics, fast changes in technology, geopolitical changes,

DOI: 10.4018/979-8-3373-5776-8.ch004

and changing consumer habits have provided an environment in which traditional and rigid organizational structures and talent management practices are inadequate. This new reality has made the skill to change, become innovative, and be fast and agile to respond as a competitive advantage. The chapter explores the notion of Agile Talent as paradigm shift in organizational approach to workforce, replacing the fixed job descriptions and hierarchical models with flexible and adaptable and goal-oriented teams. Agile Talent is not just a buzzword; it is a strategic necessity to survive and develop in the VUCA era. The conventional model of talent that was based on the Industrial Age was founded on the assumption of predictability and specialization. They hired employees with a well-defined role that had specific duties and career development was through a limited, pre-determined ladder. This model was effective in the business environment that was steady and the changes were slow and incremental. But in the VUCA world we are in today, it is a weakness of this model. The skills that are of value today might not be of value tomorrow. A strict organizational hierarchy may result in the blocking of communication and it may also lead to slow decision making, as well as cross-functional teamwork required to address complex issues. Agile Talent concept provides a very effective antidote to these issues. It transforms talent into a dynamic resource that can be mobilized, re-trained and redirected to business requirements on an on-demand basis. It is about creating a force of work that is not merely competent, but also tough, inquisitive and internalized to study and evolve.

Volatility

This is the rate and the extent of change. The market may change overnight; a new player may appear unexpectedly and change of tastes of consumers will take place within a moment. Such volatility makes it extremely hard to plan and predict in the long term (Syamsir et al., 2025). In the case of talent management, this implies that the skills and roles required in a project or a business unit can vary very quickly. An agile workforce, thus, can be made of people who are not merely skilled at their jobs at hand but are also in a position to learn new skills very fast and adjust to new requirements.

Uncertainty

This means the absence of predictability. Although volatility is concerned with the speed of change, uncertainty is concerned with the inability to know the future. The old career route, which was an undisputed and distinct route is now shrouded in doubt. Employees are also seeking new ways to develop and learn and not necessarily ascend a corporate ladder. Agile talent management solves this through continuous learning and development that empowers the employees to have a skill portfolio that can help them in the uncertain future and are thus resilient.

Complexity

This is the interrelationship of different factors. A seemingly easy problem can be connected to one dozen of various elements including global supply chains, local laws, or even social media trends. Complex issues can be addressed using a multidisciplinary approach. The previous paradigm of isolated departments and specialized professionals does not stand a chance of this task. Complexity, in its turn, is the core of Agile Talent, which promotes cross-functional teams (Singh & Singh, 2022). It unites people who might have different backgrounds and skill sets to work and share knowledge and innovate in a manner that cannot be achieved under a traditional and hierarchical structure.

Ambiguity

It is the absence of clarity. In numerous cases, there exists no correct solution, there is no definite cause-effect correlation. Businesses are presented with new issues that have never been experienced before. Such ambiguity demands a workforce that is easy to experiment, iterate and learn in failure. Agile Talent encourages psychological safety culture, which allows employees to feel at ease to take risks, express their views, and criticize the existing status without the fear of being punished.

The Agile Talent Core Principles

Agile Talent is not a universal solution but an attitude that is created on a number of basic principles. The principles can be regarded as a guiding principle in organizations that would like to develop a dynamic and strong workforce.

Emphasise the Skills and not the Roles: In the traditional model, the worth of an individual was determined by what he or she was doing. Agile Talent drastically changes this approach and puts it in the personal capability of the individual with their skills, their competencies and their potential. Valuing the skills that an employee will bring to the table does not mean that the value can be determined by a single and constant role. This enables increased flexibility in the deployment of talent wherever it is most required and the employees to keep on increasing their expertise.

Dynamic Teaming and Project-Based Work: Agile organizations use dynamic and project-based work teams, rather than a fixed department structure. These are cross-functional and self-organizing teams that unite people with the appropriate skills to address a certain issue (Shet, 2024; Supina & Singh, 2024). After the completion of the project the team is disbanded and the team members are shifted to other projects. Such a model can be as flexible as possible and make sure that the appropriate talent is always busy with the most urgent business tasks.

Constant Learning and Re-skilling: In a VUCA world, skills are becoming shorter lived. Agile Talent is established based on continuous learning. Organizations are compelled to spend a lot of money in training and development, and employees have to learn to own their growth. This is by establishing a culture in which learning does not happen once a year in a training session. It is empowering employees to develop new skills either through enrolling in training programs, through on-job training or mentorship.

Empowerment and Autonomy: The Agile Talent is based on trust and empowerment. The leaders in this model are not micro managers but facilitators and coaches. They give a purpose and resources required by teams and step aside. This independence encourages the feeling of ownership, responsibility and inner motivation resulting in increased rates of engagement and innovation.

LITERATURE REVIEW

Agile organizations are mission-oriented, and the purpose is evident in their mission statements that bonds and motivates the employees. When employees have a sense of attachment to the purpose of their work, they become resilient, flexible and ready to go the extra mile. This culture of purpose is the binding factor that agile workforce has. Continuing on the theoretical background of Agile Talent, the actual strength of the new paradigm is manifested in the practice. Going beyond the abstract principles, Agile Talent Framework in action is full re-engineering of the full employee lifecycle, including the identification of potential candidate until the further development and delivery of value (Ambardar et al., 2023). It is a paradigm shift whereby organizations have to break down the existing structures and restructure them with flexibility, speed, and constant learning being the fundamental aspect.

Practical Transformations

This part explores the action plan and practical transformations that render the Agile Talent Framework in practice which redefine the process of talent acquisition, performance management, and organizational culture. The exploration starts with a radical re-strategy of acquiring talent and onboarding. The conventional method of employment, which recruits with specific roles that are narrow-minded, is essentially opposing the expectations of a VUCA environment. Practically, Agile Talent Framework is a reflection that instead of hiring to fill a job title, one hires based on a skill set. This includes seeing past the resume of a candidate and evaluating his or her potential, learning agility and flexibility. Companies that base their recruitment on this model pay more attention to those who have growth mentality, curiosity, and readiness to take up new challenges (Singh & Hassan, 2024). The interview process itself is made more agile, typically consisting of team-based simulations with projects, in which prospective workers have to work together with current team members to address real-world problems. This is not only assessing their technical abilities but also their teamwork and communication skills as well. Once a candidate has been hired, onboarding is no longer a one-time, unchanging event. Rather it is an experience that immerses the new employee into a dynamic team, and gets them a comprehensive idea of the purpose of the company as well as a direct contribution to a project of importance. This fast-tracked integration will make sure that the new talent is productive and engaged on the first day, and the learning processes are not as lengthy as it would be with a traditional onboarding.

Performance Management and Feedback

The Agile Talent Framework in practice is based on such a cornerstone as the transformation of performance management and feedback (Turan & Cinnioğlu, 2022; Singh, 2025). The speed of business makes the annual performance review, a legacy of the industrial era, irrelevant. Instead, agile organizations have continuous feedback loops which are timely, specific and development oriented instead of judgment oriented. This is the movement towards a peer-to-peer feedback model as opposed to a top-down feedback model that was hierarchical. Managers transform into evaluators by becoming coaches who have frequent one on one discussions with each other in order to give advice, eliminate obstacles and applaud the achievements. This ongoing feedback is usually associated with agile sprints or milestones of a project, so it is always related directly to the work in question (Singh, 2024). It does not focus on giving a numerical rating but in building a culture of continuous growth and betterment. Moreover, the agile performance management tends to use the 360-degree feedback where employees are provided with a set of reviewing sources (peers, subordinates, superiors, etc.) to have a comprehensive picture of their influence. This will make them feel a collective responsibility to perform and develop and empower all the team members to make their colleagues succeed. Lastly, the most remarkable and transformative aspect of the Agile Talent Framework practice is the development of a psychological safety and an experimenting culture (Kaivo et al., 2018). This forms the foundation upon which other agile practices are created. In its absence, staff will be cautious to venture out, to express an opinion, or to question the status quo all which are critical factors in innovation in a complex world. Companies that manage to apply the given framework effectively help to create the so-called fail-forward culture in which errors are not considered failure, but rather a great learning experience. The leaders are very instrumental in demonstrating this behavior through their own mistakes openly and willing to make mistakes. Psychological safety gives the teams the ability to be self-organizing and self-sufficient enough to make choices and refine solutions without having to be monitored by a manager. This is a strong motivational strategy that results in an increased employee engagement, creativity and responsibility. It is also the key to the full potential of the dynamic teamwork at work as it enables people with different backgrounds to cooperate freely and positively and is sure that their input is going to be appreciated and esteemed. The Agile Talent Framework enables organizations to not only react to change, but to move it through the establishment of a safe environment to dialogue and experiment (Turan & Cinnioğlu, 2022). It is the very practical implementation of a work force that is not merely competent and flexible but resolute, creative and utterly dedicated on the same cause. These practices, starting in skill-based hiring all the way up to the psychological safety, ensure the success of the implementation, which is what can be used to distinguish a traditional organization that stays still, static, and traditional, and a dynamic, future-proof one.

Reinventing Talent Acquisition and Onboarding

The old-fashioned method of talent acquiring and onboarding is no longer suitable in the pursuit to develop dynamic and resilient work forces to cater to the VUCA era. It is an industrial-age mindset of having companies aiming to fill fixed, predetermined positions with candidates that have a set of particular qualifications and the career ladder. The strength of this inflexible model has turned into a weakness since the skills upon which success in the work force is based can shift within a day and nature of the work is becoming dynamic and projects-oriented. In a bid to be agile, the organization should radically restructure, turning the experience of the past to the prospects of the future and the one-way hiring system to the open, transparent ecosystem of possibility (Kavitha & Suresh, 2021). The initial and most essential part of this redefinition is the change of the role-based hiring to skill-based hiring. The old job descriptions and their laundry list of duties and years of experience is very narrow-minded and backward looking. They are interested in repeating the past success instead of looking at the future needs. Instead, agile organizations are shifting to skills-based approach. This implies that they are not looking at the experience of the Marketing Manager who has 10 years of experience but someone with a certain set of skills say, data analysis, content creation, SEO knowledge and managing online campaigns. The change has far reached consequences. It expands the talent pool by eliminating some of the unrealistic restrictions such as limited degrees of degrees or industry experience allowing organizations to take into consideration a broader pool of candidates. It is also more flexible in terms of deploying the talent. The example of a talented data analyst is not limited to the marketing department, but it could also become a valuable member of a cross-functional team that addresses a supply chain issue. The strategy renders the workforce stronger because the expertise is more mobile and enduring than an individual job position. What also goes hand-in-hand with this skills-based approach is a paradigm shift in what organizations are seeking in a candidate (Setiawati, 2021). It is not about the static experience anymore but about the potential and the possibility to learn. In the era when 50 percent of all competencies will be rendered outdated in several years, past achievements of a candidate do not forecast future success rather well as skills and attitudes toward learning.

Learning Agility

Learning agility the ability to learn in a short period of time, use it in new issues, and learn based on mistakes and achievements is the new gold standard. The practices of agile talent acquisition are expected to evaluate this characteristic by using behavioral questions, project-based interviews, and simulations that would evaluate the ability of a candidate to solve a problem in ambiguous situations. It is aimed at finding such people who do not only excel in a particular field but also possess the fundamental qualities of being curious, being robust, and not being scared of uncertainty. This attitude change makes the hiring process not only the validation of the past experience but also a prospective evaluation of the ability of a candidate to expand and adjust to the organization. The last component of this re-architectured structure is the strategic deployment of the inside talent markets (Kavitha & Suresh, 2021). Such a significant contributor to losing talent is the old form of siloed organization where the career ladder of an employee was the vertical promotion in a single department. An employee who is talented and willing to take a new challenge but cannot get a chance in his/her current team can quit the company completely. The solution to this issue is the internal talent marketplaces that are driven by AI and machine learning. They are fluid, digital platforms that make career opportunities democratic by aligning the skills, interests and career aspirations of employees with internal opportunities and within-organizational roles, projects, mentoring opportunities and short-term gigs. A worker who shows interest in data analytics, say, can be assigned a one-time project to a different department, which will provide them with new competencies and experience without leaving their job (Firdaus, 2024). This system offers a clear and transparent perspective on all possible opportunities that includes de-departmentalization and cultivates a culture of internal mobility (Singh, 2024). This is a potent tool to the organization because it offers it an effective mechanism to fill skill gaps, redeploy talent quickly and efficiently in critical projects, and considerably enhance employee engagement and retention. The talent and internal talent marketplaces turn the relationships between career as a ladder and career as an ecosystem into a dynamic growth environment that allows employees to own their development, and enables the organization to have a visible, agile, and resilient talent pipeline. It is the combination of these three practices that skill-based hiring, agility in learning, and internal markets, which allows an organization to indeed redefine the relationship with talent, developing a workforce that is not only future-ready but also future-making. The Agile Talent concept essentially reinvents the performance management process as a punitive process that looks backward at annually in a backward-oriented fashion to a continuous and forward-oriented process of development and coaching. The old annual review is not just ineffective in a VUCA environment, but literally counterproductive; the business needs of today can change within weeks. It imposes stress and tension, and employees are evaluated based on the quality of work they have completed in one year, and it is usually evaluated by the unperfective memory of a manager (Verma, 2024). Agile performance management, on the contrary, is conceived to be a continuous pulse check, a structure of constant feedback loops, which empowers staff, cultivates a growth mentality and ensures that individual contributions are strictly aligned to the fast-changing needs of the business. The most crucial and the first one is the alteration of annual reviews to the continuous feedback loops. The change also implies that the performance problems are resolved immediately before they can grow and evolve into bigger and more challenging questions. Such a continuous stream of information simplifies the process of making changes to current situations and guarantees that everyone is aligned (Aftab et al., 2022). The core of this new model is an emphasis on development and coaching, rather than evaluation. It is no longer aimed at rating or labeling the performance of an employee but assisting him/her to develop and become a better person. This model does not have managers who are judges but coaches and mentors. They are there to guide, eliminate barriers, and assist the team members to acquire the skills that are necessary to achieve the success in their present position and be prepared to face the challenges that will appear in the future (Supina & Singh, 2024). This strategy develops a culture of support and trust because employees do not think of their manager as an enemy, rather, they view him or her as a partner in their professional journey. Performance discussions are re-packaged to be on the potential of the future as opposed to the errors of the past. Such a growth orientation creates a learning atmosphere across the organization and employees are not afraid to experiment, risk, as well as learn through success and failure. Manager-as-coach model is a strong motivating force of engagement because employees feel that the organization is interested in their success in the long run.

DISCUSSION AND INTERPRETATION

Agile Talent Framework increases the feedback source as compared to the traditional manager-subordinate relationship by including peer-to-peer feedback and 360-degree feedback. In the cross-functional team work and project work environment, a single manager may not be able to see full performance of an employee (Bhanumathi & Hemavathi, 2025). The peer feedback will be helpful in understanding the level of collaboration skills, style of communication, and the contributions made by an individual in making a team successful. When used effectively and presented in a constructive manner, this feedback can serve as a potent instrument of self-awareness and self-improvement. 360-degree feedback, which incorporates the input of other employees, direct reports, and even external stakeholders will provide not just a multi-dimensional perspective of the performance and behavior of an employee. This holism approach is important in order to detect the blind spots and offer a more balanced and realistic evaluation. Collecting feedback through many sources, in turn, helps avoid the risk of bias and provides the employee with a more comprehensive image of his or her contribution to the company. The last part of this agile performing puzzle is the essential one the alignment of personal objectives to agile sprints and business performance. In a conventional environment, the goals that an employee has may be established at the start of the year and they may be fixed throughout the year, despite changes in business priorities. This will be a misalignment and wasted effort recipe in an agile environment. Agile performance management solves this by attaching individual objectives to the dynamic short term objectives of the sprints or projects of a team (Singh & Ansari, 2024). This helps in making sure that the input of each person is being directly related to the most urgent business needs. To address these goals, performance check-ins are utilized, which enable real-time changes and prioritization (Esenyel, 2024; Singh, 2024). This constant alignment makes the whole workforce be aligned towards a single direction with individual efforts being directly aimed at the overall business results of the organization. It is the change of the traditional, annual goals into the dynamic and sprint-based versions that enable an organization to be responsive, flexible, and targeted in the face of a continuous change. The Agile Talent Framework enables the transition of performance management into an engine of change and corporate resiliency by shifting to continuous, people-centered, and multi-source feedback and making individual performance and business results closely interconnected.

Psychological Safety and Experimentation

Innovation is not a luxury in the business world that is volatile, uncertain, complex, and ambiguous (VUCA), but a requirement to stay alive. However, no innovation can take place without the basis of something that is usually neglected to be done: a culture of psychological safety. Psychological safety is commonly referred to as a collective belief in the existence of a safe place in the team where people take interpersonal risks, and they are comfortable enough to call out, ask questions, and even confess when they make any mistakes without fear of punishment or embarrassment (Rozman et al., 2023). This does not entail being nice to one another, but rather establishing a climate of mutual trust and respect, under which the free flow of ideas, active questioning of the status quo and shared learning are possible. The most radical and significant change that an organization can undergo, especially within the Agile Talent framework, is the development of this culture, because it is the driving force of experimentation and a continuous improvement. The establishment of the fail-forward culture is the keystone of the psychologically safe environment. Most traditional organizations tend to punish failure, which is a negative label on the records of the employee and this factor can slow down the career advancement of the employee. This risk aversion is caused by this fear of failure, and thus the inability to move forward with what is well-known and safe, and unwillingness to test a faulty idea. Failure is redefined in a culture based on a fail-forward philosophy as an essential and unavoidable aspect of the learning process. Companies that achieve this will not only tolerate failure but also celebrate the knowledge gained out of the same. This is usually facilitated by the use of retrospective meetings where teams freely discuss what went wrong, why it went wrong and what they can do differently in future without putting their blame on the finger. Organizations can use this creative potential of its workforce by making failure a learning opportunity on its way to success and triggering a cycle of learning and innovating. Without overt and explicit involvement of leadership, this cultural change is not possible (Singh & Kumar, 2021). One of the most important elements of creating psychological safety is the leadership that should provide the models of vulnerability and risk-taking. The culture of fear and silence is formed by a leader who positions himself or herself as the one, who has all the correct answers (Esenyel, 2024). Employees will be reluctant to raise issues or novel ideas when they think that their leader is not ready to be disputed. However, agile leaders are leaders who show their vulnerability. They do not hesitate to confess that they do not know everything and they consult their teams, as well as they are ready to admit their own errors. This action conveys a very strong message that it is okay to be imperfect and the search of the common solution is much stronger than the ego of an individual. Leaders should also be the promoters of risk-taking since they should be seen to be in support and shielding teams of individuals experimenting new ideas even when they fail. Leaders give the air cover teams to go to extremes and venture into the unknown by endorsing the effort and the learning, no matter what the end result is. This is what actually makes teams agile and innovative. Once the principle of psychological safety is well established, then the teams can be empowered to decide and learn through mistakes.

Traditional Approach

The traditional approach of having a manager as the only decision-maker of his or her team is a bottleneck that kills speed and innovativeness. Teams are provided with autonomy as they are allowed to make decisions, own their projects and control their workflows in a psychologically safe environment. The strength of this empowerment is that it will make a team feel more like they own and have a sense of responsibility. When an error occurs, the center of attention is not to identify who may have gone wrong but the systematic causes of the error and come up with a solution together. It is based on the assumption that the majority of errors are not caused by a lack of competence in a person but a broken system or processes (Mishra & Chakraborty, 2023). Organizations change their culture of collective accountability and perpetual enhancement by enabling groups to take decisions and to learn as they fail. It is what agility means, a workforce which is not waiting on the top-down instructions but instead actively and intelligently adjusting to the real world in the present moment. Finally, there is no denying that the connection between psychological safety and innovation is provided. Innovation is not genius, but that of a group of people who ideate, experiment and iterate. To succeed in this process, individuals must feel free to present half-baked ideas, ask dumb questions and even provide dissenting views without the fear of being subjected to any professional or social scrutiny. Different views are not only tolerated, they are being actively encouraged and welcomed in a psychologically safe environment. The ability to be creative and come up with breakthroughs is what comes out of this cognitive diversity coupled with the freedom to experiment and learn. Employees are better engaged, stronger, and willing to go an extra mile to their team and their organization when they feel safe. They are not cogs in the machine; they are intelligent, creative problem-solvers who are given the opportunity to give their full potential. Through the development of a culture of psychological safety and experimentation, organizations are not merely creating a more enjoyable workplace but a basic, long-term competitive edge with regard to the continuously changing environment.

The Agile Talent Era of Leadership

Previously, the leadership position was largely determined by a high up the hierarchy with a top-down leadership style whereby the manager dictated what to do and get compliance. The leader was the sole decision maker in everything, the origin of all information and the main manipulator of direction of a team. This classical model, in the new Agile Talent Era, is not only obsolete, but a major hindrance to the success of an organization (Khajuria et al., 2024). The VUCA environment requires a different type of leader one who is not a commander but a coach, a facilitator and a mentor. The new paradigm of leadership does not involve control, rather it involves empowerment; it does not involve having all the answers but posing the right questions; and it does not involve managing people but developing a culture where talent can flourish and create. The biggest change in the Agile Talent Era is the one between Commander and Coach. The major role undertaken by a commander is to lead, to issue orders, and to control. A coach however is a facilitator, the one who leads a team and helps the team to discover their own solutions. The Agile leader realizes that there is no way they can know all the expertise to solve every problem in such a complex fast changing world. They are actually employed to empower the people who do. This includes moving away to telling to assisting people to know how they can do it. This comes by means of active listening, powerful and open-ended questions and offering the required resources and air cover to a team to experiment and learn. The Agile leader has hope in the judgment and expertise of his team and gives them a clear purpose and autonomy to attain the same (Khajuria et al., 2024). The leader ensures that their team members feel a sense of ownership, accountability and intrinsic motivation by letting their team members self-organize, not only does she/he give the space to be addressed to more strategy-oriented and big-view questions, but also creates a sense of ownership, accountability and intrinsic motivation on the part of the team members. Such an approach to coaching develops a strong and flexible workforce that does not rely on an individual to guide it. The essence of the work is to establish trust and create a sense of purpose in the Agile leader. A firm purpose or mission can be a strong anchor in a constantly changing world in a sense that it is a north star helping a team to focus its efforts (Kavitha & Suresh, 2021). The Agile leader will be the one who defines this purpose, and it should be clear how the work of the team relates to the bigger mission of the organization. This focus of direction coupled with the confidence developed by the leader gives the structure under which a team can work independently. Consistency and transparency lead to the establishment of trust (Singh & Kumar, 2024). A leader who works in Agile mode is with the team and the organization; they are always available whenever the team is in need and they are also transparent in their decision-making. They do not hoard information but rather they share it freely thus enabling the team to make informed decisions. It is this trust that will enable a leader to release control and trust that the team will make the correct decisions based on the correct reason. Finally, the aim of the leadership in Agile Talent era is to enable teams to become self-managed. The key building blocks of an agile organization foundation are self-managing teams (Kavitha & Suresh, 2021). These are teams comprising of talented people, who are provided an actual purpose and the freedom to work out the most appropriate means to reach it. The leader of Agile does not have to run these teams but can assist them. This includes elimination of bureaucracy obstacles, availing resources required and stepping in action when specifically requested by the team. The leader ensures that his teams are highly efficient and responsive by enabling them to deal with their own work, which also releases their creativity and problem-solving skills. This is an influential innovation model of leadership because it appreciates the fact that those ideas and solutions are best when they are provided by people who are nearest to the work. It is a radical change in thinking about one leader being the source of all the wisdom to the thinking about a team, a collective power, being the driver of organizational success. The Agile Talent age is one that calls on leaders who are inspiring, coaching, and empowering rather than commanding and controlling. Such leaders are the ones who will create the vibrant, strong, and creative workforces, which will survive under the continuous change.

Agile Talent Management Tools and Technologies

Technology is not merely a facilitator of business processes in the Agile Talent area: it is the structural base of work of a flexible, fluid workforce. The old means of making functions by a fixed set of job description documents, email correspondence, and yearly performance appraisal is no longer adequate to handle an ever-changing, learning, and restructuring workforce into new teams and projects (Kavitha & Suresh, 2021). In order to develop and maintain an agile workforce, companies need to take advantage of a set of potent digital platforms, which connect individuals, enable teamwork and integrate a learning cycle right into the working process. These are the technologies behind the Agile Talent Framework that are practical and which give the visibility, flexibility and connectivity needed to survive in a world of VUCA. The most central part of this technological change is the inception of Internal Talent Marketplaces and Skill-Matching Platforms. These interfaces are the virtual version of a corporate ecosystem, which is created to dissolve the departmental silos that have been a major impediment to innovation and mobility. These systems are based on artificial intelligence and machine learning to form an open and searchable database of the skills and interests of each employee and any career goals they may have. They also serve as a hub where talent may be linked with a vast array of internal opportunities, including full-time positions and temporary project work (also known as gigs), mentorships and cross-functional teams (Kaivo et al., 2018). As an example, a software engineer who is interested in marketing could be assigned a three-month project to assist a product team to develop a new feature so that they can acquire new skills and experience without changing their job. This does not only retain talent as engaged and motivated but also gives the organization a potent real-time tool to deal with skill gaps and bring talent to the most urgent business priorities. Systems such as Gloat, Fuel50 or even home-built systems, are the future of HR, and they are turning career advancement into a multi-directional, dynamic process that is no longer vertical. These platforms democratize the career development and greatly enhance the retention of employees since they can view all the opportunities available and understand that they can develop and grow in the company. Other than talent deployment, Collaborative Tools and Communication Platforms are an essential requirement of the Agile Talent Framework that provides the smooth interaction within the framework of distributed or hybrid workforces. Such applications as Slack, Microsoft Teams, or Trello are no longer the additional elements; they represent the nervous system of an agile organization. They substitute the old, ineffective email channel with live, channel-based communication which is transparent and searchable. These sites enable quick assemblies of cross functional teams, giving them a special space that they can share files, facilitate the project workflow as well as make decisions without having to hold interminable meetings. An example is Trello, which uses a card-based visual system to organize tasks and projects, and thus, teams can easily monitor their progress and identify bottlenecks (Verma, 2024; Aftab et al., 2022). In the case of a distributed workforce, these devices are necessary to ensure that there is a feeling of team cohesiveness and understanding of the project goals.

Communication

They facilitate the asynchronous communication whereby team members in various time zones are able to work on a project at their convenience and be able to have one source of truth of all information about the project avoiding confusion and enhancing efficiency. These are the online glue that binds agile teams, and the communication is seamless, and the collaboration is smooth and transparent and manageable project workflows (Singh & Sihmar, 2025). Lastly, to maintain the workforce that is based on the continuous learning, the organizations need to take advantage of advanced Learning and Development Platforms. The previous training session model that involves one time and face-to-face session will not work with the modern business speed. The agile talent needs to be provided with an accessible, personalized, and integrated learning ecosystem, which needs to be directly embedded into the everyday workflow. The recent L&D platforms provide short lessons that are micro-learning and easy to digest and can be taken whenever necessary so that employees can learn the new skills within the limited few minutes they have in between meetings. They also apply AI to design individual learning plans and, based on the current skills of an employee, their career goals, and the needs of the team, suggest the most appropriate and effective training (Ambardar et al., 2023). This information-based practice makes sure that learning is not a mass production but a focused efficient way of investing in the development of an individual. Such platforms as Coursera Business, LinkedIn Learning, and internal systems that are built by the company can be combined with other HR and project management tools, thus learning is not a break but an extension of the work of an employee.

CASE STUDIES AND BEST PRACTICES

Theory without practice is a hollow exercise. To truly understand the power of Agile Talent, it is essential to examine real-world applications and learn from the successes and challenges of leading companies. Companies that have successfully adopted agile talent models, such as Spotify and ING, provide compelling case studies of how this framework can be implemented and scaled to transform an entire organization. These examples are not a blueprint to be copied, but a source of inspiration and a demonstration of the profound impact that a people-centric, dynamic approach can have on business outcomes. One of the most widely cited examples of an agile talent model in action is the Spotify model. While not a rigid framework to be followed to the letter, it offers a powerful set of principles for organizing a workforce around purpose and autonomy. At its core, the model breaks down the traditional hierarchy into Squads, small, autonomous, cross-functional teams that function like mini-startups, each with a specific long-term mission. These Squads are organized into "Tribes" to maintain alignment on a broader product area. This structure breaks down departmental silos and empowers teams with the freedom to choose their own agile methodologies; be it Scrum or Kanban. The success of this model lies in its ability to balance autonomy with alignment. Squads are free to innovate and experiment, but Chapters and Guilds ensure that technical standards are maintained and that knowledge is shared across the organization (Turan & Cinnioğlu, 2022; Setiawati, 2021). The best way to begin is not with a full-scale, company-wide rollout but by building a pilot program. This involves selecting a small, motivated team or business unit and empowering them to adopt the new framework (Esenyel, 2024). This pilot serves as a controlled environment to test the new practices, gather feedback, and demonstrate early wins. The final, and most critical, part of this roadmap is the continuous process of measuring success and iterating on the framework. Unlike traditional transformations with a fixed endpoint, the agile journey is an ongoing evolution. Success should not be measured solely by traditional KPIs but also by a new set of metrics that reflect agile principles.

Case Study: Agile Culture and Talent Flexibility at Netflix

Organizations operating in the volatile, uncertain, complex, and ambiguous VUCA era will be compelled to keep up with the rapid rate of technological development, changing customer demands, and high competition in the global industry. Netflix is considered to be one of the companies which have the agile workforce practices. Initially Netflix was established as a DVD rental company but has managed to be an international streaming service and entertainment production company. Such transformation demanded technological breakthrough as well as the creation of a versatile, dynamic and highly skilled labor force that could react fast to the changes in the industry (Leal et al., 2026). During the rule of Reed Hastings, Netflix developed a special organizational culture based on freedom, responsibility, and density of talent. These values have assisted the company in developing a nimble workforce that is innovative and one that makes quick decisions in the fast-changing digital entertainment sector.

Organizational Environment and Problems

Digital technologies and the emergence of streaming services have seriously shaken the entertainment industry. The new digital competitors Amazon and Disney threatened the traditional television networks and media companies. Consumers were becoming more and more concerned with on-demand content, customized suggestions and quality digital experiences. In the case of Netflix, staying relevant meant constant innovation in terms of content development, digital streaming technology and expansion of the business worldwide (Nayak & Sahoo, 2026). These issues required a labor force that was able to respond fast to evolving conditions of the market and come up with innovative solutions to difficult problems. Consequently, Netflix implemented an agile talent strategy that aimed at facilitating flexibility, collaboration, and learning.

Agile Corporation Culture

The management has implemented a unique organizational culture, which is commonly referred to as a Freedom and Responsibility culture, which is one of the key success factors of Netflix. Rather than using strict policies and highly structured decision-making, Netflix gives its employees freedom to own their work and make sound independent decisions. Employees are given trust to make decisions in the best interests of the organization even though there is accountability of their results. This culture gives the employees the power to experiment, innovate, and make calculated risks without having to worry about too much bureaucracy (Naqvi & Nair, 2026).

The organization has also stressed on transparency and free communication where employees are provided with the information needed to make effective decisions. Netflix breaks down hierarchical obstacles and promotes independence, which produces a climate in which employees are free to react quickly to the emergent issues.

Talent Density and High-Performance Teams

Talent density is another important issue about the agile workforce strategy at Netflix. The company emphasizes on recruiting very competent people who exhibit high creativity, flexibility, and problem-solving skills. Instead of having many teams with different performance rates, Netflix focuses on establishing smaller teams that consist of the most successful people. Such a strategy increases teamwork and productivity as the workers will collaborate with other employees of the same expertise and motivation (Lambert & Ozdemir, 2026). Knowledge sharing and solving of problems collectively also occurs as a result of having a high level of talent density thus the team could easily respond to complex problems. The company also feels that when employees who are talented work under a conducive atmosphere, then they are more likely to be innovative and more productive.

Flexible Work Practices and Decision-Making

The workforce management model that Netflix has implemented also involves flexible work organizations and decentralization in decision making. Projects have also been known to be structured into teams, but not necessarily along departmental lines and thus employees who belong to one discipline, say engineering, marketing and content development are able to work efficiently with others who belong to a different discipline. Such cross-functional teamwork promotes different views and hastens the generation of creative thoughts. Orders are allowed to be made fast without delays associated with long approval times. This flexibility is very vital in digital entertainment business where speed in innovation and fast reaction to the market dynamics are crucial to success.

On-the-Job Learning and Feedback

Organization in the traditional setting usually uses annual performance reviews to assess employees. Netflix, in its turn, focuses on constant feedback and candid communication. The employees communicate frequently with their managers and colleagues in terms of performance, goals, and improvement opportunities. The strategy encourages learning and development culture and enables the employees to adjust efficiently to change in the organization. Moreover, Netflix makes investments in professional growth and motivates employees to enlarge their skills in fields like data analytics, digital technology, and development of creative content. Learning continuously makes certain that the employees are up to date with the industry trends and technological changes arising.

Results and Impact of the Organization

The culture of agility and flexibility of talent at Netflix has also made the company successful worldwide. Netflix has developed a workforce through empowerment of employees, high talent density, and cross-functional coordination that can make this company an innovation driver and responsive to market shock. The company has been able to penetrate the international markets, create original content that has gained awards and come up with innovative streaming technologies that have improved the experiences of users. Besides, the agile workforce model has enhanced employee engagement and organizational resilience enabling Netflix to survive in a highly competitive and fast changing industry (Lambert & Ozdemir, 2026). The example of Netflix shows that agile talent management is a key to the organizational success in the VUCA environment. Through a culture of freedom and responsibility, an emphasis on talent density, and an emphasis on continuous learning, Netflix has created an adaptable workforce that is able to evolve in uncertainty and initiate sustained innovation. The case is an informative example to organizations who want to build agile talent strategies and stay competitive in a more complicated business environment in the world.

CONCLUSION

The future of work is agile and not something that will happen in the future, but it is something that is happening and being being influenced by the uncompromising forces of a VUCA world. The previous models of work as being static in terms of job description, fixed hierarchies and linear career paths are becoming outdated in favour of a model of work that is dynamic, fluid and adaptable, which revolves around talent, purpose and continuous learning. With the ever-increasing rate of technology, the ever-increasing interconnectedness of the markets and the accelerating rate of change, being able to be responsive and resilient in an organization will be its final competitive advantage. The future of work is not the substitute of people by automation, but it concerns collaboration between people and machines in new and collaborative forms. Human skills that are hard to automate such as creativity, critical thinking, emotional intelligence and the capacity to resolve complex, ambiguous issues will be the most valuable in this future. Agile workforce is also perfectly placed to exploit these talents. It consists of people not only highly qualified and knowledgeable in one field but of those who are lifelong learners, who are not afraid of ambiguity, and who have a strong sense of purpose. It is a workforce that is nimble enough to create cross-functional teams on a short-fuse to address a new problem, shift their skills to a new project, and usually evolve to new technologies and customer needs. The relationship between the employer and the employee has a new social contract at the center of this agile future. The traditional value proposition of life-long employment in return of loyalty has been turned over with a new one: employees contribute their complete creative and intellectual faculties to the work in exchange of an evolving purposeful culture, the ability to learn continuously, and enabling environment. The future of work is not on the management but empowering people. It is leadership that coaches and not gives orders and it is an organizational structure which is a network of independent teams and not a top-down hierarchy. This future is not always smooth.

IMPLICATIONS

The advent of agile talent as a strategic focus has dangerous consequences to organizations, leadership behaviors, people systems, and policy frameworks in the VUCA (Volatile, Uncertain, Complex, and Ambiguous) age. With the world markets constantly in flux due to technological upset, geopolitical changes, and digital revolution, companies have to essentially reconsider the manner in which they acquire, nurture, and keep talent.

Organizational Implications

Agile talent changes the organizations that have hierarchical structures to those that are flexible and networked. The conventional job description is getting phased out by the skill-oriented job listing where employees can be redeployed fast and across project. Such changes compel organizations to invest into cross-functional groups, project-based tasks and in-house talent markets. Those companies that successfully implement agility tend to exhibit faster innovation, greater resilience in times of crisis and more responsiveness to customers.

Implications of Human Resource Management.

To the HR departments, agile talent demands a shift in workforce planning as a static one to dynamic workforce strategy. Based on recruitment should be flexibility, learning responsiveness, and teamwork skills, instead of technical proficiency.

Innovation, knowledge sharing and flexibility need to be rewarded through performance management system. Furthermore, there are talent analytics and artificial intelligence-driven systems that are used by platforms like LinkedIn to map the data and use it to plan a succession strategy or skill mapping. The functions of learning and development (L&D) will also have to change.

Leadership Implications

Agile talent requires agile leadership styles. Leaders need to cease to use command and control models tracing back to facilitative and empowering models. There is decentralization of decision making whereby employees are able to react promptly to change of conditions. Therefore, the leadership development programs should focus on emotional intelligence, resilience, and competency of managing change.

Implications of Employee Well-Being and Sustainability

Although agility leads to competitiveness, it might also increase job insecurity, role ambiguity, and work pressure. Thus, to avoid burnout and ensure long-term engagement organizations need to incorporate the concepts of Sustainable Human Resource Management (S-HRM). The strike between flexibility and stability becomes important. Open communication, positive supervision, and fair rewarding systems contribute to the alleviation of the possible harm related to the constant change.

Sectors and Industries

Agile talent is especially important in service-intensive industries like the hospitality and tourism industries that are also in line with the recent research in accommodation management and green practices. Dynamic staffing models have the potential to enhance the service quality and operational efficiency particularly where there are peaks and declines in demand. Simultaneously, organizations have to be able to guarantee standardization of skills and consistency of services even in the face of fluidity in the workforce.

Policy and Educational Implications

Macro level agile talent strategies have a bearing on national workforce policies. Educational institutions should incorporate interdisciplinary and competency based as well as experiential learning to equip graduates to meet unpredictable career paths. The agile talent implications go further than HR practices to the organizational culture, the leadership paradigms, the well-being of their employees, and the national policy frameworks. To establish the dynamic workforces successfully, the holistic approach should be based on flexibility, maintenance, technological progress, and constant learning.

FUTURE RESEARCH DIRECTIONS

The rapidly increasing globalization, digitalization, socio-economic and disruptive trends have increased the topicality of agile talent management in the current VUCA (Volatile, Uncertain, Complex, and ambiguous) world. Although, current literature emphasizes on agility as a strategic HR competence, future studies need to enhance theoreticalization, methodological rigor, and cross-sectoral applicability of the findings to create dynamic and resilient workforces. The integration of agility with models of new workforce is one of the new promising directions, which should include platform-based and hybrid work structures. Future research has potential to investigate the functioning of agile talent systems in the framework of gig-based, remote and blended workforce systems. An empirical understanding on the long-term study of productivity, commitment, and innovation performance of traditional and agile structures would be beneficial. Second, studies must examine how Artificial Intelligence (AI) and workforce analytics could be used to increase talent agility.

REFERENCES

Aftab, S., Khalid, K., Waheed, A., Aftab, A., & Adnan, A. (2022). Role of agile leadership in managing inter-role conflicts for a satisfying job and life during COVID-19 in a VUCA world. *Frontiers in Psychology*, *13*, 979792. DOI: 10.3389/fpsyg.2022.979792 PMID: 36329740

Ambardar, A., Singh, A., & Singh, V. (2023). Barriers in Implementing Ergonomic Practices in Hotels- A Study on five star hotels in NCR region. *International Journal of Hospitality and Tourism Systems*, *16*(2), 11–17.

Bhanumathi, P., & Hemavathi, P. (2025). HR Agility: Embracing Change in Human Resource Practices. In *Modern Trends and Future Innovation in Human Resource Management* (pp. 197-238). IGI Global. DOI: 10.4018/979-8-3693-6402-4.ch007

Esenyel, V. (2024). Evolving leadership theories: Integrating contemporary theories for VUCA realities. *Administrative Sciences*, *14*(11), 270. DOI: 10.3390/admsci14110270

Firdaus, S. R. (2024, November). Future Leaders in VUCA Bureaucracy: Millennials and Generation Z Perspective. In *Iapa Proceedings Conference* (pp. 1349-1366).

Kaivo-Oja, J. R. L., & Lauraeus, I. T. (2018). The VUCA approach as a solution concept to corporate foresight challenges and global technological disruption. *foresight, 20*(1), 27-49. DOI: 10.1108/FS-06-2017-0022

Kavitha, R., & Suresh, M. (2021). Agile Practices in Human Resource Management. In Kumaresan, G., Shanmugam, N. S., & Dhinakaran, V. (Eds.), *Advances in Materials Research. ICAMR 2019. Springer Proceedings in Materials* (Vol. 5). Springer., DOI: 10.1007/978-981-15-8319-3_71

Khajuria, R., Maini, A., & Bukhari, S. S. (2024). Bridging the gap: HR analytics adoption in the VUCA world of Industry 5.0. *Global Knowledge, Memory and Communication*. Advance online publication. DOI: 10.1108/GKMC-06-2024-0335

Lambert, S., & Ozdemir, N. (2026). Emotional agility among clinical line managers in the VUCA world. *Higher Education, Skills and Work-based Learning*, *16*(1), 1–15. DOI: 10.1108/HESWBL-06-2025-0237

Leal, M. T., Boixadós-Porquet, A., Castro-Diez, J., García Bernardos, Á., Magaña González, C. R., & Arranz Montull, M. (2026). Integrating VUCA and agile frameworks in work-integrated learning: A higher education case study. Higher Education. *Skills and Work-Based Learning*, *16*(1), 69–81. DOI: 10.1108/HESWBL-07-2025-0307

Mishra, N., & Chakraborty, T. (2023). Employee engagement perspectives in agile organizations: Managing people in Industry 4.0. In *Agile Leadership for Industry 4.0* (pp. 139–154). Apple Academic Press. DOI: 10.1201/9781003314615-8

Naqvi, F., & Nair, M. (2026). Building Resilient Organizations: Culture, Sustainability, and Agility as Pillars of Success. In Organizational Dynamics in India: Rethinking Systemic Issues in Global Environments (pp. 141-157). Singapore: Springer Nature Singapore. DOI: 10.1007/978-981-95-1033-7_8

Nayak, D. P., & Sahoo, S. P. (2026). Workforce Agility in a Changing World: A Systematic Review and Future Research Agenda. *Thunderbird International Business Review*, tie.70098. Advance online publication. DOI: 10.1002/tie.70098

Setiawati, L. (2021). The effect of agile leadership and work environment to employees' performance in a VUCA world (Study on millennial generation employees in Jabodetabek). *International Journal of Social Science and Human Research*, *4*(11), 3123–3131. DOI: 10.47191/ijsshr/v4-i11-08

Shet, S. V. (2024). A VUCA-ready workforce: Exploring employee competencies and learning and development implications. *Personnel Review*, *53*(3), 674–703. DOI: 10.1108/PR-10-2023-0873

Singh, A. (2024). Quality of Work-Life Practices in the Indian Hospitality Sector: Future Challenges and Prospects. In Valeri, M., & Sousa, B. (Eds.), *Human Relations Management in Tourism* (pp. 208–224). IGI Global., DOI: 10.4018/979-8-3693-1322-0.ch010

Singh, A. (2025). Analysis of Perceptions on Employment of differently-abled People in the Indian Hotel Industry. *Pasos (El Sauzal)*, *23*(1), 167–183. DOI: 10.25145/j.pasos.2025.23.011

Singh, A., & Ansari, A. I. (2024). Role of Training and Development in Employee Motivation: Tourism and Hospitality Sector. In Mazurowski, T. (Ed.), *Enhancing Employee Motivation Through Training and Development* (pp. 248–261). IGI Global., DOI: 10.4018/979-8-3693-1674-0.ch011

Singh, A., & Hassan, S. C. (2024), "Identifying the Skill Gap in the Workplace and Their Challenges in Hospitality and Tourism Organisations", Thake, A.M., Sood, K., Özen, E. and Grima, S. (Ed.) *Contemporary Challenges in Social Science Management: Skills Gaps and Shortages in the Labour Market* (*Contemporary Studies in Economic and Financial Analysis, Vol. 112B*), Emerald Publishing Limited, Leeds, pp. 101-114. DOI: 10.1108/S1569-37592024000112B006

Singh, A., & Kumar, S. (2021). Identifying Innovations in Human Resources: Academia and Industry Perspectives. In Pathak, A., & Rana, S. (Eds.), *Transforming Human Resource Functions With Automation* (pp. 104–120). IGI Global., DOI: 10.4018/978-1-7998-4180-7.ch006

Singh, A., & Kumar, S. (2024). Effective Talent Management Practices Implemented in the Hospitality Sector. In Christiansen, B., Aziz, M., & O'Keeffe, E. (Eds.), *Global Practices on Effective Talent Acquisition and Retention* (pp. 126–144). IGI Global., DOI: 10.4018/979-8-3693-1938-3.ch008

Singh, A., & Kumar, V. (2025). Organizational Innovation and Adaptation in Hospitality and Tourism: Strategies for Resilience and Leadership. In C. Ramos, T. Costa, R. Madeira, & J. Ferreira do Rosário (Eds.), *Open Innovation and Technology in Tourism and Hospitality* (pp. 355-372). IGI Global Scientific Publishing. DOI: 10.4018/979-8-3693-8633-0.ch018

Singh, A., & Sihmar, P. (2025). Higher Education Institution Sustainability: Role of Green Human Resource Management. In Adu-Gyamfi, M., Boateng, F., & Atiku, S. (Eds.), *Green HRM Awareness and Training in Higher Education Institutions* (pp. 1–14). IGI Global Scientific Publishing., DOI: 10.4018/979-8-3693-2956-6.ch001

Singh, A., & Singh, V. K. (2022). The impact of ergonomic practices on housekeeping employee retention and efficiency in hotels during COVID-19 in India. Turyzm/Tourism, 32(2), 29–50. DOI: 10.18778/0867-5856.32.2.02

Singh, A., & Supina, S. (2024). Talent Acquisition and Retention in Hospitality Industry: Current Skill Gaps and Challenges. In Christiansen, B., Aziz, M., & O'Keeffe, E. (Eds.), *Global Practices on Effective Talent Acquisition and Retention* (pp. 363–379). IGI Global., DOI: 10.4018/979-8-3693-1938-3.ch020

Supina, S., & Singh, A. (2024). Exploring the Presence and Adoption of Quality of Work-Life Dimensions in the Hotel Industry? *African Journal of Hospitality, Tourism and Leisure*, *13*(2), 421–429. DOI: 10.46222/ajhtl.19770720.524

Syamsir, S., Saputra, N., & Mulia, R. A. (2025). Leadership agility in a VUCA world: A systematic review, conceptual insights, and research directions. *Cogent Business & Management*, *12*(1), 2482022. DOI: 10.1080/23311975.2025.2482022

Turan, H. Y., & Cinnioğlu, H. (2022). Agile leadership and employee performance in VUCA world. In *Agile management and VUCA-RR: opportunities and threats in industry 4.0 towards society 5.0* (pp. 27–38). Emerald Publishing Limited., DOI: 10.1108/978-1-80262-325-320220003

Verma, A. (2024). Agile leadership in the VUCA world: combating challenges of the COVID-19 pandemic. In *VUCA and Other Analytics in Business Resilience, Part A* (pp. 267-285). Emerald Publishing Limited. DOI: 10.1108/978-1-83753-902-420241013

KEY TERMS AND DEFINITIONS

Agile Talent: Agile talent refers to employees who possess the flexibility, adaptability, and continuous learning mindset required to respond effectively to rapidly changing business environments. These individuals can shift roles, acquire new skills quickly, and collaborate across functions to meet emerging organizational demands.

VUCA Environment: A VUCA environment describes conditions characterized by Volatility, Uncertainty, Complexity, and Ambiguity. Organizations operating in such environments face unpredictable market shifts, technological disruptions, and evolving customer expectations, requiring adaptive workforce strategies.

Workforce Agility: Workforce agility is the collective capability of employees within an organization to respond swiftly and effectively to change. It includes redeployment speed, cross-functional collaboration, innovation capacity, and proactive problem-solving behaviors.

Learning Agility: Learning agility is an individual's ability and willingness to learn from experiences and apply that learning to new and unfamiliar situations. It is a critical predictor of leadership potential and long-term performance in dynamic industries.

Dynamic Capabilities: Dynamic capabilities refer to an organization's ability to integrate, build, and reconfigure internal and external competencies to address rapidly changing environments. Agile talent forms the human foundation that enables these capabilities.

Talent Ecosystem: A talent ecosystem is a networked system of full-time employees, gig workers, freelancers, contractors, and technology platforms that collectively contribute to organizational objectives. Digital platforms such as Upwork and LinkedIn play a crucial role in shaping modern talent ecosystems.

Skills Fluidity: Skills fluidity refers to the ease with which employees can transfer, update, and apply their competencies across different roles or projects. It emphasizes multi-skilling, reskilling, and cross-training as mechanisms for sustaining organizational agility.

Adaptive Leadership: Adaptive leadership is a leadership approach that encourages flexibility, innovation, and responsiveness to change. Leaders practicing adaptive leadership empower teams to experiment, learn from failure, and navigate complex challenges collaboratively.

Talent Analytics: Talent analytics involves the use of data, predictive modeling, and artificial intelligence to make informed decisions about recruitment, performance management, workforce planning, and skill development. It supports evidence-based strategies for building agile workforces.

Sustainable Human Resource Management (S-HRM): Sustainable HRM is an approach to people management that balances economic performance with employee well-being, social responsibility, and environmental sustainability. In the context of agile talent, S-HRM ensures that flexibility and speed do not compromise employee engagement or long-term organizational health.

Chapter 5
Talent Management Strategy in Indian Cooperatives

Jayesh Pandey
http://orcid.org/0000-0003-4009-9677
Institute of Rural Management Anand, "Tribhuvan" Sahkari University, India

EXECUTIVE SUMMARY

This chapter examines how talent management is conceptualized and enacted within large Indian cooperatives through a qualitative multi-case study. Drawing on publicly available reports and archival sources, it analyzes three prominent cooperatives, Amul, IFFCO, and NAFED, to explore how ownership structure, governance, and strategic purpose shape people practices. The findings show that talent in cooperatives extends beyond conventional high-potential employees to include system-wide capability, institutional memory, and member-linked competence. While industrial cooperatives adopt formalized learning platforms and leadership pipelines, federated and policy-facing cooperatives rely more on embedded routines, procedural rigor, and long-term employment relationships. The chapter contributes to talent management theory by extending it beyond corporate settings and offers practical insights for cooperative leaders and policymakers seeking to strengthen capability without diluting cooperative values.

INTRODUCTION

Cooperatives matter because they sit at the meeting point of enterprise and community. At their core, cooperatives are built on the idea that people who share a common economic need can organize collectively to meet that need more fairly and

DOI: 10.4018/979-8-3373-5776-8.ch005

more sustainably than they might through individual effort alone. This is not only a moral claim, but also a practical one. In many markets, small producers, workers, and consumers face unequal bargaining power, fragmented demand, limited access to finance, and high exposure to volatility (Harilal, 2021; Zakirowa et al., 2025). Cooperative structures respond to these constraints by pooling resources, spreading risk, and creating shared assets such as procurement systems, distribution networks, storage, processing facilities, and brand platforms. What makes cooperatives especially distinctive is that the beneficiaries are also the owners, which changes the definition of success. Performance is not measured only through profit, but also through member welfare, reliability of services, long-term stability, and trust in the institution (Grashuis & Su, 2019). This design can create a stronger sense of belonging and accountability, but it can also produce governance and coordination challenges that conventional firms do not face (Österberg & Nilsson, 2009). In recent decades, the cooperative idea has gained renewed relevance globally due to debates about inclusive growth, stakeholder capitalism, and responsible business (Siedlok et al., 2024). When communities experience economic insecurity, or when value chains become concentrated in ways that squeeze smaller participants, cooperatives often emerge as credible counterweights that restore voice and agency. They also contribute to social cohesion by embedding economic activity in local relationships and shared norms, rather than treating communities as merely locations for transactions. At the same time, cooperatives are not automatically equitable or efficient simply because they are cooperatives. Their outcomes depend on how well they translate values into systems, and how effectively they build the organizational capabilities needed to compete and serve members over time (Craveiro et al., 2025). This makes cooperatives an important object of study not only for policymakers and development scholars, but also for management researchers interested in how organizations balance purpose with performance in real-world settings.

This broader significance becomes even more compelling in the Indian context, where cooperatives have long been woven into the country's development and institutional imagination. From the early roots of cooperative credit to the later emergence of large federated structures in dairy, fertilisers, sugar, handloom, fisheries, and agricultural marketing, India's cooperative movement has sought to address structural vulnerabilities in rural and semi-urban livelihoods (Gaillard & Dervillé, 2022). Cooperatives have offered mechanisms through which farmers, artisans, and workers could access markets, stabilise prices, obtain quality inputs, build processing capacity, and reduce dependence on intermediaries. Over time, cooperatives in India have expanded from being primarily local collective arrangements to becoming complex multi-tier organizations with sophisticated operations, large-scale procurement, national brands, and international partnerships. Some have become emblematic success stories, shaping not only sectoral outcomes but also popular narratives about what community-owned enterprise can achieve. Yet it is equally important to acknowledge that the cooperative landscape in India is diverse, uneven, and deeply shaped by local political economy. Cooperatives differ in their autonomy, governance quality, member participation, managerial professionalism, and relationship with the state. In several sectors, cooperatives operate in environments where regulatory oversight, political influence, and public expectations are stronger than what a private enterprise might face (Houston & Hamrick, 2025). This can create both advantages and constraints. Cooperatives may receive institutional support, legitimacy, and access to networks, but they may also face bureaucratic processes, leadership transitions driven by electoral dynamics, and tensions between member welfare and commercial imperatives. Additionally, cooperatives often function across geographically dispersed regions, requiring alignment between village-level entities, district unions, state federations, and national bodies. This multi-layered architecture can be a source of strength, because it allows local embeddedness alongside scale, but it can also make decision-making slower and accountability harder to sustain. Much of the literature on Indian cooperatives has therefore focused on governance reforms, financial viability, and policy frameworks (Mahale & Mithunraj, 2025). However, the day-to-day capacity of cooperatives to deliver value to members depends heavily on the people who run these systems, translate strategy into action, and keep the cooperative promise credible at scale. That observation provides a natural bridge to the question of talent management, which remains relatively under-discussed in cooperative scholarship despite its centrality to cooperative performance.

Talent management becomes critical in cooperatives because these organizations ask their people to perform a balancing act that is both technical and value-laden. Employees and managers in cooperatives must often pursue efficiency, competitiveness, and compliance in demanding markets while also remaining accountable to members who expect fairness, transparency, and service orientation. This dual mandate shapes what "good talent" means in a cooperative. It is not enough to hire technically competent professionals who can execute operations; cooperatives also need people who understand the cooperative identity and can work respectfully with member-owners, elected boards, and community stakeholders. In practice, this means talent management in cooperatives has to address at least three intertwined challenges. First, attracting talent can be difficult when cooperatives are perceived as slower-moving, more bureaucratic, or less glamorous than private sector employers. Compensation structures, career mobility, and location constraints, particularly for field roles, can also affect attraction. Second, development and capability building are crucial because cooperative performance depends on specialized knowledge in procurement, quality control, supply chain, agri-extension, plant operations, marketing, and increasingly, digital systems and analytics. Training cannot be treated as a one-time intervention, since cooperatives face rapid changes in consumer expectations, regulatory standards, and competitive intensity. Third, retention is not only about pay; it is also about meaningful career pathways, leadership development, organizational culture, and the credibility of governance systems. When employees perceive instability in leadership or ambiguity in decision rights, motivation and commitment can erode. These issues are amplified by the structural features of cooperatives. Cooperatives often operate through federated systems where professional managers work alongside elected representatives, which can produce blurred boundaries between governance and management (Behl et al., 2016). Talent systems must therefore clarify accountability without undermining democratic participation. Moreover, many cooperatives are currently navigating generational transitions, both among members and within their employee base. Younger professionals may seek faster learning, clearer progression, and stronger feedback cultures, while long-serving employees may value stability and institutional continuity. Managing this mix requires deliberate people strategies. In short, talent management in cooperatives is not a peripheral HR topic. It is central to how cooperatives build execution capacity, protect their legitimacy with members, and remain competitive as enterprises. Recognizing this importance leads to the need for grounded evidence on how major Indian cooperatives actually manage talent in real organizational settings.

This chapter responds to that need by presenting a multi-case study of talent management in three prominent Indian cooperatives. The inclusion of Amul reflects its iconic status and the strong familiarity it carries among practitioners and management students who associate it with cooperative success. At the same time, the chapter pairs Amul with other large cooperatives that offer richer formal documentation, enabling a more systematic analysis of talent practices through public reports and archival sources. The chapter's aim is not to produce a celebratory narrative, but to offer a realistic account of how talent management is designed and experienced within cooperative organizations that operate at scale. Across the three cases, the chapter examines how cooperatives think about talent needs, how they recruit and develop employees, how they structure roles across federated systems, and how they attempt to retain capable people while staying rooted in cooperative values. The case approach allows the chapter to capture variation rather than assume a single cooperative model. Cooperatives differ by sector, competitive pressure, regulatory environment, and organizational architecture, and these differences shape what talent management looks like on the ground. The chapter offers four kinds of value. First, it provides descriptive clarity by documenting talent practices in a setting that is often discussed in development terms but less frequently analysed as an organizational and managerial system. Second, it offers analytical insight by identifying patterns and tensions across cases, such as the recurring challenge of balancing professionalization with member accountability, or the role of training as a strategic investment rather than a welfare activity. Third, it contributes to the talent management literature by extending it beyond corporate contexts and showing how ownership and governance structures shape HR choices. Finally, it provides practical implications for cooperative leaders, policymakers, and HR professionals who want to strengthen cooperative capability without diluting cooperative identity. With this foundation, the next section outlines the methodology used in selecting cases, gathering evidence, and conducting the cross-case analysis.

METHODOLOGY

This chapter adopts a qualitative multi-case study methodology to examine talent management practices within large cooperatives in India. A case-based approach was considered appropriate because talent management in cooperatives is deeply embedded in organizational context, governance structures, and sector-specific realities, which cannot be meaningfully captured through decontextualized surveys or purely quantitative techniques (See Rana et al., 2013). The selection of cases followed a purposive logic rather than statistical representativeness. Three cooperatives were chosen based on a combination of relevance, organizational scale, sectoral diversity, and, critically, availability of reliable secondary information (See Eisenhardt, 2021). Particular emphasis was placed on cooperatives that publish annual reports, policy documents, training disclosures, and other archival materials that allow systematic examination of people management practices over time. This criterion was especially important given the significance of transparency and verifiability of sources. Data for each case were primarily drawn from publicly available documents such as annual reports, official websites, policy statements, training brochures, and credible media interviews with senior leaders. These sources were supplemented, where possible, by insights from existing case studies and institutional publications to triangulate interpretations. The analysis followed a structured within-case and cross-case process. Each case was first examined independently to understand its organizational context, talent philosophy, and people management practices. This was followed by a comparative analysis to identify recurring patterns, contrasts, and tensions across cases. Throughout the analysis, attention was paid to how cooperative values, governance arrangements, and sectoral pressures shaped talent-related decisions. The methodology is interpretive rather than evaluative in intent. The objective is not to rank cooperatives or assess best practices in an abstract sense, but to generate grounded insights into how talent management is conceptualized and enacted within cooperative enterprises operating at scale.

CASE 1: AMUL (GCMMF) AND THE "AMUL MODEL" OF TALENT MANAGEMENT

Amul, marketed by the Gujarat Cooperative Milk Marketing Federation (GCMMF), is not a single, unified corporate entity in the way most people understand large FMCG brands. It is the visible face of a federated cooperative system often described as the "Amul Model," with village dairy cooperative societies federated into district unions, and district unions federated into the state-level federation that undertakes marketing and brand management (GCMMF, 2026a). This structure matters because talent management is shaped by the logic of the institution. Amul's core capability is not only product innovation or advertising. It is the ability to coordinate an end-to-end system that links millions of producers with consumers at national scale, while keeping member interests central to the economic model. GCMMF's own organizational snapshot highlights the scale of this system, including the federation's membership of district unions and a large base of producer members and village societies (GCMMF, 2026b). From a talent management lens, this architecture immediately signals that "talent" at Amul exists in at least two forms: professional employees who run procurement, processing, quality, logistics, marketing, finance, and technology, and member-side capability that sustains milk production, quality, and reliability in the villages. This dual nature makes Amul a useful case because it broadens the usual corporate framing of talent management from "employees only" to "capability across a value-chain community," while still requiring professional management to keep the system competitive. Amul's public communication repeatedly emphasizes professional management as a necessity for cooperative competitiveness. In a chairman's speech hosted on Amul's website, a clear governance stance is articulated that cooperatives "must be headed only by professionals" with tenures long enough to implement meaningful systems (GCMMF, 2005). Even though the statement is not framed as an HR policy note, it has direct implications for talent management because it positions leadership capability, continuity, and system-building as non-negotiables. This aligns closely with strategic talent management thinking that starts with identifying "pivotal positions," meaning roles that disproportionately shape sustainable advantage. Collings and Mellahi (2009)'s definition of strategic talent management explicitly places "key positions" and a "differentiated human resource architecture" at the center of the concept. In Amul's context, pivotal positions are not limited to the apex leadership team at GCMMF. They also include roles that ensure procurement integrity, quality assurance, cold-chain reliability, plant operations, distribution planning, and brand execution across India. What is distinctive is that these pivotal roles operate within a governance environment where member interests are structurally embedded, which can be a source of strategic clarity but also a constraint that requires leaders who can manage both performance and legitimacy.

A practical way to interpret Amul's talent model is through the idea of a differentiated HR architecture. Talent management literature has long argued that organizations invest differently in different segments of human capital based on value and uniqueness, rather than applying identical HR practices to everyone (Lepak & Snell, 1999). Amul's cooperative system naturally encourages such differentiation because it includes multiple organizations and role types across the federation and unions, as well as a large member base. In corporate organizations, "differentiation" is often a deliberate HR design choice. At Amul, differentiation is partly structural. The federation focuses on brand, marketing, market development, and system coordination, while district unions focus on procurement and processing, and village societies focus on milk collection and member interface. A talent implication follows: capability building must occur at multiple levels and for different populations. For employees, it looks like recruitment, training, safety culture, and engagement systems. For members, it looks like knowledge and practice diffusion to improve productivity and quality at the farm level. The training and development page associated with an Amul dairy unit describes structured programmes for dairy farmers, including a programme designed for women dairy farmers, jointly designed with government and GCMMF, with advanced training support from Anand Agriculture University (Amul Dairy, 2026). While this is not "employee talent" in the conventional HR sense, it is a core part of Amul's capability engine and is one reason the model is often treated as institution-building rather than only brand-building.

Publicly available career communication suggests that GCMMF pays attention to recruitment integrity and candidate protection, including explicit warnings that the organization does not charge any fee at any stage of recruitment, including training (GCMMF Careers, 2026). From a talent management perspective, such signalling matters for two reasons. First, it supports employer brand credibility, particularly important for a high-visibility brand where fraudulent recruitment can dilute trust. Second, it reflects a broader cooperative emphasis on fairness and transparency that can shape organizational culture and employee expectations from the start. In talent management literature, a persistent critique is that the term "talent management" is often used loosely as a rebranding of HR activities without clarity of meaning or evidence (Lewis & Heckman, 2006). Amul's case encourages a more grounded interpretation: recruitment is not only a pipeline exercise, but part of a trust-building narrative that matches the cooperative identity. Early socialization, including induction practices, appears visible through publicly shared posts by individuals referencing induction training and leadership interaction at Anand. While such posts are not official policy documents, they reinforce a plausible picture of onboarding as a cultural immersion into the cooperative story and its rural-development identity, which can influence commitment and meaning at work.

Amul's talent development can be read through the lens of the AMO framework (Boxall & Purcell, 2016), which argues that performance emerges when employees have ability (skills), motivation (will), and opportunity (systems and voice) to contribute. Public sustainability reporting by an Amul federation dairy unit highlights "behavior-based safety" and a proactive safety culture as a foundation of daily operations, linking safety outcomes to preventive measures and "growing safety awareness among employees" (Amul Fed Dairy, 2024). It also explicitly notes the "continued importance of enhancing employee training," alongside PPE compliance and risk assessments. This is a useful talent-management signal because it positions learning not merely as skill-building but as a mechanism to shape culture and reduce risk in high-reliability operations. In many corporate organizations, talent development is discussed primarily in terms of leadership programs, competencies, and career tracks. In Amul's operational reality, a substantial part of talent development is likely embedded in operational excellence, quality systems, and safety systems that protect people and products. The same report frames inclusive employment, safe working environment, and employee engagement as part of its strategic focus, and it also mentions equal participation opportunities for women. This illustrates a practical point: in cooperatives that are tightly linked to livelihoods and public trust, development often takes the form of institutional routines and system discipline, not only classroom training calendars.

Amul's talent management resembles corporate organizations in at least three ways. First, it requires professional managers and specialists to run complex supply chains, manufacturing, quality assurance, and national marketing, which makes structured recruitment, onboarding, and capability building unavoidable. Second, it depends on leadership continuity and systems thinking, a theme explicitly emphasized in Amul's own discourse on professional leadership and tenure. Third, like strong corporate brands, Amul benefits from a distinctive employer identity that can attract talent motivated by mission and scale, not only compensation. Where Amul becomes unique is in the way talent is distributed across a federated system, and in the way "talent outcomes" are tied to member welfare and trust. Corporate talent management typically optimizes for shareholder value through human capital. Amul's cooperative system, by design, must optimize for member-owner value while still competing in consumer markets, and that creates a dual accountability environment for managers and employees. This duality also shapes the meaning of high performance. For example, talent decisions that might be straightforward in corporates, such as restructuring, plant consolidation, or aggressive cost cutting, can be more politically and socially sensitive in cooperatives because the organization is embedded in member livelihoods and regional institutions. Figure 1 presents the summary of talent management strategy of Amul.

Figure 1. Talent Management strategy of Amul

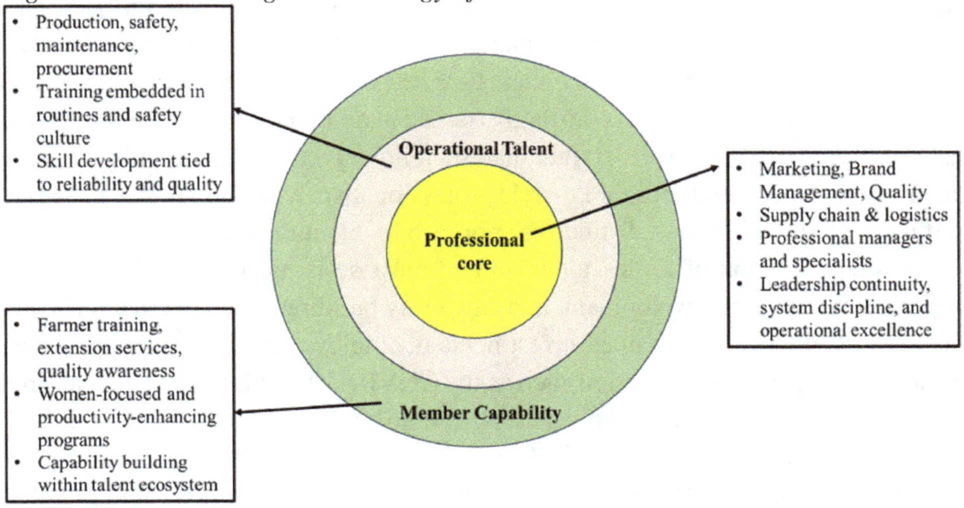

CASE 2: IFFCO AND TALENT MANAGEMENT IN A LARGE, FEDERATED INDUSTRIAL COOPERATIVE

Indian Farmers Fertiliser Cooperative Limited (IFFCO) represents a distinctive form of cooperative enterprise in which large-scale industrial operations coexist with farmer ownership and cooperative governance. Established as a multi-state cooperative, IFFCO operates extensive fertiliser manufacturing plants, logistics systems, and marketing networks while remaining formally accountable to a vast base of member cooperatives. Publicly available organizational documents consistently frame IFFCO as an institution "of farmers, by farmers, for farmers," while simultaneously emphasizing the role of professional management and skilled employees in sustaining growth and credibility (IFFCO, 2022). This dual framing is significant for understanding talent management in the organization. Employees are not positioned merely as operational resources, but as custodians of reliability, safety, and service quality in a sector that is capital intensive, technologically complex, and socially sensitive. IFFCO's annual reports explicitly describe human resources as one of the organization's most valuable assets and link organizational performance to the ability to attract, nurture, and retain capable and committed employees (IFFCO, 2022).

From a talent management perspective, this aligns with strategic talent management theory, which defines talent in relation to roles and capabilities that have a disproportionate impact on long-term organizational success (Collings & Mellahi, 2009). In IFFCO's case, such roles span plant operations, maintenance, safety, research, supply chain management, and extensive field-level engagement with farmers. The organization's scale necessitates formalized people systems similar to those found in large industrial corporations. At the same time, the cooperative ownership structure ensures that employee effort is constantly framed in relation to farmer outcomes and national agricultural priorities, rather than shareholder returns alone. This creates a talent context that blends corporate-style professionalism with cooperative purpose, setting the foundation for a distinctive approach to talent management.

This combination of professionalism and purpose is most visible in IFFCO's approach to learning, development, and capability building. The organization's annual reports document sustained investments in employee training and upskilling, even during periods of disruption such as the COVID-19 pandemic, when learning activities were shifted to virtual formats rather than being suspended (IFFCO, 2022). A notable initiative reported by IFFCO is the development of an internal digital learning platform, referred to as a Learning Hub, which offers curated content across technical, safety, maintenance, information technology, and managerial domains. This initiative reflects a system-level approach to capability development, consistent with talent management literature that emphasizes building internal talent pools for strategically important roles rather than relying on ad hoc training interventions (Lepak & Snell, 1999). In addition, IFFCO reports leadership-focused development initiatives, including structured leadership programs aimed at preparing future leaders for higher responsibility roles (IFFCO, 2022). These practices align closely with the Ability–Motivation–Opportunity framework, which argues that sustained performance emerges when employees possess the required skills, are motivated to apply them, and are given opportunities to contribute meaningfully (Boxall & Purcell, 2016). In IFFCO's case, ability is developed through technical and managerial training systems, motivation is reinforced through a strong narrative linking employee contribution to farmer prosperity, and opportunity is reflected in internal development pathways and leadership grooming. Importantly, learning and development at IFFCO are closely tied to operational imperatives such as safety, quality, and process discipline, rather than being treated as standalone HR initiatives. This integration distinguishes IFFCO's talent system from more generic corporate models that often separate leadership development from operational capability building.

The emphasis on culture, continuity, and internal progression further shapes IFFCO's talent management approach and highlights both its strengths and inherent tensions. Public disclosures describe deliberate efforts to foster a culture of openness, mutual respect, and trust, alongside employee welfare and well-being initiatives that support long-term commitment (IFFCO, 2022). Retention in this context appears to be driven not only by compensation, but also by stability, purpose alignment, and the credibility of internal career pathways. Media reports on leadership transitions at IFFCO provide visible evidence of this internal labor market orientation. The appointment of a managing director who progressed through the organization from an early-career technical role has been widely reported and underscores the value placed on long-term development and institutional knowledge (Times of India, 2025). Such internal progression is consistent with talent management research that highlights the role of internal labor markets in sustaining firm-specific human capital, particularly in organizations where trust, legitimacy, and continuity are critical (Lepak & Snell, 1999). At the same time, reliance on long tenures and internal promotion can create challenges related to generational renewal and external knowledge infusion. This tension is especially salient in cooperatives, where governance stability and professionalization must be balanced carefully. Compared with Amul's federated, brand-centric talent system, IFFCO represents a more centralized and industrially formalized talent model. Yet both cases reinforce a central insight for talent management theory: effective talent systems are deeply shaped by organizational purpose and ownership structure. IFFCO demonstrates that cooperatives can adopt sophisticated, corporate-like talent management practices while remaining anchored in cooperative values, provided those practices are clearly linked to member outcomes and long-term institutional responsibility. Figure 2 presents the summary of talent management strategy at IFFCO.

Figure 2. Talent Management Strategy of IFFCO

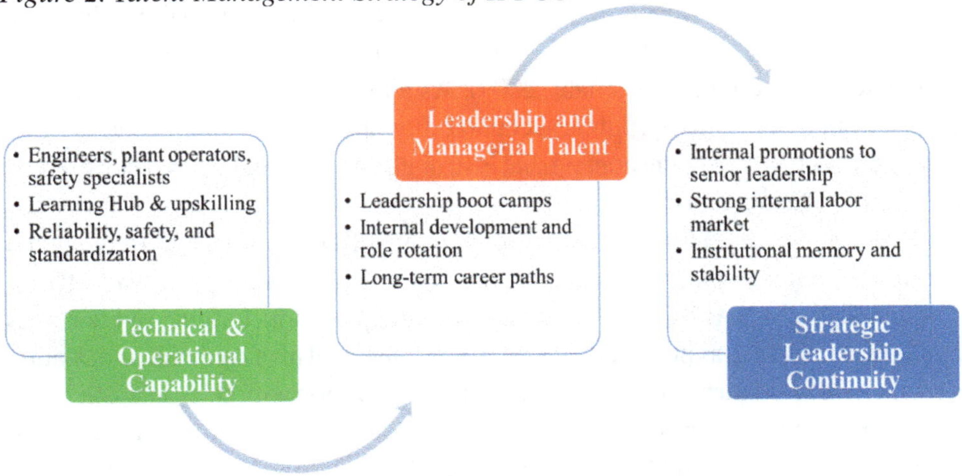

CASE 3: TALENT MANAGEMENT IN NAFED

The National Agricultural Cooperative Marketing Federation of India (NAFED) represents a distinct cooperative form that is structurally and functionally different from both Amul and IFFCO. Established as a national-level apex cooperative, NAFED's primary mandate is agricultural marketing, price stabilization, and support to farmers through procurement, storage, distribution, and market intervention operations. Its activities are closely aligned with national agricultural policy objectives, including minimum support price operations and market access for agricultural produce. Publicly available documents position NAFED as a professionally managed cooperative that operates at the intersection of markets, government policy, and farmer interests (NAFED, 2022). This positioning has direct implications for talent management. Unlike manufacturing-centric cooperatives such as IFFCO, or brand-led federated systems like Amul, NAFED's effectiveness depends heavily on managerial, commercial, and regulatory capabilities. Employees must navigate procurement operations, logistics, warehousing, financial management, and coordination with multiple government agencies, while maintaining credibility with member cooperatives and farmers. NAFED's annual reports consistently emphasize the importance of human resources in executing these complex responsibilities and explicitly acknowledge training and capacity building as necessary for organizational effectiveness (NAFED, 2022). From a talent management theory perspective, NAFED illustrates a case where "pivotal roles" are not concentrated in production or brand management, but in market intelligence, procurement planning, compliance, and inter-institutional coordination. This aligns with strategic talent management arguments that talent value is context-specific and should be defined in relation to organizational strategy and operating environment rather than generic notions of high potential (Collings & Mellahi, 2009). As a result, NAFED's talent system is shaped by policy sensitivity, public accountability, and the need for procedural rigor, creating a cooperative talent context that is strongly professionalized yet constrained by its public-facing mandate.

These contextual demands are reflected in NAFED's approach to training and capability development, which is documented in its annual reports and official communications. NAFED reports regular training programs for employees across functional areas such as procurement operations, financial management, information systems, and regulatory compliance, often in collaboration with external institutions and government agencies (NAFED, 2022). Unlike IFFCO's internally branded learning platforms or Amul's embedded capability-building across federated units, NAFED's development approach appears more episodic and compliance-oriented, reflecting its role as an implementing and coordinating agency rather than a production enterprise. From a talent management standpoint, this suggests a model where learning is closely tied to policy changes, procedural updates, and risk mitigation rather than long-term technical specialization alone. This orientation fits well with the Ability–Motivation–Opportunity framework. Ability is developed through targeted training linked to operational requirements, while opportunity is shaped by exposure to diverse assignments across regions and functions, given NAFED's nationwide presence (Boxall & Purcell, 2016). Motivation, however, is more complex. Unlike Amul's strong cooperative identity narrative or IFFCO's farmer-centric purpose combined with industrial pride, NAFED operates in a space where employee motivation must be sustained despite frequent external scrutiny, shifting policy priorities, and limited autonomy in certain decisions. This places greater emphasis on job security, institutional legitimacy, and professional recognition as motivational levers. In this sense, NAFED's talent management resembles that of public-sector or quasi-government organizations more than that of market-driven corporates, even though it remains formally a cooperative. This hybrid identity shapes how talent practices are designed and experienced, and it sets up a contrast with the other cases examined in this chapter.

The retention and career dynamics within NAFED further highlight the distinctive features of talent management in policy-facing cooperatives. Public disclosures and organizational descriptions suggest a relatively stable workforce, with emphasis on procedural continuity, institutional memory, and adherence to established systems (NAFED, 2022). From a talent management perspective, this stability can be both an asset and a constraint. On the one hand, long tenures support credibility in dealings with government agencies, member cooperatives, and market participants. On the other hand, they may limit rapid innovation, lateral talent inflow, and experimentation with new work practices. Talent management theory has long noted that organizations operating in highly regulated environments often prioritize internal labor markets and rule-based HR systems to reduce uncertainty and risk (Lepak & Snell, 1999). NAFED fits this pattern closely. Compared with Amul's distributed talent ecosystem and IFFCO's internally developed industrial leadership pipelines, NAFED represents a cooperative talent model oriented toward administrative competence, coordination capability, and procedural reliability. Yet this does not make its talent challenges any less strategic. As agricultural markets become more data-driven and supply chains more complex, NAFED's ability to attract and retain professionals with expertise in analytics, logistics, and digital platforms becomes increasingly important. The NAFED case therefore adds a critical dimension to the chapter's cross-case analysis by showing how talent management in cooperatives is shaped not only by ownership structure, but also by proximity to the state and policy apparatus. It reinforces the broader argument that cooperative talent management cannot be understood through a single template, but must be interpreted through the strategic role the cooperative plays within its ecosystem. Figure 3 presents the summary of talent management strategy at NAFED.

Figure 3. Talent Management Strategy of NAFED

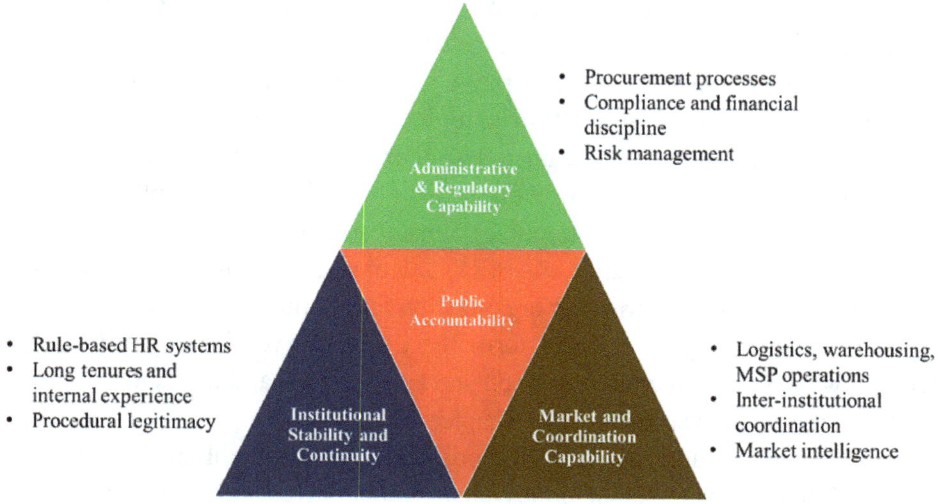

DISCUSSION

The analysis across the three cases reveals that talent management in cooperatives is deeply contingent on organizational purpose and operating logic, rather than driven by a uniform or best-practice model. Amul, IFFCO, and NAFED all recognize people as central to organizational effectiveness, yet they differ markedly in how talent is defined and managed. In Amul, talent is conceptualized as system-wide capability that spans professional employees and producer members, making talent management inherently federated and embedded in organizational identity. IFFCO, by contrast, defines talent more narrowly through industrial, technical, and managerial roles that are critical for manufacturing reliability and leadership continuity. NAFED represents a third configuration, where talent is understood primarily as administrative, coordination, and regulatory competence, reflecting its policy-facing mandate and public accountability. These differences are not incidental. They emerge from the strategic roles each cooperative plays within its ecosystem. This finding reinforces a core argument in strategic talent management literature that talent must be defined in relation to value creation and strategic context rather than generic notions of high potential. It also challenges the assumption that professionalization leads cooperatives to converge toward corporate HR models. Instead, the evidence suggests that cooperatives selectively adopt and reinterpret talent practices in ways that align with cooperative values, member accountability, and sector-specific constraints.

A second important finding concerns variation in the degree and form of talent system formalization across cooperatives. IFFCO demonstrates a highly structured and centralized talent architecture, with formal learning platforms, leadership development initiatives, and internal career pathways that resemble those of large industrial corporations. These systems support the accumulation of firm-specific human capital and provide stability in technically complex operations. Amul, in contrast, relies on a more implicit and distributed talent system, where development is embedded in operational routines, safety practices, and federated coordination rather than articulated through explicit talent frameworks. NAFED occupies an intermediate position, characterized by rule-based and procedure-oriented HR practices that emphasize compliance, continuity, and administrative reliability. Importantly, these differences do not suggest a hierarchy of effectiveness. Rather, they indicate that formalization is contingent on organizational needs and constraints. Industrial cooperatives benefit from standardized systems and centralized control, while federated cooperatives depend more on shared identity and decentralized execution. Across all three cases, however, there is a common reliance on internal labor markets and long-term employment relationships, reflecting the importance of institutional memory, trust, and legitimacy in cooperative organizations. Table 1 presents the comparison among the talent management strategies among the three cooperatives, offering a concise synthesis of these structural and strategic differences.

Table 1. Comparison of Talent Management Strategies among the three cooperatives

Dimension	Amul	IFFCO	NAFED
Core Organizational Logic	Federated, brand-led cooperative	Industrial, manufacturing-led cooperative	Policy-facing, marketing federation
Dominant Talent Philosophy	Capability across the value-chain community	Professional excellence and leadership continuity	Administrative competence and institutional stability
Definition of Talent	Employees + member capability	Employees in pivotal industrial roles	Professionals managing procurement, compliance, coordination
Degree of HR Formalization	Moderate and distributed	High and centralized	Moderate and rule-based
Talent Development Focus	Embedded learning, safety, system discipline, farmer training	Learning Hub, leadership boot camps, internal pipelines	Training linked to procedures, policy, and compliance

continued on following page

Table 1. Continued

Dimension	Amul	IFFCO	NAFED
Leadership Development	Continuity through professional leadership	Strong internal labor market and long tenures	Stability-oriented, limited acceleration
Retention Logic	Identity, purpose, cooperative belonging	Career continuity, culture, welfare	Job security, legitimacy, procedural clarity
Similarity to Corporates	Low to moderate	High	Moderate, closer to public-sector organizations
Distinct Cooperative Feature	Talent extends beyond employees to members	Farmer purpose embedded in industrial systems	Talent shaped by policy proximity and accountability

The third key finding highlights a persistent tension between continuity and renewal in cooperative talent management systems. All three cooperatives exhibit a strong preference for stability, long tenures, and internally developed leadership, albeit for different reasons. In Amul and IFFCO, leadership continuity is framed as essential for system-building, operational reliability, and long-term value creation. In NAFED, continuity underpins procedural legitimacy and credibility in policy implementation. While this emphasis on continuity strengthens institutional coherence, it also introduces challenges related to generational transition, innovation, and the integration of new capabilities. Younger professionals may seek faster progression, greater role variety, and more explicit development pathways than traditional cooperative systems have historically provided. The cases suggest that cooperatives are responding to this challenge unevenly. IFFCO appears to be investing most explicitly in leadership pipelines and scalable learning systems to manage renewal without destabilizing continuity. Amul relies more on cultural transmission and purpose-driven commitment, which can be powerful but less visible to new entrants. NAFED's rule-based systems provide stability but may limit flexibility in responding to emerging skill demands. Taken together, these findings suggest that talent management in cooperatives is best understood as an ongoing balancing act rather than a static design. This insight provides a logical bridge to the implications section, which examines what these patterns mean for theory, managerial practice, and cooperative policy.

A PROCESS MODEL OF TALENT MANAGEMENT IN COOPERATIVES

While the individual case analyses provide detailed insights into talent practices within Amul, IFFCO, and NAFED, the cross-case comparison reveals a broader pattern that can be conceptualized as a cooperative talent management process. Across the three cooperatives, talent management appears to unfold through a sequence of interconnected stages shaped by institutional context. First, the governance structure and strategic role of the cooperative influence how talent is defined. In federated systems such as Amul, talent extends beyond employees to include member capability across the value chain. In industrial cooperatives such as IFFCO, talent is primarily associated with technical and managerial roles critical to operational reliability. In policy-facing organizations such as NAFED, talent centers on administrative competence and coordination capability.

Second, once talent priorities are defined, cooperatives invest in capability development mechanisms suited to their operational context. These mechanisms include embedded learning routines, structured training programs, leadership development initiatives, and knowledge diffusion across organizational levels. Third, cooperatives rely heavily on retention and continuity mechanisms, including internal labor markets, long tenures, and purpose-driven organizational cultures. These mechanisms help preserve institutional memory and sustain trust among members and stakeholders. Finally, the interaction of these processes contributes to organizational outcomes such as operational reliability, coordination across federated systems, and credibility in markets and policy environments. Figure 4 summarizes this process model. By integrating the insights from the three cases, the model highlights how talent management in cooperatives functions not as a discrete HR activity but as an institutional capability that links human capital development with member value creation and cooperative legitimacy.

Figure 4. Talent Management Process Model for cooperatives

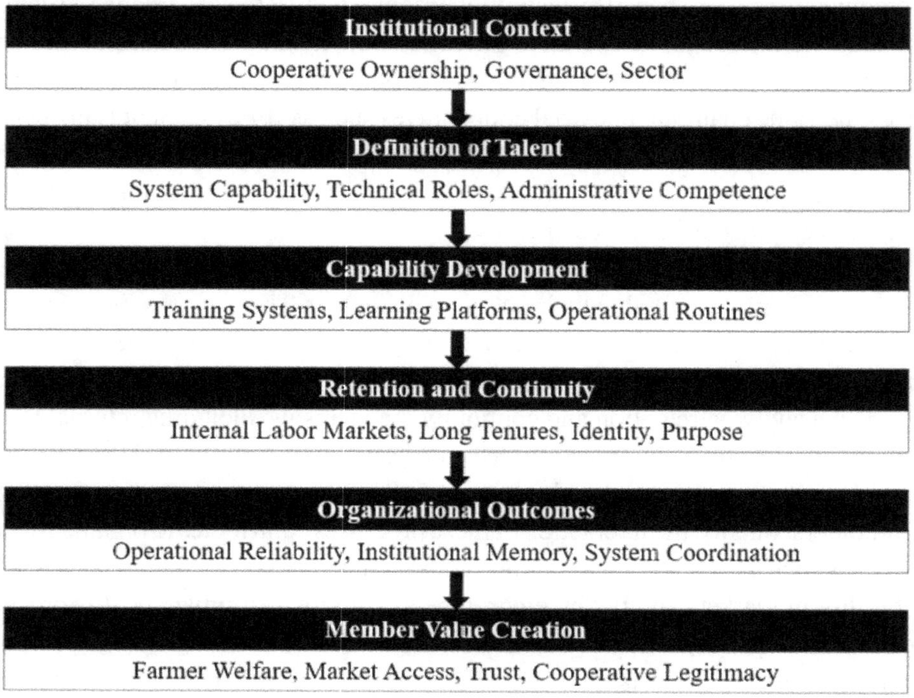

IMPLICATIONS

The findings from this multi-case analysis have important theoretical implications for talent management scholarship, particularly in how talent is conceptualized and studied beyond corporate contexts. First, the cases reinforce the argument that talent management cannot be treated as a universal set of practices that travel unchanged across organizational forms. Instead, talent must be understood as a contextually defined construct shaped by ownership structure, governance arrangements, and organizational purpose. The cooperative cases illustrate that talent is not always confined to a narrow group of high-potential employees, as is often implied in mainstream talent management literature. In Amul, talent extends to system-wide capability that includes producer members, while in NAFED it centers on administrative and coordination competence rather than accelerated leadership pipelines. These patterns suggest the need to broaden prevailing talent management frameworks to accommodate collective, distributed, and institutionally embedded forms of talent. Second, the findings invite a re-examination of dominant assumptions around professionalization and convergence. While prior research often assumes that professionalization pushes organizations toward corporate-style HR systems, the cooperative cases show selective adaptation rather than full convergence. Cooperatives adopt formal talent practices when they align with strategic needs, but retain distinct logics rooted in member accountability and long-term legitimacy. This has implications for theory building, as it underscores the importance of integrating governance and ownership variables into talent management models. Finally, the findings point to the value of studying internal labor markets and long-term employment relationships as strategic choices rather than residual features. In cooperative contexts, continuity, institutional memory, and trust emerge as central dimensions of talent value, suggesting that talent management theory would benefit from greater attention to stability-oriented strategies alongside growth- and acceleration-oriented models.

The findings also generate important implications for managerial practice and policy in cooperatives, particularly for leaders seeking to strengthen organizational capability without diluting cooperative identity. For cooperative leaders, the cases highlight the need to move away from importing corporate talent practices wholesale and instead design talent systems that are aligned with the cooperative's strategic role and governance context. Industrial cooperatives may benefit from investing in formal learning infrastructure and leadership pipelines, while federated cooperatives may need to focus on embedding capability development within operational routines and member-facing systems. Across all cooperative types, leaders must consciously manage the tension between continuity and renewal by creating visible pathways for younger professionals while preserving institutional stability. This may involve clearer role definitions, cross-functional exposure, and development mechanisms that make long-term careers in cooperatives attractive to new entrants. For policymakers, the findings suggest that cooperative performance cannot be strengthened through regulatory or financial interventions alone. Talent development deserves explicit policy attention, particularly in national-level cooperatives that play critical roles in agricultural markets and rural livelihoods. Support for training institutions, leadership development programs, and professionalization initiatives that respect cooperative values can help build durable capacity across the sector. More broadly, these implications underscore that talent management is not a peripheral concern for cooperatives, but a strategic lever that shapes their ability to remain credible, competitive, and relevant in changing economic and institutional environments.

CONCLUSION

This chapter examined talent management in Indian cooperatives through a multi-case study of Amul, IFFCO, and NAFED, demonstrating that talent management in cooperatives is neither uniform nor derivative of corporate practice. Instead, it is shaped by each cooperative's purpose, governance structure, and strategic role within its ecosystem. Across the cases, talent emerges as a form of organizational capability rather than merely a subset of high-performing individuals, with practices designed to support continuity, legitimacy, and long-term value creation for members and stakeholders. The analysis shows that cooperatives selectively adopt formal talent management systems where they align with operational and strategic needs, while retaining distinctive approaches rooted in cooperative values and accountability. At the same time, the cases reveal a persistent tension between stability and renewal, as cooperatives balance reliance on institutional memory and long tenures with the need to attract new skills and perspectives in changing environments. By situating talent management within the unique context of cooperative enterprises, this chapter extends talent management scholarship beyond corporate settings and offers practical insights for cooperative leaders and policymakers seeking to strengthen organizational capability without diluting cooperative identity.

REFERENCES

Behl, A., Pal, A., & Roy, K. K. (2016). Integrated framework for governance of cooperative: An Interpretive Structural Modeling approach. *Indian Journal of Economics and Development*, *4*, 2.

Boxall, P., & Purcell, J. (2016). *Strategy and human resource management* (4th ed.). Palgrave Macmillan. DOI: 10.1007/978-1-137-40765-8

Careers, G. C. M. M. F. (2026). *Careers and recruitment notice*. https://www.amul.com

Collings, D. G., & Mellahi, K. (2009). Strategic talent management: A review and research agenda. *Human Resource Management Review*, *19*(4), 304–313. DOI: 10.1016/j.hrmr.2009.04.001

Craveiro, E. G., dos Santos Oliveira, E., Barros de Oliveira, P. C., Bezerra, J. P., de Souza Cardoso, M., Peña, G. D., & Nascimento-e-Silva, D. (2025). Approaches And Attributes Of Management Systems and Their Implications for Cooperative Organizations. Environmental & Social Management Journal, 19(12).

Dairy, A. (2026). *Training and development initiatives*. https://www.amuldairy.com

Dairy, A. F. (2024).. . *Sustainability Report*, •••, 2024–2025. https://www.amulfeddairy.com

Eisenhardt, K. M. (2021). What is the Eisenhardt Method, really? *Strategic Organization*, *19*(1), 147–160. DOI: 10.1177/1476127020982866

Gaillard, C., & Dervillé, M. (2022). Dairy farming, cooperatives and livelihoods: Lessons learned from six indian villages. *Journal of Asian Economics*, *78*, 101422. DOI: 10.1016/j.asieco.2021.101422

GCMMF. (2005). *Chairman's speech: Annual general body meeting*. Gujarat Cooperative Milk Marketing Federation. https://www.amul.com

GCMMF. (2026a). *The Amul model*. Gujarat Cooperative Milk Marketing Federation. https://www.amul.com

GCMMF. (2026b). *Organisation overview*. Gujarat Cooperative Milk Marketing Federation. https://www.amul.com

Grashuis, J., & Su, Y. (2019). A review of the empirical literature on farmer cooperatives: Performance, ownership and governance, finance, and member attitude. *Annals of Public and Cooperative Economics*, *90*(1), 77–102. DOI: 10.1111/apce.12205

Harilal, K. N. (2021). Globalization of agriculture and atomization of farming: Small farms crisis in Asia. *Millennial Asia*, *12*(3), 298–315. DOI: 10.1177/09763996211059964

Houston, C. M., & Hamrick, J. D. (2025). Failure of cooperative self-regulation: An exploration of cooperative regulatory violations. *Annals of Public and Cooperative Economics*, *96*(2), 225–256. DOI: 10.1111/apce.12498

IFFCO. (2022). *Annual report 2021–22*. Indian Farmers Fertiliser Cooperative Limited. https://www.iffco.in

Lepak, D. P., & Snell, S. A. (1999). The human resource architecture: Toward a theory of human capital allocation and development. *Academy of Management Review*, *24*(1), 31–48. DOI: 10.2307/259035

Lewis, R. E., & Heckman, R. J. (2006). Talent management: A critical review. *Human Resource Management Review*, *16*(2), 139–154. DOI: 10.1016/j.hrmr.2006.03.001

Mahale, P., & Mithunraj, B. (2025). The National Cooperative Policy 2025—Reinvigorating India's Cooperative Sector. *International Journal of Finance and Banking Research*, *11*(4), 70–80. DOI: 10.11648/j.ijfbr.20251104.11

NAFED. (2022). *Annual report 2021–22*. National Agricultural Cooperative Marketing Federation of India Ltd. https://www.nafed-india.com

Österberg, P., & Nilsson, J. (2009). Members' perception of their participation in the governance of cooperatives: The key to trust and commitment in agricultural cooperatives. Agribusiness. *International Journal (Toronto, Ont.)*, *25*(2), 181–197.

Rana, G., Goel, A. K., & Rastogi, R. (2013). Talent management: A paradigm shift in Indian public sector. *Strategic HR Review*, *12*(4), 197–202. DOI: 10.1108/SHR-02-2013-0012

Siedlok, F., Callagher, L., & Korber, S. (2024). Reviewing worker and producer cooperative contributions toward SDG8 in developing and developed economies. In *International Business and SDG 8: Exploring the Relationship between IB and Society* (pp. 281–295). Springer Nature Switzerland. DOI: 10.1007/978-3-031-46802-5_14

Times of India. (2025). IFFCO appoints KJ Patel as managing director. *The Times of India*. https://timesofindia.indiatimes.com

Zakirova, A., Alff, H., & Schmidt, M. (2025). Unequal fields: Political ecology perspective on organic cotton production in Tajikistan. *Organic Agriculture*, *15*(2), 183–198. DOI: 10.1007/s13165-025-00491-y

Chapter 6
Managing Talent for Business Growth: A Case Study Based on Broadcom Technical Concepts

Hani Chandhana
http://orcid.org/0009-0009-7363-9925
Showcraft Events LLC, UAE

Ashima Rahman
Bankura University, India

EXECUTIVE SUMMARY

This case study defines how talent management can be used to promote organisational resilience and business development in small technical service firms with reference to the Broadcom Technical Concepts LLC, Abu Dhabi. With its operations in a dynamic ELV systems integration industry, the organisation has used workforce flexibility, retention of skilled workers, and strategic redeployment to keep its operations running even when there is havoc like the COVID-19. The development of a complementary venture, ShowCraft allowed to utilize the available technical potential in the most efficient way and thus diversify without raising the number of employees. The research brings out the role of human capital as a strategic asset within uncertain settings as well as underscoring the existence of structured talent development and succession planning in providing a long term sustainability and scalability.

DOI: 10.4018/979-8-3373-5776-8.ch006

INTRODUCTION

In the modern business world with its high rates of technological growth and digitalization, and the growing competitive level in the world, organizations have to keep revising their strategies in order to stay competitive and viable. The contemporary organizations are rapidly adopting the sophisticated technological infrastructure, computer-mediated communication networks and automated systems of operation to improve efficiency, productivity, and service delivery. Consequently, human capital has become one of the most important strategic resources of organizations due to the success of the functioning of such intricate technological systems. The past belief that the major determinants of organizational success are financial commitment or physical site is slowly being overtaken by an expanded acknowledgement that knowledge, skills, and capabilities of the employees are vital in the attainment of long term organisational performance.

The increased significance of human capital can be especially seen in those industries which depend much on the technological expertise and specialised knowledge. The organisational effectiveness relies on the capability of the employees to design, install, operate and maintain complex technological systems in such sectors. This has in turn seen organisations becoming more aware of the need to invest in both the technological infrastructure and also the training and management of their employees. This change has resulted in the adoption of talent management as a strategic organisational capability that aims at attracting, developing, retaining, and efficiently exploiting employees having valuable skills and competencies.

Talent management has adopted a crucial role in the contemporary organisational strategy due to the fact that employees have become a competitive advantage source. The literature on strategic management underlines the fact that organisations are able to gain sustained competitive advantage in case they manage their internal resources and capabilities in an efficient way (White, 2017). Human capital is one of these resources, which has been instrumental in organisational innovation, efficiency in operations and strategic flexibility. The employees do not only play a role in the technical knowledge and experience that they have but they also play a role in problem solving, teamwork and adapting to the changing business environments.

The importance of human capital is also determined in the theory of intellectual capital, which is the knowledge, expertise and capabilities that is vested on employees and organisational processes. It is a well known fact that intellectual capital is a significant creator of value in the knowledge based economies (Stewart, 1997). Those organisations that are able to develop and manage intellectual capital effectively can be in a position of improving innovation, the overall decision making process, and the competitive placement in the market. The skills of workers in technologically intensive industries are usually a key organisational resource that may not be easily copied by other players.

Resource-Based View (RBV) of the firm offers a valuable theoretical paradigm of strategic value of human capital. The RBV theory suggests that organisations attain long-term competitive advantage through the presence of resources that are valuable, rare, inimitable and non-substitutable (Barney, 1991). Proficient staff that is specialised in knowledge and technical abilities often fits these requirements and is invaluable assets to organisations. When organisations successfully create and sustain such resources by practicing talent management, organisations are able to develop capabilities that can hardly be imitated by their competitors. Consequently, talent management is a relevant process by which organisations synchronise workforce capability and strategic goals.

Talent management refers to a set of organisational practices e.g. recruitment, training, performance management, employee development and employee retention strategies. The practices are intended to make sure that organisations possess the right employees who possess the right skills to realise the organisational goals (Collings and Mellahi, 2009). Talent management systems are not only effective in enhancing the productivity of the workforce but also lead to resilience and adaptability of organisations especially those operating in an industry that is highly dynamic in terms of technology.

Whereas the concept of talent management has been extensively researched among big multinationals, limited research has been done on how talent management practices work with small and medium enterprises (SMEs). A small-scale business is likely to experience special issues with workforce management because of restricted financial means, reduced organisational designs, and less formal human resource systems. Talent management practices in most of the SMEs are usually progressive based on the needs of operations as opposed to being adopted within organizational structures (Lewis and Heckman, 2006). In spite of these constraints, SMEs tend to place much dependency on the technical skills and flexibility of their workforce to ensure that they remain competitive and sustainable as an organisation.

Effective talent management is of special significance as the emerging economies in which the company operates are characterized by the increasing demand of the skilled professionals due to the rapid technological progress and infrastructure growth. The United Arab Emirates (UAE) is one of the bright examples of such an environment. The UAE has enjoyed significant economic growth over the last 20 years to support large-scale investments in infrastructure development through massive investments in the digital transformation and smart city projects. The policies of the government to diversify the economy and innovate technologies have greatly enlarged the need of combined technological products on various industries such as construction, transportation, health care, hospitality industry, and education.

In the scope, the Extra Low Voltage (ELV) system integration market has emerged as a vital part of the current infrastructure development. ELV systems also incorporate a broad spectrum of technological technologies that comprise closed-circuit television (CCTV) surveillance systems, access control systems, enterprise networking systems, fibre optics communication infrastructure, audio-visual technologies, and building automation systems. Such systems are important in aiding security, communication and efficiency in the operations of modern buildings and facilities. Such systems are expensive and need very competent individuals with specialised technical knowledge and expertise to successfully implement and maintain them successfully.

Broadcom Technical Concepts LLC is a company that is in this technologically dynamic environment and it provides integrated ELV and IT infrastructure solutions in the United Arab Emirates. The organisation was set up in 2008 in Abu Dhabi and has expanded to be a recognised service provider providing technological infrastructure solutions in various industries, which started as a small business. The company provides numerous products such as installation of network infrastructure, surveillance systems, structured cabling solutions, fibre optic communication networks, automation systems, as well as audio-visual technologies. Broadcom Technical Concepts has over the years operated in an eclectic range of clients comprising of government organisations, commercial establishments, hospitality institutions, and educational facilities.

Growth and development of Broadcom Technical Concepts is a good opportunity to investigate how talent management practices develop in a small technical services organisation that operates in competitive and technologically intensive environment. SMEs tend to use more relaxed and less structured methods of workforce management unlike large companies with formalised human resource management systems. The relationship between talent management practices and organisational resilience and business growth can be a key area of consideration based on the manner in which such organisations are able to manage their human capital.

This chapter thus looks at how talent management is used to facilitate organisational performance and strategic flexibility in Broadcom Technical Concepts. Based on theoretical views held by the Resource-Based View, intellectual capital theory and strategic human resource management literature, the paper examines the role of workforce capabilities in organisational development and resiliency. The chapter also examines the talent management practices that change concerning organisational challenges such as market uncertainty and technological change.

Through the case of Broadcom Technical Concepts, the current study will serve as an addition to the existing body of literature concerning the management of the talent in the SMEs that work within the emerging markets. The findings offer information on how organisations can successfully exploit human capital to sustain business, innovate, and gain competitive advantage in the fast changing and changing technological landscapes.

REVIEW OF LITERATURE

The literature in strategic management lays stress on linking organisational resources and long-term strategic objectives. To keep up with the ever-changing market organisational competencies need to test their internal capabilities and external environments constantly to ensure that they remain competitive. Strategic management models emphasize that strategic success of organisations relies heavily on the capacity to efficiently utilise internal organisational resources, such as human capital in accomplishment of the strategic objectives (White, 2017). In the same breath, strategic management scholars believe that companies need to build internal capacity that is capable of responding to the forces of competition as well as industry dynamics. These competencies tend to be incorporated in the skills, knowledge and experience of employees who engage in the organisational decision making and operational efficiencies (Rumelt, Schendel and Teece, 1991).

In the strategic management view, human capital is a very important organisational resource that assists in execution of strategic initiatives. It is the responsibility of the organisations to make sure that their employees have the potential that can help in the facilitation of innovation, efficiency of operations and responsiveness in the market. Strategic management models thus emphasise the need to come up with workforce skills that resonate with organisational goals and long term strategic planning (Alizadeh *et al.*, 2016). Talent management may be considered as a process by which organisations develop employee talents and coordinate employee performance with strategic organisational objectives(Collings and Mellahi, 2009). Strategic human resource systems are thus required to develop in order to facilitate organisations to draw effective benefits out of workforce capabilities as a way of creating sustained competitive advantage.

Human capital strategic role is especially pronounced in the knowledge-based industries where organisational performance largely depends on the capability of the workers in generating, applying and relaying knowledge. Intellectual capital has become a concept that has played a key role in the development of a theoretical framework that appreciates the value of the knowledge that employees hold in the organisations. Intellectual capital is the intangible knowledge that is entrenched in employees, organisation processes and relationships that provides value creation and competitive advantage. Those organisations which successfully manage intellectual capital can increase the levels of innovation, increase the operational efficiency, and their strategic positions in the competitive markets (Stewart, 1997).

The increasing focus on the intellectual capital is part of a broader change in organisational thinking, in which knowledge resources have been identified as key drivers of organisational success. Intellectual capital does not only cover the knowledge of individual employees but also organisational systems that assist in the knowledge creation and knowledge sharing. Organisations can also increase their skill to exploit intellectual capital through workforce development and knowledge management practice which leads to better organisational performance and long-term sustainability (Capital, 1998).

Researchers studying intellectual capital have also noted the utility of the quantification and administration of knowledge resources in organisations. Literature on intellectual capital underscores the need to have structures by organisations to identify, measure and report on intangible knowledge resource so as to manage them effectively. A well managed intellectual capital helps organisations to gain a better insight into the value of employee expertise and its contribution to organisational performance (Petty and Guthrie, 2000). Also, intellectual capital is instrumental in development of organisational policy and strategic decision-making process. Such organisations have a greater ability to develop value in terms of innovation, sharing of knowledge and is the ability to deploy its resources strategically in managing intellectual capital (Brennan and Connell, 2000).

Intellectual capital measurement has also emerged as a significant field of study in the field of organisational studies. Researchers have highlighted how organisations should ensure that they have a good system of assessing the role played by intellectual capital in the performance of the organisation. Intellectual capital measurement frameworks help organisations to determine how good their workforce development programs are and what can be done to help employees improve their capabilities. Through the systematic analysis of intellectual capital, organisations are able to enhance their decision making in regard to talent development and management of knowledge (Kannan and Aulbur, 2004).

The recent studies also support the significance of intellectual capital in modern organisation settings. Intellectual capital has been cited as one of the key indicators in attaining sustainable development and resilience of organisations in knowledge based economies. When organisations make good use of intellectual capital, they have the ability to build on innovation skills, decision making and organisational flexibility in the face of volatile market conditions (Morea *et al.*, 2026). Empirical analyses also show that disclosure of intellectual capital may have a positive impact on the firm value through enhancing transparency and boosting investor confidence (Halid, Yusuf and Pilomonu, 2026). Also, intellectual capital reporting can enhance the transparency in information asymmetry between organisations and their stakeholders, which, in turn, can lead to better market valuation and organisational credibility (Yahaya, 2026).

Resource-Based View (RBV) of the firm also supports the strategic significance of human capital. According to the RBV model, organisations can attain sustained competitive advantage when they hold valuable, rare, inimitable and non-substitutable resources (Barney, 1991). Human capital especially employees who are specialised in knowledge and technical expertise meets these requirements quite often and hence is a key organisational resource. When organisations manage to develop and defend such resources successfully, they can create competitive benefits that are hard to be imitated by the competitors.

The RBV theory suggests that organisations need to concentrate on building internal capabilities, which may not be easily copied by the rivals. Such abilities are usually brought about by the summative skills and experiences of employees who make contributions towards organisational innovation and problem solving. Human capital thus emerges as one of the primary factors of organisational competitiveness especially in those industries where technological skills and specialised knowledge are central to organisational performance (Barney, 2001).

The ongoing studies still utilise RBV theory in the study of the development of strategic capabilities in competitive organisations. There is some research into the way that companies exploit internal assets like marketing capabilities, knowledge bases, and organisational learning processes as a way to increase competitive advantage (Lubis *et al.*, 2026). Equally, RBV has been furthered to analyse the role in which organisations that work in special markets contexts utilise unique organisational resources to improve strategic positioning and strategic performance results (Islam, 2026). These visions support the perception that human capital and organisational capabilities are major forces of organisational success.

Talent management practices are important in facilitating organisations to create and exploit human capital. Talent management is a continuum of organisational practices such as recruitment practice, training practice, career development practice, succession planning, and performance management. These practices serve to ensure that organisations have the right employees that have the right skills to meet the objective of organisations. Talent management systems help to enhance organisational performance and long term competitive advantage by ensuring that the capabilities of the workforce fit workforce with the strategic organisation objectives (Buckingham and Vosburgh, 2001).

Systemic approach to talent management places a lot of emphasis on the integration of different human resource practices into integrated organisational system(Lewis and Heckman, 2006). Instead of viewing the recruitment, training and performance evaluation as separate processes, organisations are advised to embrace integrated talent management systems that would enable them to realise alignment of workforce development with organisational strategy. This combined strategy would make sure that the talent development initiatives would benefit the overall organisational goals and lead to long term strategic success (Ashton and Morton, 2005).

More recent studies have gone on to elaborate the concept of talent management by laying stress on the contextual factors. According to scholars, organisational, industry and environmental conditions require the talent management strategy to be less generic. Talent management is not a universal model but should be adjusted to the unique circumstances of organisations so that it can deliver successful results (Gallardo-Gallardo, Thunnissen and Scullion, 2020). On the same note, empirical research on the practices of talent management indicates that various organisations take different practices based on leadership practices, organisational structure, and workforce traits (Thunnissen and Gallardo-Gallardo, 2019).

Another component of talent management practices that is important is performance management systems. Performance management entails systematic assessment of employee performance to make sure that individual performance fits organisational purposes. Good performance management systems give organisations useful information on the ability and development requirements of employees. Through the adoption of systematic performance appraisal mechanisms, organisations can be able to award employees who perform well and devise strategies to improve the productivity of the workforce and the company as well (Armstrong and Baron, 2005).

Another management literature that has attracted extensive discussion on performance measurement frameworks is their role in enhancing organisational performance. Performance measurement systems enable organisations to track performance in operations and the effects of workforce initiatives on organisational performance. This is achieved by combining performance measurement systems and talent management practices, which enables organisations to have an integrated approach to workforce management that can be used to make strategic decisions and facilitate organisational development (Folan and Browne, 2005).

The literature that has explored the connection between organisational performance and human resource activities has always shown that successful HR systems play a significant role in enhancing organisational performance. Companies that invest in human resource development and equipping of employees with better capacities will experience more productivity and proficiency in operations. Such employees can contribute more to organisational aims and react to the dynamic demands in the market because they have the required competencies to execute their tasks successfully (Xu and Meyer, 2013).

On the same note, research has shown that there is a close correlation between perceived organisational performance and human resource practices. Employers which offer training opportunities to employees, as well as improving on their skills and careers, have high chances of achieving sustainability in organisational growth. The workforce development initiatives allow organisations to both improve the motivation and engagement of employees and the overall performance of the organisation (Singh and Singh, 2024).

Another strategic level of talent management is employee retention. Those organisations that do not manage to retain talented employees are likely to lose knowledge and expertise to operate. It may translate to high turnover which means that the organisations will incur high employee turnover and organisational disruption. Therefore, organisations need to come up with retention plans that will facilitate employee engagement and career growth. Some of the retention strategies involve career development prospects, organisational support and well-crafted leadership practices that bring about employee commitment and satisfaction.

Employee behaviour is also significant to the performance of an organisation. Organisational citizenship behaviour (OCB) describes those actions that are voluntary performed by the employees and help organisations to be effective, but are not directly related to the job requirements. Research has shown that OCB plays an important role in the productivity, collaboration, and teamwork in organisations (Sankar *et al.*, 2026). The broader review in the literature regarding organisational citizenship behaviour also reveals the critical role of employee engagement and discretionary behaviour at workplace to assist organisational performance (Das, 2026).

The modern organisations have also been affected by the technological advancement in terms of talent management. The fast integration of digital technologies, automation, and high-quality communication systems have changed the character of work in most industries. Due to the introduction of more advanced technologies, there is a need to expose the employees to technical skills that will enable them to use and maintain these technologies. In turn, the organisations have to make investments in workforce training and development programmes that facilitate technological competence and skills development (Zuboff, 1988).

Competitive forces are a driving force behind organisational innovation and digital transformation policies, specifically in the case of small and medium-sized firms (Kanoujiya *et al.*, 2026). It has also been noted that leadership is another aspect that promotes sustainable organisational development in SMEs. Good leadership allows organisations to promote innovation, employee growth, and organisational flexibility in the dynamic business settings.

The literature of organisational behaviour also emphasises the significance of motivation of the employees, the effectiveness of the organisation leaders and organisational culture as determinants of the performance of the workforce. These behavioural dynamics are important in the development of effective talent management systems that facilitate the development of employees and organisational success (Robbins, Robbins and Judge, 2025).

The next important element of talent management is the workforce planning and the talent forecasting. Workforce planning is a methodical procedure where organisations examine the current and future workforce needs to enable it to have the required human resources to realise organisational objectives. Workforce planning enables organisations to realise the possible skills gaps, foresee the future workforce needs and formulate measures to combat the workforce gaps. Through the integration of workforce planning process with the organisational strategy, organisations are able to ensure that the talent management programs facilitate the long-run business goals.

Succession planning is one of the main elements of workforce planning and talent management. Succession planning is a process that involves the identification and development of employees who have potential to be taken up in the organisation as future leaders. Organisations can also train employees to take up more responsibilities and continuity in organisational leadership through structured leadership development programmes. The succession planning is especially relevant in organisations that are knowledge-based ones where leadership abilities are a key determinant in the organisational strategy and decision-making.

Talent management has also been transformed by the increasing significance of digital transformation. To gain an advantage in the labour market, organisations engage more in digital technologies as they can be used to conduct recruitment, assess the performance of employees, and promote the workforce development program. DHRSs can assist organisations in gathering workforce data and analysing the data to aid in making evidence-based decisions regarding talent management practices. Such technological progress enables organisations to track the performance of the employees, detect gaps in their skills, and create specific training programmes to improve the working capabilities of the employees.

In spite of the remarkable development of the research on talent management, researchers still emphasize the necessity to investigate the topic of talent management practices in the context of particular organisations. Talent management systems might be more effective or not based on the size of an organisation, industry and environmental factors. The small and medium-sized enterprises have their own specific problems connected with the workforce management because of the lack of resources and administrative capabilities. This leads to a higher level of flexible talent management being practised by SMEs that place more attention to flexibility and pragmatic decision making.

Moreover, an analysis of talent management in the emerging markets can provide more information on how organisations can adjust workforce management strategies to their local economic and institutional environments. The growth of the economy in emerging economies is usually characterized by the high pace of infrastructure development and the implementation of technology, which leads to the growing demand on technical skilled workers. The organisations in such environments should therefore be able to formulate talent management strategies that not only favour workforce capability development but equally tends to the local labour market challenges.

Through investigating the talent management practices in the realities of technical service organisations in the emerging markets, the researchers can make contributions to a better understanding of the role played by human capital resources in facilitating the organisational performance in dynamic and competitive settings. The resulting such research can also have a practical value to managers who may wish to devise effective workforce strategies to achieve organisational sustainability and long term growth.

Overall, the literature clearly shows that talent management is of strategic value in the betterment of organisational performance, continuity of leadership, and competitive advantage. Nevertheless, there continue to be serious gaps in the literature on how small technical service organisations operationalise talent management when undergoing organisational change. The case of Broadcom Technical Concepts is thus an opportunity to know how talent management practices work in specialised technical service firms that are in dynamic and competitive environments.

COMPANY BACKGROUND: BROADCOM TECHNICAL CONCEPTS LLC

Broadcom Technical Concepts LLC was founded in 2008 in Abu Dhabi at a time when the rapid infrastructural and technological change was taking place in the United Arab Emirates. The period of high-rate economic growth in the country began in the early 2000s under the impact of massive investments in the urban development, transport infrastructure, hospitality facilities, and digital communication technologies. Government organisations and the private organisations started to shift towards high technological systems with the aim of assisting security, operational efficiency, and integrated communication networks. The increasing need in modern technological infrastructure provided the chances of the specialised companies that could provide the integrated IT and Extra Low Voltage (ELV) solutions. Broadcom Technical Concepts LLC was born in the midst of this dynamic environment and its goal is to provide technology solutions to its clients to offer high-quality infrastructure services.

The vision and the determination of the founder had a strong connection with the formation of the organisation. The founder started his career as a common person with low financial means yet having great expectations to create a prosperous business in the fast-growing technological industry of the UAE. Similar to most entrepreneurs in the emergent markets, the founder had been influenced by his ambition and uncertainty. During the initial period of the business, the founder used his sheer will, familiarity in the industry and good networking effects to make a mark in the competitive technical services market.

Technological based business needs a lot of investment in terms of capital in equipments, labour and operational infrastructure. Financial constraints were also one of the most important challenges encountered by the organisation during the first years of operation. The project needed money to be continued in its operations, and it had to work hard to secure the resources to implement the project, and to compete with the established players in the industry. Irrespective of these issues, the founder stuck to the idea of creating a sustainable company that would be able to provide clients with reliable and technologically advanced solutions.

The initial work done by the organisation was rather low in scale, but has been an essential step in building the reputation of the company on the market. Every project carried out gave a chance to prove the technical ability, reliability and dedication to customers. Over time, by offering regular and quality services and the focus on the needs of its clients, the organisation earned the credibility and trust of its customers. These initial successes enabled it to get other projects and increase the number of professional contacts in the industry.

Broadcom Technical Concepts is a company that functions in the Information Technology infrastructure and ELV system integration. ELV systems form an important part of the modern building infrastructure, and they encompass technologies like surveillance systems, access control systems, networking infrastructure, structured cabling, and integrated communication systems. The systems facilitate critical operations of the current facilities such as safety surveillance, communication connectivity and automated building operation. With the growing digitalisation of urban environments, the traffic of built-in ELV systems increases in the commercial and institutional spheres.

With time, the organisation gained experience in providing a broad spectrum of technical services that are meant to facilitate the infrastructure requirements of contemporary organisations. Some of these services are IT infrastructure deployment, CCTV surveillance systems, access control technologies, automation and lighting control systems, enterprise wireless networks, fiber optic communication networks, structured cabling systems, audio-visual communication solutions, the IPTV technologies, and satellite television distribution systems (SMATV). The combination of these services is the technological support of the operational facilities today that allow organisations to work effectively and provide safe and connected environments.

The other differentiating factor of the organisation is its capability to offer turnkey solutions. The company does not provide separate technical services, but provides complete solutions of any project including the complete project life cycle. This covers system consultation, technical design, equipment purchase, installation, testing, commissioning and long term support of maintenance. These integrated services enable the organisation to offer individualised infrastructure solutions to the operational needs of individual clients. In this way, the company can operate as a service provider and, at the same time, as a long-term technology partner that is helping its clients in the digital transformation.

As the firm increased its capacity of operation, it started to serve a wide variety of industries in the UAE. The client base of the organisation comprises government institutions, shopping malls, hotels, learning institutions, health care facilities, transport infrastructure developments and business office settings. These industries are critically dependent on consolidated technological systems to facilitate safety, communication and operational efficacies. The versatility of technical ability and the management of projects is evidenced by the flexibility with which the organisation can provide the reliable infrastructure solutions in a variety of sectors.

Broadcom Technical Concepts has managed to accomplish a good number of infrastructure projects across the UAE over the years. The organisation has acted as a service provider to over 500 clients and it has proven its operational stability and long term credibility in technical services industry. Most of these projects entail the installation of intricate technology that demands highly skilled engineering knowledge and co-ordinations among the project teams, suppliers and clients. An effective implementation of such projects has enabled the company to build and enhance its image as a trusted provider of integrated technology solutions.

The other fact that has led to the growth of the company is its partnership with globally known technology manufacturers. The organisation operates as a licensed dealer of internationally established technology brands like the ITC and Ruijie in Abu Dhabi and in the overall market in the UAE.

Such alliances allow the company to offer high-quality technological products and solutions that are of international quality standards. The availability of such technologies enables the organisation to provide some innovative and dependable infrastructure systems that aid the changing demands of the modern facilities.

The list of clients served by this company features some of the top organisations that are based in the United Arab Emirates. These clients are a varied sample of industries and they comprise government authorities, commercial restaurants, hospitality groups, educational institutions, health care providers and huge corporate organisations. The high-profile clients of the organisation work with reflect the skills of the organisation to address the high standards of operations and to provide technically complex projects. These giant organisations have a lot of trust in the company and this has greatly enhanced the reputation of the company in the regional technology services market.

Although the organisation has been growing in terms of its operations and customer base, it has retained a privately owned company with an entrepreneurial vision of the founder. The founder still has a significant role to play in determining the strategic direction of the firm but at the same time keeping the core values of the organisation in line with the values upon which the organisation was initially founded. With time, the founder has diversified his entrepreneurial concerns and has come to manage numerous business operations, which are indicative of the growth and success attained due to years of hard work and sound judgement.

The adventure that started as a small-scale entrepreneurial venture and went up to become a provider of technical solutions was not a smooth one. In the initial days the company was experiencing a financial constraint, competition in the market, and uncertainty in operations which were very limiting factors. There were some times when it needed a lot of resilience and flexibility to deal with project commitments and operational stability. Nevertheless, the founder was dedicated to providing quality services and ensuring a good relationship with the clients, which enabled the organisation to overcome these difficulties with time.

With great effort and thorough planning the firm was able to steadily increase its level of human resources, technical capacity and operations. The allocation of funds towards professional staff, technical development, and high-level technological facilities helped the organisation to enrich its service provision, as well as to take on more intricate projects. This ongoing growth has enabled the organisation to be competitive in the fast changing technological environment of the UAE.

The overall technological landscape in the UAE keeps changing as the nation pours numerous resources into the smart city projects, digital infrastructure, and technologies. The government programs that support the digital transformation and innovation have boosted the need of integrated technological solutions in both the government and the business world. The companies present in the technical services sector need to constantly evolve with the new technologies and client demands as well.

To address these changing trends, Broadcom Technical Concepts has addressed its technical capabilities and intensified its technology in integrated infrastructure solutions. The organisation has been able to keep its place in the competitive market environment due to its capacity to embrace change in technology and provide dependable services to its clients. The company has been able to improve the creation of modern digital infrastructure within the UAE by integrating technical expertise with the customer-oriented strategy.

Today Broadcom Technical Concepts LLC is known as one of the suppliers of integrated IT and ELV solutions, which facilitate protected, linked and technologically developed environments in the whole of the United Arab Emirates. The experience of the organisation can be attributed to the influence of entrepreneurial insight, persistence and strategic ability to establish a successful organisation in a competitive and dynamic technological environment.

TALENT MANAGEMENT PRACTICES

The case studied under Broadcom Technical Concepts explains how talent management has transformed to aid the continuity of the organisation, its resilience, and expansion amidst a changing technological landscape. The case illustrates the way talent management practices may develop naturally in small and medium-sized enterprises (SMEs) and not be introduced by the system of a formal human resource mechanism. Hence workforce management in the organisation has over the last few years since the inception of the organisation in 2008 been influenced more by the realities of operation, the market conditions and strategic decisions of the leadership than by the traditional HR models. This trend represents the claim that has been presented in literature on talent management, which suggests that, in some cases organisations opt to use context-based strategies to manage human capital based on the size of the organisation, resources and the pressure of the environment.

The strategy towards talent management in the initial years of the organisation was more informal and reactive. At the initial stage of the company foundation, there were only five employees. At this level, the technical ability, dedication and flexibility of these people were very critical to the existence of the organisations. The workforce was very limited so that the employees had to carry out several duties at the same time. Employees engaged in different operation activities such as installation of systems, troubleshooting systems, coordination of projects, technical maintenance and support to clients. This multipurpose structure enabled the organisation to be functional even with its paucity of resources.

The capacity of the early workforce structure to be flexible demonstrates a significant element of using talents in small organisations. Rather than depending on rigid job specifications or departmental specialisation, the company aimed at ensuring that it maximised the productive ability of the existing employees. Employees were advised to develop more technical capacity and suit themselves to diverse operational problems. This strategy is indicative of the notion of human capital utilisation that is highlighted in the strategic management literature where knowledge, expertise, and adaptability of the employees are regarded as central organisational resources that work towards performance and sustainability.

When the company started to gain its image in the ELV and IT infrastructure market, the demand to its services started growing at a slow pace. The organisation started getting more project opportunities with commercial establishments and infrastructure and with institutional clients. As a measure to this growth, the company has increased its workforce gradually to satisfy the rising operation requirements. The organisation expanded to more or less forty-five employees by 2017 with an initial number of five employees.

This development stage was a major change in the way the organisation handled its work force. Although the initial years were mostly dedicated to the flexibility of the workforce and the ability to stay afloat, the expansion stage demanded a more systematic treatment of the acquisition of talents and the development of capabilities. The recruitment practices started to focus on the technical expertise and the project-specific skills. The infrastructure projects also grew intricate and therefore the organisation demanded more and more employees, who had specialised expertise in fields like network infrastructure, surveillance systems, fiber optic communication, and system integration.

Despite the fact that the formal HR systems were still not much used in this time frame, the management team started to realise the strategic value of the development of a technically competent workforce. Recruitment was also becoming more based on the ability of the organisation to provide long-term service and not short-term operational requirements. This change is indicative of the concepts of the Resource-Based View (RBV) of the firm that argues that organisations gain sustainable competitive advantage through the creation of valuable, rare, and difficult-to-imitate internal capabilities.

In the framework of Broadcom Technical Concepts, technical know-how was an important organisational asset. The employees with specialised engineer skills and system integration skills were directly related to the company successful completion of complex infrastructural projects. These skills helped the organisation to improve its functioning capacities and reputation in the market.

But, the organisational path has been significantly shaken by the international COVID-19 pandemic. Starting in 2020, the pandemic posed unprecedented challenges to most sectors across the globe, including ones that rely on the development of physical infrastructures and the provision of on-site technical services. The technical services industry was greatly impacted by government restrictions, delays in the construction works, and cutbacks in investments in infrastructure.

In the case of Broadcom Technical Concepts, the effects of the pandemic led to the reduction of the project activity and uncertainty of operations. When numerous projects were postponed or put on hold, the organisation had to re-organise its human resources to ensure that it was self-sufficient financially. As of 2021, the workforce of the company was cut by forty-five employees down to around seventeen employees.

Although downsizing is perceived as a loss to an organisation, this was also a critical moment in the way the company would treat talent management. Instead of trying to reintegrate the workforce as quickly as possible into the organisation as the conditions started stabilising, the organisation took another strategic approach. The management started laying more emphasis on retention of highly skilled and experienced employees instead of increasing the number of employees. This change was a movement of workforce growth to talent optimisation.

Those employees who were left in the organisation had a considerable amount of technical skills and knowledge of the organisation. Their experience in operations, relationship with clients and technical systems of the company allowed the organisation to proceed with delivering the services despite having fewer employees. This case proved the relevance of knowledge capital in knowledge intensive sectors. The knowledge and experience that would be instilled on employees proved to be important organisational resource that helped maintain the operations even in a time of uncertainty.

Strategically, the leadership realised that, the sustainability of the organisation was not only pegged on the size of workforce but on the proper utilisation of the available talent. The retention of the experienced professionals allowed the organisation to retain institutional knowledge that ensured that quality of services was maintained and it could also stay afloat in the face of market disruption. This move signifies the increased acknowledgement in the management literature that human capital is a strategic organisational resource that could help a firm to endure through the turbulent times.

Instead of letting the talents of the retained employees go to waste once the activity in the project reduces, the management team started to consider new options in which the workforce could play a role in the organisational development. This strategic thinking took later on to the development of a supporting business venture that specializes in audio-visual event solutions.

The setting up of ShowCraft was a diversification strategy as well as a talent management strategy. The technical skills needed in the installation of audio-visual systems, lighting control, and event technology implementation were closely similar to those that many employees already had in the organisation. The company did not hire new staff, but instead it redistributed the available workforce of the engineers and technicians to carry out the operations of its newly formed venture.

This is a strategic workforce redeployment that shows an innovative method of workforce use. The company was in a position to make full use of the available workforce and at the same time generate new revenue by deploying employees to work in both organisations. This strategy minimised the outsourcing of personnel as well as meant that precious technical skills were not lost to the organisation.

The dual-role approach produced a mechanism through which employees worked on the infrastructure development in both Broadcom Technical Concepts and event technology services in ShowCraft. This type of cross-functional use increased the professional exposure of the employees and increased their technical flexibility. The employees were exposed to various work environments in the field of technology and that also augmented their ability and flexibility.

Talent development wise, this cross-organisational deployment provided a chance of perpetual learning and skill growth. The exposure to the various project environments enabled the employees to acquire wider technical skills and problem-solving abilities. This solution is consistent with the principle of organisational learning, according to which employees constantly learn new things based on the experience and sharing of knowledge.

The strategic exploitation of the available talent also delivered a number of organisational gains. To begin with, the company was in a position to maintain its institutional knowledge pool through retention of long serving employees. Second, the organisation also minimised the operational expenses in terms of recruitment and training. Third, the cross-functional organization allowed the employees to be productive and kept working even when the infrastructural projects were minimal.

In the long run, this strategy proved to be successful as the complimentary venture started to generate more streams of revenue. ShowCraft helped in diversification of the service offerings of the organisation and at the same time enhanced value of the workforce it retained. This result is the way talent management decisions could affect more overall organisational strategy and business development.

The overall number of employees at Broadcom Technical Concepts, as well as ShowCraft, had reached about thirty five workers by the year 2026. Nonetheless, this growth was far different compared to the developed workforce growth in the past before the pandemic. Instead of concentrating more on boosting the number of employees, the organisation focused more on capability alignment and strategic use of the workforce. The decisions made by the organisation concerning the recruiting procedures were more informed by the needs of the organisation in the long-term operations and the specialised skills needed to serve the infrastructure and the event technology services.

The case of Broadcom Technical Concepts has shown that talent management in SMEs usually develops to suit practical organisational issues other than following set frameworks. Management of workforce within the organisation portrays a flexible policy that focuses on retaining the employees, skill development and strategic redeployment of the human capital.

The other significance of the talent management strategy used by the organisation is that the talent management strategy is strategy-oriented towards the nurturing of good interpersonal relationships amongst the workforce. Otherwise, in smaller organisations, leadership can be in direct contact with the employees that results in a working environment of collaboration, trust and open communication. Such intimate relations between the leadership and employees may reinforce organisational culture and increases employee engagements.

The leadership practices were also critical towards the talent management outcomes in the organisation. It also exhibited the capacity of the leadership to appreciate the strategic importance of human capital and make long-term organisational sustainability decisions. The organisation does not simply regard employees as operational resources, but as an element of its strategic capability.

Broadcom Technical Concepts case thus shows the significance of talent management that is led by the leaders in smaller organisations. Employee retention decisions, skill development decisions and cross-functional deployment decisions under leadership played a crucial role in determining how the organisation could readjust to the external challenges.

In a more general sense, experience of the organisation is indicative of some of the main themes of research in the current field of talent management. To begin with, it shows how valuable intellectual capital is in the knowledge-intensive industries. Technical expertise and problem-solving skills of employees were the key resources that helped the organisations to perform.

Second, the case demonstrates how strategic flexibility can also be used in talent management. Instead of the organisation solely using traditional HR structures, there was an adaptive approach to workforce which was necessary to keep up with the market changes.

Third, it is an approach of the organisation that emphasizes the significance of integrating talent management with business strategy. The organisational goals such as diversification and expansion of the services were closely correlated with the workforce decisions.

Lastly, the case shows that talent management may be used as an organisational resiliency driver. The retention of talented workers and redistribution of their skills to emerging business opportunities helped the organisation to overcome the wave of economic shocks as well as setting the organisation in the path of expansion.

To conclude, the talent management practices that have been noted in Broadcom Technical Concepts demonstrate how the SMEs may be managed to successfully manage human capital under challenging and swiftly changing environments. The practice of the organisation shows that resilience in the workforce, flexibility and proper strategic exploitation of employee competence can play an important role in organisational.

CRITICAL ANALYSIS

The Broadcom Technical Concepts case offers a valuable learning experience as it allows critically examining the workings of talent management in the context of the small and medium-sized enterprises in technologically dynamic settings. The experience of the organisation has shown the impact of the capabilities of the work force, technical expertise, and managerial decision-making on organisational resilience and strategic development. Simultaneously, the case indicates that there are a number of structural constraints of informal talent management systems. With the help of the theoretical models introduced in the literature review, one can determine the strengths and risks of the Broadcom workforce approaches to human capital management.

Among the most remarkable lessons of the case is associated with the use of human capital as a strategic organisational asset. The sources on strategic management make it clear that sustainable competitive advantage is attained by the organisations implementing the internal resources that facilitate the innovation process and operational efficiency properly (White, 2017). The technical skill of employees in the case of Broadcom Technical Concepts is a key organisational capability with a direct effect on service provision and operational performance. The company is in an industry where implementation of projects is highly dependent on specialised engineering knowhow with regard to IT infrastructure, ELV systems, surveillance technologies, and network integration. Consequently, the capacity to retain technically competent workforce in the organisation becomes critical in supporting the sustenance of the competitive position of the organisation in the market.

The observation is in line with the Resource-Based View (RBV) of the firm that says that organisations gain sustained competitive advantage when they possess resources that are valuable, rare, inimitable and non substitutable (Barney, 1991). Such resources may be explained as the technical potential of the workforce of Broadcom. The highly skilled system integrators, automation technologies as well as network infrastructure bring expertise that is not easily duplicated by other organisations in competition. This know-how can thus be an intellectual capital that enhances the organisational ability to operate and reputation in the technical services sector.

The significance of intellectual capital further becomes justified by the fact that researchers note the increasing role of knowledge-based resources in modern organisations. Intellectual capital refers to the knowledge, skills and experience in employees which is incorporated in organisational innovation and performance (Stewart, 1997). The skills of employees in knowledge-intensive industries like IT and integration of ELV systems can be the most important organisational resource. The Broadcom case exemplifies how intellectual capital can help organisations to survive the times of uncertainty. In the situation when the company had to cut its employee base due to the COVID-19 pandemic, the remaining staff members had enough experience to provide the services without any increased staff numbers. This shows the ability of specialised knowledge to offset the drawbacks of workforce and operational capacity.

Nevertheless, as much as the dependency on the experienced employees allowed Broadcom to continue with its operations, it also creates possible structural weaknesses. The talent management literature highlights the need to come up with systematic workforce planning and succession measures to make sure that the organisation is sustainable in the long-term (Rothwell, 1994). In Broadcom, the organisation seems to rely so much on a rather small team of professional workers whose experience is essential in the implementation of the project. This reliance presents possible risks in case the important workers quit the organisation or are unavailable because of the outside forces. The process of transferring the institutional knowledge to the new employees may be problematic without proper systems of succession planning or organised leadership development in the organisation.

This weakness is one of the major setbacks that most small and medium sized businesses have to contend with. Comparing to the large multinational organisations, which have an established human resource department, SMEs tend to use informal approaches to managing their workforce that are based on operational requirements, but not formal HR frameworks. According to the literature, talent management in SMEs is often developed in informal decision-making instead of being systemized through organizational policy (Gallardo-Gallardo, Thunnissen and Scullion, 2020). Although such flexibility enables organizations to react fast to market dynamics, it can also lessen the clarity and uniformity of workforce development procedures.

The other notable thing about the talent management strategy of Broadcom is the strategic use of flexibility of workforce. The organization also proved to be flexible in assigning its employees to various working situations especially when forming the complementary venture Show Craft. The present strategic redeployment shows how organizations can utilize the available organizational competencies to facilitate diversification and expansion of business. To assist in the development of audio-visual event services, Broadcom did not hire new staff but instead used the technical capacity of the staff it already had to develop.

Theoretically speaking, such strategy signifies the systemic approach to the talent management that is promoted by Ashton and Morton (2005) who state that the set of the talent management practices must be aligned with the organisational strategy closely. The success of this move to reassign the workers to several areas of operation enabled Broadcom to leverage its internal strengths to aid in organisational development. The development of ShowCraft enabled the business to diversify its services and at the same time keep its employees just as productive even when the infrastructure projects were not at their usual level of activity.

Moreover, cross-functional movement of the workers led to creation of the organisational learning. Organisational learning can be described as a process by which employees can learn and develop new skills based on experience and team-work (Zuboff, 1988). The workers in infrastructure project as well as audio-visual event services had to be exposed to novel technical settings that broadened their knowledge scope and developed their professional flexibility. This kind of exposure is capable of enhancing organisational capabilities by making the employees more versatile and able to deal with various technological challenges.

Irrespective of these benefits, the cross-functional workforce model also brings in some potential manageability complexities. Such employees who work in diverse roles on various areas of operation can be affected by role ambiguity and work stress. Lack of clearly stated responsibilities may cause confusion in terms of performance expectations and responsibility. Moreover, the employees working on two (or more) projects at the same time might be subjected to higher stress and fatigue levels, and, consequently, it may eventually impact job satisfaction and efficiency. These issues underscore the need to strike a balance between flexibility in the workforce and proper clarity of roles and workload.

The other weakness of the talent management strategy by Broadcom relates to the lack of formal performance management systems. It is a well-known fact that performance management is a vital tool in balancing the performance of employees with business goals and determining areas where workforce can be developed (Armstrong and Baron, 2005). Strategic rating systems enable organisations to evaluate employee capabilities in a systematic way by identifying high-performing employees and developing specific training programmes that improve the workforce performance. Without such systems, performance appraisals can be highly subjective by managers instead of being objective.

Such dependency on informal appraisal systems can result in inequity in terms of developing employees. Employees might not have good feedback on their performance or a formalized career development guidelines. In the long run, the absence of formal development channels may decline the motivation of the employees and raise the chances of them leaving the company. Career development and growth are opportunities that skilled professionals usually pursue. In case organisations fail to offer organised growth, employees will be more likely to seek employment with organisations that offer more explicit career growth.

The other critical issue is connected to the scalability of the current talent management practices of Broadcom. These informal systems to workforce management could be effective in small organisational settings where the leadership is in close contact with the employees. Nonetheless, informal systems can become more challenging to handle in case organisations grow and broaden their area of operation. According to findings in strategic human resource management, the structured HR systems are necessary to ensure the efficiency within organisations as they continue to increase their workforce and complexity in operations (Wright and Haggerty, 2005). Through such systems, organisations have the opportunity to standardise their recruitment processes, use training programmes and have a standardised evaluation framework.

In the case of Broadcom Technical Concepts, the gradual growth of the infrastructure services, as well as the event technology operations, might necessitate the creation of more formalised HR practices. Such practices may include planned recruitment measures, systematically executed training programmes, performance evaluation systems and leadership development plans. Such systems would assist the organisation to retain workforce consistency as well as sustaining long-term organisational development.

Another relationship between talent management outcomes and leadership is also pointed out in the case. Leadership is important in the development of organisational culture and workforce engagement. Studies in organisational behaviour stress the fact that leadership activities determine the motivation of employees, teamwork, and innovation (Robbins, Robbins and Judge, 2025). At Broadcom, the leaders showed the skills of acknowledging the strategic importance of employee skills and coming up with decisions that focused on workforce retention in times of uncertainty. The leadership helped in organisational resilience by retaining experienced employees and using their skills in new operational environments.

Nevertheless, the orientation of the decision-making process to the leadership can not necessarily replace organised systems in organisations. Although entrepreneurial leadership might be effective when the small organisations are in the early development stages, institutionalisation of the management practices is often essential in the long-term growth of the organisation. The development of structured HR systems would enable the organisation to retain the same practices of workforce development as the leadership roles are decentralised across the various levels of management.

The other dimension that will arise out of the case is the influence of technological change on talent management requirements. The literature highlights that the digital transformation and Industry 4.0 technologies are transforming workforce. and expertise needs (Kanoujiya et al., 2026). Companies that work in the technologically intense industries should continuously invest in workforce training and development so that they can be competitive. It is so because without the organised learning systems, organisations might fail to keep pace with the new technologies and changing market needs.

In the case of Broadcom Technical Concepts, the lack of formal learning and development programmes can restrict the capability of the organisation to actively equip the employees in the event of any future technological change. Introduction of training programs on new technology like state of the art network systems, digitalisation and automated infrastructure would greatly empower the workforce and contribute towards organisational innovation in the long term.

The case of Broadcom Technical Concepts, in general, displays a two-sided reality in the talent management practices. On the one hand, the flexible and adaptive character of using the workforce allowed the organisation to succeed in passing major difficulties in its operations and diversification of business operations. The human capital is able to work as an engine of organisational resilience as demonstrated by the strategic retention of talented workers and by its innovative redeployment of technical knowledge.

Conversely, structural constraints related to unofficial talent management systems are also present in the case. Lack of proper succession planning, performance management systems, as well as organised learning schemes can pose threat to long term organisational sustainability. These constraints will be necessary to address, in case the organisation will take care of its competitive stance in the constantly developing complex technological environment.

Summing up, in the case, it is shown that talent management is a key aspect in determining organisational adaptability, innovation, and growth. The analysis demonstrates the significant role of human capital in sustaining organisations in the knowledge-based sectors by connecting the practical organisational experiences with theoretical aspects of resource-based view, intellectual capital theory, and strategic human resource management.

RECCOMENDATIONS

Broadcom Technical Concepts analysis demonstrates that talent management remains an important component that helps sustain organisational performance and makes the organisations strategically adaptable in the context of technologically changing environments. Even though the organisation has managed to overcome operational challenges through workforce flexibility and technical expertise, the results also mean that there are areas that the talent management practices can be enhanced to enable long-term organisational sustainability. The following are, therefore, suggested to improve in the talent management structure in Broadcom without compromising the operational flexibility that has been a part and parcel of the company since its beginning.

To start with, the organisation may consider using systematic talent development programmes that are directed at structurally developing workforce capabilities. The need to stay up to date with technical knowledge and competencies is essential because of the industry in which the business functions rapidly changes the IT and ELV systems industry. Frequent technical training programmes, certifications and professional development courses would help the employees keep pace with the new technological trends. These programs might involve education of advanced networking technologies and digital automation system, integrated smart infrastructure solutions, and every integrated security solutions. Constant learning programs are especially significant in knowledge intensive industries where the technologies are innovative and change at a very fast rate. The organisation will be able to enhance its intellectual capital through investing in organised talent development programmes and in that way, the organisation will be able to maintain its workforce in the ability to provide clients with high-level technological solutions.

Secondly, formal succession planning should be introduced by the organisation to decrease the relying on the few experienced employees. As noted in the critical analysis, the present workforce structure is based on technical expertise of a few technical professionals with much organisational knowledge. As much as this knowledge has helped in ensuring that the organisation continues with its operations, it also leaves the organisation susceptible in case these employees retire or leave the organisation. Introduction of systematic succession planning procedures would enable the organisation to identify high potential employees and slowly train them to take up the future leadership and technical positions. Internal talent pipelines that maintain expertise continuity and leadership skills can be achieved through mentoring programmes, leadership training programmes and cross-functional assignments which guarantee continuity of the expertise and leadership skills.

Third, the role definitions between Broadcom Technical Concepts and the complementary venture ShowCraft could be made more transparent to increase the efficiency of the workforce and the coordination of the organisation. Though deployment of employees in cross-functional manner has helped the organisation to optimise the productivity of the workforce, it can also lead to role ambiguity and workload pressures. The well-established job roles, reporting lines and the project distribution mechanisms would lessen the guess work among the staff members and the necessary project priorities would be well handled. Defined coordination systems between the two business organizations would also enhance scheduling of projects, and allocation of resources, which would mean that future conflicts involving workforce availability would be minimized.

The other notable recommendation is the introduction of formal performance management systems. The frameworks of structured performance appraisals would help the organisation evaluate the contribution of employees in a more objective manner and determine the areas that they could work on professionally. The performance management systems usually encompass performance reviews, competency tests and feedback systems that should match individual performance with the organisational goals (Cleveland, Murphy and Williams, 1989). Implementing these systems would enable Broadcom to identify employees of high-performance, learning gaps and develop specific training programs that would result in a more effective workforce. In addition, clear evaluation procedures can reinforce employee motivation through giving them a clear impression and feedback on their performance.

Another area that needs to be developed is the planning of talents into a wider organisational strategy. Talent management is more of a strategic capability and should not be looked at as a purely administrative role but as one that is able to support organisations to grow. Strategic workforce planning will enable the organisation to predict the future skills needs especially with the current changes in technologies which are transforming the infrastructure and communication industries. The organisation can also anticipate future market trends and technological advancements by studying them so as to recruit and train employees with the necessary competencies that will assist in the future projects and service innovations.

Long term organisational resilience also involves leadership development. Leadership skills affect organisational culture, employee engagement and strategy making. Cultivating leadership skills in technical and managerial employees would enhance the capacity of the organisation to deal with future obstacles and lead organisational growth. Leadership capabilities among high potential employees can be developed through leadership training programmes, mentoring relationship and strategic decision-making workshops. These efforts are especially useful within SMEs in which leadership usually takes a leading position in the development of organisational culture and operational orientation (Conger and Fulmer, 2003).

The other suggestion entails the establishment of planned career advancement systems among the employees. Technical employees are usually willing to get a chance to progress in their career and grow professionally. Clearly defined career development opportunities may go a long way in motivating and retaining employees. The career advancement systems can incorporate set promotion standards, technical specialisation, and possession of managerial roles. Employees who have a sense of long-term career growth in their organisations are more likely to be committed towards organisational goals.

They should also enhance the knowledge management practices to maintain and pass organisational expertise. Valuable knowledge is instilled in individual employees as employees gain technical experience through the implementation of projects. The organisations that do not have mechanisms to capture and share this knowledge would easily lose expertise that was deemed to be critical by the departure of employees. Transforming individual expertise to organisational knowledge could be facilitated by the creation of knowledge sharing means, like internal training programs, technical documentation systems and joint knowledge databases. This would enhance organisational learning and decrease the reliance of the organisation on a select few.

Besides knowledge management programs, they should focus on the well-being of its workforce in order to deal with work pressures that may be linked to cross-functional jobs. Those employees that are performing in more than one area of operation might have a heavier load and pressure of work. Workforce motivation and productivity can be ensured by conducting workforce well-being programs that include balanced project innovation, fair allocation of work, and support systems to employees. A healthy working environment is part of the long term employee engagement and organisational performance.

Lastly, Broadcom Technical Concepts must also contemplate having a formalised yet adaptive talent management framework that is not too strict but yet flexible enough to meet operational flexibility. Although formal HR systems may help improve organisational efficiency and development of workforce, the issue of flexibility is also pertinent in the case of SMEs in the rapidly changing industries. The introduction of a hybrid talent management system that would put in place a framework of structured policies and dynamically make decisions would enable the organisation to scale its operations without losing the entrepreneurial flair that has made it successful so far.

By using these suggestions, Broadcom Technical Concepts will be able to enhance its talent management practices and remain flexible in its strategic decisions that have boosted its development. These would lead to further utilisation of human capital resources within the organisation as a long-term organisational sustenance and competitive advantage driver.

CONCLUSION

The case study has explored how talent management assists in promoting organisational growth, resilience, and strategic flexibility in the environment of Broadcom Technical Concepts. By working in a challenging technological landscape of a fast-growing infrastructure and ongoing innovations, the experience of the organisation demonstrates how effective use of human capital can affect organisational performance at the times of growth, decline, and diversification.

The research results indicate that talent management has been in the middle stage to ensure the continuity of operations in the organisation that has gone through profound structural changes. As opposed to using the expansion of the workforce as the only strategy to enhance the growth, Broadcom focused on the retention and strategic placement of the technically skilled employees. The skills of the experienced professionals retained in the organisation during the COVID-19 pandemic enabled it to keep providing the services even as the workforce size decreased. This finding is indicative of the concepts of the Resource-Based View, which underscores the fact that human capital may serve as a resource that is difficult to replace and has a value which can be used to sustain the competitive advantage in organisations.

Another issue that comes out in the case is the role of intellectual capital in knowledge-intensive sectors. The technical skills of the staff was a major organisational strength that facilitated service quality, customer satisfaction as well as operational effectiveness. The knowledge and experience that had been integrated in its workforce helped the organisation to sustain business continuity and venture into new business opportunities whenever there was uncertainty in the market.

The subsequent strategic diversification into complementary venture ShowCraft is another example of how the management of talent may be combined with the organisational strategic decisions. The organisation could use the redeployment of technical expertise into new areas of operation to increase service provision and create additional sources of income. This is a strategic fit between workforce potential and business diversification that proves the systemic contribution that talent management could make to organisational innovation and responsiveness.

Nevertheless, the case also shows that there are a number of weaknesses related to informal talent management practices. Although flexibility in the workforce has enabled the organisation to react better to the fluctuating market conditions, the lack of a formal succession planning, performance management systems, and programmes that are organised and structured development is a potential threat to long term sustainability. With the organisation growing and expanding its operations, creation of more structured frameworks of talent management will gain a lot of significance.

On the whole, the experience about Broadcom Technical Concepts supports the argument that talent management is an important organisational capability in knowledge-based industries. Through proper exploitation of the human capital resources and matching of the workforce capability to the strategic goals, organisations may increase their chances of managing uncertainty and long-term performance.

Moreover, the case will add to the overall knowledge of talent management practices within small and medium-sized technical services organisations, especially in the emerging markets where the flexibility and alignment of the capability of the organisation to be successful. The results emphasise that financial investment or technological infrastructure is not the only way of SMEs to become resilient and grow, and strategic use of their human capital resources can also make a difference.

To sum up, A Case of Broadcom Technical Concepts shows that talent management is not only an administrative task but a strategy that facilitates organisational responsiveness, innovation, and sustainability. Companies who acknowledge the importance of employees and establish mechanisms of boosting the capacity of employees are in a better position to react to the changing market conditions and retain the capacity to stay competitive in a business environment that is becoming more competitive.

REFERENCES

Alizadeh, R., Lund, P. D., Beynaghi, A., Abolghasemi, M., & Maknoon, R. (2016). An integrated scenario-based robust planning approach for foresight and strategic management with application to energy industry. *Technological Forecasting and Social Change*, *104*, 162–171. DOI: 10.1016/j.techfore.2015.11.030

Armstrong, M., & Baron, A. (2005). *Managing performance: performance management in action*. CIPD publishing.

Ashton, C., & Morton, L. (2005). Managing talent for competitive advantage: Taking a systemic approach to talent management. *Strategic HR Review*, *4*(5), 28–31. DOI: 10.1108/14754390580000819

Barney, J. (1991). Firm resources and sustained competitive advantage. *Journal of Management*, *17*(1), 99–120. DOI: 10.1177/014920639101700108

Barney, J. B. (2001). Resource-based theories of competitive advantage: A ten-year retrospective on the resource-based view. *Journal of Management*, *27*(6), 643–650. DOI: 10.1177/014920630102700602

Brennan, N., & Connell, B. (2000). Intellectual capital: Current issues and policy implications. *Journal of Intellectual Capital*, *1*(3), 206–240. DOI: 10.1108/14691930010350792

Buckingham, M. and Vosburgh, R. M. (2001) 'The 21st century human resources function: It's the talent, stupid!', *Human Resource Planning,* 24(4).

Capital, T. I. (1998). Exploring the concept of intellectual capital (IC). *Long Range Planning*, *31*(1), 150–453. DOI: 10.1016/S0024-6301(97)87431-6

Cleveland, J. N., Murphy, K. R., & Williams, R. E. (1989). Multiple uses of performance appraisal: Prevalence and correlates. *The Journal of Applied Psychology*, *74*(1), 130–135. DOI: 10.1037/0021-9010.74.1.130

Collings, D. G., & Mellahi, K. (2009). Strategic talent management: A review and research agenda. *Human Resource Management Review*, *19*(4), 304–313. DOI: 10.1016/j.hrmr.2009.04.001

Conger, J. A., & Fulmer, R. M. (2003). Developing your leadership pipeline. *Harvard Business Review*, *81*(12), 76–85. PMID: 14712546

Das, L. (2026). Organizational Citizenship Behavior: A Systematic Review (1983 to 2024). *Journal of Evolutionary Studies in Business*, *11*(1), 123–149. DOI: 10.1344/jesb.45416

Folan, P., & Browne, J. (2005). A review of performance measurement: Towards performance management. *Computers in Industry, 56*(7), 663–680. DOI: 10.1016/j.compind.2005.03.001

Gallardo-Gallardo, E., Thunnissen, M., & Scullion, H. (2020). *Talent management: context matters*. Taylor & Francis.

Halid, I. A., Yusuf, N., & Pilomonu, M. R. S. (2026). The Effect of Intellectual Capital and Sustainability Report Disclosure on Firm Value:(Study on the Food and Beverage Sector for the Period 2022-2024). *Majapahit Journal of Islamic Finance and Management, 6*(1), 806–823.

Islam, M. M. (2026). 'Halal resource-based view: Exploring the resource-based view from marketers' lens'. *Journal of Islamic Accounting and Business Research*, •••, 1–27. DOI: 10.1108/JIABR-03-2025-0124

Kannan, G., & Aulbur, W. G. (2004). Intellectual capital: Measurement effectiveness. *Journal of Intellectual Capital, 5*(3), 389–413. DOI: 10.1108/14691930410550363

Kanoujiya, J., Agarwal, B., Rastogi, S., Tarode, S. and Bodne, S. (2026) 'Does competitive pressures affect the Indian SMEs industry 4. O adoption: using quantile regression analysis', *Journal of Innovation and Entrepreneurship*.

Lewis, R. E., & Heckman, R. J. (2006). Talent management: A critical review. *Human Resource Management Review, 16*(2), 139–154. DOI: 10.1016/j.hrmr.2006.03.001

Lubis, N. W., Rini, E. S., Lumbanraja, P., & Sembiring, B. K. F. (2026) 'Resources Based View (RBV) for Marketing Capabilities: Literature Review: Implications for SMEs', *Business Models of the Future: How AI and Advanced Digital Transformation are Reshaping Industries*, pp. 407-414. DOI: 10.1007/978-3-031-85398-2_36

Morea, D., Iazzolino, G., Petruzelli, A. M., & Omeihe, K. O. (2026). Guest editorial: What if intellectual capital is the missing link in sustainable development? *Journal of Intellectual Capital, 27*(1), 1–7. DOI: 10.1108/JIC-01-2026-416

Petty, R., & Guthrie, J. (2000). Intellectual capital literature review: Measurement, reporting and management. *Journal of Intellectual Capital, 1*(2), 155–176. DOI: 10.1108/14691930010348731

Robbins, S., Robbins, S. P., & Judge, T. A. (2025). *Essentials of organizational behavior*. BoD–Books on Demand.

Rothwell, R. (1994). Towards the fifth-generation innovation process. *International Marketing Review, 11*(1), 7–31. DOI: 10.1108/02651339410057491

Rumelt, R. P., Schendel, D., & Teece, D. J. (1991). Strategic management and economics. *Strategic Management Journal, 12*(S2), 5–29. DOI: 10.1002/smj.4250121003

Sankar, M., Chitra, A., Mahadevan, A., Nagarajan, S., & Priya, S. K. (2026). A Systematic Analysis on Organisational Citizenship Behaviour around the World from 2005 to 2025. *International Review of Management and Marketing, 16*(1), 170–178. DOI: 10.32479/irmm.21417

Singh, S., & Singh, A. K. (2024). Role of Managerial Personality in Innovative Behavior at Workplace. *Journal of the Indian Academy of Applied Psychology, 50*(1), 261–270.

Stewart, G. (1997). Supply-chain operations reference model (SCOR): The first cross-industry framework for integrated supply-chain management. *Logistics Information Management, 10*(2), 62–67. DOI: 10.1108/09576059710815716

Thunnissen, M., & Gallardo-Gallardo, E. (2019). Rigor and relevance in empirical TM research: Key issues and challenges. *Business Research Quarterly, 22*(3), 171–180. DOI: 10.1016/j.brq.2019.04.003

White, C. (2017). *Strategic management.* Bloomsbury Publishing.

Wright, P. M., & Haggerty, J. J. (2005). Missing variables in theories of strategic human resource management: Time, cause, and individuals. *Management Review*, •••, 164–173.

Xu, D., & Meyer, K. E. (2013). Linking Theory and Context: 'Strategy Research in Emerging Economies' after Wright et al. (2005). *Journal of Management Studies, 50*(7), 1322–1346. DOI: 10.1111/j.1467-6486.2012.01051.x

Yahaya, O. A. (2026). Information asymmetry as a moderator of intellectual capital disclosure and market valuation. *Journal of Business and Management Sciences, 13*(1), 1–54.

Zuboff, S. (1988). Dilemmas of Transformation in the Age of the Smart Machine. *Pub Type, 81*, 17.

KEY TERMS & DEFINITIONS

Human Capital: The common knowledge, skills, abilities and experience the employees have that adds to the overall productivity of the organisation, innovation and long-term business performance.

Intellectual Capital: The intangible organisational assets that are incorporated into the expertise of employees, organisational processes, and knowledge system that can help in creating value, innovation and organisational competitiveness.

Organisational Learning: An ongoing cycle in which organisations improve their own power by acquiring, sharing, and putting into practice knowledge acquired in the course of experience, training, and interaction between employees.

Resource-Based View (RBV): An approach to strategic management holding that organisations attain a durable competitive edge by having valuable, rare, inimitable and non substitutable internal resources especially human capabilities and organisational knowledge.

Talent Management: A strategic organisational strategy to achieve organisational goals and stay at competitive advantage involved attracting, developing, retaining and making efficient the use of employees who have the critical skills and competencies needed to accomplish the organisational goals.

Workforce Flexibility: Capabilities of both the employees and the organisations to adjust to the evolving roles and responsibilities and operations as a result of the changing technological and business environment.

Chapter 7
Corporate Universities and Strategic Talent Architecture in the Indian Banking Industry

Prateek Dirghangi
http://orcid.org/0009-0001-9760-6054
Indian Institute of Management, Ranchi, India

EXECUTIVE SUMMARY

Corporate universities (CUs) have emerged as one of the most consequential institutional innovations in contemporary human resource development. Yet, the theoretical literature remains fragmented across disciplinary boundaries while practitioner adoption has accelerated globally. This chapter provides an integrated analysis of corporate university theory, typology, function, design, and evaluation, anchoring the review in two richly documented industry cases from India's service sector. Drawing on theoretical frameworks from human capital theory, the resource-based view, knowledge management, organisational learning, and institutional theory, the chapter traces the intellectual evolution of the CU concept from its definitional ambiguities through its emergent typologies to its strategic functions under VUCA conditions. A dedicated case analysis then examines how Axis Bank and HDFC Bank have constructed strategic talent architectures in Indian private banking, including the theoretically significant 'Hire-Train-Deploy' model.

DOI: 10.4018/979-8-3373-5776-8.ch007

INTRODUCTION

The contemporary organisational landscape is shaped by conditions of persistent volatility, uncertainty, complexity, and ambiguity, pressures collectively theorised under the VUCA framework (Bennett & Lemoine, 2014). In this environment, the half-life of knowledge has compressed dramatically. Technical skills acquired in graduate education may become obsolete within five years, regulatory frameworks shift with accelerating frequency, and competitive advantages rooted in product features are rapidly eroded by imitation. What endures as a source of sustained competitive advantage, theorists and practitioners alike have argued, is an organisation's capacity to generate, codify, and deploy knowledge faster and more intelligently than its rivals. It is within this strategic context that the corporate university (CU) has acquired renewed and intensifying significance.

The global proliferation of CUs is striking evidence of this significance. From approximately 400 entities in the United States in 1988, the number exceeded 1,800 in North America by 2000, with global estimates surpassing 4,000 by the 2010s (Kolo et al., 2013). In China alone, over 1,000 corporate universities had been identified by 2013 (Alagaraja & Li, 2015). This diffusion is not a Western export as it represents a genuinely global institutional response to a genuinely global problem, the inadequacy of traditional higher education systems to produce the organisation-specific, strategically aligned, continuously updated human capital that competitive organisations require. The corporate university has emerged as the primary institutional mechanism through which leading organisations have attempted to resolve this inadequacy.

Yet the literature on corporate universities exhibits significant tensions that this chapter seeks to address. Definitional debates remain unresolved, with scholars disagreeing about what meaningfully distinguishes a CU from a sophisticated training department. Empirical research, while growing, is fragmented across disciplines of human resource development, knowledge management, organisational learning, strategic management, and institutional theory, with limited theoretical integration. Evaluation methodologies remain underdeveloped, producing an accountability gap that simultaneously undermines practitioner confidence and scholarly rigour. Perhaps most critically, the literature retains a strong geographic bias toward North American and Western European contexts, limiting the theoretical generalisability of its findings to the rapidly growing CU landscape of Asia, South Asia, and emerging markets more broadly.

This chapter addresses these concerns by synthesising the cumulative scholarship on corporate universities through a theoretically integrative lens, situating the analysis within two richly detailed industry cases drawn from India's banking industry. These cases detail and compare how two of the largest banks in India,

Axis Bank and HDFC Bank, have used corporate universities to construct strategic talent architectures in response to the sector's acute human capital challenges. The two cases are not merely illustrative. They are analytically productive counterpoints to the Western technology and manufacturing sector exemplars that dominate the existing literature. The Indian banking cases document the emergence of the 'Hire-Train-Deploy' (HTD) model, which is a distinctive temporal inversion of the standard CU paradigm in which training substantially precedes and serves as the condition for formal employment. Both cases extend existing theory in directions the literature has not previously mapped.

CONCEPTUAL FOUNDATIONS OF CORPORATE UNIVERSITIES

A persistent challenge in the CU literature is the absence of definitional consensus. The earliest influential formulation, Meister's (1998, p. 1) characterisation of the CU as 'a centralised in-house training and education facility to address the shortened shelf life of knowledge and to align training and development with business strategies' emphasised strategic alignment but was criticised for overstating centralisation and understating institutional diversity. Allen (2002) proposed a more expansive definition 'an educational entity that is a strategic tool designed to assist its parent organisation in achieving its mission by conducting activities that cultivate both individual and organisational learning, knowledge and wisdom.' Allen's formulation extended the CU's mandate to knowledge creation rather than merely transmission and explicitly linked it to mission achievement. The Global Association of Corporate Universities and Academies (G-ACUA) subsequently refined this toward operational usability, defining the CU as 'a management tool designed to assist organisations achieve their strategic goals by conducting activities that foster individual and organizational learning and knowledge' with the twin criteria of strategic orientation and company-specificity as defining features.

Dealtry (2017) introduced a more transformational rendering, situating the CU as 'a management intervention that takes a company or organisation into a new robust and sustained phase of business development that it would not achieve with its current levels of opportunity for thought leadership and styles of learning behaviour.' Blass (2005) approached the definitional question comparatively, revealing that CUs occupy an ambiguous institutional position that mimics academic forms such as degrees, campuses, and faculties to appropriate legitimacy while remaining fundamentally different in governance, purpose, and accountability. Further, Andresen and Lichtenberger (2007) contributed the analytically productive notion of 'learning architecture', a deliberately configured, multi-level system attuned to the organisation's competitive context, which captures the constructivist ambition of mature CU practice more precisely than earlier definitions.

These definitional contributions converge on a critical analytical distinction that separates a corporate university from a conventional training department. Allen (2002, 2010) articulates that the defining characteristic is whether the learning function is proactive, anticipating and shaping organisational capability in alignment with competitive strategy, rather than reactive, addressing operational skill deficits after they manifest. Holland and Pyman's (2006) study of the Coles Myer Institute demonstrated empirically that functional CUs, operating within a 'scientific management culture of standardisation and cost reduction,' produce qualitatively different outcomes from strategic CUs that pursue 'long-term and diverse approaches to managing and investing in human resources' to differentiate capabilities. The resource-based view (Barney, 1991; Grant, 1996) provides the theoretical warrant for this distinction. Human capital developed through strategic CU investment becomes a source of sustained competitive advantage precisely because it is organisation-specific, culturally embedded, and not replicable through external hiring.

Functions of Corporate Universities

Strategic HRD and the Architecture of Capability

The most extensively researched CU function is its contribution to strategic human resource development (SHRD). Allen (2007) identifies strategic alignment as the definitional criterion that distinguishes the CU from other learning entities that are training and learning are driven by corporate strategy, goals, and major initiatives, rather than by operational deficits or individual requests. This strategic alignment function operates through several mechanisms, which include connecting learning programme design to competitive challenges identified in the strategic planning cycle; creating shared conceptual frameworks across organisational units to enable coordinated strategy execution; and building leadership pipelines calibrated to anticipated succession requirements rather than reactive vacancy filling.

Mayfield, Mayfield, and Wheeler (2016) extend this analysis by examining leadership development programs and find that strategically designed CU investments contribute to competitive advantage through what they term 'meta-capabilities,' the capacity to learn, adapt, and lead effectively under conditions of discontinuous change. In VUCA environments where specific technical skills depreciate rapidly, meta-capability building may represent the most durable CU contribution. Patrucco, Pellizzoni and Buganza's (2017) process-focused analysis demonstrates that the design phase of CU development, encompassing strategy definition, governance architecture, and programme cluster identification, is critical to whether the resulting institution delivers strategic impact. Their key finding that 'flexibility and potential recycles should be considered when configuring the process' positions CU design not as a one-Further, Lui Abel and Li (2012) distinguish four types of CU organisational processes, that includes, governance, learning delivery, operational, and partnership and demonstrates that no single configuration dominates across empirical contexts, consistent with Rademakers' (2014) argument that CU design must be contingent on strategic context rather than isomorphic best practice.

Knowledge Management Transfer, Creation and Network Functions

A second major CU function is knowledge management, which has attracted growing scholarly attention, particularly from researchers in the knowledge management tradition. Chen, Xu and Zhai's (2019) landmark analysis of ZTE College and HP University identifies three interrelated functions, including knowledge transfer, knowledge creation, and knowledge services. Scarso (2017) elaborates on this framework through a multidimensional classification that encompasses knowledge domain, cognitive goals, recipient groups, KM processes, and management structures, enabling a more precise comparison of CU configurations than aggregate typologies allow.

Empirical work by Scarso (2017) reveals that CUs serving technical knowledge domains tend to function primarily as knowledge transfer mechanisms, while those serving non-technical domains engage more heavily in knowledge creation processes, since tacit and experiential dimensions of managerial knowledge resist codification. This distinction has significant implications for evaluating the impact of technical knowledge transfer, which can be measured through competency assessments. In contrast, the impact of tacit knowledge creation requires longer time horizons and more complex measurement approaches, a tension that directly contributes to the accountability gap documented in the evaluation literature.

THE CASE OF CORPORATE UNIVERSITIES IN INDIA'S BANKING INDUSTRY

The Indian banking sector presents a compelling, underexplored context for corporate university (CU) research. Characterised by high labour-market volatility, rapid technological transformation, regulatory complexity, and aggressive expansion into new geographic markets, the sector embodies precisely the VUCA conditions under which the strategic corporate university has been theoretically most advocated. Unlike the manufacturing and technology sectors that dominate the empirical CU literature, banking is a pure service industry; its competitive advantage resides almost entirely in human capital in the knowledge, values, behavioural competencies, and relationship skills of its front-line and managerial workforce. This makes the organisation of learning not merely a supporting activity but a primary strategic function.

The Indian context adds further distinctive pressures. A rapidly growing middle class has driven unprecedented expansion in retail banking demand. India's scheduled commercial banks added thousands of new branches between 2015 and 2025, with private-sector players outpacing public-sector growth in both branch count and customer acquisition. This expansion created a structural talent demand that India's formal higher education system, oriented toward engineering, medicine, and generalist management, was structurally unprepared to meet. Banking-specific technical knowledge, compliance literacy, sales acumen, and customer orientation at the level required by private banks had to be developed by the banks themselves, creating an institutional vacuum that the corporate university model was uniquely positioned to fill.

It is within this context that Axis Bank and HDFC Bank, India's third- and first-largest private-sector banks, respectively, developed sophisticated CU architectures during the 2010s and 2020s. Their programs are not merely HR interventions; they represent deliberate institutional constructions that reshape the boundary between higher education and corporate training, engage academic partners, digital platforms, and regulatory bodies as co-producers of talent, and align learning infrastructure with strategic business objectives with a precision rarely documented in the academic CU literature. This case report analyses these architectures through the theoretical lenses established in the preceding literature review, extracting insights that both validate existing CU theory and identify its limitations in high-velocity, high-volume service-sector contexts.

Talent Landscape of the Banking Industry

Sector-Level Talent Challenges

Understanding the corporate university strategies of Indian private banks requires situating them within the distinctive structural context of the sector's talent market. Three interlocking challenges define this context, which are attrition, skill mismatch, and growth-driven demand acceleration.

Attrition in junior banking roles is among the highest in any organised sector in India. Annual voluntary turnover rates of 25–35% for frontline sales and customer-facing positions, personal bankers, and relationship managers are industry norms. Teller-grade executives are an exception. The causes are multiple, including relatively modest starting compensation, high performance pressure in sales-driven roles, limited perceived career visibility in early years, and the active lateral recruiting practices of competing banks and financial services firms. The consequence is a perpetual replacement cycle. A bank that grows its branch network while sustaining this attrition rate must effectively hire, train, and integrate a substantial fraction of its frontline workforce every year to maintain operational continuity.

Skill mismatch compounds the attrition challenge. India's general-purpose higher education system produces graduates with strong analytical foundations but limited domain-specific knowledge of banking products, regulatory frameworks, credit assessment, customer relationship management, or digital banking operations. Graduate recruits from a bank might be drawn from its campus hiring pool. Economics, commerce, and MBA graduates typically lack the operational readiness to function effectively in complex banking environments without substantial post-hire training. This gap between academic preparation and job-readiness is not merely an inconvenience but a structural market failure that imposes high costs on banks' recruits who leave within their first year after receiving expensive in-house training, representing sunk costs without returns.

The third challenge, growth-driven demand acceleration, reflects the strategic ambitions of India's leading private banks. HDFC Bank's workforce grew from approximately 98,000 employees in 2019 to over 173,000 by 2023, a 77% increase over four years, with the bank onboarding over 4,000 new employees per month at its peak. At this velocity, the traditional reactive approach to talent acquisition, hire from the market, train for months, and hope for retention, is architecturally incompatible with operational requirements. The corporate university model, which front-loads training before formal employment, produces role-ready graduates on a rolling basis and generates a pipeline that can be scaled independently of the external labour market, emerges as a structural necessity rather than a strategic preference.

THE POLICY ENVIRONMENT: SKILLING INDIA AND BANKING SECTOR PRIORITIES

The Indian government's Skill India initiative, launched in 2015 and substantially elaborated in successive Union Budgets, created an enabling policy environment for corporate universities in banking. By incentivising industry-academia partnerships for skill development, the government aligned regulatory and reputational pressures with the banks' own talent development interests, effectively creating a form of normative isomorphism (DiMaggio & Powell, 1983) that accelerated CU adoption across the financial services sector. Axis Bank explicitly positioned its hire-train-deploy programs as aligned with the 'national skilling agenda'. At the same time, HDFC's Parivartan CSR initiative, which trains approximately 2,000 rural youth in vocational banking skills, extends the CU's boundary-spanning function into the domain of national human capital formation.

The Reserve Bank of India's regulatory framework also shapes banking CU design in ways rarely noted in the international CU literature. Compliance training covering Know Your Customer (KYC) norms, anti-money laundering (AML) protocols, fair lending practices, and consumer protection regulations constitutes a mandatory knowledge domain that all bank employees must master before customer-facing deployment. This regulatory knowledge requirement creates a non-negotiable floor for training content, making external recruitment without prior training inherently risky. The corporate university, by incorporating compliance training into its standard curriculum, provides a compliance assurance function alongside its capability-building function, a dimension of CU value that is largely specific to regulated industries.

Situating the Indian Banking Case within CU Literature

The Indian banking sector's CU development closely parallels the conditions that Prince and Beaver (2002) identify as drivers of third-generation CU emergence a knowledge-intensive competitive environment, rapid organisational growth requiring scalable learning solutions, increasing complexity in the skill requirements of customer-facing roles, and a growing recognition that 'knowledge and learning are activities and processes that take place within and between individuals' requiring institutional investment rather than merely marketplace acquisition. What distinguishes the Indian banking case from the Western financial services contexts described by Lloyds TSB and NAB in the comparative literature (Blass, 2015) is the severity of the structural market failure in talent supply and the pace at which the largest banks are required to grow. The consequence is a CU model optimised for volume, velocity, and standardisation in ways that the more evolutionary Western banking CU models were not required to address at the same scale.

Theoretical Positioning Banking CUs in the Literature Framework

Before examining the specific programs of Axis Bank and HDFC Bank, it is analytically productive to position banking sector CUs within the definitional, typological, and theoretical frameworks established in the literature review. This positioning exercise serves two functions, first, it establishes the analytical lens through which the case material will be interpreted, and second, it identifies, in advance, the dimensions on which banking CUs are likely to extend, challenge, or complicate existing frameworks.

On the definitional question, banking CUs unambiguously satisfy Allen's (2002) 'strategic criterion', the defining distinction between a corporate university and a conventional training department. Both Axis Bank and HDFC Bank explicitly connect their learning programs to identified strategic growth priorities, involve senior HR leadership in program design and governance, and produce outcomes measured against business performance metrics rather than merely training efficiency indicators. HDFC's Chief HR Officer's articulation of the 'train-and-deploy model' as the 'future of hiring' at the bank represents precisely the proactive, anticipatory orientation that Allen identifies as the hallmark of genuine strategic HRD.

On Rademakers' (2005, 2014) typological framework, banking CUs occupy an interesting position. The dominant function of India's banking CUs converting large cohorts of raw graduates into deployment-ready banking professionals through structured, standardised training most closely corresponds to Rademakers' 'Training Factory' archetype, high-volume, high-standardisation, focused on explicit technical knowledge and behavioural competencies that can be reliably replicated across diverse candidate cohorts. Yet the evidence also suggests emergent 'Corporate Business School' characteristics, particularly in Axis Bank's Leadership and Coaching Academy programs and in HDFC Bank's internal mobility and culture transformation initiatives. The banking CUs examined here are thus best characterised as hybrid Training Factory + Corporate Business School models, a categorisation that Rademakers explicitly anticipates as typical of empirically encountered CUs.

The knowledge management function (Chen, Xu & Zhai, 2019; Scarso, 2017) in banking CUs is primarily one of knowledge transfer rather than knowledge creation. The goal is systematic diffusion of existing banking knowledge products, processes, compliance frameworks, and service standards to large cohorts of recruits with limited domain backgrounds. However, Axis Bank's digital platform partnerships (Coursera, Adda247) introduce a knowledge services dimension, providing employees with access to cutting-edge knowledge in data science, AI, and technology that moves beyond pure transfer toward what Chen and colleagues characterise as 'knowledge services for intrapreneurship,' equipping employees with frontier knowledge that may generate innovative applications within the organisation. This knowledge services function represents an emergent second-order CU capability that distinguishes the more sophisticated banking CU models from basic training programmes.

The Case of Axis Bank's Multi-Channel Talent Pipeline Architecture

The Axis Bank Young Bankers Program Foundational Pipeline Logic

Axis Bank's corporate university journey began in 2011 with the launch of the Axis Bank Young Bankers (ABYB) Program, developed in partnership with Manipal Global Education (Moneylife, 2011). The program's foundational design reflects a clear application of Becker's (1964) human capital theory in its strategic form rather than purchasing human capital in the open labour market acquiring graduates whose training costs have been borne by the educational system or by themselves Axis invested in producing organisation-specific human capital through a structured apprenticeship model, generating a workforce asset that would be simultaneously more capable and more loyal. This need for such a program stemmed from an earlier HR overhaul in 2010 (The Economic Times, 2010) that tied promotions to output, introduced coaching for non-performers, and even allowed termination if performance did not improve. The corporate university architecture and the bank subsequently built with Manipal evolved from an earlier capability-and-enforcement logic to mature into academies and structured pipelines.

The program's architecture precisely reflects this logic (NIIT, n.d.-a). Over twelve months, participants spend nine months in full-time residential study at Manipal's Bangalore campus, developing banking domain knowledge, regulatory literacy, financial product expertise, communication skills, and the interpersonal competencies that customer-facing banking roles demand. This is followed by three months of branch internship that functions as a supervised transition to operational practice, which Lave and Wenger (1991) would recognise as 'legitimate peripheral participation,' in which the learner progressively assumes greater operational responsibility under experienced mentorship while gradually moving from the periphery of the banking community of practice toward its centre. Participants who complete the program receive a Post-Graduate Diploma in Banking Services from Manipal University and are directly absorbed into Axis Bank at the Assistant Manager grade, an entry point that creates immediate career capital and provides a visible career trajectory from the program's first day.

The program's scale is a distinguishing feature in the Indian banking CU landscape. Over twelve years, the ABYB program has produced over 16,000 graduates, an average of approximately 1,333 trained bankers per year, every year, establishing what Pedrini (2011) characterises as a 'competence pipeline', a continuously operating institutional mechanism that converts raw human potential into deployment-ready organisational capability at predictable volume and consistent quality (NIIT, n.d.-a). This pipeline logic distinguishes the ABYB from a recruitment event or a training exercise. It is a permanent institutional architecture embedded in Axis Bank's talent strategy, not a one-time initiative that might be suspended during budget cycles or absorbed into the HR department's operational discretion. Though the relationship between Manipal and the bank was strong and significant, it also entered into tie-ups with other state universities, such as Guwahati University (Business Standard, 2016) and Benares Hindu University (The Economic Times, 2016). Thus, Axis did not merely run a single flagship pipeline; rather, it ran a multi-node institutional learning ecosystem, widening the case from a single program to a more distributed CU architecture. Further, reports suggest that Axis Bank created such an architecture to ensure a ready-made, productive talent pool from day one (The Economic Times, 2012), sharpening the CU model's underlying rationale: not just training for general capability, but compressing the time between hiring and productive contribution.

Targeted Cohorts: The Women's Batch as an Inclusive Pipeline Design

In late 2024, Axis Bank introduced a women-only cohort within the Young Bankers Program, a structural innovation that extends the pipeline logic into the domain of diversity strategy. The exclusive batch increased female participation from 31% to 38% in FY 2024-25 ABYB, bringing the cohort to 700 women trainees, addressing a talent dimension that pure-volume-oriented pipelines often neglect (CXO Today, 2024; The People Management, n.d.). Axis Bank's HR leadership framed this initiative in explicitly developmental terms. The batch was accompanied by additional programming on career development, stress management, and professional identity formation, aimed at ensuring not merely that women enter banking roles but that they develop into 'well-rounded bankers' with the support structures needed to sustain their careers through the early years, where attrition risk is highest.

From a CU theory perspective, the women's cohort exemplifies what Meister (1998) termed 'mass customisation of learning' using a standardised program structure as a base while layering targeted, cohort-specific interventions that address the particular development needs of a specific learner population. This customisation logic, which recognises that identical learning inputs produce differential outcomes for learners with different social contexts, career trajectories, and development challenges, represents a mature evolution of the Training Factory model toward a more individually responsive pedagogy. It also reflects the stakeholder theory insight (Freeman, 1984; Antonelli, Cappiello & Pedrini, 2013) that CU programs must attend to the distinct interests and circumstances of different participant groups, rather than treating 'participants' as an undifferentiated collective. Finally, to ensure women's participation in middle management and a fast-track to leadership, the bank launched the Axis-ISB Women's Leadership Programme (The Economic Times,

2013) as a targeted leadership pipeline, with pre-interview training, intensive in-house training with Axis and ISB faculty, first-cohort selection criteria, and an Axis Bank–ISB Women's Leadership Certification.

The Hire-Train-Deploy Model: A Distinctive Banking CU Innovation

Axis Bank's most theoretically significant contribution to CU practice is the elaboration of the 'Hire-Train-Deploy' (HTD) model as a systematic approach to building specialised role-specific capability. While the ABYB program is a general entry-level pipeline for broadly defined banking roles, the HTD model addresses the challenge of developing specialised expertise in strategically critical niches in Axis's initial implementation, Relationship Managers for Commercial Banking and SME business, where generic banking knowledge is insufficient and where the failure of underprepared RMs carries direct revenue consequences. The SME RM HTD program was launched in 2026 in collaboration with Adda247's Career247 platform (Axis Bank, 2026) and diverges from conventional corporate training in its epistemological orientation.

Standard training programs transmit knowledge about the domain, like banking products, client types, and credit analysis frameworks; the HTD model prioritises the development of what Schön (1983) calls 'knowledge-in-action', the practical judgment and situational intelligence that experienced practitioners exhibit, but that cannot be reliably developed through classroom instruction alone. The program achieves this through 'practice-led learning with real-life simulations and customer engagement scenarios' that create authentic practice environments within a structured educational framework, producing, as Axis Bank's HR leadership describes, 'deployment-ready RMs who can be effective from day one' (Axis Bank, 2026). This 'from day one' criterion is theoretically significant. It represents a fundamental reconceptualisation of the boundary between learning and work, which Boud and Garrick (1999) call the 'learning-work nexus.' Rather than accepting that new hires will require an extended onboarding period before contributing productively, the HTD model relocates this productive capacity development into the pre-employment phase, effectively creating a new temporal structure in which the traditional sequence (hire → train → perform) is compressed into a simultaneously occurring event (trained candidate → immediate performer). The competitive implications are direct in a sector where relationship manager quality is a primary determinant of SME lending revenue; the capacity to deploy fully competent RMs without a six-to-twelve-month ramp-up period represents a meaningful competitive advantage.

Digital Extension Coursera and Adda247 as CU Delivery Infrastructure

Axis Bank's corporate university model is distinguished from many of its Indian banking peers by its systematic use of digital learning platforms as delivery infrastructure. The Coursera partnership, deployed to upskill Axis Bank's 105,000+ employees in emerging technical domains such as data science, technology, and artificial intelligence, extends the CU's knowledge management function beyond banking-specific content into frontier knowledge that positions employees for the industry's digital transformation (Coursera, 2021). This reflects the knowledge services function identified by Chen, Xu and Zhai (2019) in their analysis of ZTE College and HP University, which provides employees with access to cutting-edge knowledge that enables the development of competitive applications within the organisation.

Reported outcomes from the Coursera partnership improved workforce empowerment, lower attrition rates, and documented cases of employee advancement are consistent with social exchange theory (Emerson, 1976; Coursera, 2021). Employees who perceive substantial organisational investment in their professional development beyond role-specific skills reciprocate with enhanced organisational commitment and reduced voluntary departure. This retention effect of strategic upskilling is an under-theorized benefit in the banking CU literature. Most analysis of attrition focuses on compensation and career progression, while learning investment as a retention mechanism has received less systematic empirical attention.

Further, Axis Academies were launched to train "digital bankers", with partners such as INSEAD, CRISIL, and INSOFE, combining banking fundamentals like credit and risk with digitisation and analytics (The Tribune, 2017). It also launched an initiative to enhance fintech capabilities through an 18-week online programme with a 7-week live project, covering Java frameworks, Spring Boot, microservices, AWS practices, and codeathons, delivered in a blended or flipped classroom format (Times of India, 2020).

Finally, its partnership with Adda247, announced in November 2024, addresses the challenge of geographic reach (Axis Bank, 2024). By leveraging Adda247's community of millions of banking aspirants across Tier-III and Tier-IV Indian cities, typically underrepresented in banking recruitment because large banks' campus programs are concentrated in metropolitan institutions, Axis Bank extends its talent pipeline into previously inaccessible talent pools. This is a boundary-spanning function (Prince & Beaver, 2002; Tushman & Scanlan, 1981) of a distinctive kind, rather than spanning the boundary between the organisation and the knowledge environment. Axis's Adda247 partnership spans the boundary between the formal banking labour market and the informal aspirational community of potential banking professionals who lack access to conventional recruitment channels.

Internal Development Architecture, Leadership, and Lifelong Learning

Axis Bank aimed to build a culture of continuous learning and development, in 2016, the bank introduced "Acelerate" as an integrated performance management and capability development system, which ditched the bell curve system of performance appraisal and explicitly used learning & development as both a performance measure and retention tool (Business Standard, 2016).

The Axis Bank Young Bankers Program and the HTD model constitute the externally oriented talent pipeline dimension of Axis's CU architecture. Complementing these is an internally-oriented development architecture focused on the continuous development of existing employees. The Axis Learning Academy offers a structured catalogue of courses across functional and leadership domains, with 127 courses available and employees averaging 54.6 training hours per year (Axis Bank, 2021-22), a metric that, while below the benchmarks of some global financial services CUs, represents a genuine investment in a continuous learning culture. Notably, 62% of these training hours were delivered digitally, reflecting the blend of technology-mediated learning into the CU model that the literature identifies as characteristic of mature third-generation CU institutions (Walton, 1999; Homan & Macpherson, 2005).

The Leadership and Coaching Academy, offering tiered programs across leadership levels, addresses the longer-cycle leadership pipeline challenge, ensuring that the volume of frontline talent entering through the ABYB and HTD programs has a development pathway toward senior roles, reducing the organisation's dependence on expensive external lateral hiring for leadership positions. This lifecycle spans from entry-level formation through leadership development, which is what Allen (2002) identifies as the distinguishing mark of a mature strategic corporate university, and it elevates Axis Bank's CU well above the 'training department' characterisation that the literature's strategic criterion is designed to interrogate.

The Case of HDFC Bank's Consortium-Based Train-and-Deploy Ecosystem

Strategic Context Scale, Speed and the Future Bankers Program

HDFC Bank's corporate university model reflects the distinctive strategic challenge of an organisation growing at a pace that renders conventional recruitment-

and-training processes structurally inadequate (Economic Times HR World, 2023). The bank's CHRO articulated this challenge in terms that directly echo the strategic HRD literature 'The future of hiring in HDFC Bank will be through a train-and-deploy model supported by a strong internal talent management programme.' This statement is remarkable for its explicitness. The bank's senior leadership has publicly committed to the corporate university model, not as an experimental initiative but as the institutional architecture of its talent function going forward.

The Future Bankers Program, launched in July 2019 in partnership with Manipal Global Academy of BFSI (HDFC Bank, 2019), represents HDFC's foundational response to this challenge. Its design logic mirrors the ABYB model in broad structure, a one-year post-graduate diploma combining academic instruction with a branch internship. Still, it is calibrated specifically for HDFC's retail banking context. The six-month residential phase at Manipal's purpose-built banking academy focuses on the knowledge, skills, and values required for HDFC's customer service philosophy, product portfolio, and compliance requirements. The subsequent six-month branch internship, functioning as a supervised operational apprenticeship, distinguishes the program epistemologically from purely academic preparation. It positions the workplace itself as a pedagogical site, embodying the work-integrated learning principles identified by Wilson (2012) and Patrick et al. (2008) as producing superior graduate employability, stronger workplace identity development, and better retention of professional knowledge.

HDFC's scale ambition for Future Bankers is explicit and data-grounded. The initial program envisaged hiring 5,000 Future Bankers over 2-3 years, a figure that positions the program not as a niche-talent experiment but as a primary channel for HDFC's retail workforce expansion (HDFC Bank, 2019). The program's graduates, awarded PG Diplomas in Sales and Relationship Banking by Manipal University and directly appointed as Personal Bankers, are designed to serve HDFC's aggressive retail branch expansion, particularly in semi-urban and Tier-II and Tier-III markets where the bank needed large volumes of trained, customer-ready staff to sustain its growth trajectory. The credential, which designs a portable, externally recognised postgraduate qualification, simultaneously serves the bank's objective and the participants' interests, creating the social exchange dynamic (Emerson, 1976) that research consistently links to post-training organisational commitment.

The Rising Bankers Program Pipeline Differentiation by Role

A distinctive feature of HDFC Bank's CU architecture is its deliberate differentiation of training pipelines by role cluster. While Future Bankers addresses the personal banking and relationship management function, the Rising Bankers Program, launched in August 2022 in collaboration with Amity Global Business School (HDFC Bank,

2022), specifically targets the customer experience and customer care cluster roles that are high-volume, high-attrition, and critical to HDFC's service reputation but have historically been difficult to staff consistently with well-prepared candidates.

The Rising Bankers design differs from Future Bankers in several analytically significant respects (HDFC Bank, 2022). Its duration of 8 months is shorter than 12 months, reflecting the more standardised, procedural nature of customer care competencies compared with the more complex relational and analytical skills required for personal banking. The 5-month residential campus period at Amity, Noida, is longer than the 3-month internship, suggesting that customer care roles benefit more from intensive initial training than from the extended operational apprenticeship required in relationship banking. The credential, a PG Diploma in Customer Experience Management from Amity, is role-specific in ways that Future Bankers' Sales and Relationship Banking credential is not, signalling a more segmented theory of human capital in which specific CU programs produce specific capability profiles rather than general banking competency.

This pipeline differentiation strategy reflects what Lepak and Snell (1999) identify in their HR architecture framework as a sophisticated approach to human capital management, recognising that different employee groups create value through different mechanisms and therefore require different investment strategies. By developing separate training architectures for relationship bankers and customer care executives, HDFC Bank implicitly acknowledges that 'one size fits all' corporate university designs are strategically suboptimal in organisations with diverse role profiles and diverse sources of value creation.

The ACE Program and Multi-Provider Consortium Logic

The HDFC Bank ACE (Assistant Manager) Program, delivered through NIIT (NIIT, n.d.-b; MarketScreener, 2023), represents a third node in HDFC's multi-provider CU network. Its design is a compressed six-week residential intensive that prepares graduates for direct appointment as assistant managers. It occupies a different position in the temporal spectrum from the twelve-month Future Bankers and eight-month Rising Bankers programs. By offering a radically shorter duration, the ACE program addresses a different segment of the talent market, candidates who already possess relevant domain knowledge or professional experience and primarily require operational orientation, compliance training, and HDFC-specific process familiarisation rather than comprehensive from-scratch domain education.

The co-existence of three structurally different programs: Future Bankers program in Manipal for 12 months, ensuring a broad banking competence; Rising Bankers at Amity for 8 months, targeted at customer experience; and ACE program from NIIT of 6 weeks, aiming for a fast-track assistant manager. (HDFC Bank, 2019;

HDFC Bank, 2022; NIIT, n.d.-b) constitutes what the literature would recognise as a consortium-based CU architecture. HDFC Bank as the orchestrating intelligence, multiple academic providers as delivery nodes, each contributing distinctive institutional capabilities, and HDFC providing the strategic alignment, operational context, and post-program career pathway that gives the system its coherence.

This consortium architecture has both advantages and limitations relative to more centralised CU models. Its advantages are agility and specialisation. HDFC can scale specific programs up or down independently, add new academic partners for emerging role clusters, and leverage each partner's distinctive institutional strengths without being constrained by a single provider's capacity or curriculum design. Its limitations are the complexity of coordination and the risk of inconsistent outcomes, which ensure that graduates of programs delivered by three different institutions share common values, behavioural standards, and HDFC-specific knowledge. This requires deliberate integration mechanisms, induction protocols, culture programs, and mentorship structures that add governance overhead and introduce variability risk if not actively managed.

Internal Development and Culture Transformation

Beyond its external talent pipeline programs, HDFC Bank complements its entry-level academies with significant internal learning investment. The bank's culture transformation initiative, reportedly delivering nearly 100,000 hours of learning content in a few months (HDFC Bank Annual Report, 2022), reflects the organisational learning function (Senge, 1990) that Prince and Beaver (2002) identify as the aspirational fourth process dimension of a world-class corporate university learning processes that create a culture for learning and reflect commitment of top management. While HDFC has not established a branded internal academy comparable to Axis Bank's Learning Academy, its volume of internal training activity and its publicly stated commitment to 'robust talent management framework and internal career progression portal' for existing employees suggest an emerging internal development infrastructure that parallels the external pipeline programs in organisational significance.

The bank's Parivartan CSR initiative, which has trained approximately 2,000 rural youth in vocational banking skills (HR Katha, 2026.), extends the CU's societal function into community development. While this initiative does not directly feed HDFC's talent pipeline, it generates positive externalities for national human capital formation, as identified by Alagaraja and Li (2015) as a legitimacy resource for organisations that aspire to institutional standing beyond their sector. A CU that contributes to societal development generates public legitimacy, reinforcing its organisational authority within the institution.

Outcomes and Accountability

The Indian banking CU cases offer some of the most concrete outcome data available in the service-sector CU literature. However, the evidence base has the limitations that the accountability literature would predict. The most robust data pertain to pipeline volume, Axis 16,000+ ABYB graduates over 12 years (NIIT, n.d.-a); HDFC 4,000+ monthly new hires at peak (Economic Times HR World, 2023), credential attainment, and operational metrics. These metrics correspond to Kirkpatrick's (1998) Levels 3 (behavioural change participants successfully transition to employment) and 4 (results the organisation achieves its staffing targets), providing more robust evidence base than the reaction-level data that most CU evaluations rely on.

The specific impact metrics are revealing. Axis Bank's ABYB program has trained over 16,000 graduates in 12 years, at an average of 1,333 per year, and has introduced targeted women's cohorts, demonstrating the programme's adaptability to strategic diversity objectives (CXO Today, 2024; NIIT, n.d.-a). The company reports that upskilling initiatives reduced attrition among existing employees, resulting in a significant financial return, as each departing employee represents not only replacement cost but also the loss of the investment embodied in their CU formation (Coursera, 2021). HDFC Bank's workforce expansion from 98,000 to 173,000 in four years (Economic Times HR World, 2023), while maintaining service quality metrics sufficient to sustain its market position, would have been architecturally impossible without a parallel expansion of its training pipeline infrastructure. The statistical improbability of achieving this workforce growth through conventional reactive recruitment is itself circumstantial evidence of the pipeline's contribution to organisational performance.

Despite these impressive operational metrics, the evaluation literature's recurring critique that the most strategically significant CU outcomes remain unmeasured applies with equal force to banking CUs. The long-term contributions of CU programs to employee quality, client relationship depth, portfolio performance, and organisational culture are not systematically measured in any of the cases reviewed. The relationship between ABYB participation and long-term career progression at Axis Bank, which would be the most powerful evidence of the program's strategic value, is not publicly documented. The difference in client satisfaction scores between Future Bankers graduates and laterally hired personal bankers, which would directly validate HDFC's proposition that trained hires offer a consistent, high-quality customer service experience, is similarly unmeasured.

The banking context introduces two evaluation challenges specific to the sector. First, the compliance dimension of banking training, whose ROI is measured in regulatory penalties avoided, audit findings prevented, and reputational incidents avoided, is inherently a counterfactual claim that defies direct measurement. A bank cannot demonstrate the value of compliance training from the AML cases that did not occur. Second, the client relationship dimension of banking performance the quality of the RM's relationship with the SME client, the depth of understanding of the client's financial lifecycle, the appropriateness of the advisory judgement in complex situations is a form of tacit relational knowledge that Kirkpatrick's taxonomy was not designed to assess and that banking evaluation frameworks have not yet developed adequate tools to capture. These are not failures of institutional will but genuinely hard measurement problems that the evaluation literature has not resolved, and which banking sector researchers are particularly well positioned to contribute to.

Theoretical Contributions

The Indian banking CU cases offer a significant elaboration of Becker's (1964) human capital theory in the context of large-scale service organisations facing structural labour-market failures. Becker's framework predicts that employers will invest in general human capital only if employees bear the training cost, because general skills benefit all potential employers, removing the investor's ability to capture returns through wage suppression, and will invest in specific human capital because the employer can capture returns through the productivity-wage gap. The banking HTD model complicates this prediction. The bank invests substantially in what appears to be broadly applicable banking knowledge, a relatively general human capital investment, yet achieves acceptable returns through a combination of factors that Becker's original framework does not fully accommodate.

These factors include the earn-and-learn financial commitment that creates switching costs during training; the cohort-based socialization that builds organisation-specific networks and loyalties; the association of credentials with the sponsoring bank's brand; and the opportunity-cost advantage of guaranteed employment that makes completion uniquely attractive relative to unsupported job-seeking. Collectively, these mechanisms convert what might appear to be general human capital investment into specific human capital outcomes, consistent with Lepak and Snell's (1999) insight that the specificity of human capital is as much a function of organizational design and employment relationship architecture as of the inherent transferability of the knowledge content.

The resource-based view (Barney, 1991; Grant, 1996) would predict that CU investment generates competitive advantage only when it produces human capital that is valuable, rare, inimitable, and non-substitutable. The banking cases complicate this prediction in an interesting way: multiple major banks operate similar CU programs, while others deploy variations of the HTD model. Can any individual bank's program satisfy the rarity criterion?

The resolution lies in recognising that rarity in the banking CU context operates not at the level of program design but at the level of program execution quality and cumulative learning. Axis Bank's twelve-year track record of ABYB delivery has built an institutional knowledge base on effective curriculum design, candidate selection, internship management, graduate retention, and career progression that is not replicable for a bank initiating its first cohort. This 'learning to learn' meta-capability (Mayfield, Mayfield & Wheeler, 2016), embedded in the institutional memory of the CU organisation, constitutes a second-order competitive resource that is genuinely rare and inimitable. The implication for CU theory is that the most durable CU-based competitive advantages are not the programs themselves but the organisational capabilities for continuous program improvement that accumulate through sustained CU operation.

The banking CU cases illuminate the multi-sided value proposition that effective CU programs must sustain across diverse stakeholder groups. Allen and Meyer's framework of stakeholder interests, participants, line managers, HR leadership, senior leadership, and external stakeholders manifests in distinct ways in the banking context. Participants value not only the technical competence they develop but the portable credential that enhances their market value regardless of whether they remain with the sponsoring bank. Line managers value rapid operational readiness that reduces the productivity burden they experience when untrained recruits require extended mentoring. HR leadership values the attrition-reduction effect, the reduced replacement cost cycle, and the diversity outcomes that contribute to institutional reporting obligations. Senior leadership values strategic capability alignment and business growth enablement. External stakeholders, such as educational institutions, regulatory authorities, and the government's Skill India initiative, value the contribution to national human capital formation and sector skill development.

Nickols' (2016) argument that 'a stakeholder approach to evaluating training generates broader organisational legitimacy' is powerfully validated in the banking CU context the programs that have demonstrated sustained institutional survival and growth ABYB over twelve years, Future Bankers evolving into Future Bankers 2.0 are precisely those that have successfully maintained multi-stakeholder value propositions, adapting their design over time to address evolving stakeholder interests while preserving the core pipeline logic that senior leadership and HR leadership value most directly.

Alagaraja and Li's (2015) institutional theory analysis of CU diffusion patterns resonates directly with the Indian banking sector. The progression from ICICI Bank's pioneering corporate university programs in the late 2000s, through Axis Bank's 2011 ABYB launch, to HDFC's 2019 Future Bankers initiative, mirrors the mimetic isomorphism dynamic that DiMaggio and Powell (1983) theorise as characteristic of organisational field development under conditions of uncertainty, organisations adopt the strategies of organisations perceived as successful, progressively institutionalising the HTD model as a normative standard for talent management in the private banking sector.

The role of Manipal Global Education serving as the academic partner for both Axis's ABYB and HDFC's Future Bankers is particularly interesting from an institutional theory perspective. Manipal functions not merely as a service provider but as an institutional intermediary that legitimates the banking corporate university model by associating it with a credentialed academic institution. Its repeated selection by multiple banks suggests that it has acquired a specific form of institutional capital in the banking CU market, a reputation for reliable, high-quality banking-specific education that serves as a field-level quality signal, reducing the uncertainty individual banks might otherwise face when evaluating alternative academic partners.

Managerial Implications

For practitioners, the cases yield several actionable insights. First, the strategic criterion should function as a diagnostic for CU investment decisions. The question is not whether to brand an existing training function as a corporate university, but whether the intended institution will proactively anticipate and shape organisational capability rather than reactively address operational deficits. The distinction is observable in reporting lines, programme design processes, and performance metrics. Strategic CUs report to senior leadership, involve business units in curriculum co-design, and measure success through talent pipeline quality and strategic capability metrics rather than training volume and cost efficiency.

Second, the consortium CU model, operationalised by HDFC Bank across different institutional configurations, offers a powerful alternative to the centralised CU for organisations that require specialised expertise from multiple educational domains, seek geographic reach beyond a single campus, or require legitimacy signals from multiple credentialing partners. The governance challenge of consortium models maintaining strategic coherence and quality consistency across heterogeneous delivery partners is real. It requires deliberate integration mechanisms, unified induction protocols, shared competency frameworks, and regular cross-partner curriculum review processes that are invested in from the outset rather than retrofitted after quality inconsistencies emerge.

Third, the technology dimension deserves more deliberate strategic investment than most CU practitioners currently apply. The reach gains documented in Axis Bank's Adda247 partnership both suggest that digital learning platforms are not merely cost-reduction tools but strategic amplifiers that extend the CU's value proposition into previously inaccessible domains. Organisations that treat technology as an efficiency measure rather than a strategic capability investment consistently underutilise its potential.

FUTURE RESEARCH DIRECTIONS

The cases and theoretical analysis presented in this chapter identify several high-priority directions for future CU research. These are organised below around four thematic clusters: evaluation and impact measurement, comparative and cross-cultural extension, technological transformation, and emerging institutional forms.

Evaluation Methodology Closing the Accountability Gap

The most urgent research need in the CU literature is the development of validated, sector-specific evaluation frameworks that go beyond Kirkpatrick's (1998) generic four-level taxonomy. The accountability gap documented across all cases in this chapter, where the most strategically significant CU contributions remain unmeasured despite two decades of frameworks nominally addressing the problem, suggests that the issue is not practitioner unwillingness to evaluate but methodological inadequacy in evaluation design. Future research should develop longitudinal evaluation frameworks that track CU graduate cohorts over 5-10 year career trajectories, capturing the compounding value of initial CU formation on long-term performance, advancement, and organisational commitment.

Service industries present particular evaluation challenges that the extant literature, developed primarily in manufacturing and technology contexts, is poorly equipped to address. In banking, the most significant CU contributions are relationship quality, compliance integrity (regulatory incidents not occurring), and cultural alignment. All three are inherently counterfactual, longitudinal, and collective, defying the individual-level, short-horizon, and quantitative measurement protocols that Kirkpatrick's framework and its successors presuppose. Research partnerships between academic researchers and banking or hospitality organisations willing to provide longitudinal HR and performance data would enable the development of sector-calibrated evaluation instruments that current survey-based approaches cannot achieve.

Comparative and Cross-Cultural Extension

The CU literature's geographic bias toward North American and Western European contexts remains a significant constraint on theoretical generalisability. This chapter has demonstrated that Indian CU cases extend theory in ways that Western exemplars do not the HTD model's temporal inversion of the training-employment sequence, the federated CU's distribution of educational function across heterogeneous partners, and the dual mandate that characterises CUs in emerging market contexts are all phenomena that the existing literature, developed from GE, Motorola, and Lloyds TSB exemplars, does not adequately theorise. Future comparative research should systematically examine CU development across emerging-market contexts, including China, Southeast Asia, Latin America, and Sub-Saharan Africa, to determine whether these are genuinely distinct institutional forms or contextual adaptations of a universal strategic logic.

Sectoral comparative research is equally needed. The existing literature's privileging of technology, financial services, and manufacturing contexts has produced theoretical frameworks that perform poorly when applied to healthcare, education, public administration, and creative industries, all of which face distinctive talent-market conditions, credentialing constraints, and knowledge-creation logics. The hospitality case documented in this chapter is itself an underrepresented context, the luxury service economy's reliance on tacit, culturally embedded, behaviourally instantiated knowledge, which resists codification and requires long-cycle experiential formation, calls for CU design theory substantially different from the explicit knowledge transfer models that dominate the literature. Research that develops sector-specific CU design frameworks, grounded in the knowledge management literature's distinction between explicit and tacit knowledge, would significantly advance the field's practical applicability.

Technology, Artificial Intelligence, and the Future CU

The rapid integration of digital learning platforms, AI-assisted personalisation, and virtual simulation into CU delivery represents a transformation in the institutional form of the corporate university that the literature has tracked unevenly and theorised inadequately. The cases documented here, Axis Bank's Adda247 digital reach into Tier-III cities, and HDFC's large-scale digital content delivery, suggest that technology is not merely an efficiency amplifier of traditional CU models but a structural transformation of the CU's geographic reach, pedagogical repertoire, and talent market scope. Future research should examine whether technology-enabled CU delivery changes the fundamental human capital economics of CU investment if digital platforms reduce the marginal cost of training additional participants to near-zero, does this alter the make-versus-buy calculation at the foundation of CU strategy? And if AI-personalised learning pathways can optimise individual development trajectories in real time, does this enable a form of 'mass customisation at scale' (Meister, 1998) that was previously impossible and that changes the comparative advantage of internal versus external learning provision?

The emergence of generative AI as a learning and knowledge management tool raises additional research questions for CU theory. CUs that have historically served as primary repositories and diffusers of organisational knowledge now face a context in which large language models can compress much of this explicit knowledge-diffusion function into automated, on-demand query-response interactions. If the explicit knowledge transfer function of CUs can be substantially automated, what remains as the distinctive contribution of human-facilitated CU programming? Researchers can study whether the automation of explicit knowledge transfer will shift the strategic CU's value proposition decisively toward the development of tacit knowledge, the formation of professional judgment, relational intelligence, and cultural identity that AI cannot replicate, requiring corresponding shifts in CU design philosophy, faculty capability, and pedagogical methodology.

Emerging Institutional Forms: The Federated CU and the HTD Model

Two institutional innovations documented in this chapter warrant dedicated theoretical and empirical research programs. The 'Federated CU', in which educational functions are distributed across heterogeneous institutional partners coordinated by an orchestrating corporate intelligence, lacks a systematic theoretical treatment despite its prevalence in large service organisations operating across geographic and institutional contexts. Future research should examine how governance architectures enable strategic coherence in federated CU models. How do knowledge creation properties differ between federated and centralised CU forms? And under what conditions does the coordination overhead of federation justify itself relative to the reach, specialisation, and legitimacy benefits it provides?

The 'Hire-Train-Deploy' model, in which substantial training precedes and constitutes the condition of formal employment, similarly requires systematic theoretical and empirical investigation. Current understanding of HTD is largely practitioner-descriptive; we know what the programs look like. Approximately how many graduates they produce, but we lack rigorous evidence on comparative retention rates of HTD versus laterally hired employees, the long-term career advancement differential between the two groups, the optimal duration and design of pre-employment training for different role clusters, and the mechanisms through which pre-employment socialization generates post-employment commitment. Longitudinal cohort studies comparing HTD graduates with matched lateral hires across 3-5-year career windows, using survival analysis, performance trajectory analysis, and promotion rate comparison as outcomes, would provide the empirical foundation that HTD's growing policy significance demands.

CONCLUSION: BANKING CUS AND THE BOUNDARIES OF CU THEORY

The Axis Bank and HDFC Bank cases collectively demonstrate that the corporate university model has found a distinctive and consequential application in Indian private banking, one that both validates the foundational theoretical frameworks of the CU literature and identifies important directions for their extension.

The cases validate Allen's (2002) strategic criterion with particular clarity; both banks have constructed learning architectures that proactively anticipate competitive talent requirements rather than reactively filling vacancies after they arise. They validate the human capital theory proposition (Becker, 1964; Lepak & Snell, 1999) that employer-sponsored specific human capital investment generates returns through reduced attrition, accelerated productivity, and differentiated capabilities that cannot be achieved through market-purchased generic human capital. They validate the institutional theory account (DiMaggio & Powell, 1983; Alagaraja & Li, 2015) of CU diffusion through mimetic isomorphism, with the HTD model progressively achieving the status of a taken-for-granted organisational practice in Indian banking. And they validate the stakeholder theory proposition (Freeman, 1984; Antonelli, Cappiello & Pedrini, 2013) that CU programs that sustain multi-sided value propositions serving participants, managers, HR leadership, senior leadership, and external institutional stakeholders simultaneously achieve the organisational legitimacy required for long-term survival and growth.

The cases also identify three important extensions to existing CU theory. First, the HTD model, in which training substantially precedes the formal employment relationship, represents a temporal inversion of the standard CU paradigm that has received insufficient theoretical attention. This model's growing prevalence in high-growth, high-attrition service sector contexts warrants a dedicated theoretical treatment that goes beyond Becker's general/specific human capital distinction to address the institutional and relational mechanisms through which pre-employment training generates post-employment loyalty.

Second, the consortium-based CU architecture exemplified by HDFC Bank, in which a single organisation orchestrates multiple academic partners, each serving a distinct role cluster, represents an important structural variant between the single-institution CU and the fully federated model. The governance implications of this consortium architecture, particularly the coordination mechanisms required to maintain consistency, quality, and strategic alignment across heterogeneous delivery partners, deserve systematic scholarly attention that existing CU governance frameworks do not provide.

Third, the evaluation challenge in regulated industries, where the most significant CU outcomes are compliance-related and inherently counterfactual, and where client relationship quality constitutes the primary competitive asset but resists straightforward measurement, requires the development of sector-specific evaluation frameworks that go beyond Kirkpatrick's universal, but sector-agnostic, taxonomy. Future research that develops and validates such frameworks for banking CU contexts would represent a significant contribution to both the CU evaluation literature and the practical accountability needs of financial services organisations.

The Axis and HDFC banking cases together provide a rich empirical foundation for understanding how corporate universities adapt to service industry contexts in emerging markets. Across hospitality and banking two sectors with profoundly different competitive logics, talent profiles, and CU design imperatives the same foundational conclusion holds the organisations that have committed most deeply and most consistently to the corporate university model have built not merely training programs but institutional architectures that compound in value over time, generating competitive advantages in capability, culture, loyalty, and resilience that transactional talent markets cannot replicate. In the words of HDFC Bank's CHRO 'Educating your workforce is not a one-time expense but a continuous investment in the future of the organization.' This, ultimately, is the case for the corporate university.

This chapter has argued that the corporate university has evolved from a contested institutional curiosity into one of the most consequential strategic HR innovations available to contemporary organisations and that its full theoretical significance is only visible when the analysis moves beyond Western technology and manufacturing exemplars to encompass the service-sector, emerging-market contexts in which it is growing most rapidly and adapting most inventively. The Axis Bank and HDFC Bank cases demonstrate that even in high-velocity, high-attrition contexts where the luxury of long-cycle development seems unavailable, the strategic CU, anchored in the HTD model's temporal innovation and the consortium model's institutional agility, can address structural talent-market failures that no amount of reactive recruitment can.

Across cases, the foundational theoretical proposition of the strategic CU literature is confirmed with empirical force that educating your workforce is not a one-time expense but a continuous, compounding investment in organisational capability that generates returns in talent quality, retention, service consistency, and competitive positioning that accelerate over time as institutional learning accumulates and pipeline depth increases. The organisations that have committed most deeply and consistently to this investment have built not merely training programs but capability architectures that compound in value, creating competitive advantages that rivals cannot rapidly replicate regardless of their financial resources. For researchers, the mandate is to develop the theoretical frameworks, evaluation methodologies, and comparative empirical databases that can make this proposition testable with the rigour it deserves, given its strategic importance.

REFERENCES

Alagaraja, M., & Li, J. (2015). Utilizing institutional perspectives to investigate the emergence, rise, and (relative) decline of corporate universities. *Human Resource Development International, 18*(1), 4–23. DOI: 10.1080/13678868.2014.979003

Allen, M. W. (Ed.). (2002). *The corporate university handbook: Designing, managing, and growing a successful program.* AMACOM.

Allen, M. W. (2007). What is a next-generation corporate university? In Allen, M. W. (Ed.), *The next generation of corporate universities* (pp. 3–16). John Wiley & Sons.

Allen, M. W. (2010). Corporate universities 2010: Globalization and greater sophistication. *Journal of International Management Studies, 5*(1), 48–52.

Andresen, M., & Lichtenberger, B. (2007). The corporate university landscape in Germany. *Journal of Workplace Learning, 19*(2), 109–123. DOI: 10.1108/13665620710728484

Antonelli, G., Cappiello, G., & Pedrini, G. (2013). The corporate university in the European utility industries. *Utilities Policy, 25*, 33–41. DOI: 10.1016/j.jup.2013.02.003

Axis Bank. (2024, November 11). Axis Bank partners with Adda247 for talent development and skill building. https://www.axisbank.com/about-us/axis-bank-partners-with-adda247-for-talent-development-and-skill-building

Axis Bank. (2026, February 25). Axis Bank collaborates with Adda Education to launch Hire-Train-Deploy programme for Commercial Banking Relationship Managers. https://www.axisbank.com/about-us/axis-bank-collaborates-with-adda-education-htd-programme

Axis Bank. (2021–22). Possibilities to nurture an engaging workplace: Annual report 2021–22. https://www.axisbank.com/investors/annual-reports

Axis Bank academies. (2017, January 25). *The Tribune*. https://www.tribuneindia.com/news/archive/prospects/axis-bank-academies-355012/

Barney, J. (1991). Firm resources and sustained competitive advantage. *Journal of Management, 17*(1), 99–120. DOI: 10.1177/014920639101700108

Becker, G. S. (1964). *Human capital: A theoretical and empirical analysis, with special reference to education*. University of Chicago Press.

Bennett, N., & Lemoine, G. J. (2014). What a difference a word makes: Understanding threats to performance in a VUCA world. *Business Horizons*, *57*(3), 311–317. DOI: 10.1016/j.bushor.2014.01.001

Blass, E. (2005). The rise and rise of the corporate university. *Journal of European Industrial Training*, *29*(1), 58–74. DOI: 10.1108/03090590510576217

Blass, E. (2015). The changing and developing role of the corporate university post-millennium. *Industry and Higher Education*, *29*(3), 167–177. DOI: 10.5367/ihe.2015.0256

Chen, Y. Q., Xu, Y. S., & Zhai, Q. G. (2019). The knowledge management functions of corporate university and their evolution. *Journal of Knowledge Management*, *23*(10), 2086–2112. DOI: 10.1108/JKM-04-2018-0228

Coursera. (2021, March). Axis Bank reduces attrition via upskilling on Coursera. https://www.coursera.org/business/case-studies/axis-bank

Dealtry, R. (2017). Corporate university developments: Managing strategic learning agility. *Journal of Workplace Learning*, *29*(5), 359–369.

DiMaggio, P. J., & Powell, W. W. (1983). The iron cage revisited: Institutional isomorphism and collective rationality in organizational fields. *American Sociological Review*, *48*(2), 147–160. DOI: 10.2307/2095101

Economic Times HR World. (2023, November 9). A growing concern in the banking industry: Here's how HDFC Bank is tackling high attrition rates! ETHRWorld. https://hr.economictimes.indiatimes.com/news/hrtech/talent-acquisition-and-management/a-growing-concern-in-the-banking-industry-heres-how-hdfc-bank-is-tackling-high-attrition-rates/105081619

Emerson, R. M. (1976). Social exchange theory. *Annual Review of Sociology*, *2*(1), 335–362. DOI: 10.1146/annurev.so.02.080176.002003

Grant, R. M. (1996). Toward a knowledge-based theory of the firm. *Strategic Management Journal*, *17*(S2), 109–122. DOI: 10.1002/smj.4250171110

HDFC Bank. (2019, July 3). HDFC Bank in partnership with Manipal Global Academy of BFSI launches Future Bankers program. https://www.hdfcbank.com/content/bbp/repositories/723fb80a-2dde-42a3-9793-7ae1be57c87f/?folderPath=/Footer/Press%20Release/Future-Bankers-program.pdf

HDFC Bank. (2022a). Embarking on cultural transformation [Annual report 2022]. https://v.hdfc.bank.in/embarking-on-cultural-transformation

HDFC Bank. (2022b, August 11). HDFC Bank launches Rising Bankers programme with Amity Global Business School. https://www.hdfcbank.com/content/api/contentstream-id/723fb80a-2dde-42a3-9793-7ae1be57c87f/rising-bankers-amity

Holland, P., & Pyman, A. (2006). Corporate universities: A catalyst for strategic human resource development? *Journal of European Industrial Training*, *30*(7), 542–553. DOI: 10.1108/03090590610643851

Katha, H. R. (2026, January 27). HDFC Bank expands Parivartan skilling initiative to Meerut. https://www.hrkatha.com/news/hdfc-bank-expands-parivartan-skilling-initiative-to-meerut

Kirkpatrick, D. L. (1998). *Evaluating training programs: The four levels* (2nd ed.). Berrett-Koehler.

Kolo, S., Reuschel, T., Hoffmann, R., & Schmidt, A. (2013). *Key facts on corporate universities: Trends, status quo, implications*. Fraunhofer Verlag.

Lave, J., & Wenger, E. (1991). *Situated learning: Legitimate peripheral participation*. Cambridge University Press. DOI: 10.1017/CBO9780511815355

Lepak, D. P., & Snell, S. A. (1999). The human resource architecture: Toward a theory of human capital allocation and development. *Academy of Management Review*, *24*(1), 31–48. DOI: 10.2307/259035

Lui Abel, A., & Li, J. (2012). Exploring the corporate university phenomenon: Development and implementation of a comprehensive survey. *Human Resource Development Quarterly*, *23*(1), 103–128. DOI: 10.1002/hrdq.21122

MarketScreener. (2023, May 24). HDFC Bank opens doors to recruits with a special recruitment programme. https://www.marketscreener.com/quote/stock/HDFC-BANK-LIMITED-9059482/news/HDFC-BANK-Opens-Doors-to-New-Recruits-with-a-Special-Recruitment-Programme-43838285

Mayfield, M., Mayfield, J., & Wheeler, C. (2016). Talent development for top leaders: Three HR initiatives for competitive advantage. *Human Resource Management International Digest*, *24*(6), 4–7. DOI: 10.1108/HRMID-07-2015-0120

Meister, J. C. (1998). *Corporate universities: Lessons in building a world-class work force* (rev. ed.). McGraw-Hill.

Moneylife. (2011, December 1). Axis Bank launches 'Young Bankers' program for banking aspirants. https://www.moneylife.in/article/axis-bank-launches-young-bankers-program-for-banking-aspirants/28563.html

NIIT. (n.d.-a). Axis Bank Young Bankers Program. https://learnforjobs.niit.com/india/axisbankyb

NIIT. (n.d.-b). HDFC Bank ACE Banker Program. https://www.niit.com/en/banking-financial-services-insurance/hdfc-bank-ace-banker-program

Patrucco, A., Pellizzoni, E., & Buganza, T. (2017). The design process of corporate universities: A stakeholder approach. *Journal of Workplace Learning*, *29*(4), 304–318. DOI: 10.1108/JWL-04-2016-0024

Pedrini, G. (2011). The corporate university phenomenon and the competences pipeline. *Journal of US-China Public Administration*, *8*(9), 1004–1015.

Prince, C., & Beaver, G. (2002). Redefining the role of the corporate university: A case study of the National Australia Bank. *Industry and Higher Education*, *16*(4), 213–220. DOI: 10.5367/000000002101296315

Rademakers, M. (2005). Corporate universities: Driving force of knowledge innovation. *Journal of Workplace Learning*, *17*(1/2), 130–136. DOI: 10.1108/13665620510574513

Rademakers, M. (2014). *Corporate universities: Drivers of the learning organization*. Routledge. DOI: 10.4324/9780203073988

Scarso, E. (2017). Corporate universities as knowledge management tools. *VINE Journal of Information and Knowledge Management Systems*, *47*(4), 538–554. DOI: 10.1108/VJIKMS-12-2016-0074

Schön, D. A. (1983). *The reflective practitioner: How professionals think in action*. Basic Books.

Senge, P. M. (1990). *The fifth discipline: The art and practice of the learning organization*. Doubleday.

The People Management. (n.d.). Manipal Academy of BFSI and Axis Bank launch women-exclusive Young Bankers cohort to advance gender inclusion in banking. https://thepeoplemanagement.com/manipal-academy-of-bfsi-and-axis-bank-launch-women-exclusive-young-bankers-cohort

Today, C. X. O. (2024, December 17). Manipal Academy of BFSI and Axis Bank launch women-exclusive Young Bankers cohort to advance gender inclusion in banking. https://cxotoday.com/press-release/manipal-academy-of-bfsi-and-axis-bank-launch-women-exclusive-young-bankers-cohort

Tushman, M. L., & Scanlan, T. J. (1981). Boundary spanning individuals: Their role in information transfer and their antecedents. *Academy of Management Journal*, *24*(2), 289–305. DOI: 10.2307/255842

Walton, J. (1999). Human resource development and the corporate university. In Walton, J. (Ed.), *Strategic human resource development* (pp. 412–437). Pearson Education.

Wilson, T. (2012). *A review of business–university collaboration*. Department for Business, Innovation and Skills.

Wu, F. (2013). Corporate university development in China: A review of the literature and research agenda. *Journal of Chinese Human Resource Management*, *4*(2), 134–149.

Chapter 8

Inclusive Talent Management in Sports Organizations:

Talent Leadership and Strategy in Ambiguous Environments

Vaishali Rahate
http://orcid.org/0000-0001-6277-1685
Datta Meghe Institute of Management Studies, India

Neha Dhule
http://orcid.org/0009-0001-4410-4085
Datta Meghe Institute of Management Studies, India

V. Lakshmi Prasanna
http://orcid.org/0000-0003-0774-3694
Gokaraju Rangaraju Institute of Engineering and Technology, India

P. Selvakumar
http://orcid.org/0000-0002-3650-4548
Department of Science and Humanities, Nehru Institute of Technology, Coimbatore, India

Vijay Kumar
http://orcid.org/0000-0002-6532-0430
Shoolini University, India

T. C. Manjunath
http://orcid.org/0000-0003-2545-9160
Rajarajeswari College of Engineering, Bengaluru, India

EXECUTIVE SUMMARY

In today's dynamic and globalized world, the sports industry has become a powerful platform for cultural exchange, social integration, and human development. Within this context, the importance of inclusive talent management in sports cannot be overstated. Inclusive talent management refers to the strategic approach of identifying, nurturing, and advancing talent from a diverse range of backgrounds, abilities, genders, ethnicities, and socio-economic circumstances, ensuring that opportunities

DOI: 10.4018/979-8-3373-5776-8.ch008

are accessible to all individuals regardless of their differences. This philosophy goes beyond traditional merit-based selection and performance metrics, recognizing the value of fostering diverse perspectives, experiences, and skill sets to drive innovation, competitiveness, and long-term success in sports organizations. First and foremost, inclusive talent management contributes significantly to the democratization of sports. Historically, access to elite training, coaching, and competitive opportunities has often been limited to individuals from certain demographic groups.

INTRODUCTION

In today's dynamic and globalized world, the sports industry has become a powerful platform for cultural exchange, social integration, and human development. Within this context, the importance of inclusive talent management in sports cannot be overstated. Inclusive talent management refers to the strategic approach of identifying, nurturing, and advancing talent from a diverse range of backgrounds, abilities, genders, ethnicities, and socio-economic circumstances, ensuring that opportunities are accessible to all individuals regardless of their differences. This philosophy goes beyond traditional merit-based selection and performance metrics, recognizing the value of fostering diverse perspectives, experiences, and skill sets to drive innovation, competitiveness, and long-term success in sports organizations. First and foremost, inclusive talent management contributes significantly to the democratization of sports. Historically, access to elite training, coaching, and competitive opportunities has often been limited to individuals from certain demographic groups, leading to underrepresentation of minorities, women, disabled athletes, and those from lower socio-economic backgrounds. By actively dismantling barriers to participation and creating pathways for diverse talent, inclusive talent management helps level the playing field, providing equitable access to resources and opportunities. This not only enriches the talent pool but also helps correct systemic inequalities that have persisted in the sports sector for decades. Moreover, diversity and inclusion in sports talent management enhance team performance and organizational resilience. A wide body of research across various industries, including sports, has demonstrated that diverse teams outperform homogenous ones in problem-solving, creativity, and adaptability. In the highly competitive and rapidly evolving world of sports, where innovation in strategy, training methodologies, and fan engagement is key to success, drawing from a broad range of perspectives gives teams a distinct advantage.

Additionally, embracing inclusive talent management is essential for aligning with the broader societal values and expectations of today's audiences. Fans, sponsors, and stakeholders increasingly demand that sports organizations reflect and promote social justice, equality, and human rights. Inclusive practices in talent management demonstrate a commitment to these values, enhancing the reputation and brand of sports organizations. They help build stronger connections with diverse fan bases and communities, driving engagement and commercial success. In contrast, organizations that fail to prioritize inclusion risk alienating stakeholders and facing public backlash. An important component of inclusive talent management is the recognition and accommodation of varying needs and experiences among athletes and staff. This involves implementing policies and practices that support mental health, gender equity, disability access, and cultural sensitivity. For instance, providing tailored coaching for para-athletes, addressing the unique challenges faced by LGBTQ+ athletes, ensuring gender-sensitive facilities and equipment, and promoting work-life balance are all integral to creating an inclusive environment. Furthermore, training for coaches, managers, and support staff on unconscious bias and inclusive leadership is essential to sustain meaningful change and ensure that all individuals can thrive. From a governance perspective, embedding inclusive talent management within the strategic priorities of sports organizations requires commitment from leadership, clear accountability, and continuous evaluation. This includes setting measurable diversity and inclusion goals, collecting and analyzing relevant data, and involving diverse voices in decision-making processes. Establishing partnerships with grassroots organizations, schools, and community groups can also help identify and develop talent from the importance of inclusive talent management in sports transcends individual organizations and has far-reaching societal implications. Sports possess a unique ability to inspire, unite, and drive social serve as a powerful example for other sectors and contribute to building more equitable and inclusive societies.

DEFINING INCLUSIVE TALENT MANAGEMENT: UNDERSTANDING INCLUSIVE TALENT MANAGEMENT

Talent leadership is a critical dimension of effective sports organizations in today's highly competitive and globalized environment. It refers to the ability of leaders—whether coaches, team managers, directors, or executives—to strategically identify, develop, and leverage human potential to drive (Kaliannan M. et al. 2023) sustained performance and organizational success. In the fast-evolving world of sports, where innovation, resilience, and adaptability are paramount, sound talent leadership principles provide the foundation for cultivating high-performing athletes, cohesive teams, and vibrant organizational cultures. Understanding and applying these principles is essential for sports leaders who seek to maintain competitive advantage, foster personal and professional growth, and promote values of excellence, integrity, and inclusion. At the heart of talent leadership is a commitment to a growth mindset. Leaders must believe in the potential of individuals to improve, develop, and exceed expectations through effort, learning, and perseverance. This contrasts with static views that regard talent as fixed or innate. A growth-oriented staff to adapt to challenges, overcome setbacks, and achieve their fullest potential. Sports leaders who embody and promote this mindset create a culture where striving for excellence is embedded in daily routines and long-term strategies. Another fundamental principle is individualized development. Effective talent leadership recognizes that each athlete (Holden et al. 2025) and staff member possess unique strengths, motivations, learning styles, and developmental requires deep understanding of each person's capabilities and aspirations, often achieved through regular dialogue, performance reviews, and mentorship. By fostering personalized growth, talent leaders help individuals unlock new levels of performance and well-being, which collectively elevate the entire organization. Clear vision and purpose are also key components of successful talent leadership. Sports organizations that articulate compelling missions and shared values provide their members with a strong sense of direction and belonging. Talent leaders must communicate these guiding principles consistently and authentically, ensuring alignment between organizational goals and personal ambitions. This alignment drives motivation, commitment, and cohesion within teams. (Anlesinya A. et al. 2020) Moreover, it empowers individuals to understand how their contributions fit into the broader objectives, fostering a deeper sense of meaning and engagement.

In addition, talent leadership involves creating an environment of psychological safety—a space where individuals feel respected, valued, and free to express themselves without fear of ridicule or reprisal. (Tahmasebi R. et al. 2024) In psychologically safe environments, athletes and staff are more likely to take risks, share ideas, admit mistakes, and seek help when needed—all of which are essential for innovation, learning, and continuous improvement. Leaders must actively build trust, model vulnerability, and encourage open communication to cultivate such environments, ultimately driving higher performance and stronger relationships. Feedback and accountability form another pillar of effective talent leadership. Constructive, timely, and balanced feedback helps individuals understand their strengths and areas for improvement. Leaders must develop the skills to deliver feedback in ways that inspire growth and resilience rather than defensiveness or demotivation. At the same time, maintaining accountability ensures that high standards of performance, effort, and behavior are consistently upheld. Talent leaders must strike a careful balance between support and challenge, creating cultures of both compassion and excellence. A principle increasingly recognized as essential is inclusive leadership—ensuring that talent development practices are equitable, unbiased, and supportive of diversity in all forms. Sports organizations must actively seek out and nurture talent from varied backgrounds, creating pathways for underrepresented groups and addressing structural barriers to advancement. (Cooper J. N. et al. 2020) Inclusive talent leadership not only enhances fairness but also enriches team dynamics, promotes innovation, and reflects the values of modern societies. Leaders must be aware of unconscious biases, advocate for inclusive policies, and demonstrate cultural competence in their interactions and decisions.

BENEFITS OF INCLUSIVE TALENT MANAGEMENT

Inclusive talent management is a forward-thinking and strategic approach to attracting, developing, retaining, and promoting individuals within an organization—ensuring that opportunities are accessible (Worley C. et al. 2020) to people of all backgrounds, identities, and abilities. Unlike traditional talent management models, which often focus narrowly on technical skills or past performance, inclusive talent management takes into account the broader social, cultural, and structural factors that influence access to opportunity and success. It recognizes that true organizational excellence and innovation stem from the rich diversity of people, perspectives, and experiences within a workforce, and that barriers—whether explicit or implicit—must be addressed to unlock the full potential of talent. In this way, inclusive talent management is not merely an HR initiative; it is a holistic, values-driven philosophy that shapes organizational culture, leadership practices, and strategic outcomes. At its core, inclusive talent management seeks to identify and mitigate systemic inequities that have historically limited participation and advancement for certain groups. These inequities may be based on gender, race, ethnicity, socioeconomic background, age, disability, sexual orientation, gender identity, religion, or other factors. In many industries and sectors, unconscious bias and structural discrimination continue to create unequal playing fields, these dynamics by promoting equitable access to opportunities—whether in hiring, training, mentorship, promotion, or leadership development. It involves intentional design of processes and practices that ensure all individuals, regardless of their background, (Tushabe et al. 2025) have the opportunity to thrive. An essential component of inclusive talent management is the broadening of the definition of "talent" itself. In traditional frameworks, talent is often measured by narrow, predefined criteria—such as specific degrees, certifications, or elite institutional affiliations. Inclusive talent management, by contrast, recognizes that potential can take many forms and that valuable contributions come from a wide range of experiences. This more expansive view embraces different learning styles, lived experiences, leadership approaches, and problem-solving abilities, allowing organizations to tap into a deeper and more diverse pool of candidates. It challenges outdated assumptions about what makes someone "qualified" or "high-potential," fostering a more dynamic and innovative talent ecosystem. Further, inclusive talent management emphasizes the importance of cultivating a sense of belonging within the organization. It is not enough to simply recruit diverse talent; organizations must also create an environment in which all individuals feel respected, (Baran et al. 2020) valued, and supported in contributing their best work. Psychological safety—where individuals can express themselves without fear of negative consequences—is central to this effort.

Another important dimension is equity in career development and advancement. Research consistently shows that underrepresented groups often face hidden barriers to progression, including limited access (Kotte K. R. et al. 2025) to influential networks, sponsorship, high-visibility assignments, and leadership pathways. Inclusive talent management proactively addresses these disparities through transparent career development processes, mentorship and sponsorship programs, leadership training tailored to diverse needs, and accountability measures to monitor progress. It also involves critically examining organizational structures—such as promotion criteria, performance evaluation systems, and leadership succession planning—to ensure they do not inadvertently disadvantage certain groups. Data-driven decision-making is a hallmark of effective inclusive talent management. Organizations must collect, analyze, and act on relevant data related to diversity, equity, and inclusion (DEI). This includes not only demographic data but also qualitative insights from employee engagement surveys, focus groups, and feedback channels. Data enables organizations to identify gaps, measure progress, and inform targeted interventions. It also fosters transparency and accountability, demonstrating a genuine commitment to continuous improvement in inclusion and equity. Inclusive talent management also extends beyond the internal workings of the organization (Sakthivel M. et al. 2025) to influence external relationships and brand reputation. Today's employees, customers, investors, and other stakeholders increasingly expect organizations to stand for social responsibility and inclusivity.

CREATING AN INCLUSIVE CULTURE: STRATEGIES FOR CREATING AN INCLUSIVE CULTURE

The benefits of inclusive talent management extend far beyond ethical considerations—they touch every aspect of organizational performance, culture, and long-term sustainability. Inclusive practices (Maheswaran K. et al. 2025) help build more innovative, resilient, and competitive organizations by ensuring that talent from all backgrounds is welcomed, valued, and empowered to thrive. As organizations in every sector—from corporate enterprises to sports teams, government agencies, and nonprofits—face increasing complexity, diversity of stakeholders, and rapid change, inclusive talent management provides a strategic advantage that is essential for sustained success. One of the most widely recognized benefits of inclusive talent management is its positive impact on innovation and creativity. Research consistently shows that diverse teams outperform homogenous ones when it comes to problem-solving and idea generation. (Shollen et al. 2025) This is because individuals with different backgrounds, experiences, perspectives, and thinking styles approach challenges in varied ways, leading to richer discussions, more innovative solutions, and reduced risk of "groupthink." When talent management practices are inclusive, they create environments where all voices are heard and valued—making it possible to tap into the full creative potential of a workforce. In industries where innovation is a key driver of competitive advantage—such as technology, healthcare, and sports—this benefit is particularly significant. Enhanced decision-making is another critical advantage. Diverse teams bring broader perspectives to the table, helping organizations make more informed, well-rounded decisions. Inclusive practices ensure that diverse viewpoints are actively sought out and considered, leading to better risk management, greater insight into complex issues, and decisions that resonate with a wider range of stakeholders. In today's globalized world, where organizations must navigate cultural nuances and shifting societal expectations, this ability to make informed, inclusive decisions is invaluable. Inclusive talent management also drives higher levels of employee engagement, satisfaction, and retention. (Hubballi R. B. et al. 2025) When employees feel respected, valued, and included, they are more likely to be engaged in their work, loyal to their organization, and committed to its goals. Inclusive workplaces foster psychological safety—where individuals feel comfortable expressing their ideas, taking risks, and being themselves.

Broader access to talent is another major benefit. In an increasingly competitive labor market, organizations that limit themselves to narrow definitions of "fit" or "qualification" risk missing out on vast pools of talent. (Thirunagalingam. et al. 2025) Inclusive talent management helps break down barriers to entry and advancement, enabling organizations to attract candidates from a wider range of backgrounds. This not only enriches the talent pool but also helps address critical skills shortages—particularly in fields where demand for specialized expertise is high. In addition, inclusive organizations are more likely to appeal to younger generations of workers, who increasingly prioritize diversity and social responsibility in their employment choices. From a performance standpoint, inclusive practices can lead to higher overall organizational effectiveness. Studies by consulting firms such as McKinsey & Company and Deloitte have found strong correlations between diversity in leadership and better financial performance. Organizations with inclusive cultures tend to be more adaptable, better able to respond to changing market conditions, and more likely to capture new market opportunities. They are also better positioned to build relationships with diverse customers, partners, and communities—enhancing brand reputation and opening new avenues for growth. Improved organizational reputation and brand equity are further benefits of inclusive talent management. In an era where transparency and social responsibility are increasingly important to consumers, investors, and other stakeholders, organizations that demonstrate a genuine commitment to diversity and inclusion enjoy stronger public trust and goodwill. (Upadhyaya A. N. et al. 2025) They are viewed as employers of choice by top talent, and as ethical, progressive brands by customers.

EFFECTIVE TALENT LEADERSHIP IN SPORTS: PRINCIPLES OF EFFECTIVE TALENT LEADERSHIP

Creating an inclusive culture is a transformative process that goes beyond simple policy changes or public statements—it requires deliberate strategies that reshape organizational mindsets, behaviors, structures, (Soundariya A. et al. 2025) and everyday interactions. An inclusive culture is one where every individual, regardless of background, identity, or experience, feels valued, respected, supported, and empowered to contribute fully. It is marked by a sense of belonging, psychological safety, fairness, and mutual respect. Building such a culture involves a holistic and sustained commitment, led by senior leadership, embraced by all levels of the organization, and reinforced through consistent actions, policies, and accountability mechanisms. The first critical strategy in creating an inclusive culture is securing visible, authentic commitment from leadership. Senior leaders must champion inclusion not just through words but through actions—allocating resources, setting clear expectations, modeling inclusive behaviors, and holding themselves accountable. Leadership must articulate a compelling vision for inclusion and embed it into the organization's mission, values, and strategic priorities. When leaders consistently demonstrate their commitment—such as by participating in inclusion training, (Nese et al. 2025) sponsoring employee resource groups (ERGs), and prioritizing DEI in decision-making—they send a strong signal that inclusion is a core organizational value, not a fleeting initiative. A second key strategy is developing inclusive leadership capabilities at all levels. While top-down commitment is essential, true cultural change requires that managers, team leads, and frontline supervisors are equipped to foster inclusion in their daily practices. This involves providing targeted training on topics such as unconscious bias, cultural competence, inclusive communication, emotional intelligence, and conflict resolution. Inclusive leadership also requires self-awareness—encouraging leaders to reflect on their own biases and privileges and a commitment to continuous learning. When leaders at every level demonstrate empathy, fairness, and respect, they help create a culture where all employees feel (Samal A. et al. 2025) valued and included.

Embedding inclusion into core processes and systems is another vital strategy. Policies related to hiring, promotion, performance evaluation, compensation, and career development should be designed with equity in mind. (Chib S. et al. 2025) This may involve revising job descriptions to eliminate biased language, using structured interviews to reduce subjectivity, implementing blind resume reviews, and ensuring that promotion criteria are transparent and fair. It also includes providing equitable access to leadership development programs, mentorship opportunities, and stretch assignments. By institutionalizing inclusive practices, organizations ensure that inclusion is not dependent on individual goodwill, but is woven into the fabric of everyday operations. Fostering psychological safety is central to creating an inclusive culture. Employees need to feel that they can speak up, share ideas, admit mistakes, and challenge the status quo without fear of ridicule or retaliation. Leaders can promote psychological safety by actively encouraging diverse viewpoints, responding constructively to feedback, and modeling vulnerability themselves. Regular team check-ins, anonymous feedback channels, and open (Le Roy et al. 2025) forums can help surface concerns and build trust. When employees trust that their voices will be heard and respected, they are more likely to engage fully and contribute to a dynamic and innovative workplace. Representation matters—not only in terms of demographic diversity but also in reflecting a range of experiences, perspectives, and voices. Organizations should set measurable goals for increasing diversity in hiring, leadership, and board composition. But numbers alone are not enough; it is essential to create an environment where diverse talent feels welcomed, supported, and empowered. ERGs, affinity groups, and mentorship programs can provide valuable support networks for underrepresented employees, helping them navigate the organization and build connections. Another effective strategy is to foster open dialogue and (Abid & Polo, 2025) continuous education around inclusion. Organizations should create safe spaces for conversations about race, gender, disability, LGBTQ+ inclusion, and other aspects of identity and experience.

BUILDING TRUST AND RAPPORT: BUILDING TRUST WITH ATHLETES AND STAFF

Effective talent leadership in sports is a dynamic, multifaceted discipline that shapes the success of athletes, teams, and entire organizations. It goes far beyond traditional coaching or management; it requires a deep (Samuel. et al. 2025) understanding of human potential, team dynamics, organizational strategy, and the evolving cultural and social landscape of modern sports. In today's competitive environment—where performance margins are razor-thin and the expectations of athletes, fans, and stakeholders are continually rising—leaders who master the principles of effective talent leadership can unlock extraordinary levels of performance, resilience, and innovation. These principles provide a framework for identifying, nurturing, and maximizing the capabilities of individuals and teams, ensuring both immediate success and sustainable long-term development. One of the core principles of effective talent leadership is adopting a growth mindset. Great sports leaders understand that talent is not a fixed attribute but a capacity that can be developed through effort, learning, and perseverance. They reject limiting beliefs about innate ability and instead cultivate environments where athletes and staff are encouraged to embrace challenges, (Ziegler et al. 2025) learn from setbacks, and continuously improve. This mindset fosters resilience, adaptability, and a passion for learning—qualities essential for sustained high performance in an ever-evolving sports landscape. Individualized development is another key principle. Effective talent leaders recognize that each athlete is unique, with distinct strengths, motivations, learning styles, and personal circumstances. Rather than applying a uniform approach, they tailor training, feedback, and support to meet the specific needs of each individual. This involves building trusting relationships, understanding each athlete's personal and professional goals, and designing development plans that align with both the individual's potential and the team's objectives. By focusing on personalized growth, leaders help athletes achieve their best while fostering deeper engagement and loyalty. Building a strong, shared vision is central to effective talent leadership. Leaders must articulate clear, inspiring goals and values that unite individuals and teams around a common purpose. This vision should go beyond (Hill. et al. 2025) winning games or medals—it should encompass broader values such as integrity, teamwork, respect, and community impact.

Psychological safety is a (Raetze S. et al. 2025) vital principle in talent leadership. In high-pressure sports environments, where performance is constantly scrutinized, athletes need to feel safe to take risks, voice concerns, admit mistakes, and express vulnerability. Leaders who cultivate psychological safety create a foundation for trust, open communication, and continuous improvement. They listen actively, respond empathetically, and encourage honest dialogue. When athletes know they are supported and valued as whole individuals—not just for their on-field performance—they are more likely to take the kinds of risks and creative actions that drive innovation and peak performance. Constructive feedback and accountability are essential components of effective talent leadership. (Gabrišová et al. 2025) Athletes require timely, specific, and balanced feedback to understand their strengths and areas for growth. Leaders must develop the ability to deliver feedback in ways that inspire improvement rather than defensiveness. At the same time, maintaining high standards of effort, behavior, and professionalism is crucial. Leaders must hold individuals accountable, modeling consistency and fairness. This balance of support and challenge helps athletes and teams reach higher levels of excellence while maintaining a positive and respectful culture. Inclusivity and equity are increasingly recognized as foundational principles of talent leadership in sports. Leaders must be intentional about creating environments where all individuals—regardless (Avrillia S. et al. 2025) of gender, race, ethnicity, sexual orientation, socioeconomic background, or ability—feel welcome, valued, and supported. Inclusive leadership broadens the talent pool, enriches team dynamics, and enhances innovation.

EMPOWERING ATHLETES AND STAFF: EMPOWERING ATHLETES AND STAFF

Building trust and rapport with athletes and staff is a foundational element of effective leadership in sports. Without trust, even the most technically skilled coaches, managers, or directors will struggle to inspire, (Mueller. et al. 2025) motivate, and develop their teams. Trust serves as the bedrock upon which strong relationships, open communication, psychological safety, and collective performance are built. It is the invisible glue that binds individuals to a common purpose and fosters the sense of belonging that fuels both personal growth and team success. In an environment as emotionally charged and high-stakes as sports—where athletes often face intense physical demands, public scrutiny, and personal pressures—leaders must be intentional, consistent, and authentic in cultivating trust and rapport at every level. The first step in building trust is demonstrating authenticity and integrity. Athletes and staff quickly discern whether a leader is genuine or merely performing a role. Leaders who are authentic—who speak honestly, acknowledge their own limitations, and act consistently with their stated values—are more likely to earn respect and trust. Integrity is equally crucial; it involves doing what is right even when it is difficult, honoring commitments, and ensuring fairness and transparency in decision-making. When athletes see that their leaders operate with integrity, they feel safer, respected, and more inclined to commit fully to (Solomons. et al. 2025) the team's vision. Active listening and empathy are core behaviors that foster trust and rapport. Athletes and staff want to feel heard, understood, and valued—not just for their performance, but as whole people.

Figure 1. Life Cycle of Talent Management

Consistency and reliability are also critical for trust. Athletes and staff must know that they can count on their leaders—not just (Esposito. et al. 2025) during victories and good times, but especially when things are difficult. Leaders who are consistent in their actions, decisions, and communication create an environment of predictability and security. This includes providing regular, honest feedback; setting clear expectations; and applying rules and standards fairly to all team members. Inconsistency, favoritism, or erratic behavior can quickly erode trust, especially in high-pressure sports settings where stability and clarity are vital. Respecting individual differences is another key to building trust. Each athlete and staff member brings a unique background, identity, and set of experiences to the team. Effective leaders demonstrate respect for these differences by recognizing and valuing diverse perspectives, avoiding stereotypes, and being culturally competent. They create an inclusive environment where everyone feels welcomed and appreciated. This respect extends to honoring personal boundaries, maintaining confidentiality, (Purnomo et al. 2025) and supporting work-life balance. When people feel that their individuality is respected, trust and rapport deepen naturally. Creating opportunities for genuine connection outside of formal coaching or work contexts also helps build trust. Leaders who take the time to engage with athletes and staff on a personal level—celebrating milestones, acknowledging personal achievements, or participating in informal conversations—help humanize relationships. These moments of connection reinforce the idea that leaders care about their people beyond their roles or output, fostering loyalty and camaraderie. Another crucial factor is demonstrating competence and professionalism. Trust is not built on good intentions alone—athletes and staff need to believe in their leader's ability to guide them toward success. Leaders must demonstrate strong technical knowledge, strategic thinking, and effective management skills. (Grall. et al. 2025) They should stay updated on advancements in sports science, coaching techniques, and leadership practices, and continually invest in their own development. When leaders exhibit both competence and a willingness to learn, they earn the respect and trust of those they lead. Psychological safety is a cornerstone of trust-building.

NAVIGATING AMBIGUITY IN SPORTS ORGANIZATIONS: STRATEGIES FOR NAVIGATING AMBIGUITY

Navigating ambiguity in sports organizations is an essential leadership capability in today's fast-evolving and high-pressure athletic environment. Sports, by their very nature, involve uncertainty—outcomes are unpredictable, (Griesinger. et al. 2025) athlete performance can fluctuate, external factors such as competition rules, governing body decisions, sponsorship dynamics, and public expectations are in constant flux. Beyond the inherent unpredictability of competition, modern sports organizations face ambiguity in areas like athlete well-being, technological integration, diversity and inclusion initiatives, globalization, and the influence of social media. Events like global pandemics, political unrest, and economic shifts further add to this complexity. Therefore, leaders in sports must embrace ambiguity and develop strategies that foster organizational agility, resilience, and clarity amid uncertainty. Mastering this capability ensures that ambiguity becomes an opportunity for learning, innovation, and growth rather than a source of fear or dysfunction. (Huyler et al. 2025) The first crucial strategy for navigating ambiguity is to establish and communicate a strong organizational purpose and shared values. When faced with uncertainty, athletes and staff look to their leaders for stability. Clear values—such as integrity, teamwork, excellence, fairness, inclusion, and athlete-centeredness—serve as a moral compass that guides behavior even when external circumstances are unclear. A well-articulated purpose gives meaning to day-to-day actions and helps individuals stay focused on what truly matters, regardless of short-term ambiguity. Leaders who consistently reinforce purpose and values foster trust and cohesion, enabling their teams to move forward confidently despite uncertainty. Fostering a growth mindset and culture of learning is another key strategy. Ambiguity often demands adaptation and creative problem-solving. Leaders must promote a mindset where challenges and uncertainty are seen as opportunities for learning and growth rather than threats. This involves encouraging curiosity, experimentation, and resilience. Athletes and staff should be supported in taking calculated risks, trying new approaches, and learning from setbacks. (Redondo-Duarte S. et al. 2025) Leaders should model this mindset themselves—demonstrating openness to feedback, willingness to adapt, and a commitment to continuous improvement.

Transparent and consistent communication is essential to managing ambiguity effectively. In uncertain situations, lack of information can lead to fear, speculation, and reduced morale. Leaders should proactively (Holden et al. 2025) communicate with athletes and staff—sharing what is known, acknowledging what is unknown, and explaining the rationale behind decisions. Honesty about the limitations of current knowledge builds credibility. It is better to say, "Here is what we know and what we're doing to learn more," than to remain silent or pretend to have all the answers. Regular updates and open forums for questions and dialogue help maintain trust and engagement during periods of uncertainty. Empowering athletes and staff to take ownership and contribute solutions is another powerful way to navigate ambiguity. Rather than trying to control every outcome, effective leaders distribute leadership by encouraging individuals at all levels to take initiative and share responsibility for navigating challenges. This fosters a sense of agency and ownership, builds collective intelligence, and enables the organization to respond more flexibly to changing circumstances. Athletes can be engaged in co-creating training adaptations, staff can be empowered to innovate in their domains, and leadership can tap into the creativity of the broader organization. Scenario planning and proactive preparation help organizations anticipate and respond to uncertainty. Leaders should engage teams in considering various possible futures, identifying risks and opportunities, and developing contingency plans. For example, how might a major competition be disrupted? How might new technology affect training methods? (Tushabe et al. 2025) What if a key sponsor withdraws support? Thinking through these possibilities builds mental flexibility and readiness. Athletes can use visualization and mental rehearsal techniques to prepare for unexpected changes in competition formats or conditions.

ADAPTING TO CHANGE: ADAPTING TO CHANGING ENVIRONMENTS

Navigating ambiguity in sports organizations is an essential leadership capability in today's fast-evolving and high-pressure athletic environment. Sports, by their very nature, involve uncertainty—outcomes are unpredictable, (Shollen et al. 2025) athlete performance can fluctuate, external factors such as competition rules, governing body decisions, sponsorship dynamics, and public expectations are in constant flux. Beyond the inherent unpredictability of competition, modern sports organizations face ambiguity in areas like athlete well-being, technological integration, diversity and inclusion initiatives, globalization, and the influence of social media. Events like global pandemics, political unrest, and economic shifts further add to this complexity. Therefore, leaders in sports must embrace ambiguity and develop strategies that foster organizational agility, (Galanti et al. 2025) resilience, and clarity amid uncertainty. A well-articulated purpose gives meaning to day-to-day actions and helps individuals stay focused on what truly matters, regardless of short-term ambiguity. Leaders who consistently reinforce purpose and values foster trust and cohesion, enabling their teams to move forward confidently despite uncertainty. (Ziegler et al. 2025) Fostering a growth mindset and culture of learning is another key strategy. Ambiguity often demands adaptation and creative problem-solving. Leaders must promote a mindset where challenges and uncertainty are seen as opportunities for learning and growth rather than threats. This involves encouraging curiosity, experimentation, and resilience.Transparent and consistent communication is essential to managing ambiguity effectively. In uncertain situations, lack of information can lead to fear, speculation, and reduced morale. Leaders should proactively (Huyler et al. 2025) communicate with athletes and staff—sharing what is known, acknowledging what is unknown, and explaining the rationale behind decisions. Organizations can develop flexible operational plans that can pivot quickly when circumstances shift. Building psychological safety and emotional resilience is foundational for navigating ambiguity. (Galanti et al. 2025) Sports organizations must create environments where athletes and staff feel safe to voice concerns, ask questions, experiment, and admit mistakes.

MANAGING UNCERTAINTY: MANAGING UNCERTAINTY IN SPORTS

Adapting to changing environments is a core competency for modern sports organizations, athletes, and staff. In today's fast-paced, increasingly complex world of sport, change is constant and often unpredictable. (Le Roy et al. 2025).Change often brings uncertainty, disruption, and emotional stress. Leaders should prioritize the development of resilience among athletes and staff—providing training and resources in areas such as stress management, emotional intelligence, mindfulness, and mental well-being. Organizations should also provide robust support networks, including access to sports psychologists, (Nese et al. 2025) mentors, and peer support groups. When individuals are mentally strong and emotionally supported, they are better equipped to handle the demands of change, maintain focus on their goals, and sustain high performance even during turbulent times.Clear and transparent communication is vital during periods of change. When change occurs, uncertainty can create anxiety, rumors, and disengagement. Leaders must communicate openly about the nature of the change, the reasons (Gabrišová et al. 2025) behind it, the expected impacts, and the path forward. When people feel that they have a voice and a role in driving change, they are more likely to support it enthusiastically and work to make it successful. Shared leadership and participatory approaches to change are particularly effective in building organizational adaptability. Developing organizational agility through flexible systems and processes is another key enabler of adaptation. Rigid structures, overly bureaucratic processes, and narrow job roles can hinder an organization's ability to respond to change. Leaders should design workflows, decision-making processes, staffing models, and resource allocation systems that can pivot quickly as circumstances evolve. Agile project management techniques, cross-functional teams, and iterative planning cycles all contribute to organizational agility. Flexibility should be embedded in both strategic and operational levels of the (Purnomo et al. 2025) organization so that it can adjust rapidly to external or internal changes.

HOLISTIC ATHLETE DEVELOPMENT: HOLISTIC APPROACH TO ATHLETE DEVELOPMENT

Managing uncertainty is an essential capability for success in modern sports. By its very nature, the sports environment is inherently unpredictable—athletic performance fluctuates, opponents' strategies evolve, injuries occur, and competitions unfold with countless variables that defy full control. (Kaliannan M. et al. 2023) Beyond the field of play, sports organizations face constant uncertainty in areas such as governance changes, sponsorship dynamics, regulatory shifts, technological disruptions, societal trends, and global events like pandemics or geopolitical instability. This begins with adopting a growth mindset—where challenges are embraced as learning experiences and where failure is viewed as feedback, not defeat. Athletes and staff who (Tahmasebi R. et al. 2024) understand that uncertainty is a natural and inevitable part of the sports world are better prepared to respond constructively when unexpected events occur. When circumstances change rapidly, and when specific outcomes cannot be guaranteed, athletes and staff rely on a shared sense of purpose and core principles to guide their actions. Leaders should continually articulate the organization's mission and values—whether (Anlesinya A. et al. 2020) focused on excellence, integrity, teamwork, athlete development, or community impact. These values serve as a constant "north star," helping individuals make decisions and maintain motivation even when the future is unclear.

Transparent and consistent communication is another fundamental strategy. In uncertain times, ambiguity and lack of information can lead to confusion, fear, and disengagement. Leaders must communicate openly and frequently (Cooper J. N. et al. 2020) with athletes and staff—sharing what is known, acknowledging what is unknown, and explaining the rationale behind decisions. When leaders admit uncertainty with honesty and humility, they foster trust and credibility. Providing regular updates, creating forums for dialogue, and listening actively to concerns all contribute to a transparent communication culture. Clarity does not require having all the answers—it requires being truthful, consistent, and empathetic. Building psychological safety is crucial for managing uncertainty effectively. Athletes and staff must feel safe to express concerns, ask questions, and propose ideas—even when outcomes are unclear. Psychological safety enables open dialogue, experimentation, and collaborative problem-solving. Leaders should encourage curiosity, tolerate ambiguity, and reward initiative. They must model vulnerability themselves (Worley C. et al. 2020), demonstrating that it is acceptable not to have all the answers. Team-based approaches to uncertainty encourage innovation and resilience—allowing athletes and staff to adapt together rather than in isolation. Trust and cohesion within teams are powerful buffers against the stress of uncertainty, enabling faster and more effective responses. Empowering individuals to take ownership and initiative further strengthens organizational adaptability. (Baran et al. 2020) Leaders should encourage athletes and staff to be proactive in managing uncertainty—identifying potential risks, proposing solutions, and adapting their practices as needed.

SUPPORT SYSTEMS FOR ATHLETES: SUPPORT SYSTEMS FOR ATHLETES

Holistic athlete development is an approach that recognizes and nurtures the entire person—not just the athlete's physical and technical abilities, but also their mental, emotional, social, and ethical dimensions. (Kotte K. R. et al. 2025) In today's sports landscape, where demands on athletes are higher than ever, a purely performance-focused model is insufficient. Long-term success—both in sport and in life—requires developing well-rounded individuals who can sustain excellence, adapt to challenges, and contribute meaningfully beyond the field of play. This sense of respect and validation strengthens motivation, well-being, and long-term engagement with sport. Physical development remains a vital component of holistic athlete development, encompassing not only sport-specific skills and fitness but also injury prevention, recovery, and overall physical health. A well-rounded physical program attends to the individual needs of each athlete, adapting training loads, techniques, and recovery strategies to support sustainable performance. (Sakthivel M. et al. 2025) It also emphasizes long-term athlete health, recognizing that many athletes will live decades beyond their competitive careers. Attention to nutrition, sleep, and physical literacy contributes to lifelong wellness and helps athletes maintain their quality of life after sport.Equally important is mental and emotional development. The mental aspects of performance—such as focus, confidence, resilience, and coping with pressure—are critical to success in sport. Holistic development programs integrate mental (Maheswaran K. et al. 2025) skills training, mindfulness, visualization, and psychological resilience-building into regular practice. Coaches and leaders have a responsibility to model and community engagement help athletes develop a strong moral compass. Character development contributes not only to personal growth but also to the creation of positive team cultures and broader societal impact. Personal identity and purpose are central to sustaining athletes' well-being and long-term engagement. (Hubballi R. B. et al. 2025).

CAREER TRANSITION AND POST-ATHLETIC LIFE

Support systems for athletes are critical to fostering both high performance and long-term well-being in the demanding world of sport. As the physical, mental, and emotional pressures on athletes continue to intensify—driven (Thirunagalingam. et al. 2025) by rising competitive standards, public scrutiny, technological advances, and the growing year-round demands of elite sport—the presence of robust, multi-dimensional support networks is more important than ever. Effective support systems help athletes manage stress, recover from setbacks, balance personal and professional commitments, and develop holistically as both performers and individuals. These systems also serve as protective buffers against the risks of burnout, injury, mental health challenges, and identity foreclosure. In a well-designed support ecosystem, athletes are empowered to pursue excellence sustainably, knowing that they are not alone on their journey. At the heart of an athlete's support system is the coach-athlete relationship. Coaches are often the most influential figures in an athlete's development, providing technical instruction, strategic guidance, emotional support, and moral leadership. The quality of this relationship is a key predictor of both performance outcomes and personal well-being. Effective coaches foster trust, communicate openly, (Upadhyaya A. N. et al. 2025) and demonstrate genuine care for the athlete as a whole person—not just a performer. They balance the drive for results with empathy and respect, creating psychologically safe environments where athletes can thrive. Coaches who are attuned to the emotional needs of their athletes can detect early signs of stress or burnout and intervene appropriately. Mental health and psychological support is an essential component of modern athlete support systems. The stigma surrounding mental health in sports has begun to fade, as athletes and organizations increasingly recognize the central role that psychological well-being plays in performance and life. Access to qualified sports psychologists, counselors, and mental performance coaches helps athletes build resilience, manage anxiety, develop coping strategies, and address personal challenges. Ongoing mental health support—not just crisis intervention—enables athletes to sustain optimal performance and well-being throughout their careers. Encouraging open dialogue about mental health and (Soundariya A. et al. 2025) integrating psychological support into regular training routines normalizes the importance of caring for the mind as well as the body.

Medical and physiotherapy support is equally vital. High-level sport places enormous physical demands on the body, and the risk of injury is ever-present. Comprehensive medical support systems provide athletes (Samal A. et al. 2025) with access to sports physicians, physiotherapists, athletic trainers, massage therapists, and rehabilitation specialists. These professionals work collaboratively to prevent injuries, optimize recovery, and manage both acute and chronic health conditions. In the event of injury, an integrated medical team can guide the athlete's return-to-play process, balancing performance goals with long-term health. The best systems also address the often-overlooked aspects of injury recovery—such as mental health support and reintegration into team environments—ensuring that athletes receive holistic care. Strength and conditioning coaches and sport scientists contribute to an athlete's physical preparation and performance optimization. These professionals develop evidence-based training programs tailored to the individual athlete's needs, goals, and physiological profile. They monitor performance metrics, manage workload, and implement periodization strategies to promote peak performance (Abid K. et al. 2025) and reduce injury risk. The integration of sport science—covering biomechanics, nutrition, sleep, recovery, and data analytics—enhances training effectiveness and supports informed decision-making by both athletes and coaches. Addressing issues such as disordered eating, energy availability, and body image is an important part of this support, particularly in sports where appearance or weight categories can contribute to unhealthy behaviors. Social and peer support is often overlooked but profoundly important. (Chib S. et al. 2025) Strong relationships with teammates, family, friends, and mentors provide emotional grounding and a sense of belonging.

BEST PRACTICES IN INCLUSIVE TALENT MANAGEMENT: BEST PRACTICES.

Supporting athletes through career transitions and into post-athletic life is a vital but often underappreciated responsibility of sports organizations, coaches, and leaders. The transition out of competitive sport is (Samuel. et al. 2025) one of the most challenging phases in an athlete's life, marked by profound shifts in identity, routine, purpose, financial stability, social connections, and physical activity. Whether triggered by retirement, injury, deselection, or personal choice, this transition is often accompanied by psychological stress, uncertainty, and vulnerability. For some athletes, especially those who have invested their entire identity and sense of self-worth in their sporting career, this period can lead to feelings of loss, depression, anxiety, or a lack of direction. Conversely, when managed well, this transition can open new pathways for growth, purpose, and personal fulfillment. Comprehensive, proactive support for career transitions is essential not only for the long-term well-being of athletes but also for maintaining the ethical integrity of sports organizations and contributing positively to society. Understanding the complexity of career transitions is the first step in providing effective support. Athletic careers are often short, and for (Raetze S. et al. 2025) many athletes, the exit from sport can feel abrupt and unplanned. Career planning should begin long before an athlete retires from competition. Sports organizations and educational partners should encourage and facilitate dual-career (Hill. et al. 2025) pathways, enabling athletes to pursue academic or vocational qualifications alongside their sporting commitments. Lifelong learning should be promoted as an integral part of the athletic journey.

Psychological support plays a central role in helping athletes manage the emotional aspects of transition. Access to sports psychologists, counselors, and peer support groups allows athletes to process feelings of loss, anxiety, (Avrillia S. et al. 2025) and uncertainty. Structured transition programs can include workshops on identity exploration, resilience, coping strategies, and building self-esteem beyond athletic performance. Tailored guidance should consider the unique strengths, experiences, and passions of each athlete, helping them align their next career steps with their personal interests and values. Recognizing and validating the transferable skills gained through sport—such as discipline, teamwork, leadership, and perseverance—helps athletes market themselves confidently in new contexts. Financial planning and literacy are critical areas of support. Many athletes face significant changes in income post-retirement, and some may have little experience in managing personal finances. Financial counseling on topics such as budgeting, investment, insurance, and retirement planning helps athletes build a secure financial foundation. Early education on managing sponsorship income, contract earnings, and long-term savings prepares athletes to navigate financial realities with (Mueller. et al. 2025) greater confidence and stability. Addressing financial literacy as a proactive component of athlete development reduces vulnerability and supports independence. Fostering social connections and community engagement mitigates the isolation that can accompany transition.

THE FUTURE OF TALENT MANAGEMENT IN SPORTS: FUTURE TRENDS AND DIRECTIONS

Inclusive talent management (ITM) has become an essential priority for modern sports organizations, as diversity, equity, and inclusion (DEI) are now widely recognized as drivers of innovation, performance, (Solomons. et al. 2025) and ethical responsibility. Best practices in inclusive talent management aim to attract, retain, develop, and empower athletes, coaches, and staff from a broad range of backgrounds, ensuring that everyone has equal access to opportunities and support. The goal is not merely to "diversify the numbers," but to cultivate an inclusive culture where all individuals can thrive and contribute fully to organizational success. In the context of sports—where talent pipelines, recruitment practices, leadership structures, and cultural norms have historically excluded or marginalized certain groups—systematic and intentional action is required to embed inclusive principles into every aspect of talent management. The first best practice is to establish inclusive talent management as a leadership priority. Senior leaders and boards must articulate a clear and compelling vision for inclusion and ensure that this vision is embedded in the organization's mission, values, and strategic objectives. DEI should not be treated as an "add-on" or compliance exercise, but as a core element of organizational success. Leaders must be visible champions of inclusion, holding themselves accountable for progress and modeling inclusive behaviors. Leadership commitment creates a mandate for change, mobilizes resources, and signals to all stakeholders that inclusion matters. Data-driven approaches are fundamental to inclusive talent management. Organizations must collect, analyze, and transparently report data on the diversity of their athlete pools, coaching staff, leadership ranks, and talent pipelines. Demographic data should be complemented by qualitative insights into experiences of inclusion, belonging, and psychological safety. (Esposito. et al. 2025)

Inclusive recruitment and selection practices are critical to building diverse talent pipelines. Job descriptions, recruitment materials, and selection criteria should be reviewed for bias and framed to attract candidates from a wide range of backgrounds. Proactive outreach to underrepresented communities, (Grall. et al. 2025) partnerships with diverse educational institutions, and inclusive hiring panels help ensure that recruitment processes are equitable. Unconscious bias training for all individuals involved in selection decisions reduces the influence of stereotypes and promotes fair evaluation. Transparency in selection criteria and feedback mechanisms builds trust with candidates and supports continuous improvement. Equity in access to development opportunities is another best practice. Historically marginalized groups often face structural barriers to advancement—such as limited access to mentoring, coaching, high-performance pathways, or leadership development programs. Organizations must ensure that all athletes and staff have equitable access to these opportunities. Targeted development initiatives, sponsorship (as opposed to mere mentorship), and structured progression pathways help level the playing field. Organizations should also monitor participation rates and outcomes (Redondo-Duarte S. et al. 2025) to identify and address disparities. Creating psychologically safe environments is vital to supporting inclusion. Athletes, coaches, and staff must feel safe to express their identities, voice concerns, and contribute ideas without fear of discrimination or retaliation. Psychological safety fosters innovation, collaboration, and performance. Building such environments requires proactive leadership, open communication, and visible responses to instances of bias or exclusion. Training in cultural competence, inclusive leadership, and active bystander skills equips all members of the organization to contribute to a positive culture. Addressing systemic barriers and inequities is a central component of inclusive talent management. This involves critically examining and reforming organizational policies, structures, and practices that may inadvertently disadvantage certain groups. (Griesinger. et al. 2025) Organizations should engage with affected groups to understand barriers and co-create solutions. Addressing systemic issues moves inclusion beyond superficial representation to genuine equity.

CONCLUSION

The future of talent management in sports is poised to evolve in transformative ways, shaped by rapid technological advancements, shifting social expectations, globalization, and the growing emphasis on holistic athlete well-being. As the sporting landscape becomes more complex and interconnected, talent management strategies must adapt to meet the evolving needs of athletes, coaches, and organizations. No longer confined to traditional models focused solely on physical performance and competition outcomes, modern talent management will increasingly prioritize human-centered, inclusive, and sustainable approaches. It will also embrace data-driven personalization, lifelong development, and proactive transition planning. In short, the future of talent management in sports lies in creating environments where diverse individuals can thrive across all dimensions of life—athletic, personal, professional, and social. One of the most significant trends shaping the future is the integration of advanced technologies into talent management. Wearable sensors,

AI-powered analytics, biometric monitoring, virtual reality (VR), and augmented reality (AR) training tools are revolutionizing how athletes are recruited, developed, and supported. Real-time data on physical performance, recovery, and well-being enables hyper-personalized training programs that optimize individual progress while minimizing injury risk. AI-driven scouting and talent identification tools are expanding the reach and accuracy of talent pipelines. Virtual coaching environments and immersive learning platforms will make elite-level training accessible to a broader range of athletes, democratizing talent development. However, alongside these innovations, sports organizations must navigate challenges related to data privacy, ethics, and equitable access to technology—ensuring that technological advancements enhance rather than exacerbate existing inequalities. Another key direction is the growing emphasis on holistic athlete development and well-being. Future talent management models will move beyond a narrow focus on winning to prioritize the long-term mental, emotional, physical, and social health of athletes. Programs will integrate mental health support, life skills education, career planning, and identity development as core components of athlete pathways. Athlete-centered approaches that promote psychological safety, empowerment, and meaningful participation will become the standard. The emerging field of athlete-centered coaching—rooted in empathy, autonomy, and personal growth—will shape coaching philosophies and practices. Furthermore, sports organizations will increasingly recognize their ethical responsibility to prepare athletes for life beyond sport, embedding career transition planning into the fabric of talent management from an early stage.Diversity, equity, and inclusion (DEI) will play an even more central role in the future of talent management. As societal expectations around DEI continue to rise, sports organizations will face increasing pressure to address systemic barriers, promote equitable access, and build truly inclusive cultures. Future talent pipelines will reflect greater gender diversity, racial and cultural diversity, LGBTQ+ inclusion, and representation of athletes with disabilities. Intersectional approaches will ensure that the unique experiences and needs of all athletes are acknowledged and supported. Best practices in inclusive talent management—such as equitable recruitment, inclusive leadership development, and culturally competent coaching—will become non-negotiable elements of organizational success. Furthermore, sports organizations will need to engage authentically with the communities they serve, building trust and accountability through transparent action on DEI. Globalization will continue to reshape talent management. The cross-border movement of athletes, coaches, and expertise will accelerate, creating more diverse and dynamic sporting environments. Talent identification will expand beyond traditional geographic strongholds, leveraging global scouting networks, digital platforms, and international partnerships.

REFERENCES

Abid, K., & Polo, F. (2025). Narrative review on talent management: Evaluating two decades and exploring future research directions. *Journal of Global Mobility*, *13*(1), 1–31. DOI: 10.1108/JGM-07-2024-0076

Anlesinya, A., & Amponsah-Tawiah, K. (2020). Towards a responsible talent management model. *European Journal of Training and Development*, *44*(2/3), 279–303. DOI: 10.1108/EJTD-07-2019-0114

Avrillia, S., Hakim, L., Sulfia, S., & Anshori, M. I. (2025). Hybrid leadership and organizational performance: A literature review approach. *Implementasi Manajemen & Kewirausahaan*, *5*(1), 14–30. DOI: 10.38156/imka.v5i1.540

Baran, B. E., & Woznyj, H. M. (2020). Managing VUCA: The human dynamics of agility. *Organizational Dynamics*, •••, 100787. PMID: 32843777

Chib, S., Mehta, A. K., Saravanan, A., Mishra, B. R., & Manjunath, T. C. (2025). Mental Health Challenges and Solutions in High-Pressure Work Environments. In Harriott, S. (Ed.), *Innovative Approaches to Managing Conflict and Change in Diverse Work Environments* (pp. 247–272). IGI Global Scientific Publishing. DOI: 10.4018/979-8-3693-9556-1.ch011

Cooper, J. N., Newton, A. C., Klein, M., & Jolly, S. (2020). A call for culturally responsive transformational leadership in college sport: An anti-ism approach for achieving equity and inclusion. *Frontiers in Sociology*, *5*, 65. DOI: 10.3389/fsoc.2020.00065 PMID: 33869471

Esposito, G., De Bernardi, P., Bertello, A., & Vrontis, D. (2025). Value tensions and actionable knowledge in grassroots innovation: A study of invitational ambiguity and implementation challenges. *Journal of Knowledge Management*, *29*(2), 372–392. DOI: 10.1108/JKM-04-2024-0385

Gabrišová, I., Koman, G., Soviar, J., & Holubčík, M. (2025). The Adoption of Modern Sports Technologies from Professional Settings to Everyday Life. *Administrative Sciences*, *15*(7), 249. DOI: 10.3390/admsci15070249

Galanti, T., & Fantinelli, S. (2025). Managing the future of talents: Digital innovation in learning organizations. *The Learning Organization*, *32*(4), 554–580. DOI: 10.1108/TLO-06-2023-0096

Grall, M., Charue-Duboc, F., & BenMahmoud-Jouini, S. (2025). Bridging project management and design thinking: Evidence from digital transformation projects. *Project Management Journal*, *56*(3), 390–410. DOI: 10.1177/87569728251337426

Griesinger, A. N., Ehnold, P., Hoffmann, A., & Schlesinger, T. (2025). Integrating scientific recommendations for the development and promotion of junior elite athletes in Germany–an analysis of sports policy documents. *International journal of sport policy and politics, 17*(1), 61-79.

Hill, I., & Sallai, D. (2025). Diversity, Equity and Inclusion in Human Resource Management. *Diversity, Equity and Inclusion for Business & Management*, 91.

Holden, J., Wagstaff, C. R., Wadey, R., & Brown, P. (2025). Navigating athlete development in elite sport: Understanding the barriers to the provision of performance lifestyle service in England. *Psychology of Sport and Exercise*, *77*, 102779. DOI: 10.1016/j.psychsport.2024.102779 PMID: 39551251

Hubballi, R. B., Seenivasan, R., & Basava Aradhya, S. G., Dinesh, N., & Seelam, P. K. (2025). Overview of Current AI Technologies in Education. In L. Kyei-Blankson & E. Ntuli (Eds.), *Transformative AI Practices for Personalized Learning Strategies* (pp. 1-26). IGI Global Scientific Publishing.

Huyler, D., Gomez, L., Rocco, T. S., & Plakhotnik, M. S. (2025). Leading Different Generational Cohorts in the Workplace: Focus on Situational and Inclusive Leadership. *New Horizons in Adult Education and Human Resource Development*, *37*(1), 6–19. DOI: 10.1177/19394225241297230

Kaliannan, M., Darmalinggam, D., Dorasamy, M., & Abraham, M. (2023). Inclusive talent development as a key talent management approach: A systematic literature review. *Human Resource Management Review*, *33*(1), 100926. DOI: 10.1016/j.hrmr.2022.100926

Kotte, K. R., Attaluri, V., & Selvakumar, P. (2025). Revolutionising Retail Banking with AI and Virtual Technologies AI-Driven Financial Training. In Nair, A. J., Manohar, S., Limbu, Y. B., & Huhmann, B. A. (Eds.), *Intersecting Natural Language Processing and FinTech Innovations in Service Marketing* (pp. 421–440). IGI Global Scientific Publishing. DOI: 10.4018/979-8-3693-9944-6.ch020

Le Roy, J., Meier, O., & Paquier, M. C. (2025). Redefining employee performance in a VUCA World: Constructing a new typology–Positive deviant behavior. @. *GRH*, *54*(1), 11–37.

Maheswaran, K., Selvakumar, P., Shaikh, M., Shashank, G., Gupta, S., & Manjunath, T. C. (2025). The Evolution of Smart Urban Mobility With Emerging Technologies. In Ponnusamy, S., Assaf, M., Youssef, B., Jeon, G., & Kalyanaraman, S. (Eds.), *Leveraging VANETs and Blockchain Technology for Urban Mobility* (pp. 1–28). IGI Global Scientific Publishing. DOI: 10.4018/979-8-3373-0265-2.ch001

Mueller, M., & Kubatova, J. (2025). A systematic review of managerial burnout and personal crisis: Navigating the interplay of individual, organizational, and environmental factors. *German Journal of Human Resource Management*, 23970022251315650.

Nese, R. N., Nese, J. F., Santiago-Rosario, M. R., Izzard, S., Newson, A., Pimentel-Mannan, I., Lissman, D. C., Daza, T., Triplett, D., & Malose, S. (2025). Improving classroom engagement and reducing exclusionary discipline: A quasi-experimental study of the Inclusive Skill-Building Learning Approach during COVID-19. *Journal of Education, 205*(2), 114–129. DOI: 10.1177/00220574241309893

Purnomo, H., Soejoko, D. K. H., & Leksono, P. Y. (2025). RECENT TRENDS IN HUMAN RESOURCE MANAGEMENT IN THE DIGITAL AGE. *INTERNATIONAL JOURNAL OF FINANCIAL ECONOMICS, 2*(1), 159–172.

Raetze, S., Steputat-Raetze, A., Mueller, H., Maynard, M. T., & Schmutz, J. B. (2025). Teamwork under adversity: an integrative review and future research agenda. *Academy of Management Annals*, (ja), annals-2022.

Redondo-Duarte, S., & Santa-Marina, S. E. (2025). Empowering Students for Working in Culturally Rich and Psychologically Nourishing Work Environments. In *Developing Effective and High-Performing Teams in Higher Education* (pp. 57–88). IGI Global.

Sakthivel, M., Jaganathan, A., & Mohanraj, M. Mohit, & Manjunath, T. (2025). Brand Loyalty through AI and Personalisation AI-Generated Content for Financial Marketing. In A. J Nair, S. Manohar, Y. B. Limbu, & B. A. Huhmann (Eds.), *Intersecting Natural Language Processing and FinTech Innovations in Service Marketing* (pp. 77-96). IGI Global Scientific Publishing.

Samal, A., & Misra, L. I. Mohit, Pougajendy, S., Chandel, P. S., Manjunath, T. C., (2025). Musealization and Tourism Practices. In S. Oflazoğlu & M. Dora (Eds.), *Preserving Cultural Heritage in Post-Disaster Urban Renewal* (pp. 115-142). IGI Global Scientific Publishing.

Samuel, H. S., Etim, E. E., Nweke-Maraizu, U., & Okibe, G. (2025). Building Collaborative and Interdisciplinary Teams: Strategies for Effective Talent Management. In *Cultivating Creativity and Navigating Talent Management in Academia* (pp. 23-38). IGI Global Scientific Publishing.

Shollen, S. L., & Hanold, M. (2025). Game Changers: Leadership Lessons From Popular Sport Icons. *New Directions for Student Leadership, 2025*(185), 25–31. DOI: 10.1002/yd.20655 PMID: 40020219

Solomons, J., Bekker, S., Groom, R., & Kraak, W. (2025). Insights into coaching effectiveness: Perspectives from coaches and players in South African Women's Rugby. *International Journal of Sports Science & Coaching*, *20*(1), 8–21. DOI: 10.1177/17479541241283625

Soundariya, A., Behera, N. K., Chandel, P. S., Gupta, S., & Manjunath, T. C. (2025). AI and Environmental Ethics: The Role of AI in Addressing Climate Change Ethical Considerations in AI-Driven Environmental Solutions. In Chakraborty, S. (Ed.), *Human Values, Ethics, and Dignity in the Age of Artificial Intelligence* (pp. 321–346). IGI Global Scientific Publishing. DOI: 10.4018/979-8-3693-9035-1.ch013

Tahmasebi, R., & Nijs, S. (2024). A paradox perspective on talent management: A multi-level analysis of paradoxes and their responses in talent management. *International Journal of Human Resource Management*, *35*(3), 507–562. DOI: 10.1080/09585192.2023.2250261

Thirunagalingam, A., & Selvakumar, P. (2025). Application of Automation and Robotics in the Oil and Gas Industry. In Abdullayev, V., & Khang, A. (Eds.), *Revolutionizing AI and Robotics in the Oil and Gas Industry* (pp. 229–244). IGI Global Scientific Publishing. DOI: 10.4018/979-8-3693-8156-4.ch011

Tushabe, M., Kyambade, M., Namatovu, A., & Oyella, S. (2025). Advancing gender diversity in leadership: The role of work-life balance and gender participation in Ugandan public universities. *Cogent Social Sciences*, *11*(1), 2486553. DOI: 10.1080/23311886.2025.2486553

Upadhyaya, A. N., Debnath, P., Rani, P., Manjunath, T. C., & Bhattacharya, S. (2025). AI-Based Disaster Prediction and Early Warning Systems. In Mobo, F. (Ed.), *AI and Emerging Technologies for Emergency Response and Smart Cities* (pp. 55–74). IGI Global Scientific Publishing. DOI: 10.4018/979-8-3693-9770-1.ch003

Worley, C. G., & Jules, C. (2020). COVID-19's uncomfortable revelations about agile and sustainable organizations in a VUCA world. *The Journal of Applied Behavioral Science*, *56*(3), 279–283. DOI: 10.1177/0021886320936263

Ziegler, A., Naujoks-Schober, N., Vialle, W., & Stoeger, H. (2025). Analyzing National Talent Support Systems: The Case for a Resource-Oriented Approach. *Sustainability (Basel)*, *17*(13), 5896. DOI: 10.3390/su17135896

Chapter 9

Resilient Ethical Governance and Talent Well-Being in Hybrid, Sport, Family, Startup, and Ambiguous Ecosystems

Jose De Jesus Reyes-Sánchez
http://orcid.org/0000-0002-3866-2363
TECNM Instituto Tecnologico Superior De Fresnillo, Mexico

EXECUTIVE SUMMARY

This work integrates evidence and frameworks to articulate a resilient ethical governance that sustains performance and talent well-being in hybrid ecosystems where high-performance sports, family businesses and startups converge. The central thesis is that the decisive factor is not the workplace, but the alignment between purpose, coordination rules, metrics for results, and data safeguards, in order to protect dignity, agency, and psychological safety without sacrificing innovation. The analysis connects self-determination theory and demands-resources with stakeholder governance, proposing explainable analytics (dashboards, wearables), granular consent, traceability, and auditing. Integrity reforms and safeguarding protocols in sports, the operationalization of socio-emotional wealth in business families and social license in startups are discussed.

DOI: 10.4018/979-8-3373-5776-8.ch009

INTRODUCTION

Resilient ethical governance and talent well-being become strategic when sports organizations, family businesses, and startups operate with hybrid work and high public visibility, because distributed coordination reconfigures the relationship between results, integrity, and subjective work experience; in this scenario, institutional quality is expressed in the ability to translate values into verifiable rules, anchor trust in psychological safety practices, and maintain motivation through task designs and metrics consistent with the collective purpose (Edmondson & Bransby, 2023; Gagné et al., 2022). The shift towards hybrid modalities has shown differentiated effects on performance and retention according to the clarity of coordination rules, the competence of virtual leadership and the alignment between autonomy and evaluation by results; When work design specifies presences by purpose, verifiable standards, and learning paces, productivity is preserved without penalizing the choice to work remotely, while operational ambiguity fuels proximity biases and relational attrition (Bell et al., 2023; Gibbs et al., 2023).

In terms of collaboration, geographic distance and asynchrony restructure networks and information flows, so teams must combine face-to-face blocks for exploration with remote spans for execution, in addition to safeguards that maintain intergroup bridges and avoid network rigidity; Collective performance improves when shared sense is cultivated as an explicit practice of interpretation under uncertainty and transitions between tasks are managed with review routines that are understandable to all (Yang et al., 2022; Choudhury et al., 2021; Eckstein, 2024).

The expansion of people, board, and wearable analytics promises more informed decisions about burden, risk, and development, but also introduces dilemmas about purpose, proportionality, explainability, and consent; Organizational trust and social license depend on frameworks that combine independent bias audits, traceability understandable to non-technical audiences, and usability assessment, integrated with regulatory obligations that make algorithmic risk management demonstrable (Giermindl et al., 2022; Helminski et al., 2024).

In high-performance sport, the combination of immersive technologies, monitoring metrics and media exposure requires protocols that separate the functions of attention and discipline, delimit the uses and limits of biometric data and ensure independent reporting channels; Hybrid coordination in competitive calendars becomes sustainable when protection and performance coevolve under clear rules and forums with a true agency for athletes and support teams (Arzubiaga et al., 2021; Boers & Andersson, 2023).

In startups and platform economies, the pressure for rapid iterations and capital can normalize forms of control that shift judgment towards opaque systems, so responsible governance requires appeal mechanisms, pedagogical explanations and granular consent, in addition to public reflection on the social effects of algorithmic design; contemporary discussion on platform-mediated work, strategic ambiguity, and applied ethics offers tools to balance innovation, efficiency, and dignity (Raghavan et al., 2020; Harsin, 2024; Santoni de Sio & Mecacci, 2024).

In all the ecosystems analyzed, psychological safety is confirmed as an infrastructure for learning and error prevention, because it allows dissent without fear, requesting help and documenting decisions to review them with evidence; When articulated with clear objectives, role standards, and virtual leadership practices, it mitigates the costs of hybrid coordination and anchors procedural justice experiences that impact participation and retention (Cao et al., 2024; Helminski et al., 2024).

At the level of organizational capabilities, the combination of hybrid coordination, deliberate learning, and stakeholder governance requires maintaining meaning-making practices that integrate technical, narrative, and metric signals, and that avoid tactical oscillations under time pressure; This interpretive work is strengthened when it is institutionalized in reports after critical events and in explicit roles that safeguard the minority perspective, maintaining coherence between ends and means in visible environments (Choudhury et al., 2021; Beckel & Fisher, 2022).

STATEMENT OF THE PROBLEM

The underlying problem in hybrid ecosystems where high-performance sport, family businesses, and startups converge is not only adjusting where work gets done, but governing the interdependence between performance, integrity, and well-being when coordination is fragmented and asymmetries of power and visibility are amplified. In the absence of clear rules and fair procedures, climates of silence and attrition emerge that erode trust and cooperation, especially when performance judgment occurs at a distance and under time pressure (Edmondson & Bransby, 2023; Gibbs et al., 2023).

The growing reliance on people analytics, sensors, and management dashboards exposes risks of invasive surveillance, opacity, and distribution brains if purposes, thresholds, and appeals are not governed by clear standards. These environments need data traceability, technical and pedagogical explainability, and audits that prevent disproportionate use, in dialogue with regulatory frameworks such as the European AI Act. When the information that feeds into employment decisions does not become understandable and controversial, legitimacy falls and psychosocial health deteriorates; On the other hand, evidence-based transparency improves the acceptance and quality of human-machine judgment (Gagné et al., 2022). In sport, public visibility and the emotional density of bonds make it essential to translate safeguarding into operational protocols with care functions separate from the discipline and with secure reporting channels (Little, 2024; Ho et al., 2024; Chadwick, 2022).

The persistent ambiguity typical of hybrid agreements requires the construction of meaning to decide with incomplete information, protect voice, and maintain coordination between teams that alternate face-to-face exploration and remote execution. When networks become rigid and attention is fragmented, learning and repairing after mistakes fail; Therefore, the problem statement should incorporate psychosocial review and support routines, along with work designs that combine autonomy with relational anchors and verifiable standards of outcomes (Maitlis & Christianson, 2014; Eckstein, 2024; Choudhury et al., 2021; Kelloway et al., 2023).

Finally, the problem requires multi-criteria and integrated panels that assess technical results, equity and talent well-being, with explainability of models and usability evaluation for non-technical audiences. The absence of these devices turns disagreements into power disputes; their presence, on the other hand, facilitates justified and auditable decisions in contexts of high scrutiny and rapid technological iteration (Marín Díaz et al., 2023; Cao et al., 2024).

BACKGROUND

Genealogy of Ethical Governance in Sport, Family Business and Entrepreneurship

In recent years, a cross-sectoral genealogy of ethical governance has coalesced around the protection of individuals, organisational transparency and practical redress mechanisms in high-visibility arenas such as sports federations, multigenerational family businesses and venture-backed startups, reflecting broader shifts in corporate governance doctrine and AI accountability towards verifiable duty of care practices and explainability of decisions (Cheong, 2024). Integrity reforms in sport have shifted from punitive manuals to risk-based safeguarding and organisational learning, codifying operational definitions of interpersonal violence, independent reporting channels and explicit responsibilities for governing bodies to protect both minor and adult athletes (Tuakli-Wosornu et al., 2024; Tak et al., 2024).

In parallel, family businesses have strengthened the independence of ethics and governance bodies and linked reputational management to strong indicators of workplace well-being and psychological monitoring, while evidence links positive perceptions of employee responsibility programs to improved pride and outcomes when integrated into credible systems (Schaefer et al., 2024). Among startups, accountability commitments are increasingly appearing on performance dashboards that integrate psychosocial and diversity metrics alongside material ESG indicators, supported by emerging indicator frameworks tailored to early-stage companies (Ryan et al., 2024).

Overall, international casuistry has taken governance beyond mere legal compliance, towards risk-oriented and learning-oriented models that foster sustained cooperation between stakeholders with divergent interests and time horizons (Tuakli-Wosornu et al., 2024).

Integrity and Governance Reforms in Federations and Leagues With a Focus on Protecting People

Recent developments in sports integrity set higher duty of care thresholds, moving from general statements to enforceable guidelines with safe avenues for reporting, investigation criteria and explicit responsibilities of the regulatory body. The International Olympic Committee's consensus on interpersonal violence in sport standardizes, recommends independent reporting systems, and calls for coordination across clinical, legal, and management disciplines to ensure prevention and redress, thereby strengthening public trust and social license to operate (Cleary et al., 2019; Debicki et al., 2016). In parallel, the updated positions of medical academies have detailed the role of health personnel in early identification, care, and institutional advocacy, which accelerates the incorporation of reporting and learning procedures after critical events (Tuakli-Wosornu et al., 2024; Little, 2024).

Evolution of Codes of Conduct and Ethics Committees in Multigenerational Households

Family businesses have evolved from codes of conduct focused on intra-family trust to independent control structures, conflict management criteria and protection mandates that cover psychosocial risks, biases in decision-making and traceability of disciplinary processes. Recent studies underline that socio-emotional wealth, understood as a priority for continuity and reputation, becomes a lever for integrating standards of ethics and well-being when connected with purpose frameworks and non-financial performance metrics (Papagiannidis et al., 2025).

Emergence of Responsibility Commitments in Venture-Capital-Driven Startups

The recent entrepreneurial ecosystem is transitioning from informal principles to accountability commitments embedded in roadmaps and investor agreements, including well-being metrics, data governance, and cultural risk prevention. The lessons of reputational crises in technology platforms and on-demand services have underscored that legitimacy cannot be maintained without internal oversight structures, diversity in decision-making teams, and listening mechanisms for the user community and for staff. At the same time, regulations on AI and data in different jurisdictions have prompted startups to anticipate transparency, explainability, and impact assessment requirements, with implications for how products are experienced and scaled (Ho et al., 2024).

International Casuistry That Motivated Standards of Prevention and Reparation of Damage

The sequence of cases involving systemic omissions of protection in sport and cultural failures in technology companies showed that the absence of operational protocols, reliable registries and independent review bodies produces irreparable damage for individuals and organizations. From these experiences have emerged standards that require reporting pathways, psychosocial risk assessment frameworks, data governance audits, and redress mechanisms that include clinical care, compensation, and structural changes (Howcroft, 2025). Similarly, research on organizational legitimacy on digital platforms has documented that incomplete narratives and the concealment of critical practices deteriorate trust and precipitate regulatory and social reactions that affect business continuity (Little, 2024; Harsin, 2024; Tuakli-Wosornu et al., 2024).

Evolution of Remote Work and Hybrid Work in High-Performing Industries

The first waves of formal teleworking made it possible to measure changes in production, hours and coordination, with results showing increases in connected time and slight drops in productivity in some collaboration-intensive occupations, highlighting the role of communication architecture and fatigue in meetings. With the advancement of hybrid schemes, asynchronous coordination practices, digital coexistence rules, collaborative technologies, and focused presence calendars have become entrenched, reducing the cost of coordination and improving focus on deep cognitive tasks. In creative and product work, the combination of face-to-face blocks for exploration and remote sessions for execution has favored collective learning and review rituals that preserve autonomy, while satisfaction and retention assessments describe gains for profiles that value flexibility and time control (Beckel & Fisher, 2022).

Evidence on Retention, Satisfaction, and Career Mobility in Mixed Arrangements

Accumulating evidence indicates that mixed arrangements can improve satisfaction, work-life balance, and perception of autonomy, but that retention and mobility depend on deliberate mentoring practices, socialization, and performance visibility. When companies define clear presence rules based on their purpose, invest in asynchronous collaboration tools, and limit meeting saturation, better promotion trajectories and less attrition are observed, especially in groups facing costly care burdens and travel. Studies also show that proximity bias can mitigate these benefits if leaders lack training and if performance metrics are not transparent and comprehensive about task diversity (Dimoff, & Gilbert, 2023; McPhail & Fisher, 2024).

Consolidation of Psychological Safety in Teams With Public Visibility

Psychological safety has ceased to be a diffuse trait to consolidate itself as a condition that facilitates voice, learning and sustained performance in units with public exposure, from sports campuses to product teams in startups. Recent literature describes how post-critical event reporting improves learning in sensitive operations and reduces the impact of errors on staff well-being, translating clinical and emergency practices to corporate and sports contexts (Koopmann, Lin, & Cooper, 2024). The adoption of climate frameworks for psychosocial safety underscores the importance of clear rules for respectful treatment, workload and participation in decisions, which decreases silence and authority biases. In accelerated iteration cycles typical of tech companies, combining psychological safety with a focus on outcomes allows hypotheses to be explored without punitive fear and quickly corrected based on shared evidence. (Kelloway et al., 2023).

Post-Critical Event Review Practices in Sensitive Operations

Following clinical events or operational incidents, high-risk teams have institutionalized structured reviews that integrate root cause analysis, applicable lessons, and psychosocial support, with effects observed in a culture of safety, trust, and coordination. These practices have been adapted through guidelines that recommend combining on-the-course of review with post-review to maintain continuous learning and avoid the accumulation of emotional burdens. It has been observed that the quality of the report depends on competent facilitation, space neutrality, and documentation of improvement commitments, which in turn strengthens accountability without resulting in blame (Papagiannidis et al., 2025).

History of International Standards for Governance and Psychological Health

The emergence of governance and psychological health standards provides a common scaffolding for organizations of different natures. The Organisational Governance Standard emphasises purpose, value to stakeholders and effective governance control, while the guide for managing psychosocial risks offers practical recommendations for identifying risks, designing controls and measuring progress. The International Standards Board's Sustainability Disclosure Framework addresses materiality for investors and integrates labour and cultural risks, while multilateral bodies publish guidelines to protect and promote mental health at work (Howcroft, 2025). In parallel, the regulation of artificial intelligence in Europe defines the obligations of explainability, data governance, and impact assessment, which directly affect organizations that use people analysis systems and work assignment algorithms (Little, 2024; Harsin, 2024).

Recent History of People Analytics and Data Ethics at Work

People analytics went from descriptive reports to the adoption of predictive models, and from there to applications with explainability and traceability that allow auditable decisions to be made about selection, rotation, and development. This transition has sparked debates about informed consent, proportionality, and data minimization, as well as the need to incorporate principles of fairness and transparency to prevent indirect discrimination. Recent reviews warn of the risks of invasive surveillance, opacity, and displacement of professional judgment when delegated to opaque systems, and therefore recommend incorporating independent audits and participatory governance that integrates staff and their representatives (Giermindl et al., 2022).

Development of Explainability and Traceability Practices in Management Panels

Integrated dashboards have evolved into visualizations that combine financial, social, and occupational health metrics, with an emphasis on multi-criteria that facilitate collective decisions. In health, recent literature describes evaluations of the adoption and usability of dashboards and their impact on inequalities, while in technology management, multi-criteria decision-making approaches are proposed that allow the benefits, risks, and costs of adoption to be weighed against incomplete data (Gallifant et al., 2023). For people analytics, the advancement of technical and pedagogical explainability in turnover or absenteeism models favors the comprehensibility of the factors that drive decisions and allows the revision of assumptions by non-technical actors. These developments are increasingly necessary due to regulatory frameworks and societal expectations for transparency, making analytical maturity and quality of data governance strategic. (Helminski et al., 2024; Cao et al., 2024; Marín Díaz et al., 2023).

Emergence of Independent Audits to Mitigate Bias in Internal Algorithms

Internal and external algorithmic audits have become emerging practices to detect biases, errors and disproportionate uses of data in work contexts, with a particular focus on performance evaluation systems, productivity tracking and mobility recommendations. Recent studies on ethics and regulation of artificial intelligence point to traceability, explainability and governance obligations that require these audits to be professionalized and to establish clear responsibilities on the board of directors. Research on the impact of algorithmic systems on workers highlights the emotional effects of opacity and remote management, which is why they recommend internal codes with non-retaliation clauses and the participation of affected people in the design of safeguards (Newlands, 2021; Santoni de Sio & Mecacci, 2024).

Socio-Emotional Wealth and Its Effects on Family Business Decisions

Recent research shows that socio-emotional wealth (SEW) functions as a compass for continuity, control, and prestige in family businesses, and channels long-term sustainability and responsibility strategies beyond immediate financial horizons (Reina et al., 2023). These preferences shape fundamental decisions about succession, professionalization, and openness to external talent; Empirical work also links structured governance to greater resilience and social acceptance. Clear rules that balance affection with organizational discipline, as well as evaluation systems that recognize legacy without penalizing innovation, reduce intra-family conflicts, and support strategic renewal (Dayan et al., 2019; Li et al., 2023).

Wearable Technology and Biometric Metrics in Sport and Employment

A rapidly maturing evidence base shows that physiological sensors can estimate the risk of loading, fatigue and injury with increasing accuracy, but with modality-specific limitations: heart rate is usually accurate, step counts are often reliable, while energy expenditure and some contexts remain error-prone. Systematic reviews emphasize the need for validated devices, transparent error reporting, and protocols for consent, access, and governance, especially to mitigate bias and ensure equity in skin tones, age, and abilities (Canali et al., 2022). Immersive and extended reality (XR) tools are increasingly being used for load training and visualization; Meta-analytic evidence indicates that VR training can outperform conventional approaches on average, but effectiveness varies depending on task design and measurement rigor, so safeguards against overexposure, poor fit, and biased metrics are essential (Howard et al., 2021; Radianti et al., 2020).

In workplaces, regulators insist that health-related biometric and wearable data should be used for preventive and benefit-sharing programs, rather than punitive control. The UK ICO guidance calls for necessity/proportionality, data protection impact assessments, and transparency on data flows and access; in the U.S., the EEOC warns that the use of wearable device-derived biometrics in employment decisions may implicate the ADA and anti-discrimination laws, requiring accommodations and careful management. Together, these frameworks reinforce organizational duty of care, explainability of decisions, and fair remediation when harm occurs (Fuller et al., 2020; Zhang et al., 2020).

Interest-Oriented and Purpose-Oriented Government as the Axis of Legitimacy

Actor-oriented governance has strengthened its influence on strategy by providing mechanisms to solve problems of collective action in joint value creation. Recent contributions propose deliberative processes and value distribution mechanisms that maintain cooperation and trust between parties with heterogeneous objectives, in line with sustainability disclosure frameworks that demand coherence between financial risk and social materiality. This orientation translates into multi-criteria metrics that integrate the economic, social, and well-being performance of talent, and that reinforce legitimacy by demonstrating coherence between discourse and practice (Gómez-Mejía & Herrero, 2022).

Lessons From Reputational Crises in Tech Leagues and Companies

Analyses of failures by omission in athlete protection protocols and of cultural errors in technology companies have shown that the denial, opacity, and exclusive prioritization of growth metrics deteriorate legitimacy and create sustained risks of harm. Recent literature documents reform processes that include the strengthening of independent bodies, the diversification of boards of directors, new reporting avenues, and public commitments to measurable objectives (Little, 2024; Harsin, 2024). In the technology field, studies on the organizational legitimacy of platforms describe how the concealment of critical elements of the business model and the aggressive management of conflicts with regulators undermines trust and forces a rethink of narratives and structures. In both fields, honest communication, external audits, and the integration of learning into permanent policies are revealed as conditions for restoring cooperation and sustaining operations (Howcroft, 2025).

Organizational Ambiguity and Historical Strategies to Navigate it

Organizational ambiguity characterizes contexts in which signals are incomplete and where relevant information is collectively constructed through processes of shared meaning. Recent research on sense formation offers frameworks for alignmental interpretations and actions when goals are multiple and resources are limited, through structured conversations, prudent experimentation, and continuous review. In hybrid arrangements, the paradox between flexible schedules and the need for face-to-face cohesion is managed by coordination devices that allow decisions to be prioritized with partial information and clear rules (Turner et al., 2023).

THEORETICAL FRAMEWORK

Self-Determination Theory Applied to Distributed Coordination

The theory of self-determination serves as a structure to explain why teams operating in hybrid and distributed modalities are sustained by agreements that reinforce autonomy, competence and social bonding. In sports contexts with high public visibility, in family businesses where identity is inherited, and in startups with accelerated iteration rates, work design that grants meaningful choice over time and place favors the internalization of objectives, as long as there is clarity in the role and access to useful feedback (Eckstein, 2024). Recent evidence shows that practices that foster basic motivational needs in remote and virtual work are associated with stable performance and well-being, even as interdependence and technological uncertainty intensify. Flexible location decisions and work-from-anywhere arrangements, when volunteered and accompanied by close leadership, tend to maintain productivity and retention without impairing collaborative learning if bonds of belonging are fostered (Selivanovskikh et al., 2025).

Model of Labor Demands and Resources With a Focus on Tasks and Stations

The resource demands model states that people's loss and flourishing depend on the dynamic balance between demands and support. In hybrid and competitive ecosystems, that balance is seasonal and localized to tasks, with peaks before a competition, during an investment round, or at the end of a product sprint. Accurately managing cognitive, emotional, and temporal burdens requires mapping workflows by role, anticipating bottlenecks, and designing seasonally adjusted structural and social resources. Recent reviews of the theory show that sustained overload without recovery predicts burnout, while resources such as autonomy, learning, and team support activate motivational mechanisms that sustain performance. In hybrid regimes, the distribution of resources must take into account asynchronous coordination and the reduction of social signals, since remote work modifies collaboration networks and can rigidify information circuits (Yang et al., 2022; Bell et al., 2023)

Psychological Safety as a Basis for Learning and Repair

Psychological safety functions as an invisible infrastructure that allows respectful disagreement, difficult questions and requests for help, necessary conditions for learning and repairing mistakes made. In sports teams, technical teams, and product cells working in hybrid agreements, this security depends on explicit rules and leadership modeling, especially when the error is visible to external audiences (Edmondson & Bransby, 2023). Recent literature documents that psychological safety has matured into a category with established constructs, measures, and practices, and that its absence translates into organizational silences with costs in innovation, integrity, and mental health. Voice and silence reviews indicate that, in hierarchical systems, people filter what they say in the face of reputational and professional risks, which makes it crucial to create post-event review rituals that shift blame and focus on learning (Morrison, 2023; Bell et al., 2023).

Stakeholder-Centric Governance for Complex Decisions

Stakeholder-oriented governance provides a framework for decision-making when economic, sporting, family and social interests converge. This approach requires identifying communities affected by high-impact human impact decisions, establishing iterative negotiation procedures under constraints, and establishing prioritization criteria when objectives clash. At the level of principles, international standards place purpose, value generation, supervision, and accountability as pillars of good governance applicable to any organization, including clubs, federations, business families, and startups (Sandberg & Tsoukas, 2020; Christianson & Barton, 2021). Sustainability disclosure standards add guidelines on how to report on risks and opportunities that affect the ability to generate future flows, and require showing the relationship between governance and strategy in environmental and social matters (Raghavan et al., 2020).

Multiple Institutional Logics in Sport and Family Ecosystems

Sports ecosystems and family businesses operate under multiple institutional logics that coexist and are stressed. In sports, the rules of the game, tradition and the market coexist, while in the family business the affective, ownership and entrepreneurial logics are intertwined. Recent studies in sport management show how the agency of actors navigating institutions influences regulatory changes and responses to market and geopolitical pressures, while empirical reviews trace decades of research on institutional theory in the sector (Boers & Andersson, 2023). In family businesses, research on members acting as hybrid managing owners describes areas in which contradictory logics are balanced, from editorial decisions in family media to innovation investment strategies (Chadwick, 2022).

Theory of Meaning in Crises and Ambiguous Scenarios

Meaning theory explains how teams construct shared narratives to guide action under incomplete cues. In hybrid arrangements, ambiguity is amplified by asynchrony and technological mediation, which require meaning-making rituals that link performance to action. In prolonged crises, such as those experienced by sports and technology systems, recent studies emphasize that meaning-making is affected when attention resources are exhausted and sources of information are fragmented, so it is advisable to design pauses and relational reviews that articulate what is known, what is not known, and what will remain uncertain (Maitlis & Christianson, 2014).

Organizational and Procedural Fairness in Evaluation and Data

Organizational justice, and in particular procedural justice, is central to evaluating performance, allocating burdens, and making data-driven decisions in high-exposure contexts. The adoption of people analysis and algorithmic tools in the selection, promotion, and assignment of tasks complicates the task of explaining criteria, thresholds, and appeals. Recent research warns that automated systems in recruitment can perpetuate bias if they are not designed with safeguards from conception, and that the use of staff data without clarity of purpose, proportionality, and participation undermines trust (Giermindl et al., 2022; Avery et al., 2023)

Socio-Emotional Wealth and Psychological Contract in Business Families

In the family business, socio-emotional wealth includes the non-financial values linked to identity, continuity and control, and conditions the psychological contract between family and talent. Recent research shows heterogeneous configurations of this wealth and how they are connected to entrepreneurial orientation and to decisions about risk and innovation. Studies in emerging markets and in small and medium-sized family businesses suggest that socio-emotional wealth can drive proactivity and innovation when balanced with government professionalization, while its rigidity tends to elevate conservatism in critical decisions (Arzubiaga et al., 2021; Cambrea et al., 2022; Boers & Andersson, 2023)

Algorithmic Ethics for the Analysis of People With Real Impact

Algorithmic ethics applied to talent management require data traceability, documentation of automated decisions, and independent technical and social audits. In people analytics, risks include indirect bias, measurement errors, and overappropriation of sensitive data. Recent literature proposes frameworks to mitigate bias in procurement systems and underlines the duty of granular consent, minimisation and proportionality, as well as clear limits on secondary reuse. Regulatory reviews and frameworks also recommend independence in audits, disclosure of modeling assumptions, and stakeholder participation in the design of management panels (Raghavan et al., 2020; Giermindl et al., 2022).

Dynamic Capabilities to Orchestrate Hybrid Mode

The effective orchestration of hybrid work can be read from dynamic capabilities, understood as the ability to detect opportunities and threats, take advantage of them and reconfigure assets. In sports, family, and entrepreneurial settings, this perspective helps structure practice portfolios that balance exploration and exploitation, with rapid redesigns based on product phase, competitive calendar, or capital cycle. The strategic literature underscores that environment sensing and reconfiguration are critical management tasks to maintain advantages in turbulent markets (Teece, 2016; Bell et al., 2023; Yang et al., 2022).

Responsible Leadership Oriented to the Care of Talent

Responsible leadership integrates purpose with performance and well-being metrics, ensures dignity in demanding cycles, and makes value-based decisions when there is pressure to deliver. Recent evidence shows that leadership has an impact on the mental health of staff and can become a buffer against psychosocial risks if they practice active listening, boundary recognition and load adjustment. In virtuality and hybrid arrangements, specific behaviors are recommended that include establishing human contact routines, clarifying availability and boundaries, and recognizing invisible work that occurs outside of synchronous channels (Kelloway et al., 2023; Bell et al., 2023).

CHALLENGES FACED BY ORGANIZATIONS OR INSTITUTIONS

In hybrid ecosystems that combine professional sports, family businesses, and tech entrepreneurship, organizations face simultaneous tensions of coordination, legitimacy, and attention to talent. What is decisive is not to list obstacles, but to translate them into clear operational needs: norms anchored in the task, psychosocial safeguards, ethical data and verifiable and purposeful governance. What follows identifies these needs and supports them with the evidence and frameworks already present in the base document.

The design needs of hybrid work begin by anchoring presence and distance to the nature of the task, with explicit coordination rules that reduce synchronization costs and protect development paths. Experimental and quasi-experimental evidence shows that clear agreements on remote days, outcome-focused metrics, and learning rituals can sustain performance and reduce turnover, provided that leadership masters virtual collaboration and outcomes management practices, and that effects on productivity and cooperative networks are monitored (Choudhury et al., 2021).

For hybrids to be sustainable, organizations must protect recovery times, define coordination cadences, and establish availability limits that reduce fatigue and defensive microhandling. Psychosocial health requires proportional norms and controls aligned with international guidelines, as well as climates that allow voice and the request for help without reprisals. Integrating these requirements involves training leaders in caring behaviors, institutionalizing post-critical event reviews, and measuring overload risks as part of the board's dashboard. (Beckel & Fisher, 2022; ISO 45003, 2021; Edmondson, 2023).

Procedural fairness in assessment and data requires explaining criteria, thresholds, and avenues of appeal when using people analytics and algorithmic systems. Explainability and auditing practices are needed to avoid bias in hiring, performance, and promotion, along with guarantees of proportionality, minimization, and informed consent (Raghavan et al., 2020; Giermindl et al., 2022; Avery et al., 2023).

When wearable and biometric technologies are incorporated into sport and employment, the primary need is granular, understandable and revocable consent, with transparency in purposes, thresholds and secondary use; In addition, veto rights and participation of athletes and collaborators in the design of the system (Tuakli-Wosornu et al., 2024; Little, 2024; Le Noury, Patel, Beaven, & Driller, 2022).

In ecosystems with high public scrutiny, legitimacy depends on stakeholder-oriented governance that connects purpose and value creation with verifiable commitments. Organizations need deliberative processes that distribute benefits and risks, as well as disclosure frameworks that reveal how the strategy addresses relevant societal issues (Ho et al., 2024).

Family businesses, traversed by socio-emotional wealth, need governance rules that balance continuity with openness and merit, avoiding favoritism and silences that hinder innovation and voice. This translates into deliberative forums that legitimize dissent, transparent criteria for promotion and professionalization of committees with effective independence. These measures connect identity and reputation to long-term decisions and attract non-family talent without eroding shared purpose. (Arzubiaga et al., 2021; Berrone, Cruz, & Gómez-Mejía, 2012;).

In ambiguous and volatile contexts, meaning management demands rituals of collective interpretation and updated role maps that transform weak signals into coordinated actions. Organizations need structured pauses, honest narratives about what is known and what is uncertain, and reports that turn surprises into learning. These sense-making capabilities must be combined with a continuous assessment of assumptions and the accessibility of critical information to tactical decision-makers. (Maitlis & Christianson, 2014).

Governing with data without losing legitimacy requires dashboards that integrate financial results with indicators of occupational health, equity, and well-being, along with explainability and traceability practices understandable to non-specialists. In addition, it is necessary to monitor distributional impacts with disparity instruments and evaluate the adoption and usability of the panels in clinical and occupational contexts. In people analysis, explainability favors acceptance and improves combined human-machine judgment. (Cao et al., 2024).

EXAMPLES OF IMPLEMENTATION IN COMPANIES OR ORGANIZATIONS

Microsoft redesigned coordination routines after observing that fully remote work made internal collaboration networks more static and isolated. The answer was to reduce redundant meetings, reinforce asynchronous documentation, protect concentration blocks and train managers in virtual leadership, practices consistent with the evidence on management competencies in distributed environments and with voice and silence frameworks that avoid penalizing autonomy when performance is evaluated by results. (Yang et al., 2022; Morrison, 2023).

Trip.com a randomized controlled trial of hybrid work was applied with face-to-face days for exploration and social bonding, and remote days for execution, measuring productivity, satisfaction and turnover. The results showed stabilization of performance and reduction of voluntary departures, with differential effects according to distance of travel and gender, provided that the objectives were clear and the evaluation focused on the results. Evidence supports the training of middle managers to coordinate hybrid interdependencies and anchor work design in basic psychological needs (Bloom et al., 2024).

The International Olympic Committee issued a consensus on protection against interpersonal violence that national federations took as the basis for independent reporting, informed consent and separation of responsibilities and disciplines protocols. High-performance centers also incorporated extended reality for technical training under criteria of data use and ethical evaluations (Tuakli-Wosornu et al., 2024; Edmondson & Bransby, 2023; Little, 2024)

Uber in Paris faced regulatory and social tensions that made visible the need for explainable algorithmic governance and appeals for automated decisions. On work platforms, algorithmic monitoring and opaque allocation can shift risk to the margins, so audits and disparity dashboards help monitor effects by groups and document critical business model assumptions with a focus on stakeholders and procedural fairness. (Harsin, 2024; Raghavan et al., 2020).

The U.S. Patent and Trademark Office demonstrated that a work-from-anywhere regime can sustain or increase productivity when verifiable tasks and goals are redesigned, interdependence is regulated, and self-determination is supported without eroding accountability for results. This pattern offers a replicable template for public administrations and professional services firms by articulating autonomy with performance metrics and virtual leadership. (Bell et al., 2023; Morrison, 2023)

RESULTS

Comparative results indicate that hybrid arrangements with clear coordination rules, competent virtual leadership, outcome-focused metrics, and learning rituals preserve productivity and stabilize retention, as long as coordination costs are mitigated and occupational health is covered. The dominant pattern is that satisfaction and permanence improve when autonomy is accompanied by clarity in the role and psychosocial support, avoiding penalties in visibility and career for opting for mixed schemes. This effect is manifested more intensely in knowledge work and in product cells that alternate face-to-face exploration and remote execution (Bell et al., 2023; Beckel & Fisher, 2022).

In contrast by ecosystem, high-performance sport stands out for the centrality of protection and reparation, where recent consensuses specify definitions, reporting pathways, and separation of care and discipline functions. Startups have tensions between speed of delivery and procedural fairness, which are cushioned when governance is stakeholder-oriented and decision-making assumptions are transparent. Family businesses turn socio-emotional wealth into an advantage when they professionalize their deliberative forums and clarify merit criteria, which reduces favoritism and maintains intergenerational legitimacy (Tuakli-Wosornu et al., 2024; Boers & Andersson, 2023; Ho et al., 2024). In all contexts, voice and learning indicators improve when psychological safety is consolidated with explicit treatment rules and post-critical event reporting.

The use of people analytics and integrated dashboards produces better decisions when technical and pedagogical explainability allows non-specialists to understand the factors that guide predictions, auditing biases and monitoring disparities by group. Organizations that incorporate dashboard evaluation frameworks and eliminate variables with unintended correlations increase trust and engagement, especially when managing mobility and performance in hybrid cycles. The literature warns that, without proportional traceability and consent, the risks of invasive surveillance and inequitable decisions increase (Giermindl et al., 2022).

Regulation and social license emerge as conditions of possibility for scaling technology at work. The European Artificial Intelligence Act sets out documentation and risk management obligations that translate into better data governance practices. Organizations obtain sustained cooperation when they show coherence between purpose and social effects, especially in markets that react to the precariousness and asymmetries introduced by allocation platforms and algorithms. Opaque surveillance reduces trust and precipitates regulatory responses that affect business continuity. In collaborative networks, bulk remote strengthens connections and reduces intergroup exploration, so results are superior when bridges are protected and synchronous meetings are limited. Work-from-anywhere regimes maintain or increase productivity by redesigning verifiable tasks and standards, as long as the assessment is results-based and virtual leadership competencies are formed (Yang et al., 2022; McPhail & Fisher, 2024).

In sport, the responsible adoption of wearable technologies and immersive environments improves training and prevention as long as there are explicit purposes, thresholds of use and granular consent with separation between care and discipline. The active defense of athletes and the training of medical and technical teams in psychological safety increase confidence and facilitate early notification, reducing critical events and organizational recovery times. The most legitimate cases share documentation of decisions and independent review mechanisms (Tuakli-Wosornu et al., 2024; Little, 2024).

CONCLUSIONS

To conclude, integrated evidence confirms that sustainable performance in hybrid ecosystems with high public exposure depends less on where the work is done and more on how the interdependence between outcomes, integrity, and talent well-being is governed. This requires translating purpose into verifiable norms, protecting voice and psychological safety, and subjecting people analytics to standards of explainability, traceability, and reparation, especially in high-performance sports, family businesses, and startups that are experiencing accelerated rates of iteration (Edmondson & Bransby, 2023; Tuakli-Wosornu et al., 2024). Qualitative findings show a strong pattern: hybrid arrangements preserve productivity and stabilize retention when there are clear rules of coordination by task, competent virtual leadership, outcome-focused metrics, and learning rituals that legitimize disagreement and asking for help; Performance suffers when asynchrony stiffens networks and physical proximity becomes an evaluation bias. Adherence to these principles is especially fertile in knowledge product and work cells, where the combination of face-to-face blocks for exploration and remote sections for execution harmonizes autonomy with belonging (Beckel & Fisher, 2022).

The legitimacy of the use of labor and wearable data depends on a non-negotiable triangle: explicit and proportional purpose, technical and pedagogical explainability understandable to non-specialists, and independent audits that allow for the correction of biases and the documentation of decisions. Organizations that combine integrated dashboards with usability evaluation and group disparity monitoring increase the acceptance and quality of human-machine judgment; the absence of traceability precipitates perceptions of surveillance and regulatory responses (Giermindl et al., 2022; Gallifant et al., 2023; Helminski et al., 2024). In high-performance sport, protection requires operational protocols with independent reporting channels, separation between care and discipline, detailed consent and limits on the secondary use of biometric data; When this is true, trust and cooperation between athletes, medical teams and coaches increases. In startups, social licensing is based on stakeholder-oriented governance and transparency about decision assumptions; In family businesses, socio-emotional wealth is activated when deliberative forums are professionalized and merit criteria are established that avoid favoritism (Avery et al., 2023; Newlands, 2021; Howcroft, 2025).

Procedural justice emerges as a condition of possibility to evaluate performance and make decisions with the support of algorithms: explaining criteria and thresholds, enabling channels of appeal without reprisals, minimizing and segmenting consents, and involving affected groups in the design of safeguards. When these norms are installed, defensive silences decrease and the perception of fairness increases, with effects on motivation and retention; where they are lacking, opacity generates moral damage and public dispute (Raghavan et al., 2020).

Mental safety ceases to be a diffuse ideal to function as a learning infrastructure: reports after critical events, explicit rules of treatment and leadership that models competent vulnerability. This infrastructure cushions the ambiguity of hybrid coordination and facilitates collective meaning-making in cycles of time pressure, allowing for rapid correction without punitiveness and sustaining development trajectories even with high scrutiny (Edmondson & Bransby, 2023; Maitlis & Christianson, 2014; Morrison, 2023).

In summary, the resilient ethical governance that these ecosystems demand takes the form of three complementary movements: institutionalizing interactive safeguards in people analytics and wearable technology; install learning and repair routines that protect the minority voice and avoid blame; and align purpose with integrated metrics under the effective oversight of the regulatory body. This tripod turns trust into a verifiable attribute and creates the conditions for innovation and dignity to coexist in high-visibility contexts (Lepri et al., 2018; Tuakli-Wosornu et al., 2024).

RECOMMENDATIONS FOR FUTURE RESEARCH

Prioritize designs that identify causal effects of hybrid work on performance, innovation, and retention through field experiments, random assignment of face-to-face days by purpose, and models with interaction between tasks and asynchronous coordination, comparing product cells, sports units, and family businesses; It complements with network analysis to map proximity dependency and its bias in performance evaluation.

To develop validated instruments in Spanish to measure psychological safety, voice and mental load in contexts of high public exposure and fluctuating demand, with scales sensitive to distributed coordination and the combination of human and algorithmic evaluation; integrate experience journals and critical post-event reports with longitudinal analyses to capture learning and repair processes (Edmondson & Bransby, 2023; Maitlis & Christianson, 2014).

Build assessment frameworks for people analytics and integrated dashboards that combine understandable technical explainability for non-specialist audiences, bias audits with pool capital metrics, and usability testing in real talent decisions, documenting traceability and granular consent in line with the requirements of the European Artificial Intelligence Act.

Evaluate protection protocols in high-performance sports that separate care and discipline functions and define limits of use of immersive and biometric technologies, with implementation analyses that measure confidence, propensity to report, and organizational repair times, comparing disciplines, competition levels, and hybrid training arrangements (Tuakli-Wosornu, Mountjoy, Budgett, et al., 2024; Little, 2024; Dowling et al., 2024).

Analyze how socio-emotional wealth is operationalized in merit rules, deliberative forums, and non-financial metrics in family businesses, and under what conditions such wealth is aligned with stakeholder governance and transparency in succession and mobility decisions, avoiding favoritism and preserving intergenerational legitimacy.

To study the interaction between algorithmic governance, platform economies and social license, incorporating geopolitical tensions and information asymmetries in the distribution of risks and benefits; It combines institutional analysis with technical audits and consent frameworks, including instability scenarios and effective appeal mechanisms.

Compare multi-criteria methods for prioritizing decisions with human and technical effects, assessing their impact on transparency, understandability, and acceptance by diverse groups; It measures how panel design and stakeholder engagement modify distributional commitments and outcomes in occupational health, equity, and performance.

Explore how collaboration is reorganized with remote and work-from-anywhere arrangements, using ethical telemetry and network analysis to identify intergroup bridges, structural rigidity, and proximity effects, and design intentional presences that balance face-to-face exploration with distributed execution (Yang et al., 2022; Choudhury et al., 2021; Beckel & Fisher, 2022).

Deepen the theory and practice of meaning-making in environments of persistent ambiguity, combining digital ethnographies, episodic interviews, and decision analysis to understand how data translates into action and how coherence between ends and means is preserved in cycles of time pressure (Eckstein, 2024; Turner et al., 2023; Sandberg & Tsoukas, 2020; Christianson & Barton, 2021).

REFERENCES

Arzubiaga, U., Iturralde, T., Maseda, A., & Kotlar, J. (2021). Big Data in Family Businesses: A Socio-Emotional Perspective on Wealth. *European Management Journal, 39*(3), 308–321. DOI: 10.1016/j.emj.2020.10.006

Avery, D. R., Hall, A. V., Preston, M., Ruggs, E. N., & Washington, E. (2023). Is justice colorblind? A review of rational-ethnic differences in the workplace through the prism of organizational justice. *Annual Review of Organizational Psychology and Organizational Behavior, 10*, 389–412. DOI: 10.1146/annurev-orgpsych-120920-052627

Beckel, J. L., & Fisher, G. G. (2022). Teleworking and occupational health and well-being. *International Journal of Environmental Research and Public Health, 19*(7), 3879. DOI: 10.3390/ijerph19073879 PMID: 35409563

Bell, B. S., McAlpine, K. L., & Hill, N. S. (2023). Leading virtually. *Annual Review of Organizational Psychology and Organizational Behavior, 10*(1), 339–362. DOI: 10.1146/annurev-orgpsych-120920-050115

Bloom, N., Han, R., & Liang, J. (2024). Hybrid work from home improves retention without hurting performance. *Nature, 630*(8018), 920–925. DOI: 10.1038/s41586-024-07500-2 PMID: 38867040

Boers, B., & Andersson, T. (2023). Family members as hybrid owners and managers in family recurring businesses: Managing multiple institutional logics. *Journal of Family Business Management, 13*(2), 523–543. DOI: 10.1108/JFBM-06-2021-0065

Canali, S., Porcheron, M., & Lucivero, F. (2022). Challenges and recommendations for wearable devices in digital health: Data quality, interoperability, health equity, equity. *PLOS Digital Health, 1*(10), e0000104. DOI: 10.1371/journal.pdig.0000104 PMID: 36812619

Cao, B., Hamamoto, Y., Wang, Y., & Zhang, H. (2024). A new integrated approach to preliminary and multi-criteria decision-making. *PeerJ Informática, 10*, e2096. DOI: 10.7717/peerj-cs.2096 PMID: 38983217

Chadwick, S. (2022). From utilitarianism and neoclassical management of sport to a new geopolitical economy of sport. *European Sport Management Quarterly, 22*(5), 685–704. DOI: 10.1080/16184742.2022.2032251

Cheong, B. C. (2024). Transparency and Accountability in AI Systems: Safeguarding Well-Being in the Age of Algorithmic Decision-Making. *Frontiers in Human Dynamics*. https://doi.org/DOI: 10.3389/fhumd.2024.1421273

Choudhury, P., Foroughi, C., & Larson, B. Z. (2021). Working from anywhere: The productivity effects of geographic flexibility. *Strategic Management Journal*, *42*(4), 655–683. DOI: 10.1002/smj.3251

Christianson, M. K., & Barton, M. A. (2021). Understanding in times of COVID-19. *Journal of Management Studies*, *58*(2), 572–576. DOI: 10.1111/joms.12658

Cleary, P., Quinn, M., Moreno, A., & Marqués, P. (2019). Organisational legitimacy, sustainability reporting and print management in a resource-constrained environment. *Journal of Family Business Strategy*, *10*(2), 100229. DOI: 10.1016/j.jfbs.2018.11.002

Dayan, M., Ng, P. Y., & Ndubisi, N. O. (2019). Mindfulness, socio-emotional richness and environmental strategy of family businesses. *Business Strategy and the Environment*, *28*(3), 466–481. DOI: 10.1002/bse.2222

Debicki, B. J., Kellermanns, F. W., Chrisman, J. J., Pearson, A. W., & Spencer, B. A. (2016). Development of a Socio-Emotional Importance of Wealth (SEWi) Scale for Research in Family Businesses. *Journal of Family Business Strategy*, *7*(1), 47–57. DOI: 10.1016/j.jfbs.2016.01.002

Dowling, M., Robertson, J., Washington, M., Leopkey, B., & Ellis, D. (2024). Agency and institutions in sport. *European Sport Management Quarterly*, *24*(1), 1–7. DOI: 10.1080/16184742.2023.2292102

Eckstein, G. (2024). Thirty-five years of business and management sense. *Business Research*, *17*, 555–577. DOI: 10.1007/s11301-024-00458-5

Edmondson, A. C., & Bransby, D. P. (2023). Psychological safety comes of age: Themes observed in an established literature. *Annual Review of Organizational Psychology and Organizational Behavior*, *10*(1), 55–78. DOI: 10.1146/annurev-orgpsych-120920-055217

Fuller, D., Colwell, E., Low, J., Orychock, K., Tobin, M. A., Simango, B., & Buote, R. (2020). Reliability and Validity of Commercially Available Wearable Devices for Measuring Steps, Energy Expenditure, and Heart Rate: A Systematic Review. *JMIR mHealth and uHealth*, *8*(9), e18694. DOI: 10.2196/18694 PMID: 32897239

Gagné, M., Parker, S. K., Griffin, M. A., Dunlop, P. D., Knight, C., Klonek, F. E., & Parent Rocheleau, X. (2022). Understand and shape the future of work with self-determination theory. *Nature Reviews Psychology*, *1*(7), 378–392. DOI: 10.1038/s44159-022-00056-w PMID: 35574235

Gallifant, J., Kistler, E. A., Nakayama, L. F., Ntatin, A., Fernandez, L., Zera, C., Bates, D., Dankwa-Mullan, I., & Celi, L. A. (2023). Disparity Panels An evaluation of the literature and framework for improving health equity. *The Lancet. Digital Health, 5*(11), e831–e839. DOI: 10.1016/S2589-7500(23)00150-4 PMID: 37890905

Gibbs, M., Mengel, F., & Siemroth, C. (2023). Working from home and productivity. *Journal of Microeconomic Political Economy, 1*(1), 7–54. DOI: 10.1086/721803

Giermindl, L. M., Strich, F., Christ, O., Leicht-Deobald, U., & Redzepi, A. (2022). The dark sides of people analytics. *European Journal of Information Systems, 31*(3), 410–435. DOI: 10.1080/0960085X.2021.1927213

Gómez-Mejía, L. R., & Herrero, I. (2022). Going back to the starting point: The measure of socio-emotional wealth. *Journal of Family Business Strategy, 13*(3), 100480. DOI: 10.1016/j.jfbs.2021.100480

Harsin, J. (2024). Taxis against Uber in Paris, technological capital and collaborative economy. *Labor History, 65*(6), 784–800. DOI: 10.1080/0023656X.2024.2327461

Helminski, D., Sussman, J. B., Pfeiffer, P. N., Kokaly, A. N., Ranusch, A., Renji, A. D., Damschroder, L. J., Landis-Lewis, Z., & Kurlander, J. E. (2024). Development, implementation, and evaluation methods for health care panels. Review of scope. *JMIR Medical Informatics, 12*, e59828. DOI: 10.2196/59828 PMID: 39656991

Ho, S. S. H., Mishra, A., & Kim, P. H. (2024). Can corporate social responsibility lead to social freedom to operate? *Journal of Management Studies, 61*(5), 1202–1231. DOI: 10.1111/joms.12863

Howard, M. C., Gutworth, M. B., & Jacobs, R. R. (2021). A meta-analysis of virtual reality training programs. *Computers in Human Behavior, 121*, 106808. DOI: 10.1016/j.chb.2021.106808

Howcroft, D., & Leaver, A. (2025). Unstable platforms. *Accounting Forum, 49*(1), 1–23. DOI: 10.1080/01559982.2024.2309018

Kelloway, E. K., Dimoff, J. K., & Gilbert, S. (2023). Mental health at work. *Annual Review of Organizational Psychology and Organizational Behavior, 10*(1), 363–387. DOI: 10.1146/annurev-orgpsych-120920-050527

Li, J., Wang, Y., Yao, N. C., & Cui, X. (2023). Exploring the effects of socio-emotional wealth on the environmental strategies of family businesses in China: An integrative perspective. *Business Strategy and the Environment, 32*(8), 5368–5381. DOI: 10.1002/bse.3425

Little, K. (2024). Defence of athletes. *Journal of Physical Education, Recreation & Dance, 95*(9), 34–41. DOI: 10.1080/00913847.2024.2440821 PMID: 39648878

Maitlis, S., & Christianson, M. (2014). Understanding it in organizations: Taking stock and moving forward. *The Academy of Management Annals, 8*(1), 57–125. DOI: 10.5465/19416520.2014.873177

Marín Díaz, G., Gómez Ruiz, I., García-Villena, R., & Palazón, M. (2023). Analyze employee turnover using explainable AI. *Mathematics, 11*(22), 4677. DOI: 10.3390/math11224677

McPhail, R., & Fisher, R. (2024). Remote work after the pandemic and its impact. *International Journal of Human Resource Management, 35*(9), 1721–1750. DOI: 10.1080/09585192.2023.2221385

Morrison, E. W. (2023). Voice and silence of employees, taking stock, living with dualities and moving forward. *Annual Review of Organizational Psychology and Organizational Behavior, 10*, 79–107. DOI: 10.1146/annurev-orgpsych-120920-054654

Newlands, G. (2021). Algorithmic surveillance in the collaborative economy: The organization of work through space conceived by Lefebvri. *Organization, 28*(1), 74–95. DOI: 10.1177/0170840620937900

Papagiannidis, E., Mikalef, P., & Conboy, K. (2025). Responsible governance of artificial intelligence: A framework for review and research. *The Journal of Strategic Information Systems, 34*(2), 101885. DOI: 10.1016/j.jsis.2024.101885

Radianti, J., Majchrzak, T. A., Fromm, J., & Wohlgenannt, I. (2020). A systematic review of immersive virtual reality applications for higher education: Design elements, lessons learned, and research agenda. *Computers & Education, 147*, 103778. DOI: 10.1016/j.compedu.2019.103778

Raghavan, M., Barocas, S., Kleinberg, J., & Levy, K. (2020). Mitigating Bias in Algorithmic Recruitment: Evaluating Claims and Practices. *2020 Conference Proceedings on Fairness, Accountability, and Transparency*, 469–481. https://doi.org/ DOI: 10.1145/3351095.3372828

Reina, W., Pla-Barber, J., & Villar, C. (2023). Socio-emotional richness in family business research: A systematic review of the literature on its definition, roles, and dimensions. *European Management Journal, 41*(6), 1000–1020. DOI: 10.1016/j.emj.2022.10.009

Ryan, M., Popa, E., Blok, V., & IJsselsteijn, W. (2024). Start doing the right thing: Indicators for socially responsible start-ups and investors. *Journal of Responsible Technology, 20*, 100094. DOI: 10.1016/j.jrt.2024.100094

Sandberg, J., & Tsoukas, H. (2020). Reconsideration of the understanding of meaning: Towards a broader understanding through phenomenology. *Theory of Organization, 1*(1), 1–34. DOI: 10.1177/2631787719879937

Santoni de Sio, F., & Mecacci, G. (2024). Artificial intelligence and the future of work. *The Journal of Ethics, 28*(3), 1–25. DOI: 10.1007/s10892-024-09493-6

Schaefer, S. D., Cunningham, P., Diehl, S., & Terlutter, R. (2024). Employees' positive perception of corporate social responsibility generates beneficial results for companies and their employees: Organizational pride as a mediator. *Corporate Social Responsibility and Environmental Management, 31*(3), 2574–2587. DOI: 10.1002/csr.2699

Selivanovskikh, L., Maltseva, E., & Isada, F. (2025). Strategic ambiguity. *Management Decision, 63*(2), 345–372. DOI: 10.1108/MD-05-2024-1021

Tak, M., Deutsch, R., Kavanaugh, E., Lynch, M., & Tuakli-Wosornu, Y. A. (2024). Secure Sports Reporting Systems: A Qualitative Study of How Athletes Navigate Notification. *Journal of Global Sports Management.* https://doi.org/DOI: 10.1080/19406940.2024.2323011

Teece, D. J. (2016). Dynamic Capacities and Entrepreneurial Management in Large Organizations: Towards a Theory of the Entrepreneurial Firm. *European Economic Review, 86*, 202–216. DOI: 10.1016/j.euroecorev.2015.11.006

Tuakli-Wosornu, S., Mountjoy, M., & Budgett, R.. (2024). IOC Consensus on Interpersonal Violence Against Athletes. *British Journal of Sports Medicine, 58*(9), 506–520. DOI: 10.1136/bjsports-2024-108766 PMID: 39586634

Tuakli-Wosornu, Y. A., Burrows, K., Fasting, K., Hartill, M., Hodge, K., Kaufman, K., & Rhind, D. J. A. (2024). IOC Consensus Statement: Interpersonal Violence and Protection in Sport. *British Journal of Sports Medicine, 58*(22), 1322–1344. DOI: 10.1136/bjsports-2024-108766 PMID: 39586634

Turner, J. R., Gray, B., & Bishop, W. (2023). The multifaceted theory of the formation of meaning. *Sistemas, 11*(3), 145. DOI: 10.3390/systems11030145

Yang, L., Holtz, D., Jaffe, S., Suri, S., Sinha, S., Weston, J., Joyce, C., Shah, N., Sherman, K., Hecht, B., & Teevan, J. (2022). The effects of remote work on collaboration among information workers. *Nature Human Behaviour, 6*(1), 43–54. DOI: 10.1038/s41562-021-01196-4 PMID: 34504299

Zhang, Y., Weaver, R. G., Armstrong, B., Burkart, S., Zhang, S., & Beets, M. W. (2020). Validity of wrist-based photoplethysmography devices for measuring heart rate: A systematic review and meta-analysis. *Journal of Sports Sciences*, *38*(17), 1939–1947. DOI: 10.1080/02640414.2020.1767348 PMID: 32552580

Chapter 10
Rethinking Performance Management in a Hybrid World

A. Rahmath Nisha
http://orcid.org/0009-0001-5146-2411
Saveetha School of Management, Saveetha Institute of Medical and Technical Sciences, Chennai, India

A. K. Subramani
http://orcid.org/0000-0003-0783-7113
Saveetha School of Management, Saveetha Institute of Medical and Technical Sciences, Chennai, India

V. S. Deepthi
http://orcid.org/0009-0006-3161-1316
Saveetha School of Management, Saveetha Institute of Medical and Technical Sciences, Chennai, India

EXECUTIVE SUMMARY

The transition to hybrid work has radically upset the traditional performance management (PM) frameworks, unveiling fundamental visibility, equity, feedback rhythm, and goal alignment gaps to enhance the quality of life — the overall well-being and satisfaction of employees in their work and personal spheres. This paper discusses the way the hybrid and remote work structure opposes the traditional appraisal, highlighting the necessity to reconsider PM to fit agile processes, collaborating digitally, and changing employee expectations. The study is based on empirical research, case studies, and new practices points to such fundamental problems as proximity bias, rigidity of KPIs, erosion of trust, and burnout, as well as focusing on the innovative methodologies such as real-time feedback, outcome measures,

DOI: 10.4018/979-8-3373-5776-8.ch010

emotional intelligence and inclusive evaluation practices. The paper proposes a reimagined PM paradigm grounded in fairness, transparency, flexibility, and inclusion supported by ethical use of technology and strategic agility.

1. INTRODUCTION

1.1. Evolution of Traditional vs. Hybrid Work Models

In the past decades, the traditional work model where employees commute to a shared location to work, has seen changes (Sampat et al., 2022). (Iqbal et al., 2021) argue that the traditional system of work is not the most effective method of working. Indeed, hybrid work as a phenomenon has gained a lot of attention globally in recent research (e.g. Kossek et al., 2015; Iqbal et al., 2021). The change in the nature of work and the development of technology have enabled organizations to adopt work models in which employees have the ability to work remotely outside of the traditional office environment (Allen et al., 2015). Hybrid work combines both traditional and remote working models and thus provides employees the flexibility to work from an office or a remote location (Iqbal, et al., 2021).

1.2. Importance of Performance Management Systems (PMS)

Understanding organizational performance is difficult. Multiple ambiguities are involved, for instance measuring the achievement of diverging goals and targets (Vakkuri, 2010). Organizations establish a performance management system (PMS) where performance is regularly measured and the results are used for various purposes, ranging from internal planning, decision-making and control to external accountability issues. Performance information (PI) covers data on inputs, processes, outputs and outcomes. It focuses on past and future performance events and therefore it comprises performance targets, as well as performance indicators.

A well-designed PMS will give a good picture of the financial performance of an organization, as well providing information about non-financial aspects using a variety of tools (Performance appraisals, Benchmarking, Evaluation techniques, Balanced scorecard tools etc). To get a meaningful picture of a hybrid's performance is a more complicated exercise than measuring the performance of pure public or pure private entities (Grossi et al., 2017). Moreover, the shift to hybrid work has also emphasized the importance of employees' overall quality of life. Quality of life refers to an individual's overall well-being, encompassing physical health, psychological state, work–life balance, and satisfaction with their work environment. In hybrid settings, performance management must therefore integrate not only productivity metrics but also well-being indicators to ensure sustainable employee engagement.

2. CHALLENGES IN HYBRID PERFORMANCE MANAGEMENT

2.1. Visibility Bias: Remote Workers Overlooked

The discourse on visibility in hybrid work remains divided between technological optimism and managerial skepticism. While early studies (Kossek et al., 2015; Richardson & Kelliher, 2015) linked remote work to reduced recognition and exclusion from key decision processes, recent scholarship argues that digital ecosystems may redefine rather than reduce visibility (Groysberg et al., 2023). Output-based dashboards, asynchronous collaboration tools and real-time are also present in digitally mediated settings. performance analytics is said to democratize visibility by allowing contributions to be traced across locations. Yet, such an algorithmic visibility brings about new inequities- favoring employees that. are numerically expressive or calculably quantifiable on those practicing relational work of a subtle nature that is out of metrics (Biron et al., 2024).

This predicament implies that even hybrid spaces are not about visibility as seen or as not seen. but a managerially interpreted, data transparency, trust-dependent socially constructed outcome. cultures. Theory of social exchange and control provide rival explanations, the former focuses on the former. The latter put more emphasis on accountability that can be measured, although relational recognition is considered to be more important (Blau, 1964; Ouchi, 1979). The solution to this paradox in efficient hybrid performance management should be the encouragement of contextual visibility- recognizing the traces of digital and not tangible contributions. Thus, rather than through technological fixes alone, visibility equity needs to be incorporated in the inclusive leadership non-screen performance signals which are reflected in practices and reflexive appraisal systems time or activity metrics.

2.1.1. Ethical AI and Fairness in Remote Monitoring

These responsible AI adoption in the HR practices always based on issues of ethics like prevention of prejudice and the protection of confidential information (Deepthi et al., 2024). Additionally, they worry that a greater amount of remote labor may make their contributions less visible (Chidambaram and Tung, 2005) and impede their ability to advance in their careers (Richardson and Kelliher, 2015). These worries stem from the worry that coworkers or managers might believe that work is not being done if they are not physically there (Bailey and Kurland, 1999).

Lack of visibility continues to be a problem for management control even as trust in remote workers is growing (Eckhardt et al., 2019; Sewell and Taskin, 2015)

2.2. One-Size-Fits-All KPIs: Inflexible Measurement

Different industries have different processes that need to be assessed, KPIs can differ from one another. According to (Lindberg et al., 2015), KPIs may be used to measure performance and find waste in several sectors of a business. KPIs assist decision makers in assessing how well a particular stated goal is being achieved (Gonzalez et al., 2017). In order to assure meaningful measurement, academic research emphasizes utilizing outcome-based frameworks such as OKRs and customizing KPIs to roles and context. KPIs that are outcome-oriented, transparent, and customized encourage adaptability while maintaining accountability (Tawalbeh, 2025).

2.2.1. Infrequent Feedback Cycles Misaligned With Agile Workflows

A year-long grounded-theory study of remote-first and hybrid software teams was carried out. Grounded-theory feedback in a year. research on remote-first and hybrid software team was conducted. They found out they were not going the same direction coordination failure particularly in asynchronous was brought about by feedback and delays in communication. processes. This led to the rejection of Scrum by the teams in favour of more flexible and reactive approaches similar to Kanban (de Souza Santos and Ralph, 2022).

2.2.2. Lack of Data Granularity in Remote Settings

Workers who works at home communicated with each other more their core relationships and less cross silos, as of 2021 Microsoft research of over 61,000 workers. This reduction of bridge contacts made it difficult to propagate knowledge and the capacity to real-time identification of performance indicators (Yang et al., 2022). In the study, absence of is also demonstrated. Remote software teams were found to have coordination anomalies as a result of process visibility, poor communication, waiting in the line, and job ambiguity. Managers find it difficult to determine each contribution or identify bottlenecks with legacy measures of performance where none exist clear information about the flows of collaboration (de Souza Santos and Ralph, 2022).

2.2.3. Overemphasis on Output Over Outcomes

Once work is done, the work is measured to find out the results establish the contribution of each individual towards the end product. These are the common results that are used by managers and supervisors to determine how their employees are doing. This is consistent with many telework research that emphasizes on management by objectives (MBO) to measure workers will be able to deliver performance despite their physical distance between each other (Perez et al., 2005). Managers can materials of the review offered on the basis of digital collaboration technologies (Groysberg et al., 2022) or to achieve results, sent through email (Mazmanian et al., 2013). Supervisors will be able to analyze and provide effectively asynchronous or synchronous comments on the results of watching them, because the work can be broken down into small portions responsibilities or massive teamwork activities (Malhotra et al., 2007). Also, these tools can be utilized by managers to showcase and express team achievements since the type of engagement can be indirect (Mulki et al., 2009).

2.3 Trust and Appraisal Fairness: Balancing Transparency and Psychological Safety

The connection between trust and appraisal equity in hybrid work environments is less normative than. linear. The classical paradigms focus on procedural justice, which is just rules, openness, and uniformity because it is the basis of trust in an organization (Hubbell and Chory, 2005). However, recent studies indicate that there is a possibility of. that too much transparency can actually be counterproductive in the sense that it is seen by the employees as police surveillance, or micromanagement (Biron et al., 2024; Mathur et al., 2024). This creates a "fairness fear paradox" of hybrid performance management: systems aimed at equity-assurance can at the same time undermine psychological safety without mediation by empathy and conversation.

Theoretically, the Control Theory (Ouchi, 1979), as well as the Social Exchange Theory (Blau, 1964). Control based frameworks promote. Data-driven supervision and standardization so as to achieve equity; exchange point-of-view is focused on relational reciprocity and perceived benevolence. In mixed situations, both extremes are not enough. Algorithms appraisal can ensure formal equality and not relational justice, whereas unconditioned trust alone can ensure such justice-based systems are prone to inconsistency and nepotism. Especially applicable in this case is the idea of trust asymmetry (Korsgaard et al., 2015) once trust is harmed by opaque or penal assessments, repair must be done by an unproportional management effort.

2.3.1. Blended Onsite and Remote Presence

Hybrid workplaces create a blended paradigm that seeks to strike a balance between autonomy and collaboration by alternating periods of onsite presence with remote work. High employee happiness and retention are made possible by hybrid models that incorporate digital tools and flexible workspaces to facilitate simultaneous work at home and in the office, according to qualitative research of hybrid events and organizational settings. About 75% of workers say that having flexible time and space arrangements has enhanced their job satisfaction in hybrid settings (Yeke & Özveren, 2024).

2.3.2. Increased Autonomy and Flexibility

Greater autonomy and flexibility in task scheduling, location, and manner are features of hybrid work that have been demonstrated to enhance job satisfaction and performance. In distant settings, autonomy is a key predictor of satisfaction, less work-family conflict, and less emotional tiredness, according to (Charalampous et al., 2019; Gajendran & Harrison, 2007). These findings are dependent on self-discipline and remote readiness (Allen et al., 2024).

2.3.3. Shift From Activity-Based to Outcome-Based Work

Recurring meetings and coordination artifacts are repurposed to provide outcome transparency teams utilize sprint reviews and backlogs to measure progress instead of tracking time logged per session (Christensen et al., 2025). Agile software teams making the shift to hybrid work offer a striking example. Instead of depending on synchronous presence, (de Souza Santos & Ralph 2022) demonstrate that when tasks were explicitly assigned and associated with results, coordination in remote-first teams improved. Table 1 summarizes the synthesized challenges and emerging managerial interventions aligned with the FTFI framework.

Table 1. Challenges and Emerging Solutions in Hybrid Performance Management

	Key Challenges in Hybrid Performance Management	Emerging Solutions / Managerial Interventions	Framework Alignment (FTFI)
1	**Visibility Bias** — Remote employees often feel overlooked due to lack of physical presence and informal visibility.	Implement output-based evaluation, AI-driven collaboration analytics, and regular recognition check-ins to ensure equitable visibility.	Fairness, Transparency
2	**One-Size-Fits-All KPIs** — Traditional, static KPIs fail to capture diverse hybrid contributions.	Adopt customized OKRs and role-specific performance dashboards that emphasize outcomes and collaboration quality.	Flexibility, Transparency
3	**Delayed or Irregular Feedback** — Annual reviews create lag and demotivation.	Introduce continuous feedback loops and real-time recognition platforms using digital tools like Slack/ Workday.	Flexibility, Inclusion
4	**Lack of Trust and Psychological Safety** — Employees fear surveillance and biased appraisal.	Build trust-based evaluation systems emphasizing coaching and feedback literacy among managers.	Fairness, Inclusion
5	**Technology Overload and Data Misuse** — Overreliance on tracking tools harms engagement.	Establish ethical data governance policies and transparent AI-based evaluation criteria.	Transparency, Fairness
6	**Poor Manager Enablement** — Managers lack hybrid coaching and empathy skills.	Implement manager training in empathy, inclusive feedback, and data-driven coaching methods.	Inclusion, Fairness
7	**Burnout and Work–Life Imbalance** — Hybrid flexibility often blurs work boundaries.	Create personalized performance goals integrating well-being metrics and workload calibration tools.	Flexibility, Inclusion
8	**Limited Cross-Cultural Consistency** — Global hybrid teams face differing fairness perceptions.	Use culturally adaptive PM frameworks with clear communication and transparent criteria.	Fairness, Transparency, Inclusion
9	**Lack of Developmental Focus** — Ratings over learning reduce growth motivation.	Shift from ratings to strengths-based development plans and career conversations.	Flexibility, Inclusion
10	**Unclear Ethical Boundaries in AI Use** — Employees unsure how performance data is used.	Introduce AI ethics charters and employee consent mechanisms for transparency in performance analytics.	Transparency, Fairness

Source: (Author's conceptual synthesis, 2025)

3. EMERGING SUCCESS INDICATORS IN HYBRID CONTEXTS

3.1. Collaboration and Emotional Intelligence

Higher emotional intelligence promotes effective conflict resolution, open communication of ideas, and team cohesion in a variety of contexts, including IT and healthcare, according to research showing a favorable association between emotional intelligence and workplace collaboration (Atif et al., 2024). In a similar vein, in knowledge-intensive professions, emotional intelligence is closely associated with both task performance and creative performance, especially when under stress or role overload. These results show that emotional intelligence is relevant in promoting synergy of creativity and interpersonal harmony (Stawicki et al., 2023). It is a useless task to know how one feels in one situation or another, and it is especially so in verbal communication, which can be achieved with the help of facial expression recognition and analysis (Tamilselvi, 2024). In the evolving AI-enabled HRM environment, HR executives are transforming their methods of leadership, adopting more flexible styles, allowing workers which have more autonomy, and improving the lines of communication (Baruah et al., 2024).

3.2. Role of Digital Tools and Analytics

Specifically, sentiment analysis provides a sophisticated look into psychological safety and team mood (Obaidi et al., 2025) conducted systematic mapping research of sentiment tools in software engineering. According to research, when data analytics dashboards were incorporated into performance systems, companies that used collaboration platforms like Slack and Microsoft Teams experienced gains in engagement and productivity of 20–25% (Dowling et al., 2022).

3.3. Diversity and Inclusion: Ensuring Equity Across Locations, Demographics, and Personalities

In order to close these disparities, inclusive leadership is essential. Regardless of physical location, inclusive leaders that promote psychological safety, ask for feedback from everyone, and value different viewpoints improve employee engagement, creativity, and well-being, according to empirical study in Asian IT businesses (Nembhard & Edmondson, 2006). Personality and neurodiversity are included in equity, which transcends the demographic classifications. Research indicates that personality is determined by the environment. diversity differences in individuals' ways of demonstrating the Big Five traits-enhances the task performance, contextual, consciousness, and acclimatization (Park & Park, 2021)

3.4. Operating Under VUCA (Volatility, Uncertainty, Complexity, Ambiguity)

3.4.1. Volatility: Agility as Survival, Stability as Credibility

Volatility indicates the increasingly rapid change technological disruption, talent mobility and. changing the expectations of stakeholders. The hybrid teams are also able to recalibrate fast with Agile practices like sprint reviews and fast-paced goal iterations (Baran & Woznyj, 2020). But agility would too much disintegrate, direction, creating whiplash on a strategic level. Delivery in a performance system that is constantly in flux is dangerous, destroying confidence of employees and memory of the organization. There is empirical evidence in the software and service sectors that has demonstrated that teams possessing limited agility, such as those where adaptation in the long term has a short-term anchor become more resilient (Christensen et al., 2025).

3.4.2. Uncertainty: From Predictive Control to Sense-Making

When there is a lack of clarity in causal relations, there is uncertainty. Conventional PM systems undertake to inflict predictive control using standardized metrics and fixed KPIs; however, hybrid teams act. between asynchronous and cross-cultural boundaries where foresight is restricted. Drawing on (Weick, 1995) effective hybrid PM replaces prediction with interpretive alignment, sense-making theory continuous communication where the managers and employees are jointly creating meaning about changing objectives. This move makes the manager a narrative facilitator rather than an evaluator so that ambiguity is ensured happens to be a mutual education process instead of a stressor.

3.4.3. Complexity: Managing Interdependence Through Systems Thinking

Complexity is the non-linear interdependence between teams, technologies and markets. In performance failures hybrid structures, not an individual incompetence often leads to performance failures systemic misalignments are timely dependencies, incompatible digital processes, or overloaded communication channels. It is proposed through systems theory (Bititci et al., 1998) to measure the performance at several levels-individual, team, and ecosystem to prevent attribution bias. Network based-benefits are therefore received by Hybrid PM analytics which reflect relational and collaborative measures (e.g., Cross-team knowledge flows, digital coordination density).

3.4.4. Ambiguity: The Limits of Data and the Role of Judgment

Ambiguity is not the same as uncertainty because there are facts available but they are not interpreted. Hybrid PM often interprets online information, such as the activity feed, sentiment board, or engagement rating, out of context objective truths. However, these measurements hide the situational inputs like emotional tone, cultural, variation, or informal learning. In this case, the human judgment is essential. Making a decision under ambiguity demands integrating data mining with management sense-ethics, a reflexive realization of when to trust numbers and in which cases to favor dialogue or intuition (Bennett and Lemoine, 2014).

3.4.5. Integrative Perspective: Toward Dynamic Equilibrium in Hybrid PM

The hybrid PM should be a dynamic equilibrium system across VUCA dimensions and not a system. fixed control apparatus. Volatility requires agility; uncertainty requires sense-making; complexity. demands systemic coherence; and ambiguity demands reflective judgment. Such balance conforms to the adaptation-performance theory (Pulakos et al., 2000), which perceives effectiveness, not as adherence to rules but as being receptive to change. Organizations that embed into adaptive indicators, learning velocity, feedback responsiveness and psychological safety.

3.5. Regular Check-ins

(Brewster et al., 2016) It has been shown that regular feedback enables staff members to quickly modify their behavior, decreasing recurrent mistakes and boosting productivity. According to Gallup and Deloitte polls, employees who have regular development talks are also far more engaged; companies that do regular check-ins claim a 27–30% decrease in employee turnover and a 14% boost in productivity.

3.6. Forward-Looking Conversations

In CPM, forward-looking discussions move the emphasis from analyzing historical performance to jointly preparing for future expansion. Instead of assessing previous performance, these conversations focus on new objectives, development requirements, and stretch assignments proactively preparing staff for changing responsibilities as stated by (De Leede and Kraijenbrink, 2014). Forward dialogues take place every three months or at project milestones, during which the manager and staff together define SMART goals, develop development roadmaps, and describe future duties (Locke & Latham, 2002)

3.7. Real-Time Feedback Loops

According to a recent empirical study, prompt, positive feedback greatly improves subsequent task performance in all roles and cultures, but negative or delayed feedback had less of an effect (Goller & Späth, 2023)

4. GOAL AGILITY AND CONTINUOUS DEVELOPMENT FOCUS

4.1. OKRs and Forward-Looking Conversations

According to goal-setting theory, employees are more motivated and perform better when they have clear, difficult goals and receive feedback on them (Locke & Latham, 2002). Middle-management's ability to translate high-level objectives into concrete tasks and transparent tracking is crucial, according to research on OKR adoption in big software teams. Better uptake and effect were observed by organizations that made investments in learning communities, OKR alignment forums, and goal communication pipelines. Organizations can practically combine OKRs with CPM by monitoring progress during routine check-ins, creating progress dashboards, and working together to change priorities. When it comes to converting strategic intent into team-level OKRs, middle managers are essential liaisons (Butler et al., 2024)

4.2. Feedback Evolution

4.2.1. Focusing on Growth Rather Than Ratings

(Aguinis et al., 2012) compared strength-oriented response to traditional Weakness-based appraisals, proving that pointless to emphasize that people have their weaknesses are not the only thing that motivates interaction, the practice of skills, and labor but their strength satisfaction.

4.2.2. Personalized Career Trajectories

New data-driven systems such as job Composer underscore the necessity of. individual-based path mapping, namely, career decisions optimized according to individual preferences wider data trends, though no more career trajectory research. Career paths that are in line with individual purpose, skill, and opportunity can be created by combining these tools with strengths-based frameworks (Obaidi et al., 2022).

Employers can encourage intrinsic motivation and retention by having staff members identify their signature qualities and then build their career growth around them. It has been demonstrated that interventions like signature-strengths spotting, in which managers receive training on identifying and fostering both strong and emerging strengths, improve coaching behavior and developmental support (Fatien & Otter, 2015)

4.2.3. Collaboration Heatmaps

In order to detect irregularities and inefficiencies in work processes, a recent open-access study presented the Workspace Performance Measurement (WPM) technique, which integrates comprehensive behavioral data, such as interaction patterns, tool use, and activity flow. As part of these digital monitoring tools, collaboration heatmaps show cold zones (such isolated contributors or underutilized experts) and hotspots in collaboration (like those inundated with cross-team requests) (Nesterak et al., 2024).

4.2.4. Work Pattern Analysis

In order to identify irregularities in process flow and individual performance deviations, it records detailed workspace activity and physiological measurements (e.g. unexpected delays, frequent task switching). These can be used by managers to locate systemic. bottlenecks exceeding the measures of output (Nesterak et al., 2024). Remote work pattern analysis. or hybrid spaces may unveil such issues as post-hours working, divided attention, or context exchange overload variables correlated with burnout based on the Job Demands-Resources model (Bakker & Demerouti, 2007)

4.2.5. Nudges for Feedback and Recognition

Subtle interface-based treatments known as digital "Nudges" are intended to promote actions like giving feedback or praising colleagues. Nudges may be used in workplace platforms to remind staff members to provide feedback, thank a teammate after a project, or follow up on objectives (Ruehle, 2023). A growing body of nudge research looks at workplace applications, but much of it concentrates on consumer behavior. Small-to-medium effect sizes (Hedges' $g = 0.32$) were discovered in a meta-analysis of digital nudges in privacy-related domains for enhancing desired sharing behaviors (Ioannou et al., 2021). Ethics experts warn that badly thought-out nudges can erode trust, particularly if they are interpreted as manipulative. Users dislike nudges that aren't clear and serve platform goals or financial interests (Grön, 2025). The study suggests moral standards for digital nudging that prioritize free will, purpose clarity, and voluntary involvement (Meske & Amojo, 2020)

4.2.6. Integrating Wellness Into Goal Setting

Hope, resilience, self-efficacy, and optimism are all components of psychological capital (PsyCap), which has substantial positive relationships with performance, citizenship behavior, engagement, and satisfaction and negative correlations with burnout and turnover intention. Integrating PsyCap-enhancing objectives (such as stress management and resilience building) into individual development discussions promotes performance and well-being (Avey et al., 2011)

4.3. Strength-Based and Career-Focused PM

Performance has been strongly associated with job engagement, which is described as a positive, fulfilled state of mind relating to work that is marked by vigor, devotion, and absorption. For instance, more engaged flight attendants perform better both in and out of their roles, while hospitality industry workers exhibit greater client loyalty and pleasure (Salanova & Schaufeli, 2008). Through vocal behaviors, psychological safety indirectly promotes participation. Employee engagement levels increase through empowered involvement in teams where workers feel comfortable speaking up (Ge, 2020)

4.4. Trust, Transparency, and Culture-Building Remotely

Frameworks for building trust in virtual teas emphasize clarity, consistency, and relational touchpoints (Soomar, 2020). More coordination, cohesiveness, and contentment are reported by teams who devote time to trust-building practices, such as frequent, open updates, individual sharing, and norm-setting meetings. Job satisfaction and performance can be negatively impacted by coordination problems such ambiguity, mistrust, role confusion, and isolation, according to research on remote-first and hybrid software teams (de Souza Santos & Ralph, 2022). Although psychological safety encourages creativity, too much of it can impair performance in everyday tasks; hence, transparency and group accountability assist strike a balance (team rules, clear expectations) (Eldor et al., 2023)

5. CASE STUDIES

5.1: Global Technology Firm

Challenge: Remote Employees Felt Disconnected From Strategic Goals (Iseal et al., 2024)

The case study revolves around a technology company that specializes in developing software solutions for the finance industry. The project in question involved the development and launch of a new software product designed to meet the needs of a large-scale financial institution. The project had a tight deadline, limited resources, and several complex technical challenges that required cross-functional collaboration between the development, marketing, and customer support teams.

Solution: Shifted to Dynamic OKRs and Weekly Team Check-ins

The correlation of the OKRs departments helped promote cross-functional collaboration, especially. a partnership between the software development, sales and the customer support teams. Regular check-ins helped to find dependencies early and teams collaborated to identify troubleshoot problems, including technical. early adopters' bugs or feature requests. The OKRs also offered an organized system of communication where all teams knew each other. their advancement and trouble. Meeting weekly to discuss OKRs facilitated the clarification of expectations. clear up any misunderstandings.

Outcome: Improved clarity, Accountability, and Morale

The introduction of OKRs provided more clarity in the roles, as the team members knew how they will work contribution to the success of the product was made by work. Each team had major results that they were responsible about. periodic reports on the progress made sure that any deviations were promptly addressed. However, there were there were examples of situations when team members experienced the burden of personal responsibility, which occasionally resulted in stress and burn out, especially in the development team that does bug fixes.

5.2. CASE 2: Financial Services

The analysis is mainly devoted to the factors in general influence on the performance of employees working in the banking field as compensation, organizational culture, leadership, job satisfaction and work-life balance. While it addresses such issues as the digital transformation and high competition in the banking sphere industry (Ng et al., 2024)

Solution: Introduced AI-Based Contribution Analytics and Peer Feedback

Trust Propagation Model: This is a model that is based on a graph and it is much more accurate (AUC and ACC) compared to baselines and EM as more productive in determining credible student assessors and are giving more assuring results.

The use of Linguistic Information: The use of textual feedback and linguistic information of. will assist in gauging the trust in the reviews and reduce the impact of strategic spammers through higher values of AUC and ACC (Tarigan et al., 2023)

Outcome: Reduced Attrition and Improved Trust in Appraisal Fairness

Minimized turnover and enhanced confidence in the fairness of appraisals. The major result is the building up of an imaginary structure that seeks to increase the equity and performance evaluation process effectiveness. This framework would be tailored to offer a holistic awareness of crucial dimensions and operating factors that cause subjective bias which serves as one of the tools to unwind and solve fairness issues based on performance appraisal practices (Tarigan et al., 2023).

5.3. CASE 3: Healthcare Sector

Challenge: Managers Struggled With Assessing Team Performance Across Locations

The paper points out to a lack of performance measures and data in dispersed teams. essential dilemma of performance measurement in these networks, it is difficult to obtain consenting and clever performance measures, particularly in a situation where different services are involved. several teams located in different areas. Evaluation was also a problem that troubled managers in these networks. performance because of the highly entrenched professional cultures and "Epistemic communities" which establish the definition of what is considered a good practice and performance (Ferlie et al., 2010).

Solution: Trained Managers on Coaching and Emotional Intelligence, Integrated 360-Feedback

The 360-degree survey feedback as a leadership development tool. Evaluation of emotional intelligence in leaders. Self-other rating agreement and leadership effectiveness. While 360-degree performance assessment could involve the use of feedback, which is not mentioned in the study teams located geographically far apart, nor does it provide strategies on ways to counter the particular challenges of performance measurement in other places, e.g., data gathering, cultural variations or. problems with technological integration (Gregory et al., 2017).

Outcome: Enhanced Manager–Employee Relationships and Engagement

The feedback process became used in determining specific areas to recruit leaders on the basis of EI scores.

Influence on self-other rating agreement: The study added to the knowledge about the dynamics of. agreement of self-other rating of leadership testing, especially on emotional intelligence.

Leadership development opportunities: The results indicate that these feedback processes may prove useful. self-awareness promotion tools and the process of leading the leaders to better their emotional intelligence, and is an essential element of an effective leader (Markos and Sridevi, 2010).

6. *(FAIRNESS–TRANSPARENCY–INCLUSION CYCLE) FRAMEWORK*

Figure 1. Conceptually integrates these four dimensions as a cyclical model driving equitable and adaptive PM practices.

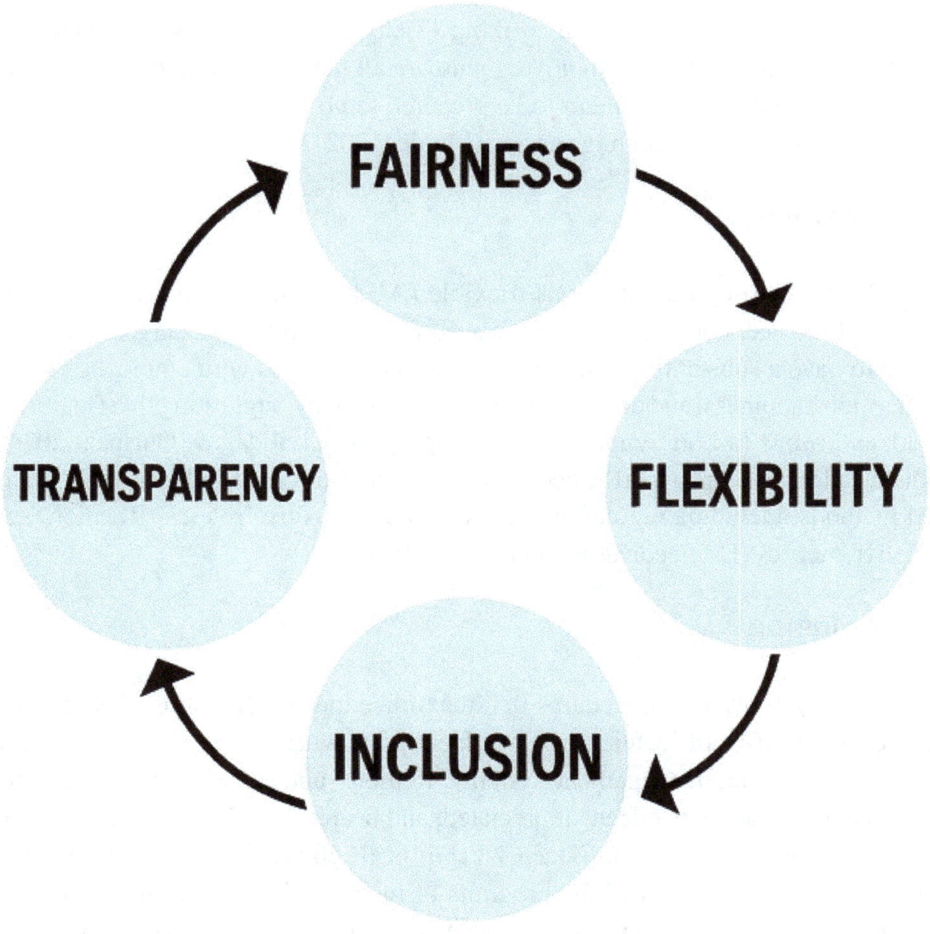

Source: (Author, 2025)

6.1. Fairness

Organizational justice, particularly distributive and procedural justice, is essential to fair performance management since it influences employee motivation, attitudes, and trust. (Greenberg, 1987) believe that assessments should be outcome-based rather than face-time in remote and hybrid situations. Performance objectives must be role-specific, outcome-linked, and in line with agile work cycles as opposed to conventional office-based measures (De Leede & Kraijenbrink, 2014)

According to a thorough analysis, fairness in PM systems is supported by openness, yet in hybrid environments, fairness is rarely discussed directly. Employee engagement and trust are undermined when systems disregard remote workers' "Office hours" or other styles of working (Tichy, 2021). Employee Engagement can be characterized by the employees who are all being committed towards their organization and that helps them to be prepared to go beyond their expectation in order to deliver the outstanding service (Monica, 2021)

6.2. Flexibility

In VUCA and hybrid situations, flexible PM dynamically modifies goals and cadence to reflect changing business needs. Flexible working arrangements were found to have a substantial positive association (r = 0.596) with employee performance, job happiness, and organizational commitment by, suggesting that flexibility is advantageous to both employers and employees (Çivilidağ & Durmaz, 2024). Other academics emphasize the need of development-oriented and forward-looking PM methods, including regular check-ins, context-sensitive role clarification, and adaptive metrics (De Leede & Kraijenbrink, 2014).

6.3. Inclusion

Designing tools and procedures that maximize the contributions of every employee, irrespective of location, role, or identity, is what is meant by inclusion in hybrid performance management systems. Remote, underrepresented, or quieter perspectives are acknowledged, appreciated, and heard in performance discussions thanks to inclusive frameworks (Deepalakshmi et al., 2025). Empathy, transparency, and cooperative decision-making are traits of inclusive leadership that have been repeatedly demonstrated to boost employee engagement and spur creativity (Hirak et al., 2012). It also provides a model that connects inclusion to engagement and performance; they pinpoint eight crucial inclusion elements that are necessary for productive, psychologically secure workplaces (Radziwill & Benton, 2024). (Zhao et al., 2025) carried performed a meta-analysis of D&I initiatives and found that training, workplace modifications, and fair feedback systems improve retention, inclusion, and performance.

6.4. Transparency

Transparency fosters participation, clarity, and trust while improving the perception of organizational justice. Employees are more likely to accept evaluations when they are aware of the decision-making process, the metrics being utilized, and how they relate to rewards (Tichy, 2021). Transparency in enabling rather than coercive PM systems gives workers access to benchmark standards and organizational objectives in addition to their personal ambitions (global transparency), promoting self-regulation and alignment (Ahrens & Chapman, 2004; Naranjo-Gil & Hartmann, 2006).

7. GLOBAL TRENDS AND FUTURE DIRECTIONS

7.1. Role of Technology

7.1.1. Choose Tools That are Scalable, Inclusive, and Actionable

Scalability ensures that systems are scalable is capable of supporting growing teams without altering the user experience during the selection. solutions of project management. Real-time goal dashboards, peer recognition platforms facilitate these and 360-degree feedback democratize performance insights in a distributed, remote, and hybrid environment workers. Inclusive features to multilingual interfaces, by allowing every voice to be heard accessible design, anonymous feedback options, and less visibility bias through anonymous feedback options (Liu et al., 2023).

7.1.2. Avoid Micromanagement Systems; Prioritize Trust and Outcome Focus

According to (Shamspour et al., 2024), micromanagement has a negative correlation with organizational commitment and dramatically raises job stress. According to their research on Iranian industrial workers, micromanagement was linked to higher levels of stress, which in turn reduced employee loyalty and retention intentions. Meanwhile, actual studies conducted in public sector contexts show that task performance is much improved by perceived autonomy and fairness (Oakman et al., 2024)

7.1.3. Balance Automation With Human Judgment

Robust human-in-the-loop models guarantee that managers, who are able to take ethical and qualitative factors into account, confirm AI discoveries contextually.

When designers use delegation well, human-AI collaboration improves performance and happiness. AI manages routine patterns, while humans handle exceptions, moral quandaries, or context-specific judgment (Hemmer et al., 2023). Because people remain involved and collaborate with AI to make better decisions, research suggests that flawed automation (60–80% reliability) may actually produce better results than flawless systems (Maltz & Shinar, 2004).

7.2. Building a Feedback Culture

7.2.1. Normalize Feedback as Part of Daily Work

Gallup research supports this view by revealing that that frequent feedback of the manager has a high rate of staff motivation and retention. Organizations are motivated to incorporate feedback behaviors within weekly or biweekly individual meetings and project rituals, an elaboration of goal-setting theory. The insertion of such a rhythm decreases fear and strengthens the. feedback value through providing feedback as a standard practice of work (Locke and Latham, 2002)

7.2.2. Reward Feedback-Giving, not Just Output

Traditional performance systems emphasize feedback-giving, as opposed to output focus on outcomes, although feedback is also an effective collaboration and cultural tool. According to cognitive evaluation theory, while material rewards run the danger of eroding intrinsic motivation, informational positive feedback that is given with autonomous support can strengthen it and reinforce competence (Deci & Ryan, 2013)

7.2.3. Recognize contributions in real time

When recognition is instantaneous and connected to a particular conduct, it has the greatest impact. According to studies, giving praise soon after an event rather than months later increases motivation, encourages repeating actions, and builds emotional ties. The importance of prompt acknowledgment was confirmed in hospital settings where leadership walk rounds and fast feedback were linked to increased engagement and decreased (Sexton et al., 2018). In the meantime, studies in clinical psychology show that well-performing teams have high positive-to-negative feedback ratios (about 5:1 or 6:1), emphasizing the value of regular affirmation over criticism (Cox, 2016)

7.3. Manager Enablement

7.3.1. Upskill Managers for Remote Coaching and Inclusive Evaluation

Beyond standard task monitoring, leadership in telework environments necessitates the development of trust and facilitation abilities. Key qualities identified by a systematic assessment of virtual leadership include managing diversity remotely, facilitating participation, building team trust, and offering social support all of which are positively correlated with both team and individual performance (Wakefield et al., 2008; Kashive et al., 2022; Soon & Salamzadeh, 2021)

7.3.2. Provide Tools for Managing Distributed Performance

Technology solutions that highlight alignment, progress, and dependency hazards are helpful to managers of hybrid teams. However, tools by themselves are insufficient; in order to successfully comprehend goal dashboards, peer feedback data, and collaborative analytics while retaining human judgment, training is required. Strong time management, technological proficiency, and soft skills are essential for distant leaders to preserve team unity and clarity, as hybrid leadership study highlights (Coffey & Wolf, 2018; Hayashi & Soo, 2012; Wong & Nordengen Berntzen, 2019)

7.3.3. Hold Leaders Accountable for Equitable Development

The equitable distribution of growth opportunities, such as stretch assignments, mentoring, and promotions, across demographics, locales, and work modes is guaranteed by leadership accountability. The study of responsible leadership places a strong emphasis on principles like stakeholder trust, ethical justice, and open accountability (Maak & Pless, 2009; Haque et al., 2019). Similarly, self-awareness, openness, and moral conduct are emphasized by authentic leadership theory as being essential to promoting responsibility and productive work environments (Avolio et al., 2009)

7.3.4. Cultural Inertia Towards Legacy Appraisal Models

It is still very difficult to overcome resistance to changing performance management models, especially when it comes to ingrained cultural inertia and managers' unease with new feedback standards. Because traditional appraisal frameworks are ingrained in routines, culture, and performance expectations, organizations frequently stick to them. The legacy evaluation models are challenging to replace because organizational culture has a significant inertia, effectively maintaining the status quo even when external contexts change quickly (Marquis & Tilcsik, 2013)

7.4. Data Misuse and Surveillance Concerns

7.4.1. Excessive Monitoring Leads to Mistrust

Unrestricted staff surveillance, such as tracking mobility, biometrics, screen time, or keystrokes, can seriously damage an organization's reputation and well-being. Aggressive surveillance has been repeatedly associated in studies with increased stress, decreased job satisfaction, and diminished autonomy. According to study conducted in post-pandemic settings, employees who feel that monitoring is intrusive are less satisfied with their jobs and will resort to counterproductive measures (such taking unapproved breaks) in an attempt to regain their independence (Alge, 2001; Staats et al., 2017; Siegel et al., 2022)

7.4.2. Ethical AI Deployment is Essential

Misuse of personal data, from performance scoring to behavioral analytics, can reinforce bias, violate privacy, and harm workplace culture, according to a growing body of research on AI ethics in HR (Mathur et al., 2024). Scholars contend that AI must function within frameworks of openness and fairness and should never take the place of human judgment in crucial decisions like promotions or terminations (Chen et al., 2021; Mathur et al., 2024). Unchecked worker surveillance, particularly after hours or via invasive digital channels, can violate privacy and dignity and run the danger of facing legal and cultural repercussions, according to the OECD policy brief (Hickok & Maslej, 2023)

7.5. Ambiguity in Goal-Setting

7.5.1. Hybrid Work Often Blurs Role Boundaries

Goal clarity is crucial for performance since hybrid work frequently blurs traditional job boundaries and increases role stress through ambiguity and overload. Reduced in-person engagement and more asynchronous operations might exacerbate role ambiguity in hybrid environments. Workers might not know what is expected of them, who is responsible for what, or how success is determined. Role ambiguity is defined by research as a lack of knowledge about duties or performance expectations that causes dissatisfaction and disengagement (Rushing et al., 1965; Cooper et al., 2001)

7.5.2. Overloaded Workers May Struggle to Prioritize

Role overload is a result of hybrid workers frequently juggling several demands, including as tight deadlines, cross-functional coordination, and fluctuating priorities. When anticipated obligations surpass existing resources or limitations, an overload happens (Peterson et al., 1995; Cooper et al., 2001). Without excellent leader-member communication or job autonomy, for example, employees find it difficult to effectively prioritize and self-regulate (Tang & Vandenberghe, 2021)

7.6. Strategic Agility in PM

7.6.1. Employee Voice and Adaptability as Performance Markers

Indicators of strategic readiness that go beyond production measurements include adaptable performance and employee voice, both restrictive and promotional. Employees who provide ideas or speak up constructively in dynamic work situations enable the company to change and innovate (Ou et al., 2018). Flexibility, innovative problem-solving, and stress resistance are traits of adaptive performance that enable workers to flourish in the face of change. High adaptability performers are more capable of performing in unclear hybrid environments (Pulakos et al., 2000).

7.7. Integrating Employee Experience Into PM

7.7.1. Combining EX, Well-Being, and Productivity Metrics

In this context, the concept of quality of Life becomes central. It represents the overall well-being and satisfaction of employees in both their professional and personal domains. In support of these conclusions, IPA research demonstrates that well-being is improved by structured work-family reconciliation policies, which in turn boost motivation and reduce stress, improving performance (Medina-Garrido et al., 2017)

7.7.2. PM as a Tool for Employee Retention and Employer Branding

According to empirical research, over 90% of the variation in retention in banking contexts may be explained by career development, feedback, and empowerment. Also, employer branding breeds retention and engagement. that is anchored on a strong internal experience, which is work design, career advancement, and psychological assistance (Ahmed et al., 2022)

8. CONCLUSION

With hybrid work becoming a new norm and not an exception, old performance management systems. work that is meant to be done simultaneously and to be geographically localized will have to be reconsidered. This study highlights the fact that old methods such as annual appraisals, generic KPIs, and output-based methods are outdated appraisals do not fit well with remote teams and agile processes. The new reality is the hybrid one performance indicators including flexibility, quality of collaboration, EI, and digital engagement, which need active and consistent context-insensitive feedback and collaborative evaluation processes. The study calls upon the concern of making PM consistent with the values of fairness, transparency. flexibility, and inclusion. Ethical use of technology, real-time feedback, manager enablement, and integration of employee well-being appears as key to developing trust-based, high performing cultures. Proactive, developmental strategies, like check-ins, learning plans, and customized career paths are the core to growth and retention. Ultimately, there is more than adopting existing systems to rethink performance management in a hybrid world it needs an alteration in the culture to human-focused, dynamic, and resilient models that facilitate organizations and individuals to succeed in the complexity and change.

REFERENCES

Aguinis, H., Gottfredson, R. K., & Joo, H. (2012). Using performance management to win the talent war. *Business Horizons*, *55*(6), 609–616. DOI: 10.1016/j.bushor.2012.05.007

Ahmed, R. R., Azam, M., Qureshi, J. A., & Hashem, E. (2022). The relationship between internal employer branding and talent retention: A theoretical investigation for the development of a conceptual framework. *Frontiers in Psychology*, *13*, 859614. DOI: 10.3389/fpsyg.2022.859614 PMID: 35369242

Ahrens, T., & Chapman, C. S. (2004). Accounting for flexibility and efficiency: A field study of management control systems in a restaurant chain. *Contemporary Accounting Research*, *21*(2), 271–301. DOI: 10.1506/VJR6-RP75-7GUX-XH0X

Alge, B. J. (2001). Effects of computer surveillance on perceptions of privacy and procedural justice. *The Journal of Applied Psychology*, *86*(4), 797–804. DOI: 10.1037/0021-9010.86.4.797 PMID: 11519663

Allen, K. S., Grelle, D., Lazarus, E. M., Popp, E., & Gutierrez, S. L. (2024). Hybrid is here to stay: Critical behaviors for success in the new world of work. *Personality and Individual Differences*, *217*, 112459. DOI: 10.1016/j.paid.2023.112459

Allen, T. D., Golden, T. D., & Shockley, K. M. (2015). How effective is telecommuting? Assessing the status of our scientific findings. *Psychological Science in the Public Interest*, *16*(2), 40–68. DOI: 10.1177/1529100615593273 PMID: 26403188

. Atif, S., Jehangir, S., & Latifi, T. T. (2024). Emotional Intelligence and its Role in Enhancing Workplace Collaboration. *Archives of Management and Social Sciences, 1(4),* 40-47. Vol. 1 No. 4 (2024): Archive of Management and Social Sciences

Avey, J. B., Reichard, R. J., Luthans, F., & Mhatre, K. H. (2011). Meta-analysis of the impact of positive psychological capital on employee attitudes, behaviors, and performance. *Human Resource Development Quarterly*, *22*(2), 127–152. DOI: 10.1002/hrdq.20070

. Avolio, B. J., Walumbwa, F. O., & Weber, T. J. (2009). Leadership: Current theories, research, and future directions. *Annual review of psychology, 60(1),* 421 449. DOI: 10.1146/annurev.psych.60.110707.163621

Bailey, N. B. K. D. E., & Kurland, N. B. (1999). The advantages and challenges of working here, there, anywhere, and anytime. *Organizational Dynamics*, *28*(2), 53–68. DOI: 10.1016/S0090-2616(00)80016-9

Bakker, A. B., & Demerouti, E. (2007). The job demands-resources model: State of the art. *Journal of Managerial Psychology, 22*(3), 309–328. DOI: 10.1108/02683940710733115

Baran, B. E., & Woznyj, H. M. (2020). Managing VUCA: The human dynamics of agility. *Organizational Dynamics, 50*(4), 100787. DOI: 10.1016/j.orgdyn.2020.100787 PMID: 32843777

Baruah, A., Shaikh, M., Kumar, R. M., Shaikh, I. A. K., & Thomas, S. N. (2024, April). Artificial Intelligence Influence on Leadership Styles in Human Resource Management for Employee Engagement. In *2024 Ninth International Conference on Science Technology Engineering and Mathematics (ICONSTEM)* (pp. 1-5). IEEE. DOI: 10.1109/ICONSTEM60960.2024.10568819

Bennett, N., & Lemoine, G. J. (2014). What a difference a word makes: Understanding threats to performance in a VUCA world. *Business Horizons, 57*(3), 311–317. DOI: 10.1016/j.bushor.2014.01.001

Biron, M., Boon, C., Farndale, E., & Bamberger, P. A. (2024). *Human resource strategy: Formulation, implementation, and impact.* Routledge., DOI: 10.4324/9781003402176

Bititci, U., Carrie, A., & Turner, T. (1998). Diagnosing the integrity of your performance measurement system. *Control, 24*(3), 9–14. https://strathprints.strath.ac.uk/id/eprint/32935

Blau, P. M. (1964). *Exchange and power in social life*. Wiley.

Brewster, C., Gooderham, P. N., & Mayrhofer, W. (2016). Human resource management: The promise, the performance, the consequences. *Journal of Organizational Effectiveness: People and Performance, 3*(2), 181–190. DOI: 10.1108/JOEPP-03-2016-0024

Butler, J. L., Zimmermann, T., & Bird, C. (2024, April). Objectives and key results in software teams: Challenges, opportunities and impact on development. In *Proceedings of the 46th International Conference on Software Engineering: Software Engineering in Practice* (pp. 358-368). DOI: 10.1145/3639477.3639747

Charalampous, M., Grant, C. A., Tramontano, C., & Michailidis, E. (2019). Systematically reviewing remote e-workers' well-being at work: A multidimensional approach. *European Journal of Work and Organizational Psychology, 28*(1), 51–73. DOI: 10.1080/1359432X.2018.1541886

Chen, J., Storchan, V., & Kurshan, E. (2021). Beyond fairness metrics: Roadblocks and challenges for ethical ai in practice. *arXiv preprint arXiv:2108.06217.* https://doi.org//arXiv.2108.06217DOI: 10.48550

Chidambaram, L., & Tung, L. L. (2005). Is out of sight, out of mind? An empirical study of social loafing in technology-supported groups. *Information Systems Research, 16*(2), 149–168. DOI: 10.1287/isre.1050.0051

Christensen, E. L., Paasivaara, M., & Salman, I. (2025, April). Hybrid Work in Agile Software Development: Recurring Meetings. In *2025 IEEE/ACM 18th International Conference on Cooperative and Human Aspects of Software Engineering (CHASE)* (pp. 120-130). IEEE.DOI: 10.1109/CHASE66643.2025.00023

Çivilidağ, A., & Durmaz, Ş. (2024). Examining the relationship between flexible working arrangements and employee performance: A mini review. *Frontiers in Psychology, 15*, 1398309. DOI: 10.3389/fpsyg.2024.1398309 PMID: 39027052

Coffey, R., & Wolf, L. (2018). *The challenge and promise of remote work: A brief study of remote work and best practices (No. ANL/ALCF-18/4). Argonne National Lab.* ANL., DOI: 10.2172/1487022

. Cooper, C. L., Dewe, P., & O'Driscoll, M. P. (2001). Organizational stress: A review and critique of theory, research, and applications. DOI: 10.4135/9781452231235

. Cox, S. (2016). Give the gift of feedback. *Nursing Management, 47(5),* 44-48. https://doi.org/. 92871.eaDOI: 10.1097/01.NUMA.0000482528

De Leede, J., & Kraijenbrink, J. (2014). The mediating role of trust and social cohesion in the effects of new ways of working: a Dutch case study. In *Human resource management, social innovation and technology* (pp. 3–20). Emerald Group Publishing Limited., DOI: 10.1108/S1877-636120140000014006

de Souza Santos, R. E., & Ralph, P. (2022, May). A grounded theory of coordination in remote-first and hybrid software teams. *In Proceedings of the 44th International Conference on Software Engineering* (pp. 25-35). DOI: 10.1145/3510003.3510105

Deci, E. L., & Ryan, R. M. (2013). *Intrinsic motivation and self-determination in human behavior.* Springer Science & Business Media., DOI: 10.1007/978-1-4899-2271-7

. Deepalakshmi, N., Sathana Priya, M., Radhakrishnan, G. V., Arya, S., & Suraj, P. G. (2025). The role of inclusive leadership in enhancing employee engagement. *Journal of Information Systems Engineering and Management, 10(35),* 1062-1074.. v10i35s.6190DOI: <ALIGNMENT.qj></ALIGNMENT>10.52783/jisem

Deepthi, P., Shaikh, M., Nargunde, A. S., Faldu, R., & Goli, G. (2024, April). Deep learning-enabled human resource analytics in predicting employee performance. In *2024 Ninth International Conference on Science Technology Engineering and Mathematics (ICONSTEM)* (pp. 1-5). IEEE. https://doi.org/DOI: 10.1109/ICONSTEM60960.2024.10568716

Dowling, B., Goldstein, D., Park, M., & Price, H. (2022). Hybrid work: Making it fit with your diversity, equity, and inclusion strategy. *The McKinsey Quarterly*, *4*, 1–9.

. Eckhardt, Andreas, Florian Endter, Anthony Giordano, and Paul Somers. "Three stages to a virtual workforce." *MIS Quarterly Executive 18, no. 1* (2019) .. https://doi.org/ DOI: 10.17705/2msqe.00006

Eldor, L., Hodor, M., & Cappelli, P. (2023). The limits of psychological safety: Nonlinear relationships with performance. *Organizational Behavior and Human Decision Processes*, *177*, 104255. DOI: 10.1016/j.obhdp.2023.104255

Fatien, P., & Otter, K. (2015). Wearing multiple hats? Challenges for managers-as-coaches and their organizations. *International Leadership Journal*, *7*(3), 24–35.

. Ferlie, E., Fitzgerald, L., McGivern, G., Dopson, S., & Exworthy, M. (2010). Networks in health care: a comparative study of their management, impact and performance. Report for the National Institute for Health Research Service Delivery and Organisation Programme.

Gajendran, R. S., & Harrison, D. A. (2007). The good, the bad, and the unknown about telecommuting: Meta-analysis of psychological mediators and individual consequences. *The Journal of Applied Psychology*, *92*(6), 1524–1541. DOI: 10.1037/0021-9010.92.6.1524 PMID: 18020794

Ge, Y. (2020). Psychological safety, employee voice, and work engagement. *Social Behavior and Personality*, *48*(3), 1–7. DOI: 10.2224/sbp.8907

Goller, D., & Späth, M. (2023). 'Good job! 'The impact of positive and negative feedback on performance. *arXiv preprint arXiv:2301.11776.* https://doi.org//arXiv.2301.1177DOI: 10.48550

Gonzalez, E., Nanos, E. M., Seyr, H., Valldecabres, L., Yürüşen, N. Y., Smolka, U., Muskulus, M., & Melero, J. J. (2017). Key performance indicators for wind farm operation and maintenance. *Energy Procedia*, *137*, 559–570. DOI: 10.1016/j.egypro.2017.10.385

Greenberg, J. (1987). A taxonomy of organizational justice theories. *Academy of Management Review*, *12*(1), 9–22. DOI: 10.2307/257990

Gregory, P. J., Robbins, B., Schwaitzberg, S. D., & Harmon, L. (2017). Leadership development in a professional medical society using 360-degree survey feedback to assess emotional intelligence. *Surgical Endoscopy*, *31*(9), 3565–3573. DOI: 10.1007/s00464-016-5386-8 PMID: 28039648

. Grön, J. (2025). Digital Nudging in B2C E-commerce. DOI: 10.1007/s10660-024-09825-6

Grossi, G., Reichard, C., Thomasson, A., & Vakkuri, J. (2017). Theme: Performance measurement of hybrid organizations–emerging issues and future research perspectives. *Public Money & Management*, *37*(6), 379–386. DOI: 10.1080/09540962.2017.1344007

Groysberg, B., Haas, D., & Lin, E. (2023). Now You See Me, Now I'm Gone. *MIT Sloan Management Review*, *64*(2), 70–75.

Haque, A., Fernando, M., & Caputi, P. (2019). Responsible leadership, affective commitment and intention to quit: An individual level analysis. *Leadership and Organization Development Journal*, *40*(1), 45–64. DOI: 10.1108/LODJ-12-2017-0397

Hayashi, C., & Soo, A. (2012). Adaptive leadership in times of crisis. *Prism*, *4*(1), 78–86.

Hemmer, P., Westphal, M., Schemmer, M., Vetter, S., Vössing, M., & Satzger, G. (2023, March). Human-AI collaboration: the effect of AI delegation on human task performance and task satisfaction. *In Proceedings of the 28th International Conference on Intelligent User Interfaces* (pp. 453-463). DOI: 10.1145/3581641.3584052

Hickok, M., & Maslej, N. (2023). A policy primer and roadmap on AI worker surveillance and productivity scoring tools. *AI and Ethics*, *3*(3), 673–687. DOI: 10.1007/s43681-023-00275-8 PMID: 37360144

Hirak, R., Peng, A. C., Carmeli, A., & Schaubroeck, J. M. (2012). Linking leader inclusiveness to work unit performance: The importance of psychological safety and learning from failures. *The Leadership Quarterly*, *23*(1), 107–117. DOI: 10.1016/j.leaqua.2011.11.009

Hubbell, A. P., & Chory-Assad, R. M. (2005). Motivating factors: Perceptions of justice and their relationship with managerial and organizational trust. *Communication Studies*, *56*(1), 47–70. DOI: 10.1080/0008957042000332241

Ioannou, A., Tussyadiah, I., Miller, G., Li, S., & Weick, M. (2021). Privacy nudges for disclosure of personal information: A systematic literature review and meta-analysis. *PLoS One*, *16*(8), e0256822. DOI: 10.1371/journal.pone.0256822 PMID: 34449821

Iqbal, K. M. J., Khalid, F., & Barykin, S. Y. (2021). Hybrid workplace: The future of work. In *Handbook of Research on Future Opportunities for Technology Management Education* (pp. 28–48). IGI Global. DOI: 10.4018/978-1-7998-8327-2.ch003

. Iseal, S., Wasiu, R., & Taiwo, I. (2024). The Impact of OKRs on Team Dynamics in Challenging Projects: A Case Study Approach

Kashive, N., Khanna, V. T., & Powale, L. (2022). Virtual team performance: E-leadership roles in the era of COVID-19. *Journal of Management Development*, *41*(5), 277–300. DOI: 10.1108/JMD-05-2021-0151

Korsgaard, M. A., Brower, H. H., & Lester, S. W. (2015). It isn't always mutual: A critical review of dyadic trust. *Journal of Management*, *41*(1), 47–70. DOI: 10.1177/0149206314547521

Kossek, E. E., Thompson, R. J., & Lautsch, B. A. (2015). Balanced workplace flexibility: Avoiding the traps. *California Management Review*, *57*(4), 5–25. DOI: 10.1525/cmr.2015.57.4.5

Lindberg, C. F., Tan, S., Yan, J., & Starfelt, F. (2015). Key performance indicators improve industrial performance. *Energy Procedia*, *75*, 1785–1790. DOI: 10.1016/j.egypro.2015.07.474

Liu, J., Zhu, Y., & Wang, H. (2023). Managing the negative impact of workforce diversity: The important roles of inclusive HRM and employee learning-oriented behaviors. *Frontiers in Psychology*, *14*, 1117690. DOI: 10.3389/fpsyg.2023.1117690 PMID: 36844330

Locke, E. A., & Latham, G. P. (2002). Building a practically useful theory of goal setting and task motivation: A 35-year odyssey. *The American Psychologist*, *57*(9), 705–717. DOI: 10.1037/0003-066X.57.9.705 PMID: 12237980

Maak, T., & Pless, N. M. (2009). Business leaders as citizens of the world. Advancing humanism on a global scale. *Journal of Business Ethics*, *88*(3), 537–550. DOI: 10.1007/s10551-009-0122-0

Malhotra, A., Majchrzak, A., & Rosen, B. (2007). Leading virtual teams. *The Academy of Management Perspectives*, *21*(1), 60–70. DOI: 10.5465/amp.2007.24286164

Maltz, M., & Shinar, D. (2004). Imperfect in-vehicle collision avoidance warning systems can aid drivers. *Human Factors*, *46*(2), 357–366. DOI: 10.1518/hfes.46.2.357.37348 PMID: 15359683

. Markos, S., & Sridevi, M. S. (2010). Employee engagement: The key to improving performance. *International journal of business and management, 5(12),* 89. https:// doi.org/. v5n12p89DOI: 10.5539/ijbm

Marquis, C., & Tilcsik, A. (2013). Imprinting: Toward a multilevel theory. *The Academy of Management Annals*, *7*(1), 195–245. DOI: 10.5465/19416520.2013.766076

Mathur, M., Pramanik, B., Rosalyn, S., Thulaseedharan, A., Mirzani, Y., & Namdeo, S. (2024). Ethical implications of AI in HRM: Balancing efficiency and privacy in employee monitoring systems. *Nanotechnology Perceptions*, •••, 4490–4496. DOI: 10.62441/nano-ntp.vi.3870

Mazmanian, M., Orlikowski, W. J., & Yates, J. (2013). The autonomy paradox: The implications of mobile email devices for knowledge professionals. *Organization Science*, *24*(5), 1337–1357. DOI: 10.1287/orsc.1120.0806

Medina-Garrido, J. A., Biedma-Ferrer, J. M., & Ramos-Rodríguez, A. R. (2017). Relationship between work-family balance, employee well-being and job performance. *Academia (Caracas)*, *30*(1), 40–58. DOI: 10.1108/ARLA-08-2015-0202

Meske, C., & Amojo, I. (2020). Ethical guidelines for the construction of digital nudges. *arXiv preprint arXiv:2003. 05249.* /arXiv.2003.05249.DOI: 10.24251/ HICSS.2020.480

Monica, B. S. (2021). The Effect of IT Employees' Engagement on Work Attitudes through Cloud Computing Services. In *Recent Advances in Technology Acceptance Models and Theories* (pp. 497–507). Springer International Publishing., DOI: 10.1007/978-3-030-64987-6_29

Mulki, J., Bardhi, F., Lassk, F., & Nanavaty-Dahl, J. (2009). Set up remote workers to thrive. *MIT Sloan Management Review*.

Naranjo-Gil, D., & Hartmann, F. (2006). How top management teams use management accounting systems to implement strategy. *Journal of Management Accounting Research*, *18*(1), 21–53. DOI: 10.2308/jmar.2006.18.1.21

Nembhard, I. M., & Edmondson, A. C. (2006). Making it safe: The effects of leader inclusiveness and professional status on psychological safety and improvement efforts in health care teams. *Journal of Organizational Behavior: The International Journal of Industrial. Journal of Organizational Behavior*, *27*(7), 941–966. DOI: 10.1002/job.413

Nesterak, J., Szelągowski, M., & Radziszewski, P. (2024). Workplace performance measurement: Digitalization of work observation and analysis. *Journal of Intelligent Manufacturing*, •••, 1–17. DOI: 10.1007/s10845-024-02419-x

Ng, C., Wider, W., Yang, C., Jiang, L., Vasudevan, A., Bhandari, P., & Lee, H. P. T. (2024). Keys factor affecting employee performance in the banking sector: A Delphi study. *Cogent Business & Management, 11*(1), 2409942. DOI: 10.1080/23311975.2024.2409942

Oakman, J., Lambert, K. A., Rogerson, S., & Bell, A. (2024). We know it doesn't work: Why do we still use how to lift training for the prevention of musculoskeletal disorders*? International Journal of Industrial Ergonomics, 100*, 103542. DOI: 10.1016/j.ergon.2023.103542

Obaidi, M., Nagel, L., Specht, A., & Klünder, J. (2022). Sentiment analysis tools in software engineering: A systematic mapping study. *Information and Software Technology, 151*, 107018. DOI: 10.1016/j.infsof.2022.107018

Ou, Z., Chen, T., Li, F., & Tang, P. (2018). Constructive controversy and creative process engagement: The roles of positive conflict value, cognitive flexibility, and psychological safety. *Journal of Applied Social Psychology, 48*(2), 101–113. DOI: 10.1111/jasp.12494

Ouchi, W. G. (1979). A conceptual framework for the design of organizational control mechanisms. *Management Science, 25*(9), 833–848. DOI: 10.1287/mnsc.25.9.833

Park, C., & Park, Y. (2021). The effect of personality diversity on life satisfaction and job performance: The mediate effect of mastery approach goal orientation. *Korean Journal of Industrial and Organizational Psychology, 34*(2), 287–318. DOI: 10.24230/kjiop.v34i2.287-318

Peterson, M. F., Smith, P. B., Akande, A., Ayestaran, S., Bochner, S., Callan, V., & Viedge, C. (1995). Role conflict, ambiguity, and overload: A 21-nation study. *Academy of Management Journal, 38*(2), 429–452. DOI: 10.2307/256687

Pulakos, E. D., Arad, S., Donovan, M. A., & Plamondon, K. E. (2000). Adaptability in the workplace: Development of a taxonomy of adaptive performance. *The Journal of Applied Psychology, 85*(4), 612–624. DOI: 10.1037/0021-9010.85.4.612 PMID: 10948805

Radziwill, N., & Benton, M. C. (2024). Unleashing excellence through inclusion: Navigating the engagement-performance paradox. *arXiv preprint arXiv:2407.09987.* https://doi.org//arXiv.2407.09987DOI: 10.48550

Richardson, J., & Kelliher, C. (2015). Managing visibility for career sustainability: A study of remote workers. *Handbook of research on sustainable careers*, 116 130. DOI: 10.4337/9781782547037.00013

Ruehle, R. C. (2023). The moral permissibility of digital nudging in the workplace: Reconciling justification and legitimation. *Business Ethics Quarterly*, *33*(3), 502–531. DOI: 10.1017/beq.2023.4

Rushing, W. A. (1965). Kahn, wolfe, quinn, and snoek: Organizaitonal stress: Studies in role conflict and ambiguity (book review). *Social Forces*, *43*(4), 591. DOI: 10.2307/2574480

Salanova, M., & Schaufeli, W. B. (2008). A cross-national study of work engagement as a mediator between job resources and proactive behaviour. *International Journal of Human Resource Management*, *19*(1), 116–131. DOI: 10.1080/09585190701763982

Sampat, B., Raj, S., Behl, A., & Schöbel, S. (2022). An empirical analysis of facilitators and barriers to the hybrid work model: A cross-cultural and multi-theoretical approach. *Personnel Review*, *51*(8), 1990–2020. DOI: 10.1108/PR-02-2022-0176

Sewell, G., & Taskin, L. (2015). Out of sight, out of mind in a new world of work? Autonomy, control, and spatiotemporal scaling in telework. *Organization Studies*, *36*(11), 1507–1529. DOI: 10.1177/0170840615593587

Sexton, J. B., Adair, K. C., Leonard, M. W., Frankel, T. C., Proulx, J., Watson, S. R., Magnus, B., Bogan, B., Jamal, M., Schwendimann, R., & Frankel, A. S. (2018). Providing feedback following Leadership Walk Rounds is associated with better patient safety culture, higher employee engagement and lower burnout. *BMJ Quality & Safety*, *27*(4), 261–270. DOI: 10.1136/bmjqs-2016-006399 PMID: 28993441

Shamspour, H. R., Kamali, M., & Narouei, B. (2024). Impact of micromanagement on organizational commitment through mediating role of job stress, moderating effect of hostile attribution bias. *International Journal of Business and Management Sciences*, *5*(3), 56–77. https://www.ijbms.org/

Siegel, R., König, C. J., & Lazar, V. (2022). The impact of electronic monitoring on employees' job satisfaction, stress, performance, and counterproductive work behavior: A meta-analysis. *Computers in Human Behavior Reports*, *8*, 100227. DOI: 10.1016/j.chbr.2022.100227

Soomar, Z. (2020). A framework for building and maintain trust in remote and virtual teams. *F1000 Research*, *9*(1187), 1187. DOI: 10.12688/f1000research.26626.1

Soon, C. C., & Salamzadeh, Y. (2021). The impact of digital leadership competencies on virtual team effectiveness in MNC companies in Penang, Malaysia. *Journal of Entrepreneurship. Business Economics (Cleveland, Ohio)*, *8*(2), 219–253. http://orcid.org/0000-0002-6917-2754

. Staats, B. R., Dai, H., Hofmann, D., & Milkman, K. L. (2017). Motivating process compliance through individual electronic monitoring: An empirical examination of hand hygiene in healthcare. *Management Science, 63(5),* 1563-1585.Cox, S. (2016. DOI: 10.1287/mnsc.2015.2400

Stawicki, C., Krishnakumar, S., & Robinson, M. D. (2023). Working with emotions: Emotional intelligence, performance and creativity in the knowledge-intensive workforce. *Journal of Knowledge Management, 27*(2), 285–301. DOI: 10.1108/JKM-07-2021-0556

Tamilselvi, M. (2024, April). Human facial emotion recognition using graphical cascaded convolutional neural network. In *2024 Ninth International Conference on Science Technology Engineering and Mathematics (ICONSTEM)* (pp. 1-8). IEEE. DOI: 10.1109/ICONSTEM60960.2024.10568797

Tang, W. G., & Vandenberghe, C. (2021). Role overload and work performance: The role of psychological strain and leader–member exchange. *Frontiers in Psychology, 12*, 691207. DOI: 10.3389/fpsyg.2021.691207 PMID: 34093378

. Tarigan, A., Gustomo, A., & Bangun, Y. R. (2023). Enhancing fairness in performance appraisals: A conceptual framework through a systematic literature review. *Journal of Advances in Humanities Research ISSN, 2948,* 4863.https://doi.org/. v2i3.176DOI: 10.56868/jadhur

. Tawalbeh, J. (2025). Remote and hybrid work models: Enhancing employee engagement and redefining performance management in a new era. *Journal of Posthumanism, 5(3),* 101-116.https://doi.org/. v5i3.715DOI: 10.63332/joph

Tichy, N. (2021). The Role of Transparency & Fairness in Performance Management-A Review and a Research Agenda. *In Academy of Management Proceedings (Vol. 2021, No. 1, p. 13230).* Briarcliff Manor, NY 10510. *Academy of Management Journal.* Advance online publication. DOI: 10.5465/AMBPP.2021.13230

. Vakkuri, J. (2010), Struggling with ambiguity: public managers as users of NPM-oriented management instruments. *Public Administration,* 88, 4, pp. 999–1024. https://doi.org/ . 01856.xDOI: 10.1111/j.1467-9299.2010

Wakefield, R. L., Leidner, D. E., & Garrison, G. (2008). Research note—A model of conflict, leadership, and performance in virtual teams. *Information Systems Research, 19*(4), 434–455. DOI: 10.1287/isre.1070.0149

Weick, K. E. (1995). *Sensemaking in organizations.* Sage.

Wong, S. I., & Berntzen, M. N. (2019). Transformational leadership and leader–member exchange in distributed teams: The roles of electronic dependence and team task interdependence. *Computers in Human Behavior*, *92*, 381–392. DOI: 10.1016/j.chb.2018.11.032

Yang, L., Holtz, D., Jaffe, S., Suri, S., Sinha, S., Weston, J., Joyce, C., Shah, N., Sherman, K., Hecht, B., & Teevan, J. (2022). The effects of remote work on collaboration among information workers. *Nature Human Behaviour*, *6*(1), 43–54. DOI: 10.1038/s41562-021-01196-4 PMID: 34504299

Yeke, S., & Özveren, C. G. (2024). Enabling the management of diverse employees in the hybrid work model: A qualitative study. *Revista Brasileira de Gestão de Negócios*, *26*(1), e20230128. DOI: 10.7819/rbgn.v26i01.4254

Zhao, K., Hsieh, W., Faulkner, N., & Smith, L. (2025). A systematic meta-review of organizational diversity and inclusion interventions and their associated outcomes. *Equality, Diversity and Inclusion*, *44*(9), 53–71. DOI: 10.1108/EDI-02-2024-0085

KEY TERMS AND DEFINITIONS

Hybrid Work: It is a flexible work model where employees share their time between their working in a traditional office and as well as remotely like home or other locations.

Performance Management: It is a continuous process that aligns employee actions with the organizational goals in order to enhance efficiency and effectiveness.

Employee Engagement: It refers to the emotional commitment and connection for the employees feel towards their work.

Performance Metrics: It is referred as quantifiable measurements used to track, assess, and evaluate the performance of individuals, teams, or organizations against established goals and objectives

Emotional Intelligence: It is the ability to understand and manage your own emotions, as well as recognize and influence the emotions of others.

Employee Well-Being: It refers to the overall health and happiness of the employees, enclosing their mental, physical, social, and financial well-being.

Quality of Life: It is the overall well-being of an individual or group, reflecting their physical health, psychological state, level of independence, social relationships, and satisfaction with their environment and life circumstances.

Compilation of References

Abid, K., & Polo, F. (2025). Narrative review on talent management: Evaluating two decades and exploring future research directions. *Journal of Global Mobility*, *13*(1), 1–31. DOI: 10.1108/JGM-07-2024-0076

Aftab, S., Khalid, K., Waheed, A., Aftab, A., & Adnan, A. (2022). Role of agile leadership in managing inter-role conflicts for a satisfying job and life during COVID-19 in a VUCA world. *Frontiers in Psychology*, *13*, 979792. DOI: 10.3389/fpsyg.2022.979792 PMID: 36329740

Aguinis, H., Gottfredson, R. K., & Joo, H. (2012). Using performance management to win the talent war. *Business Horizons*, *55*(6), 609–616. DOI: 10.1016/j.bushor.2012.05.007

Ahmed, R. R., Azam, M., Qureshi, J. A., & Hashem, E. (2022). The relationship between internal employer branding and talent retention: A theoretical investigation for the development of a conceptual framework. *Frontiers in Psychology*, *13*, 859614. DOI: 10.3389/fpsyg.2022.859614 PMID: 35369242

Ahrens, T., & Chapman, C. S. (2004). Accounting for flexibility and efficiency: A field study of management control systems in a restaurant chain. *Contemporary Accounting Research*, *21*(2), 271–301. DOI: 10.1506/VJR6-RP75-7GUX-XH0X

Al Ariss, A., Cascio, W. F., & Paauwe, J. (2014). Talent management: Current theories and future research directions. *Journal of World Business*, *49*(2), 173–179. DOI: 10.1016/j.jwb.2013.11.001

Alagaraja, M., & Li, J. (2015). Utilizing institutional perspectives to investigate the emergence, rise, and (relative) decline of corporate universities. *Human Resource Development International*, *18*(1), 4–23. DOI: 10.1080/13678868.2014.979003

Alge, B. J. (2001). Effects of computer surveillance on perceptions of privacy and procedural justice. *The Journal of Applied Psychology*, *86*(4), 797–804. DOI: 10.1037/0021-9010.86.4.797 PMID: 11519663

Alizadeh, R., Lund, P. D., Beynaghi, A., Abolghasemi, M., & Maknoon, R. (2016). An integrated scenario-based robust planning approach for foresight and strategic management with application to energy industry. *Technological Forecasting and Social Change*, *104*, 162–171. DOI: 10.1016/j.techfore.2015.11.030

Allen, K. S., Grelle, D., Lazarus, E. M., Popp, E., & Gutierrez, S. L. (2024). Hybrid is here to stay: Critical behaviors for success in the new world of work. *Personality and Individual Differences*, *217*, 112459. DOI: 10.1016/j.paid.2023.112459

Allen, M. W. (2007). What is a next-generation corporate university? In Allen, M. W. (Ed.), *The next generation of corporate universities* (pp. 3–16). John Wiley & Sons.

Allen, M. W. (2010). Corporate universities 2010: Globalization and greater sophistication. *Journal of International Management Studies*, *5*(1), 48–52.

Allen, M. W. (Ed.). (2002). *The corporate university handbook: Designing, managing, and growing a successful program*. AMACOM.

Allen, T. D., Golden, T. D., & Shockley, K. M. (2015). How effective is telecommuting? Assessing the status of our scientific findings. *Psychological Science in the Public Interest*, *16*(2), 40–68. DOI: 10.1177/1529100615593273 PMID: 26403188

Ambardar, A., Singh, A., & Singh, V. (2023). Barriers in Implementing Ergonomic Practices in Hotels- A Study on five star hotels in NCR region. *International Journal of Hospitality and Tourism Systems*, *16*(2), 11–17.

AmCham Slovenia. (2023). Partnership for Change. https://amcham.si/zagovornistvo/partnerstvo-za-spremembe/

Anderson-Meli, L., & Koshy, S. (2020). *Public relations crisis communication: A new model*. Routledge. DOI: 10.4324/9780429287763

Andresen, M., & Lichtenberger, B. (2007). The corporate university landscape in Germany. *Journal of Workplace Learning*, *19*(2), 109–123. DOI: 10.1108/13665620710728484

Anlesinya, A., & Amponsah-Tawiah, K. (2020). Towards a responsible talent management model. *European Journal of Training and Development*, *44*(2/3), 279–303. DOI: 10.1108/EJTD-07-2019-0114

Antonelli, G., Cappiello, G., & Pedrini, G. (2013). The corporate university in the European utility industries. *Utilities Policy*, *25*, 33–41. DOI: 10.1016/j.jup.2013.02.003

Armenakis, A. A., & Bedeian, A. G. (1999). Organizational change: A review of theory and research in the 1990s. *Journal of Management*, *25*(3), 293–315. DOI: 10.1177/014920639902500303

Armenakis, A. A., & Harris, S. G. (2009). Reflections: Our journey in organizational change research and practice. *Journal of Change Management, 9*(2), 127–142. DOI: 10.1080/14697010902879079

Armstrong, M., & Baron, A. (2005). *Managing performance: performance management in action.* CIPD publishing.

Arndt, J. (1967). Role of product-related conversations in the diffusion of a new product. *JMR, Journal of Marketing Research, 4*(3), 291–295. DOI: 10.1177/002224376700400308

Arrawatia, R., Dawar, V., Maitra, D., & Dash, S. R. (2019). Asset quality determinants of Indian banks: Empirical evidence and policy issues. *Journal of Public Affairs, 19*(4), e1937. DOI: 10.1002/pa.1937

Arzubiaga, U., Iturralde, T., Maseda, A., & Kotlar, J. (2021). Big Data in Family Businesses: A Socio-Emotional Perspective on Wealth. *European Management Journal, 39*(3), 308–321. DOI: 10.1016/j.emj.2020.10.006

Ashton, C., & Morton, L. (2005). Managing talent for competitive advantage: Taking a systemic approach to talent management. *Strategic HR Review, 4*(5), 28–31. DOI: 10.1108/14754390580000819

Avery, D. R., Hall, A. V., Preston, M., Ruggs, E. N., & Washington, E. (2023). Is justice colorblind? A review of rational-ethnic differences in the workplace through the prism of organizational justice. *Annual Review of Organizational Psychology and Organizational Behavior, 10*, 389–412. DOI: 10.1146/annurev-orgpsych-120920-052627

Avey, J. B., Reichard, R. J., Luthans, F., & Mhatre, K. H. (2011). Meta-analysis of the impact of positive psychological capital on employee attitudes, behaviors, and performance. *Human Resource Development Quarterly, 22*(2), 127–152. DOI: 10.1002/hrdq.20070

Avrillia, S., Hakim, L., Sulfia, S., & Anshori, M. I. (2025). Hybrid leadership and organizational performance: A literature review approach. *Implementasi Manajemen & Kewirausahaan, 5*(1), 14–30. DOI: 10.38156/imka.v5i1.540

Axis Bank academies. (2017, January 25). *The Tribune.* https://www.tribuneindia.com/news/archive/prospects/axis-bank-academies-355012/

Axis Bank. (2021–22). Possibilities to nurture an engaging workplace: Annual report 2021–22. https://www.axisbank.com/investors/annual-reports

Axis Bank. (2024, November 11). Axis Bank partners with Adda247 for talent development and skill building. https://www.axisbank.com/about-us/axis-bank-partners-with-adda247-for-talent-development-and-skill-building

Axis Bank. (2026, February 25). Axis Bank collaborates with Adda Education to launch Hire-Train-Deploy programme for Commercial Banking Relationship Managers. https://www.axisbank.com/about-us/axis-bank-collaborates-with-adda-education-htd-programme

Azhar, A., Rehman, N., Majeed, N., & Bano, S. (2024). Employer branding: A strategy to enhance organizational performance. *International Journal of Hospitality Management, 116*, 103618. DOI: 10.1016/j.ijhm.2023.103618

Backhaus, K., & Tikoo, S. (2004). Conceptualizing and researching employer branding. *Career Development International, 9*(5), 501–517. DOI: 10.1108/13620430410550754

Bailey, N. B. K. D. E., & Kurland, N. B. (1999). The advantages and challenges of working here, there, anywhere, and anytime. *Organizational Dynamics, 28*(2), 53–68. DOI: 10.1016/S0090-2616(00)80016-9

Bakker, A. B., & Demerouti, E. (2007). The job demands-resources model: State of the art. *Journal of Managerial Psychology, 22*(3), 309–328. DOI: 10.1108/02683940710733115

Bal, P. M., Chiaburu, D. S., & Jansen, P. G. W. (2010). Psychological contract breach and work performance: Is social exchange a buffer or an intensifier? *Journal of Managerial Psychology, 25*(3), 252–273. DOI: 10.1108/02683941011023730

Baran, B. E., & Woznyj, H. M. (2020). Managing VUCA: The human dynamics of agility. *Organizational Dynamics, 100787*. Advance online publication. DOI: 10.1016/j.orgdyn.2020.100787 PMID: 32843777

Barney, J. (1991). Firm resources and sustained competitive advantage. *Journal of Management, 17*(1), 99–120. DOI: 10.1177/014920639101700108

Barney, J. B. (2001). Resource-based theories of competitive advantage: A ten-year retrospective on the resource-based view. *Journal of Management, 27*(6), 643–650. DOI: 10.1177/014920630102700602

Baruah, A., Shaikh, M., Kumar, R. M., Shaikh, I. A. K., & Thomas, S. N. (2024, April). Artificial Intelligence Influence on Leadership Styles in Human Resource Management for Employee Engagement. In *2024 Ninth International Conference on Science Technology Engineering and Mathematics (ICONSTEM)* (pp. 1-5). IEEE. DOI: 10.1109/ICONSTEM60960.2024.10568819

Baruch, Y., & Rousseau, D. M. (2019). Integrating psychological contracts and ecosystems in career studies and management. *The Academy of Management Annals, 13*(1), 84–111. DOI: 10.5465/annals.2016.0103

Beckel, J. L., & Fisher, G. G. (2022). Teleworking and occupational health and well-being. *International Journal of Environmental Research and Public Health, 19*(7), 3879. DOI: 10.3390/ijerph19073879 PMID: 35409563

Becker, G. S. (1964). *Human capital: A theoretical and empirical analysis, with special reference to education*. University of Chicago Press.

Behl, A., Pal, A., & Roy, K. K. (2016). Integrated framework for governance of cooperative: An Interpretive Structural Modeling approach. *Indian Journal of Economics and Development, 4*, 2.

Bell, B. S., McAlpine, K. L., & Hill, N. S. (2023). Leading virtually. *Annual Review of Organizational Psychology and Organizational Behavior, 10*(1), 339–362. DOI: 10.1146/annurev-orgpsych-120920-050115

Bennett, N., & Lemoine, G. J. (2014). What a difference a word makes: Understanding threats to performance in a VUCA world. *Business Horizons, 57*(3), 311–317. DOI: 10.1016/j.bushor.2014.01.001

Benoit, W. L. (1997). Image repair discourse and crisis communication. *Public Relations Review, 23*(2), 177–187. DOI: 10.1016/S0363-8111(97)90023-0

Berthon, P., Ewing, M., & Hah, L. L. (2005). Captivating company: Dimensions of attractiveness in employer branding. *International Journal of Advertising, 24*(2), 151–172. DOI: 10.1080/02650487.2005.11072912

Bhanumathi, P., & Hemavathi, P. (2025). HR Agility: Embracing Change in Human Resource Practices. In *Modern Trends and Future Innovation in Human Resource Management* (pp. 197-238). IGI Global. DOI: 10.4018/979-8-3693-6402-4.ch007

Biron, M., Boon, C., Farndale, E., & Bamberger, P. A. (2024). *Human resource strategy: Formulation, implementation, and impact*. Routledge., DOI: 10.4324/9781003402176

Bititci, U., Carrie, A., & Turner, T. (1998). Diagnosing the integrity of your performance measurement system. *Control, 24*(3), 9–14. https://strathprints.strath.ac.uk/id/eprint/32935

Blass, E. (2005). The rise and rise of the corporate university. *Journal of European Industrial Training, 29*(1), 58–74. DOI: 10.1108/03090590510576217

Blass, E. (2015). The changing and developing role of the corporate university post-millennium. *Industry and Higher Education*, *29*(3), 167–177. DOI: 10.5367/ihe.2015.0256

Blau, P. M. (1964). *Exchange and power in social life*. Wiley.

Bloom, N., Han, R., & Liang, J. (2024). Hybrid work from home improves retention without hurting performance. *Nature*, *630*(8018), 920–925. DOI: 10.1038/s41586-024-07500-2 PMID: 38867040

Boers, B., & Andersson, T. (2023). Family members as hybrid owners and managers in family recurring businesses: Managing multiple institutional logics. *Journal of Family Business Management*, *13*(2), 523–543. DOI: 10.1108/JFBM-06-2021-0065

Boselie, P., & Thunnissen, M. (2017). Talent management in the public sector: Managing tensions and dualities.

Boxall, P., & Purcell, J. (2016). *Strategy and human resource management* (4th ed.). Palgrave Macmillan. DOI: 10.1007/978-1-137-40765-8

Brennan, N., & Connell, B. (2000). Intellectual capital: Current issues and policy implications. *Journal of Intellectual Capital*, *1*(3), 206–240. DOI: 10.1108/14691930010350792

Brewster, C., Gooderham, P. N., & Mayrhofer, W. (2016). Human resource management: The promise, the performance, the consequences. *Journal of Organizational Effectiveness: People and Performance*, *3*(2), 181–190. DOI: 10.1108/JOEPP-03-2016-0024

Buckingham, M. and Vosburgh, R. M. (2001) 'The 21st century human resources function: It's the talent, stupid!', *Human Resource Planning,* 24(4).

Butler, J. L., Zimmermann, T., & Bird, C. (2024, April). Objectives and key results in software teams: Challenges, opportunities and impact on development. In *Proceedings of the 46th International Conference on Software Engineering: Software Engineering in Practice* (pp. 358-368). DOI: 10.1145/3639477.3639747

Canali, S., Porcheron, M., & Lucivero, F. (2022). Challenges and recommendations for wearable devices in digital health: Data quality, interoperability, health equity, equity. *PLOS Digital Health*, *1*(10), e0000104. DOI: 10.1371/journal.pdig.0000104 PMID: 36812619

Cao, B., Hamamoto, Y., Wang, Y., & Zhang, H. (2024). A new integrated approach to preliminary and multi-criteria decision-making. *PeerJ Informática*, *10*, e2096. DOI: 10.7717/peerj-cs.2096 PMID: 38983217

Capital, T. I. (1998). Exploring the concept of intellectual capital (IC). *Long Range Planning*, *31*(1), 150–453. DOI: 10.1016/S0024-6301(97)87431-6

Careers, G. C. M. M. F. (2026). *Careers and recruitment notice*. https://www.amul.com

Chadwick, S. (2022). From utilitarianism and neoclassical management of sport to a new geopolitical economy of sport. *European Sport Management Quarterly*, *22*(5), 685–704. DOI: 10.1080/16184742.2022.2032251

Charalampous, M., Grant, C. A., Tramontano, C., & Michailidis, E. (2019). Systematically reviewing remote e-workers' well-being at work: A multidimensional approach. *European Journal of Work and Organizational Psychology*, *28*(1), 51–73. DOI: 10.1080/1359432X.2018.1541886

Chen, J., Storchan, V., & Kurshan, E. (2021). Beyond fairness metrics: Roadblocks and challenges for ethical ai in practice. *arXiv preprint arXiv:2108.06217.* https://doi.org//arXiv.2108.06217DOI: 10.48550

Chen, Y. Q., Xu, Y. S., & Zhai, Q. G. (2019). The knowledge management functions of corporate university and their evolution. *Journal of Knowledge Management*, *23*(10), 2086–2112. DOI: 10.1108/JKM-04-2018-0228

Cheong, B. C. (2024). Transparency and Accountability in AI Systems: Safeguarding Well-Being in the Age of Algorithmic Decision-Making. *Frontiers in Human Dynamics*. https://doi.org/DOI: 10.3389/fhumd.2024.1421273

Chib, S., Mehta, A. K., Saravanan, A., Mishra, B. R., & Manjunath, T. C. (2025). Mental Health Challenges and Solutions in High-Pressure Work Environments. In Harriott, S. (Ed.), *Innovative Approaches to Managing Conflict and Change in Diverse Work Environments* (pp. 247–272). IGI Global Scientific Publishing. DOI: 10.4018/979-8-3693-9556-1.ch011

Chidambaram, L., & Tung, L. L. (2005). Is out of sight, out of mind? An empirical study of social loafing in technology-supported groups. *Information Systems Research*, *16*(2), 149–168. DOI: 10.1287/isre.1050.0051

Chinmulgund, A., & Tapas, P. (2025). Organisational anthropomorphism and its antecedents: A literature review and proposed framework. *The International Journal of Organizational Analysis*, *33*(5), 1312–1323. DOI: 10.1108/IJOA-01-2024-4197

Chong, D., & Druckman, J. N. (2007). Framing theory. *Annual Review of Political Science*, *10*(1), 103–126. DOI: 10.1146/annurev.polisci.10.072805.103054

Choudhury, P., Foroughi, C., & Larson, B. Z. (2021). Working from anywhere: The productivity effects of geographic flexibility. *Strategic Management Journal, 42*(4), 655–683. DOI: 10.1002/smj.3251

Christensen, E. L., Paasivaara, M., & Salman, I. (2025, April). Hybrid Work in Agile Software Development: Recurring Meetings. In *2025 IEEE/ACM 18th International Conference on Cooperative and Human Aspects of Software Engineering (CHASE)* (pp. 120-130). IEEE.DOI: 10.1109/CHASE66643.2025.00023

Christianson, M. K., & Barton, M. A. (2021). Understanding in times of COVID-19. *Journal of Management Studies, 58*(2), 572–576. DOI: 10.1111/joms.12658

Çivilidağ, A., & Durmaz, Ş. (2024). Examining the relationship between flexible working arrangements and employee performance: A mini review. *Frontiers in Psychology, 15*, 1398309. DOI: 10.3389/fpsyg.2024.1398309 PMID: 39027052

Cleary, P., Quinn, M., Moreno, A., & Marqués, P. (2019). Organisational legitimacy, sustainability reporting and print management in a resource-constrained environment. *Journal of Family Business Strategy, 10*(2), 100229. DOI: 10.1016/j.jfbs.2018.11.002

Cleveland, J. N., Murphy, K. R., & Williams, R. E. (1989). Multiple uses of performance appraisal: Prevalence and correlates. *The Journal of Applied Psychology, 74*(1), 130–135. DOI: 10.1037/0021-9010.74.1.130

Coffey, R., & Wolf, L. (2018). *The challenge and promise of remote work: A brief study of remote work and best practices (No. ANL/ALCF-18/4). Argonne National Lab.* ANL., DOI: 10.2172/1487022

Collings, D. G., & Mellahi, K. (2009). Strategic talent management: A review and research agenda. *Human Resource Management Review, 19*(4), 304–313. DOI: 10.1016/j.hrmr.2009.04.001

Collings, D. G., Mellahi, K., & Cascio, W. F. (2019). Global talent management and performance in multinational enterprises: A multilevel perspective. *Journal of Management, 45*(2), 540–566. DOI: 10.1177/0149206318757018

Conger, J. A., & Fulmer, R. M. (2003). Developing your leadership pipeline. *Harvard Business Review, 81*(12), 76–85. PMID: 14712546

Conway, N., & Briner, R. B. (2005). *Understanding psychological contracts at work: A critical evaluation of theory and research.* Oxford University Press. DOI: 10.1093/acprof:oso/9780199280643.001.0001

Coombs, W. T. (1995). Choosing the right words: The development of guidelines for the selection of the "appropriate" crisis-response strategies. *Management Communication Quarterly*, *8*(4), 447–476. DOI: 10.1177/0893318995008004003

Coombs, W. T. (2007). Ongoing crisis communication: Planning, managing, and responding. *Sage (Atlanta, Ga.)*.

Coombs, W. T. (2007). Protecting organization reputations during a crisis: The development and application of situational crisis communication theory. *Corporate Reputation Review*, *10*(3), 163–176. DOI: 10.1057/palgrave.crr.1550049

Coombs, W. T. (2014). *Ongoing crisis communication: Planning, managing, and responding*. Sage Publications.

Coombs, W. T. (2019). *Ongoing Crisis Communication: Planning, Managing, and Responding* (5th ed.). SAGE Publications.

Cooper, J. N., Newton, A. C., Klein, M., & Jolly, S. (2020). A call for culturally responsive transformational leadership in college sport: An anti-ism approach for achieving equity and inclusion. *Frontiers in Sociology*, *5*, 65. DOI: 10.3389/fsoc.2020.00065 PMID: 33869471

Coursera. (2021, March). Axis Bank reduces attrition via upskilling on Coursera. https://www.coursera.org/business/case-studies/axis-bank

Craveiro, E. G., dos Santos Oliveira, E., Barros de Oliveira, P. C., Bezerra, J. P., de Souza Cardoso, M., Peña, G. D., & Nascimento-e-Silva, D. (2025). Approaches And Attributes Of Management Systems and Their Implications for Cooperative Organizations. Environmental & Social Management Journal, 19(12).

Dairy, A. (2026). *Training and development initiatives*. https://www.amuldairy.com

Dairy, A. F. (2024).. . *Sustainability Report*, •••, 2024–2025. https://www.amulfeddairy.com

Das, L. (2026). Organizational Citizenship Behavior: A Systematic Review (1983 to 2024). *Journal of Evolutionary Studies in Business*, *11*(1), 123–149. DOI: 10.1344/jesb.45416

Dayan, M., Ng, P. Y., & Ndubisi, N. O. (2019). Mindfulness, socio-emotional richness and environmental strategy of family businesses. *Business Strategy and the Environment*, *28*(3), 466–481. DOI: 10.1002/bse.2222

De Leede, J., & Kraijenbrink, J. (2014). The mediating role of trust and social cohesion in the effects of new ways of working: a Dutch case study. In *Human resource management, social innovation and technology* (pp. 3–20). Emerald Group Publishing Limited., DOI: 10.1108/S1877-636120140000014006

de Souza Santos, R. E., & Ralph, P. (2022, May). A grounded theory of coordination in remote-first and hybrid software teams. *In Proceedings of the 44th International Conference on Software Engineering* (pp. 25-35). DOI: 10.1145/3510003.3510105

Dealtry, R. (2017). Corporate university developments: Managing strategic learning agility. *Journal of Workplace Learning*, *29*(5), 359–369.

Debicki, B. J., Kellermanns, F. W., Chrisman, J. J., Pearson, A. W., & Spencer, B. A. (2016). Development of a Socio-Emotional Importance of Wealth (SEWi) Scale for Research in Family Businesses. *Journal of Family Business Strategy*, *7*(1), 47–57. DOI: 10.1016/j.jfbs.2016.01.002

Deci, E. L., & Ryan, R. M. (2013). *Intrinsic motivation and self-determination in human behavior*. Springer Science & Business Media., DOI: 10.1007/978-1-4899-2271-7

Deepthi, P., Shaikh, M., Nargunde, A. S., Faldu, R., & Goli, G. (2024, April). Deep learning-enabled human resource analytics in predicting employee performance. In *2024 Ninth International Conference on Science Technology Engineering and Mathematics (ICONSTEM)* (pp. 1-5). IEEE. https://doi.org/DOI: 10.1109/ICONSTEM60960.2024.10568716

DiMaggio, P. J., & Powell, W. W. (1983). The iron cage revisited: Institutional isomorphism and collective rationality in organizational fields. *American Sociological Review*, *48*(2), 147–160. DOI: 10.2307/2095101

Dowling, B., Goldstein, D., Park, M., & Price, H. (2022). Hybrid work: Making it fit with your diversity, equity, and inclusion strategy. *The McKinsey Quarterly*, *4*, 1–9.

Dowling, M., Robertson, J., Washington, M., Leopkey, B., & Ellis, D. (2024). Agency and institutions in sport. *European Sport Management Quarterly*, *24*(1), 1–7. DOI: 10.1080/16184742.2023.2292102

Dries, N. (2013). The psychology of talent management: A review and research agenda. *Human Resource Management Review*, *23*(4), 272–285. DOI: 10.1016/j.hrmr.2013.05.001

Dries, N., & Kaše, R. (2023). Do employees find inclusive talent management fairer? It depends. Contrasting self-interest and principle. *Human Resource Management Journal*, *33*(3), 702–727. DOI: 10.1111/1748-8583.12501

Eckstein, G. (2024). Thirty-five years of business and management sense. *Business Research, 17*, 555–577. DOI: 10.1007/s11301-024-00458-5

Economic Times HR World. (2023, November 9). A growing concern in the banking industry: Here's how HDFC Bank is tackling high attrition rates! ETHRWorld. https://hr.economictimes.indiatimes.com/news/hrtech/talent-acquisition-and-management/a-growing-concern-in-the-banking-industry-heres-how-hdfc-bank-is-tackling-high-attrition-rates/105081619

Edmondson, A. C., & Bransby, D. P. (2023). Psychological safety comes of age: Themes observed in an established literature. *Annual Review of Organizational Psychology and Organizational Behavior, 10*(1), 55–78. DOI: 10.1146/annurev-orgpsych-120920-055217

Eisenhardt, K. M. (2021). What is the Eisenhardt Method, really? *Strategic Organization, 19*(1), 147–160. DOI: 10.1177/1476127020982866

Eldor, L., Hodor, M., & Cappelli, P. (2023). The limits of psychological safety: Nonlinear relationships with performance. *Organizational Behavior and Human Decision Processes, 177*, 104255. DOI: 10.1016/j.obhdp.2023.104255

Emerson, R. M. (1976). Social exchange theory. *Annual Review of Sociology, 2*(1), 335–362. DOI: 10.1146/annurev.so.02.080176.002003

Esenyel, V. (2024). Evolving leadership theories: Integrating contemporary theories for VUCA realities. *Administrative Sciences, 14*(11), 270. DOI: 10.3390/admsci14110270

Esposito, G., De Bernardi, P., Bertello, A., & Vrontis, D. (2025). Value tensions and actionable knowledge in grassroots innovation: A study of invitational ambiguity and implementation challenges. *Journal of Knowledge Management, 29*(2), 372–392. DOI: 10.1108/JKM-04-2024-0385

Etter, M., Ravasi, D., & Colleoni, E. (2019). Social media and the formation of organisational reputation. *Academy of Management Review, 44*(1), 28–52. DOI: 10.5465/amr.2014.0280

European Commission. (2023). *Strategic foresight report: Navigating the green and digital transitions.*

Fatien, P., & Otter, K. (2015). Wearing multiple hats? Challenges for managers-as-coaches and their organizations. *International Leadership Journal, 7*(3), 24–35.

Firdaus, S. R. (2024, November). Future Leaders in VUCA Bureaucracy: Millennials and Generation Z Perspective. In *Iapa Proceedings Conference* (pp. 1349-1366).

Folan, P., & Browne, J. (2005). A review of performance measurement: Towards performance management. *Computers in Industry*, *56*(7), 663–680. DOI: 10.1016/j.compind.2005.03.001

Frkal, R., & Lewis, M. S. (2025). Strategic leader or impulsive billionaire: Elon Musk's early moves to turnaround Twitter. *The CASE Journal*, *21*(4), 828–838. DOI: 10.1108/TCJ-07-2024-0191

Fuller, D., Colwell, E., Low, J., Orychock, K., Tobin, M. A., Simango, B., & Buote, R. (2020). Reliability and Validity of Commercially Available Wearable Devices for Measuring Steps, Energy Expenditure, and Heart Rate: A Systematic Review. *JMIR mHealth and uHealth*, *8*(9), e18694. DOI: 10.2196/18694 PMID: 32897239

Gabrišová, I., Koman, G., Soviar, J., & Holubčík, M. (2025). The Adoption of Modern Sports Technologies from Professional Settings to Everyday Life. *Administrative Sciences*, *15*(7), 249. DOI: 10.3390/admsci15070249

Gagné, M., Parker, S. K., Griffin, M. A., Dunlop, P. D., Knight, C., Klonek, F. E., & Parent Rocheleau, X. (2022). Understand and shape the future of work with self-determination theory. *Nature Reviews Psychology*, *1*(7), 378–392. DOI: 10.1038/s44159-022-00056-w PMID: 35574235

Gaillard, C., & Dervillé, M. (2022). Dairy farming, cooperatives and livelihoods: Lessons learned from six indian villages. *Journal of Asian Economics*, *78*, 101422. DOI: 10.1016/j.asieco.2021.101422

Gajendran, R. S., & Harrison, D. A. (2007). The good, the bad, and the unknown about telecommuting: Meta-analysis of psychological mediators and individual consequences. *The Journal of Applied Psychology*, *92*(6), 1524–1541. DOI: 10.1037/0021-9010.92.6.1524 PMID: 18020794

Galanti, T., & Fantinelli, S. (2025). Managing the future of talents: Digital innovation in learning organizations. *The Learning Organization*, *32*(4), 554–580. DOI: 10.1108/TLO-06-2023-0096

Gallardo-Gallardo, E. (2018). The meaning of talent in the world of work. *Global talent management*, 33-58.

Gallardo-Gallardo, E., Thunnissen, M., & Scullion, H. (2020). *Talent management: context matters*. Taylor & Francis.

Gallifant, J., Kistler, E. A., Nakayama, L. F., Ntatin, A., Fernandez, L., Zera, C., Bates, D., Dankwa-Mullan, I., & Celi, L. A. (2023). Disparity Panels An evaluation of the literature and framework for improving health equity. *The Lancet. Digital Health*, *5*(11), e831–e839. DOI: 10.1016/S2589-7500(23)00150-4 PMID: 37890905

GCMMF. (2005). *Chairman's speech: Annual general body meeting*. Gujarat Co-operative Milk Marketing Federation. https://www.amul.com

GCMMF. (2026a). *The Amul model*. Gujarat Cooperative Milk Marketing Federation. https://www.amul.com

GCMMF. (2026b). *Organisation overview*. Gujarat Cooperative Milk Marketing Federation. https://www.amul.com

Ge, Y. (2020). Psychological safety, employee voice, and work engagement. *Social Behavior and Personality*, *48*(3), 1–7. DOI: 10.2224/sbp.8907

Gibbs, M., Mengel, F., & Siemroth, C. (2023). Working from home and productivity. *Journal of Microeconomic Political Economy*, *1*(1), 7–54. DOI: 10.1086/721803

Giermindl, L. M., Strich, F., Christ, O., Leicht-Deobald, U., & Redzepi, A. (2022). The dark sides of people analytics. *European Journal of Information Systems*, *31*(3), 410–435. DOI: 10.1080/0960085X.2021.1927213

Gómez-Mejía, L. R., & Herrero, I. (2022). Going back to the starting point: The measure of socio-emotional wealth. *Journal of Family Business Strategy*, *13*(3), 100480. DOI: 10.1016/j.jfbs.2021.100480

Gonzalez, E., Nanos, E. M., Seyr, H., Valldecabres, L., Yürüşen, N. Y., Smolka, U., Muskulus, M., & Melero, J. J. (2017). Key performance indicators for wind farm operation and maintenance. *Energy Procedia*, *137*, 559–570. DOI: 10.1016/j.egypro.2017.10.385

Government of the Republic of Slovenia. (2025). Reform of the public sector pay system.

Grall, M., Charue-Duboc, F., & BenMahmoud-Jouini, S. (2025). Bridging project management and design thinking: Evidence from digital transformation projects. *Project Management Journal*, *56*(3), 390–410. DOI: 10.1177/87569728251337426

Grant, R. M. (1996). Toward a knowledge-based theory of the firm. *Strategic Management Journal*, *17*(S2), 109–122. DOI: 10.1002/smj.4250171110

Grashuis, J., & Su, Y. (2019). A review of the empirical literature on farmer cooperatives: Performance, ownership and governance, finance, and member attitude. *Annals of Public and Cooperative Economics*, *90*(1), 77–102. DOI: 10.1111/apce.12205

Greenberg, J. (1987). A taxonomy of organizational justice theories. *Academy of Management Review*, *12*(1), 9–22. DOI: 10.2307/257990

Gregory, P. J., Robbins, B., Schwaitzberg, S. D., & Harmon, L. (2017). Leadership development in a professional medical society using 360-degree survey feedback to assess emotional intelligence. *Surgical Endoscopy*, *31*(9), 3565–3573. DOI: 10.1007/s00464-016-5386-8 PMID: 28039648

Griesinger, A. N., Ehnold, P., Hoffmann, A., & Schlesinger, T. (2025). Integrating scientific recommendations for the development and promotion of junior elite athletes in Germany–an analysis of sports policy documents. *International journal of sport policy and politics, 17*(1), 61-79.

Grossi, G., Reichard, C., Thomasson, A., & Vakkuri, J. (2017). Theme: Performance measurement of hybrid organizations–emerging issues and future research perspectives. *Public Money & Management*, *37*(6), 379–386. DOI: 10.1080/09540962.2017.1344007

Groysberg, B., Haas, D., & Lin, E. (2023). Now You See Me, Now I'm Gone. *MIT Sloan Management Review*, *64*(2), 70–75.

Guest, D. E. (2004). The psychology of the employment relationship: An analysis based on the psychological contract. *Applied Psychology*, *53*(4), 541–555. DOI: 10.1111/j.1464-0597.2004.00187.x

Gupta, P., & Panagariya, A. (2023). Privatization of public sector banks in India: why, how and how far. National Council of Applied Economic Research (NCAER)| Working Paper No.: WP, 141.

Hajjami, O., & Crocco, O. S. (2024). Evolving approaches to employee engagement: Comparing antecedents in remote work and traditional workplaces. *European Journal of Training and Development*, *48*(3-4), 375–392. DOI: 10.1108/EJTD-10-2022-0103

Halid, I. A., Yusuf, N., & Pilomonu, M. R. S. (2026). The Effect of Intellectual Capital and Sustainability Report Disclosure on Firm Value:(Study on the Food and Beverage Sector for the Period 2022-2024). *Majapahit Journal of Islamic Finance and Management*, *6*(1), 806–823.

Haque, A., Fernando, M., & Caputi, P. (2019). Responsible leadership, affective commitment and intention to quit: An individual level analysis. *Leadership and Organization Development Journal*, *40*(1), 45–64. DOI: 10.1108/LODJ-12-2017-0397

Harilal, K. N. (2021). Globalization of agriculture and atomization of farming: Small farms crisis in Asia. *Millennial Asia*, *12*(3), 298–315. DOI: 10.1177/09763996211059964

Harsin, J. (2024). Taxis against Uber in Paris, technological capital and collaborative economy. *Labor History*, *65*(6), 784–800. DOI: 10.1080/0023656X.2024.2327461

Hayashi, C., & Soo, A. (2012). Adaptive leadership in times of crisis. *Prism*, *4*(1), 78–86.

HDFC Bank. (2019, July 3). HDFC Bank in partnership with Manipal Global Academy of BFSI launches Future Bankers program. https://www.hdfcbank.com/content/bbp/repositories/723fb80a-2dde-42a3-9793-7ae1be57c87f/?folderPath=/Footer/Press%20Release/Future-Bankers-program.pdf

HDFC Bank. (2022a). Embarking on cultural transformation [Annual report 2022]. https://v.hdfc.bank.in/embarking-on-cultural-transformation

HDFC Bank. (2022b, August 11). HDFC Bank launches Rising Bankers programme with Amity Global Business School. https://www.hdfcbank.com/content/api/contentstream-id/723fb80a-2dde-42a3-9793-7ae1be57c87f/rising-bankers-amity

Helminski, D., Sussman, J. B., Pfeiffer, P. N., Kokaly, A. N., Ranusch, A., Renji, A. D., Damschroder, L. J., Landis-Lewis, Z., & Kurlander, J. E. (2024). Development, implementation, and evaluation methods for health care panels. Review of scope. *JMIR Medical Informatics*, *12*, e59828. DOI: 10.2196/59828 PMID: 39656991

Hemmer, P., Westphal, M., Schemmer, M., Vetter, S., Vössing, M., & Satzger, G. (2023, March). Human-AI collaboration: the effect of AI delegation on human task performance and task satisfaction. *In Proceedings of the 28th International Conference on Intelligent User Interfaces* (pp. 453-463). DOI: 10.1145/3581641.3584052

Hickok, M., & Maslej, N. (2023). A policy primer and roadmap on AI worker surveillance and productivity scoring tools. *AI and Ethics*, *3*(3), 673–687. DOI: 10.1007/s43681-023-00275-8 PMID: 37360144

Hill, I., & Sallai, D. (2025). Diversity, Equity and Inclusion in Human Resource Management. *Diversity, Equity and Inclusion for Business & Management*, 91.

Hirak, R., Peng, A. C., Carmeli, A., & Schaubroeck, J. M. (2012). Linking leader inclusiveness to work unit performance: The importance of psychological safety and learning from failures. *The Leadership Quarterly*, *23*(1), 107–117. DOI: 10.1016/j.leaqua.2011.11.009

Hofstede, G. (1980). *Culture's consequences: International differences in work-related values*. Sage Publications.

Holden, J., Wagstaff, C. R., Wadey, R., & Brown, P. (2025). Navigating athlete development in elite sport: Understanding the barriers to the provision of performance lifestyle service in England. *Psychology of Sport and Exercise*, *77*, 102779. DOI: 10.1016/j.psychsport.2024.102779 PMID: 39551251

Holland, P., & Pyman, A. (2006). Corporate universities: A catalyst for strategic human resource development? *Journal of European Industrial Training*, *30*(7), 542–553. DOI: 10.1108/03090590610643851

Horney, N., Pasmore, B., & O'Shea, T. (2010). Leadership agility: A business imperative for a VUCA world. *People & Strategy*, *33*(4), 32–38.

Ho, S. S. H., Mishra, A., & Kim, P. H. (2024). Can corporate social responsibility lead to social freedom to operate? *Journal of Management Studies*, *61*(5), 1202–1231. DOI: 10.1111/joms.12863

Houston, C. M., & Hamrick, J. D. (2025). Failure of cooperative self-regulation: An exploration of cooperative regulatory violations. *Annals of Public and Cooperative Economics*, *96*(2), 225–256. DOI: 10.1111/apce.12498

Howard, M. C., Gutworth, M. B., & Jacobs, R. R. (2021). A meta-analysis of virtual reality training programs. *Computers in Human Behavior*, *121*, 106808. DOI: 10.1016/j.chb.2021.106808

Howcroft, D., & Leaver, A. (2025). Unstable platforms. *Accounting Forum*, *49*(1), 1–23. DOI: 10.1080/01559982.2024.2309018

Hubballi, R. B., Seenivasan, R., & Basava Aradhya, S. G., Dinesh, N., & Seelam, P. K. (2025). Overview of Current AI Technologies in Education. In L. Kyei-Blankson & E. Ntuli (Eds.), *Transformative AI Practices for Personalized Learning Strategies* (pp. 1-26). IGI Global Scientific Publishing.

Hubbell, A. P., & Chory-Assad, R. M. (2005). Motivating factors: Perceptions of justice and their relationship with managerial and organizational trust. *Communication Studies*, *56*(1), 47–70. DOI: 10.1080/0008957042000332241

Huyler, D., Gomez, L., Rocco, T. S., & Plakhotnik, M. S. (2025). Leading Different Generational Cohorts in the Workplace: Focus on Situational and Inclusive Leadership. *New Horizons in Adult Education and Human Resource Development*, *37*(1), 6–19. DOI: 10.1177/19394225241297230

IFFCO. (2022). *Annual report 2021–22*. Indian Farmers Fertiliser Cooperative Limited. https://www.iffco.in

Ingraham, P. W., Selden, S. C., & Moynihan, D. P. (2000). People and performance: Challenges for the future public service—The report from the Wye River Conference. *Public Administration Review*, *60*(1), 54–60. DOI: 10.1111/0033-3352.00062

International Organization for Standardization. (2017). *ISO 22316:2017: Security and resilience –Organizational resilience – Principles and attributes*. ISO.

Ioannou, A., Tussyadiah, I., Miller, G., Li, S., & Weick, M. (2021). Privacy nudges for disclosure of personal information: A systematic literature review and meta-analysis. *PLoS One*, *16*(8), e0256822. DOI: 10.1371/journal.pone.0256822 PMID: 34449821

Iqbal, K. M. J., Khalid, F., & Barykin, S. Y. (2021). Hybrid workplace: The future of work. In *Handbook of Research on Future Opportunities for Technology Management Education* (pp. 28–48). IGI Global. DOI: 10.4018/978-1-7998-8327-2.ch003

Islam, M. M. (2026). 'Halal resource-based view: Exploring the resource-based view from marketers' lens'. *Journal of Islamic Accounting and Business Research*, •••, 1–27. DOI: 10.1108/JIABR-03-2025-0124

Janssen, H., & Rudeloff, C. (2025). Exploring the role of influencers in shaping employer brands: A comparative study of corporate and third-party influencers. *Corporate Reputation Review*, *28*(1), 57–70. DOI: 10.1057/s41299-023-00177-9

Junça Silva, A., & Dias, H. (2023). The relationship between employer branding, corporate reputation and intention to apply to a job offer. *The International Journal of Organizational Analysis*, *31*(8), 1–16. DOI: 10.1108/IJOA-01-2022-3129

Kaivo-Oja, J. R. L., & Lauraeus, I. T. (2018). The VUCA approach as a solution concept to corporate foresight challenges and global technological disruption. *foresight, 20*(1), 27-49. DOI: 10.1108/FS-06-2017-0022

Kaliannan, M., Darmalinggam, D., Dorasamy, M., & Abraham, M. (2023). Inclusive talent development as a key talent management approach: A systematic literature review. *Human Resource Management Review*, *33*(1), 100926. DOI: 10.1016/j.hrmr.2022.100926

Kamath, K. V., Kohli, S. S., Shenoy, P. S., Kumar, R., Nayak, R. M., Kuppuswamy, P. T., & Ravichandran, N. (2003). Indian banking sector: Challenges and opportunities. *Vikalpa*, *28*(3), 83–100. DOI: 10.1177/0256090920030308

Kannan, G., & Aulbur, W. G. (2004). Intellectual capital: Measurement effectiveness. *Journal of Intellectual Capital*, *5*(3), 389–413. DOI: 10.1108/14691930410550363

Kanoujiya, J., Agarwal, B., Rastogi, S., Tarode, S. and Bodne, S. (2026) 'Does competitive pressures affect the Indian SMEs industry 4. O adoption: using quantile regression analysis', *Journal of Innovation and Entrepreneurship*.

Kashive, N., Khanna, V. T., & Powale, L. (2022). Virtual team performance: E-leadership roles in the era of COVID-19. *Journal of Management Development*, *41*(5), 277–300. DOI: 10.1108/JMD-05-2021-0151

Katha, H. R. (2026, January 27). HDFC Bank expands Parivartan skilling initiative to Meerut. https://www.hrkatha.com/news/hdfc-bank-expands-parivartan-skilling-initiative-to-meerut

Kavitha, R., & Suresh, M. (2021). Agile Practices in Human Resource Management. In Kumaresan, G., Shanmugam, N. S., & Dhinakaran, V. (Eds.), *Advances in Materials Research. ICAMR 2019. Springer Proceedings in Materials* (Vol. 5). Springer., DOI: 10.1007/978-981-15-8319-3_71

Kelley, H. H., & Michela, J. L. (1980). Attribution theory and research. *Annual Review of Psychology, 31*(1), 457–501. DOI: 10.1146/annurev.ps.31.020180.002325 PMID: 20809783

Kelloway, E. K., Dimoff, J. K., & Gilbert, S. (2023). Mental health at work. *Annual Review of Organizational Psychology and Organizational Behavior, 10*(1), 363–387. DOI: 10.1146/annurev-orgpsych-120920-050527

Khajuria, R., Maini, A., & Bukhari, S. S. (2024). Bridging the gap: HR analytics adoption in the VUCA world of Industry 5.0. *Global Knowledge, Memory and Communication*. Advance online publication. DOI: 10.1108/GKMC-06-2024-0335

Kirkpatrick, D. L. (1998). *Evaluating training programs: The four levels* (2nd ed.). Berrett-Koehler.

Kolo, S., Reuschel, T., Hoffmann, R., & Schmidt, A. (2013). *Key facts on corporate universities: Trends, status quo, implications*. Fraunhofer Verlag.

Korsgaard, M. A., Brower, H. H., & Lester, S. W. (2015). It isn't always mutual: A critical review of dyadic trust. *Journal of Management, 41*(1), 47–70. DOI: 10.1177/0149206314547521

Kossek, E. E., Thompson, R. J., & Lautsch, B. A. (2015). Balanced workplace flexibility: Avoiding the traps. *California Management Review, 57*(4), 5–25. DOI: 10.1525/cmr.2015.57.4.5

Kotte, K. R., Attaluri, V., & Selvakumar, P. (2025). Revolutionising Retail Banking with AI and Virtual Technologies AI-Driven Financial Training. In Nair, A. J., Manohar, S., Limbu, Y. B., & Huhmann, B. A. (Eds.), *Intersecting Natural Language Processing and FinTech Innovations in Service Marketing* (pp. 421–440). IGI Global Scientific Publishing. DOI: 10.4018/979-8-3693-9944-6.ch020

Kotter, J. P. (1996). *Leading change*. Harvard Business School Press.

Kozjek, T., & Franca, V. (2020). Talent management in the public sector. *Cent. Eur. Pub. Admin. Rev., 18*, 53.

Kravariti, F., & Johnston, K. (2020). Talent management: A critical literature review and research agenda for public sector human resource management. *Public Management Review*, *22*(1), 75–95. DOI: 10.1080/14719037.2019.1638439

Kuoppakangas, P., Hagman, S., Stenvall, J., & Kinder, T. (2024). Social Learning and Reputation Management in an Espionage Crisis. *Corporate Reputation Review*, *27*(4), 271–282. DOI: 10.1057/s41299-023-00171-1

Lambert, S., & Ozdemir, N. (2026). Emotional agility among clinical line managers in the VUCA world. *Higher Education, Skills and Work-based Learning*, *16*(1), 1–15. DOI: 10.1108/HESWBL-06-2025-0237

Laufer, D., & Coombs, W. T. (2006). How should a company respond to a product harm crisis? The role of corporate reputation and consumer-based cues. *Business Horizons*, *49*(5), 379–385. DOI: 10.1016/j.bushor.2006.01.002

Lave, J., & Wenger, E. (1991). *Situated learning: Legitimate peripheral participation*. Cambridge University Press. DOI: 10.1017/CBO9780511815355

Lawrence, K. (2013). Developing leaders in a VUCA environment. UNC Executive Development. Retrieved from https://www.kenan-flagler.unc.edu/executive-development/custom-programs/~/media/DF696ABE19F74015BC753316749A930A.ashx

Le Roy, J., Meier, O., & Paquier, M. C. (2025). Redefining employee performance in a VUCA World: Constructing a new typology–Positive deviant behavior. @. *GRH*, *54*(1), 11–37.

Leal, M. T., Boixadós-Porquet, A., Castro-Diez, J., García Bernardos, Á., Magaña González, C. R., & Arranz Montull, M. (2026). Integrating VUCA and agile frameworks in work-integrated learning: A higher education case study. Higher Education. *Skills and Work-Based Learning*, *16*(1), 69–81. DOI: 10.1108/HESWBL-07-2025-0307

Lepak, D. P., & Snell, S. A. (1999). The human resource architecture: Toward a theory of human capital allocation and development. *Academy of Management Review*, *24*(1), 31–48. DOI: 10.2307/259035

Lewin, K. (1951). *Field theory in social science: Selected theoretical papers*. Harper & Row.

Lewis, R. E., & Heckman, R. J. (2006). Talent management: A critical review. *Human Resource Management Review*, *16*(2), 139–154. DOI: 10.1016/j.hrmr.2006.03.001

Li, J., Wang, Y., Yao, N. C., & Cui, X. (2023). Exploring the effects of socio-emotional wealth on the environmental strategies of family businesses in China: An integrative perspective. *Business Strategy and the Environment*, *32*(8), 5368–5381. DOI: 10.1002/bse.3425

Lilly, J., Durr, D., Grogan, A., & Super, J. F. (2021). Wells Fargo: Administrative evil and the pressure to conform. *Business Horizons*, *64*(5), 587–597. DOI: 10.1016/j.bushor.2021.02.028

Lindberg, C. F., Tan, S., Yan, J., & Starfelt, F. (2015). Key performance indicators improve industrial performance. *Energy Procedia*, *75*, 1785–1790. DOI: 10.1016/j.egypro.2015.07.474

Little, K. (2024). Defence of athletes. *Journal of Physical Education, Recreation & Dance*, *95*(9), 34–41. DOI: 10.1080/00913847.2024.2440821 PMID: 39648878

Liu, J., Zhu, Y., & Wang, H. (2023). Managing the negative impact of workforce diversity: The important roles of inclusive HRM and employee learning-oriented behaviors. *Frontiers in Psychology*, *14*, 1117690. DOI: 10.3389/fpsyg.2023.1117690 PMID: 36844330

Locke, E. A., & Latham, G. P. (2002). Building a practically useful theory of goal setting and task motivation: A 35-year odyssey. *The American Psychologist*, *57*(9), 705–717. DOI: 10.1037/0003-066X.57.9.705 PMID: 12237980

Lock, I., & Jacobs, S. (2025). Drivers of Reputation and Legitimacy of a Highly Visible Public Sector Organization: Surveying Citizens' Perceptions: I. Lock, S. Jacobs. *Corporate Reputation Review*, •••, 1–15. DOI: 10.1057/s41299-025-00230-9

Lubis, N. W., Rini, E. S., Lumbanraja, P., & Sembiring, B. K. F. (2026) 'Resources Based View (RBV) for Marketing Capabilities: Literature Review: Implications for SMEs', *Business Models of the Future: How AI and Advanced Digital Transformation are Reshaping Industries*, pp. 407-414. DOI: 10.1007/978-3-031-85398-2_36

Lui Abel, A., & Li, J. (2012). Exploring the corporate university phenomenon: Development and implementation of a comprehensive survey. *Human Resource Development Quarterly*, *23*(1), 103–128. DOI: 10.1002/hrdq.21122

Maak, T., & Pless, N. M. (2009). Business leaders as citizens of the world. Advancing humanism on a global scale. *Journal of Business Ethics*, *88*(3), 537–550. DOI: 10.1007/s10551-009-0122-0

Mahale, P., & Mithunraj, B. (2025). The National Cooperative Policy 2025—Reinvigorating India's Cooperative Sector. *International Journal of Finance and Banking Research*, *11*(4), 70–80. DOI: 10.11648/j.ijfbr.20251104.11

Maheswaran, K., Selvakumar, P., Shaikh, M., Shashank, G., Gupta, S., & Manjunath, T. C. (2025). The Evolution of Smart Urban Mobility With Emerging Technologies. In Ponnusamy, S., Assaf, M., Youssef, B., Jeon, G., & Kalyanaraman, S. (Eds.), *Leveraging VANETs and Blockchain Technology for Urban Mobility* (pp. 1–28). IGI Global Scientific Publishing. DOI: 10.4018/979-8-3373-0265-2.ch001

Maitlis, S., & Christianson, M. (2014). Understanding it in organizations: Taking stock and moving forward. *The Academy of Management Annals*, *8*(1), 57–125. DOI: 10.5465/19416520.2014.873177

Makumbe, W. (2025). The mediating effect of employer branding on the relationship between transformational leadership and organisational commitment in the South African telecoms sector. *African Journal of Economic and Management Studies*.

Malhotra, A., Majchrzak, A., & Rosen, B. (2007). Leading virtual teams. *The Academy of Management Perspectives*, *21*(1), 60–70. DOI: 10.5465/amp.2007.24286164

Maltz, M., & Shinar, D. (2004). Imperfect in-vehicle collision avoidance warning systems can aid drivers. *Human Factors*, *46*(2), 357–366. DOI: 10.1518/hfes.46.2.357.37348 PMID: 15359683

Marín Díaz, G., Gómez Ruiz, I., García-Villena, R., & Palazón, M. (2023). Analyze employee turnover using explainable AI. *Mathematics*, *11*(22), 4677. DOI: 10.3390/math11224677

MarketScreener. (2023, May 24). HDFC Bank opens doors to recruits with a special recruitment programme. https://www.marketscreener.com/quote/stock/HDFC-BANK-LIMITED-9059482/news/HDFC-BANK-Opens-Doors-to-New-Recruits-with-a-Special-Recruitment-Programme-43838285

Marquis, C., & Tilcsik, A. (2013). Imprinting: Toward a multilevel theory. *The Academy of Management Annals*, *7*(1), 195–245. DOI: 10.5465/19416520.2013.766076

Maslow, A. H. (1943). A theory of human motivation. *Psychological Review*, *50*(4), 370–396. DOI: 10.1037/h0054346

Mathur, M., Pramanik, B., Rosalyn, S., Thulaseedharan, A., Mirzani, Y., & Namdeo, S. (2024). Ethical implications of AI in HRM: Balancing efficiency and privacy in employee monitoring systems. *Nanotechnology Perceptions*, •••, 4490–4496. DOI: 10.62441/nano-ntp.vi.3870

Mayfield, M., Mayfield, J., & Wheeler, C. (2016). Talent development for top leaders: Three HR initiatives for competitive advantage. *Human Resource Management International Digest*, *24*(6), 4–7. DOI: 10.1108/HRMID-07-2015-0120

Mazmanian, M., Orlikowski, W. J., & Yates, J. (2013). The autonomy paradox: The implications of mobile email devices for knowledge professionals. *Organization Science*, *24*(5), 1337–1357. DOI: 10.1287/orsc.1120.0806

McPhail, R., & Fisher, R. (2024). Remote work after the pandemic and its impact. *International Journal of Human Resource Management*, *35*(9), 1721–1750. DOI: 10.1080/09585192.2023.2221385

Medina-Garrido, J. A., Biedma-Ferrer, J. M., & Ramos-Rodríguez, A. R. (2017). Relationship between work-family balance, employee well-being and job performance. *Academia (Caracas)*, *30*(1), 40–58. DOI: 10.1108/ARLA-08-2015-0202

Meister, J. C. (1998). *Corporate universities: Lessons in building a world-class work force* (rev. ed.). McGraw-Hill.

Meske, C., & Amojo, I. (2020). Ethical guidelines for the construction of digital nudges. *arXiv preprint arXiv:2003. 05249.* /arXiv.2003.05249.DOI: 10.24251/HICSS.2020.480

Meyers, M. C., van Woerkom, M., Paauwe, J., & Dries, N. (2020). HR managers' talent philosophies: Prevalence and relationships with perceived talent management practices. *International Journal of Human Resource Management*, *31*(4), 562–588. DOI: 10.1080/09585192.2019.1579747

Mishra, N., & Chakraborty, T. (2023). Employee engagement perspectives in agile organizations: Managing people in Industry 4.0. In *Agile Leadership for Industry 4.0* (pp. 139–154). Apple Academic Press. DOI: 10.1201/9781003314615-8

Mohan, R. (2005). Financial sector reforms in India: Policies and performance analysis. *Economic and Political Weekly*, *40*(12), 1106–1121.

Mohan, R., & Ray, P. (2018). Indian financial sector: Structure, trends, and turns. In *Routledge Handbook of Banking and Finance in Asia* (pp. 54–75). Routledge. DOI: 10.4324/9781315543222-4

Moneylife. (2011, December 1). Axis Bank launches 'Young Bankers' program for banking aspirants. https://www.moneylife.in/article/axis-bank-launches-young-bankers-program-for-banking-aspirants/28563.html

Monica, B. S. (2021). The Effect of IT Employees' Engagement on Work Attitudes through Cloud Computing Services. In *Recent Advances in Technology Acceptance Models and Theories* (pp. 497–507). Springer International Publishing., DOI: 10.1007/978-3-030-64987-6_29

Morea, D., Iazzolino, G., Petruzelli, A. M., & Omeihe, K. O. (2026). Guest editorial: What if intellectual capital is the missing link in sustainable development? *Journal of Intellectual Capital, 27*(1), 1–7. DOI: 10.1108/JIC-01-2026-416

Morrison, E. W. (2023). Voice and silence of employees, taking stock, living with dualities and moving forward. *Annual Review of Organizational Psychology and Organizational Behavior, 10*, 79–107. DOI: 10.1146/annurev-orgpsych-120920-054654

Morrison, E. W., & Robinson, S. L. (1997). When employees feel betrayed: A model of how psychological contract violation develops. *Academy of Management Review, 22*(1), 226–256. DOI: 10.2307/259230

Mueller, M., & Kubatova, J. (2025). A systematic review of managerial burnout and personal crisis: Navigating the interplay of individual, organizational, and environmental factors. *German Journal of Human Resource Management*, 23970022251315650.

Mulki, J., Bardhi, F., Lassk, F., & Nanavaty-Dahl, J. (2009). Set up remote workers to thrive. *MIT Sloan Management Review*.

Nadales-Gallego, A., Galindo-Reyes, F., & Garrido-Moreno, A. (2025). Connecting Internal Communication and Employee Engagement in Organisation: A Systematic Literature Review. *SAGE Open, 15*(4), 21582440251399773. DOI: 10.1177/21582440251399773

NAFED. (2022). *Annual report 2021–22*. National Agricultural Cooperative Marketing Federation of India Ltd. https://www.nafed-india.com

Najm, & Sabreen. (2023). The Role of Employer Brand on E-Recruitment during COVID-19 in Egypt. Journal of Administrative, Financial and Quantitative Research, 3(1), 161-181.

Nanjundeswaraswamy, T. S., Bharath, S., & Nagesh, P. (2025). Employer branding: design and development of a scale. *Journal of economic and administrative sciences*, 41(1), 88-113.

Naqvi, F., & Nair, M. (2026). Building Resilient Organizations: Culture, Sustainability, and Agility as Pillars of Success. In Organizational Dynamics in India: Rethinking Systemic Issues in Global Environments (pp. 141-157). Singapore: Springer Nature Singapore. DOI: 10.1007/978-981-95-1033-7_8

Naranjo-Gil, D., & Hartmann, F. (2006). How top management teams use management accounting systems to implement strategy. *Journal of Management Accounting Research, 18*(1), 21–53. DOI: 10.2308/jmar.2006.18.1.21

Nayak, D. P., & Sahoo, S. P. (2026). Workforce Agility in a Changing World: A Systematic Review and Future Research Agenda. *Thunderbird International Business Review*, tie.70098. Advance online publication. DOI: 10.1002/tie.70098

Nembhard, I. M., & Edmondson, A. C. (2006). Making it safe: The effects of leader inclusiveness and professional status on psychological safety and improvement efforts in health care teams. *Journal of Organizational Behavior: The International Journal of Industrial. Journal of Organizational Behavior*, *27*(7), 941–966. DOI: 10.1002/job.413

Nese, R. N., Nese, J. F., Santiago-Rosario, M. R., Izzard, S., Newson, A., Pimentel-Mannan, I., Lissman, D. C., Daza, T., Triplett, D., & Malose, S. (2025). Improving classroom engagement and reducing exclusionary discipline: A quasi-experimental study of the Inclusive Skill-Building Learning Approach during COVID-19. *Journal of Education*, *205*(2), 114–129. DOI: 10.1177/00220574241309893

Nesterak, J., Szelągowski, M., & Radziszewski, P. (2024). Workplace performance measurement: Digitalization of work observation and analysis. *Journal of Intelligent Manufacturing*, •••, 1–17. DOI: 10.1007/s10845-024-02419-x

Newlands, G. (2021). Algorithmic surveillance in the collaborative economy: The organization of work through space conceived by Lefebvri. *Organization*, *28*(1), 74–95. DOI: 10.1177/0170840620937900

Ng, C., Wider, W., Yang, C., Jiang, L., Vasudevan, A., Bhandari, P., & Lee, H. P. T. (2024). Keys factor affecting employee performance in the banking sector: A Delphi study. *Cogent Business & Management*, *11*(1), 2409942. DOI: 10.1080/23311975.2024.2409942

NIIT. (n.d.-a). Axis Bank Young Bankers Program. https://learnforjobs.niit.com/india/axisbankyb

NIIT. (n.d.-b). HDFC Bank ACE Banker Program. https://www.niit.com/en/banking-financial-services-insurance/hdfc-bank-ace-banker-program

Nilsen, E. R., Olafsen, A. H., & Nadeau, J. (2024). Rethinking employer attractiveness: A qualitative exploration of potential employees' perception of employer attractiveness attributes. *Corporate Reputation Review*, •••, 1–13.

Nöhammer, E., Schorn, R., & Becker, N. (2022). Optimizing the organizational crisis communication portfolio. *Corporate Reputation Review*, •••, 1.

Oakman, J., Lambert, K. A., Rogerson, S., & Bell, A. (2024). We know it doesn't work: Why do we still use how to lift training for the prevention of musculoskeletal disorders? *International Journal of Industrial Ergonomics, 100*, 103542. DOI: 10.1016/j.ergon.2023.103542

Obaidi, M., Nagel, L., Specht, A., & Klünder, J. (2022). Sentiment analysis tools in software engineering: A systematic mapping study. *Information and Software Technology, 151*, 107018. DOI: 10.1016/j.infsof.2022.107018

OECD. (2021a). *The future of the public service: Developing a public workforce fit for the future.*

OECD. (2021b). *Public Employment and Management 2021: The future of the public service.*

Oliveira, E., Abner, G., Lee, S., Suzuki, K., Hur, H., & Perry, J. L. (2024). What does the evidence tell us about merit principles and government performance? *Public Administration, 102*(2), 668–690. DOI: 10.1111/padm.12945

Österberg, P., & Nilsson, J. (2009). Members' perception of their participation in the governance of cooperatives: The key to trust and commitment in agricultural cooperatives. Agribusiness. *International Journal (Toronto, Ont.), 25*(2), 181–197.

Ouchi, W. G. (1979). A conceptual framework for the design of organizational control mechanisms. *Management Science, 25*(9), 833–848. DOI: 10.1287/mnsc.25.9.833

Ou, Z., Chen, T., Li, F., & Tang, P. (2018). Constructive controversy and creative process engagement: The roles of positive conflict value, cognitive flexibility, and psychological safety. *Journal of Applied Social Psychology, 48*(2), 101–113. DOI: 10.1111/jasp.12494

Panagariya, A. (2010). *India: The emerging giant*. Oxford University Press.

Panagiotidou, S., & Mihail, D. (2023, November). Pre-Recruiting HR Marketing for new Gen Talent Acquisition: The Mediating Role of Word of Mouth. In *European Conference on Management, Leadership and Governance*, 19(1), 505-511. DOI: 10.34190/ecmlg.19.1.1675

Panagiotidou, S., Mihail, D., & Katou, A. A. (2024). Unveiling the power of word-of-mouth in pre-recruitment employer branding strategy during COVID-19. *Employee Relations, 46*(4), 833–849. DOI: 10.1108/ER-10-2023-0540

Papagiannidis, E., Mikalef, P., & Conboy, K. (2025). Responsible governance of artificial intelligence: A framework for review and research. *The Journal of Strategic Information Systems, 34*(2), 101885. DOI: 10.1016/j.jsis.2024.101885

Park, C., & Park, Y. (2021). The effect of personality diversity on life satisfaction and job performance: The mediate effect of mastery approach goal orientation. *Korean Journal of Industrial and Organizational Psychology, 34*(2), 287–318. DOI: 10.24230/kjiop.v34i2.287-318

Patrucco, A., Pellizzoni, E., & Buganza, T. (2017). The design process of corporate universities: A stakeholder approach. *Journal of Workplace Learning, 29*(4), 304–318. DOI: 10.1108/JWL-04-2016-0024

Paul, A. (2018, September 13). *Examining the rise of Non-Performing Assets in India*. PRS Legislative Research. Retrieved March 1, 2026, from https://prsindia.org/theprsblog/examining-the-rise-of-non-performing-assets-in-india#:~:text=What%20led%20to%20the%20rise,capability%20of%20these%20corporations%20decreased

Pedrini, G. (2011). The corporate university phenomenon and the competences pipeline. *Journal of US-China Public Administration, 8*(9), 1004–1015.

Peterson, M. F., Smith, P. B., Akande, A., Ayestaran, S., Bochner, S., Callan, V., & Viedge, C. (1995). Role conflict, ambiguity, and overload: A 21-nation study. *Academy of Management Journal, 38*(2), 429–452. DOI: 10.2307/256687

Petty, R., & Guthrie, J. (2000). Intellectual capital literature review: Measurement, reporting and management. *Journal of Intellectual Capital, 1*(2), 155–176. DOI: 10.1108/14691930010348731

Pollitt, C., & Bouckaert, G. (2017). *Public management reform: A comparative analysis-into the age of austerity*. Oxford university press.

Poocharoen, O. O., & Lee, C. (2013). Talent management in the public sector: A comparative study of Singapore, Malaysia, and Thailand. *Public Management Review, 15*(8), 1185–1207. DOI: 10.1080/14719037.2013.816525

Prince, C., & Beaver, G. (2002). Redefining the role of the corporate university: A case study of the National Australia Bank. *Industry and Higher Education, 16*(4), 213–220. DOI: 10.5367/000000002101296315

Pulakos, E. D., Arad, S., Donovan, M. A., & Plamondon, K. E. (2000). Adaptability in the workplace: Development of a taxonomy of adaptive performance. *The Journal of Applied Psychology, 85*(4), 612–624. DOI: 10.1037/0021-9010.85.4.612 PMID: 10948805

Purnomo, H., Soejoko, D. K. H., & Leksono, P. Y. (2025). RECENT TRENDS IN HUMAN RESOURCE MANAGEMENT IN THE DIGITAL AGE. *INTERNATIONAL JOURNAL OF FINANCIAL ECONOMICS, 2*(1), 159–172.

Rademakers, M. (2005). Corporate universities: Driving force of knowledge innovation. *Journal of Workplace Learning*, *17*(1/2), 130–136. DOI: 10.1108/13665620510574513

Rademakers, M. (2014). *Corporate universities: Drivers of the learning organization*. Routledge. DOI: 10.4324/9780203073988

Radianti, J., Majchrzak, T. A., Fromm, J., & Wohlgenannt, I. (2020). A systematic review of immersive virtual reality applications for higher education: Design elements, lessons learned, and research agenda. *Computers & Education*, *147*, 103778. DOI: 10.1016/j.compedu.2019.103778

Raetze, S., Steputat-Raetze, A., Mueller, H., Maynard, M. T., & Schmutz, J. B. (2025). Teamwork under adversity: an integrative review and future research agenda. *Academy of Management Annals*, (ja), annals-2022.

Raghavan, M., Barocas, S., Kleinberg, J., & Levy, K. (2020). Mitigating Bias in Algorithmic Recruitment: Evaluating Claims and Practices. *2020 Conference Proceedings on Fairness, Accountability, and Transparency*, 469–481. https://doi.org/ DOI: 10.1145/3351095.3372828

Ramakrishna, G., Ramulu, M., & Kumar, B. P. (2016). Financial crisis and the performance of commercial banks: Indian experience. *Journal of International Economics*, *7*(2), 35.

Rana, G., Goel, A. K., & Rastogi, R. (2013). Talent management: A paradigm shift in Indian public sector. *Strategic HR Review*, *12*(4), 197–202. DOI: 10.1108/SHR-02-2013-0012

Reddy, Y. V. (2006). Evolving role of banks in India. Address delivered at the Bank Economists' Conference, Hyderabad.

Reddy, Y. V. (2006). Reforming India's financial sector: Changing dimensions and emerging issues. *BIS Papers*, *28*, 161–178.

Redondo-Duarte, S., & Santa-Marina, S. E. (2025). Empowering Students for Working in Culturally Rich and Psychologically Nourishing Work Environments. In *Developing Effective and High-Performing Teams in Higher Education* (pp. 57–88). IGI Global.

Reese, E., & Allison, J. E. (2023). *Unsustainable: Amazon, warehousing, and the politics of exploitation*. Univ of California Press.

Reina, W., Pla-Barber, J., & Villar, C. (2023). Socio-emotional richness in family business research: A systematic review of the literature on its definition, roles, and dimensions. *European Management Journal, 41*(6), 1000–1020. DOI: 10.1016/j.emj.2022.10.009

Reserve Bank of India. (2017, April 13). Retrieved January 10, 2026, from https://www.rbi.org.in/commonman/english/scripts/Notification.aspx?Id=2523

Reserve Bank of India. (2026, January 22). Retrieved March 2, 2026, from https://www.rbi.org.in/commonman/english/scripts/FAQs.aspx?Id=1105

Restubog, S. L. D., Hornsey, M. J., Bordia, P., & Esposo, S. R. (2008). Effects of psychological contract breach on organizational citizenship behaviour: Insights from the group value model. *Journal of Management Studies, 45*(8), 1377–1400. DOI: 10.1111/j.1467-6486.2008.00792.x

Richardson, J., & Kelliher, C. (2015). Managing visibility for career sustainability: A study of remote workers. *Handbook of research on sustainable careers*, 116 130. DOI: 10.4337/9781782547037.00013

Rita, P., António, N., & Raminhos, V. (2026). Using employee feedback to build effective employer branding strategies: A mixed method approach. *The International Journal of Organizational Analysis, 34*(1), 256–282. DOI: 10.1108/IJOA-04-2024-4469

Robbins, S., Robbins, S. P., & Judge, T. A. (2025). *Essentials of organizational behavior*. BoD–Books on Demand.

Rothwell, R. (1994). Towards the fifth-generation innovation process. *International Marketing Review, 11*(1), 7–31. DOI: 10.1108/02651339410057491

Rothwell, W. (2010). *Effective succession planning: Ensuring leadership continuity and building talent from within*. Amacom.

Rousseau, D. M. (1989). Psychological and implied contracts in organizations. *Employee Responsibilities and Rights Journal, 2*(2), 121–139. DOI: 10.1007/BF01384942

Rousseau, D. M. (1995). Psychological and organizational contracts: Understanding the ties that motivate. *The Academy of Management Executive, 4*(4), 123–139.

Ruehle, R. C. (2023). The moral permissibility of digital nudging in the workplace: Reconciling justification and legitimation. *Business Ethics Quarterly, 33*(3), 502–531. DOI: 10.1017/beq.2023.4

Rumelt, R. P., Schendel, D., & Teece, D. J. (1991). Strategic management and economics. *Strategic Management Journal, 12*(S2), 5–29. DOI: 10.1002/smj.4250121003

Rushing, W. A. (1965). Kahn, wolfe, quinn, and snoek: Organizaitonal stress: Studies in role conflict and ambiguity (book review). *Social Forces, 43*(4), 591. DOI: 10.2307/2574480

Ryan, M., Popa, E., Blok, V., & IJsselsteijn, W. (2024). Start doing the right thing: Indicators for socially responsible start-ups and investors. *Journal of Responsible Technology, 20*, 100094. DOI: 10.1016/j.jrt.2024.100094

Rys, M., Schollaert, E., & Van Hoye, G. (2024). Living the employer brand during a crisis? A qualitative study on internal employer branding in times of the COVID-19 pandemic. *PLoS One, 19*(5), e0303361. DOI: 10.1371/journal.pone.0303361 PMID: 38739576

Saini, G. K. (2020). Shoppers stop: Leveraging social media for employer branding. *Emerging Economies Cases Journal, 2*(1), 54–61. DOI: 10.1177/2516604220930394

Saini, G. K. (2023). Employer branding: A critical review and future research. *NHRD Network Journal, 16*(3), 220–232. DOI: 10.1177/26314541231170424

Sakthivel, M., Jaganathan, A., & Mohanraj, M. Mohit, & Manjunath, T. (2025). Brand Loyalty through AI and Personalisation AI-Generated Content for Financial Marketing. In A. J Nair, S. Manohar, Y. B. Limbu, & B. A. Huhmann (Eds.), *Intersecting Natural Language Processing and FinTech Innovations in Service Marketing* (pp. 77-96). IGI Global Scientific Publishing.

Salanova, M., & Schaufeli, W. B. (2008). A cross-national study of work engagement as a mediator between job resources and proactive behaviour. *International Journal of Human Resource Management, 19*(1), 116–131. DOI: 10.1080/09585190701763982

Samal, A., & Misra, L. I. Mohit, Pougajendy, S., Chandel, P. S., Manjunath, T. C., (2025). Musealization and Tourism Practices. In S. Oflazoğlu & M. Dora (Eds.), *Preserving Cultural Heritage in Post-Disaster Urban Renewal* (pp. 115-142). IGI Global Scientific Publishing.

Sampat, B., Raj, S., Behl, A., & Schöbel, S. (2022). An empirical analysis of facilitators and barriers to the hybrid work model: A cross-cultural and multi-theoretical approach. *Personnel Review, 51*(8), 1990–2020. DOI: 10.1108/PR-02-2022-0176

Samuel, H. S., Etim, E. E., Nweke-Maraizu, U., & Okibe, G. (2025). Building Collaborative and Interdisciplinary Teams: Strategies for Effective Talent Management. In *Cultivating Creativity and Navigating Talent Management in Academia* (pp. 23-38). IGI Global Scientific Publishing.

Sandberg, J., & Tsoukas, H. (2020). Reconsideration of the understanding of meaning: Towards a broader understanding through phenomenology. *Theory of Organization*, *1*(1), 1–34. DOI: 10.1177/2631787719879937

Sankar, M., Chitra, A., Mahadevan, A., Nagarajan, S., & Priya, S. K. (2026). A Systematic Analysis on Organisational Citizenship Behaviour around the World from 2005 to 2025. *International Review of Management and Marketing*, *16*(1), 170–178. DOI: 10.32479/irmm.21417

Santoni de Sio, F., & Mecacci, G. (2024). Artificial intelligence and the future of work. *The Journal of Ethics*, *28*(3), 1–25. DOI: 10.1007/s10892-024-09493-6

Scarso, E. (2017). Corporate universities as knowledge management tools. *VINE Journal of Information and Knowledge Management Systems*, *47*(4), 538–554. DOI: 10.1108/VJIKMS-12-2016-0074

Schaefer, S. D., Cunningham, P., Diehl, S., & Terlutter, R. (2024). Employees' positive perception of corporate social responsibility generates beneficial results for companies and their employees: Organizational pride as a mediator. *Corporate Social Responsibility and Environmental Management*, *31*(3), 2574–2587. DOI: 10.1002/csr.2699

Schön, D. A. (1983). *The reflective practitioner: How professionals think in action*. Basic Books.

Schreyögg, G., Sydow, J., & Holtmann, P. (2011). How history matters in organisations: The case of path dependence. *Management & Organizational History*, *6*(1), 81–100. DOI: 10.1177/1744935910387030

Schuler, R. S., Budhwar, P. S., & Florkowski, G. W. (2002). International human resource management: Review and critique. *International Journal of Management Reviews*, *4*(1), 41–70. DOI: 10.1111/1468-2370.00076

Schwarz, A. (2019). The state of strategic organizational crisis communication research in the context of global and digital communication. *Revista De La Asociación Española De Investigación De La Comunicación*, *6*(11), 279–310. DOI: 10.24137/raeic.6.11.15

Selivanovskikh, L., Maltseva, E., & Isada, F. (2025). Strategic ambiguity. *Management Decision*, *63*(2), 345–372. DOI: 10.1108/MD-05-2024-1021

Senge, P. M. (1990). *The fifth discipline: The art and practice of the learning organization*. Doubleday.

Setiawati, L. (2021). The effect of agile leadership and work environment to employees' performance in a VUCA world (Study on millennial generation employees in Jabodetabek). *International Journal of Social Science and Human Research, 4*(11), 3123–3131. DOI: 10.47191/ijsshr/v4-i11-08

Sewell, G., & Taskin, L. (2015). Out of sight, out of mind in a new world of work? Autonomy, control, and spatiotemporal scaling in telework. *Organization Studies, 36*(11), 1507–1529. DOI: 10.1177/0170840615593587

Sexton, J. B., Adair, K. C., Leonard, M. W., Frankel, T. C., Proulx, J., Watson, S. R., Magnus, B., Bogan, B., Jamal, M., Schwendimann, R., & Frankel, A. S. (2018). Providing feedback following Leadership Walk Rounds is associated with better patient safety culture, higher employee engagement and lower burnout. *BMJ Quality & Safety, 27*(4), 261–270. DOI: 10.1136/bmjqs-2016-006399 PMID: 28993441

Shafiee, M., & Goodarzi, S. (2026). The role of employer branding in talent management: Analysis of key strategies and tools. *The International Journal of Organizational Analysis, 34*(1), 99–114. DOI: 10.1108/IJOA-10-2024-4900

Shamspour, H. R., Kamali, M., & Narouei, B. (2024). Impact of micromanagement on organizational commitment through mediating role of job stress, moderating effect of hostile attribution bias. *International Journal of Business and Management Sciences, 5*(3), 56–77. https://www.ijbms.org/

Sharma, M. (Ed.). (2008). *Dynamics of Indian Banking: Views and Vistas*. Atlantic Publishers & Dist.

Shet, S. V. (2024). A VUCA-ready workforce: Exploring employee competencies and learning and development implications. *Personnel Review, 53*(3), 674–703. DOI: 10.1108/PR-10-2023-0873

Shollen, S. L., & Hanold, M. (2025). Game Changers: Leadership Lessons From Popular Sport Icons. *New Directions for Student Leadership, 2025*(185), 25–31. DOI: 10.1002/yd.20655 PMID: 40020219

Siedlok, F., Callagher, L., & Korber, S. (2024). Reviewing worker and producer cooperative contributions toward SDG8 in developing and developed economies. In *International Business and SDG 8: Exploring the Relationship between IB and Society* (pp. 281–295). Springer Nature Switzerland. DOI: 10.1007/978-3-031-46802-5_14

Siegel, R., König, C. J., & Lazar, V. (2022). The impact of electronic monitoring on employees' job satisfaction, stress, performance, and counterproductive work behavior: A meta-analysis. *Computers in Human Behavior Reports, 8*, 100227. DOI: 10.1016/j.chbr.2022.100227

Singh, A., & Hassan, S. C. (2024), "Identifying the Skill Gap in the Workplace and Their Challenges in Hospitality and Tourism Organisations", Thake, A.M., Sood, K., Özen, E. and Grima, S. (Ed.) *Contemporary Challenges in Social Science Management: Skills Gaps and Shortages in the Labour Market* (*Contemporary Studies in Economic and Financial Analysis, Vol. 112B*), Emerald Publishing Limited, Leeds, pp. 101-114. DOI: 10.1108/S1569-37592024000112B006

Singh, A., & Kumar, V. (2025). Organizational Innovation and Adaptation in Hospitality and Tourism: Strategies for Resilience and Leadership. In C. Ramos, T. Costa, R. Madeira, & J. Ferreira do Rosário (Eds.), *Open Innovation and Technology in Tourism and Hospitality* (pp. 355-372). IGI Global Scientific Publishing. DOI: 10.4018/979-8-3693-8633-0.ch018

Singh, A., & Singh, V. K. (2022). The impact of ergonomic practices on housekeeping employee retention and efficiency in hotels during COVID-19 in India. Turyzm/ Tourism, 32(2), 29–50. DOI: 10.18778/0867-5856.32.2.02

Singh, A. (2024). Quality of Work-Life Practices in the Indian Hospitality Sector: Future Challenges and Prospects. In Valeri, M., & Sousa, B. (Eds.), *Human Relations Management in Tourism* (pp. 208–224). IGI Global., DOI: 10.4018/979-8-3693-1322-0.ch010

Singh, A. (2025). Analysis of Perceptions on Employment of differently-abled People in the Indian Hotel Industry. *Pasos (El Sauzal)*, *23*(1), 167–183. DOI: 10.25145/j.pasos.2025.23.011

Singh, A., & Ansari, A. I. (2024). Role of Training and Development in Employee Motivation: Tourism and Hospitality Sector. In Mazurowski, T. (Ed.), *Enhancing Employee Motivation Through Training and Development* (pp. 248–261). IGI Global., DOI: 10.4018/979-8-3693-1674-0.ch011

Singh, A., & Kumar, S. (2021). Identifying Innovations in Human Resources: Academia and Industry Perspectives. In Pathak, A., & Rana, S. (Eds.), *Transforming Human Resource Functions With Automation* (pp. 104–120). IGI Global., DOI: 10.4018/978-1-7998-4180-7.ch006

Singh, A., & Kumar, S. (2024). Effective Talent Management Practices Implemented in the Hospitality Sector. In Christiansen, B., Aziz, M., & O'Keeffe, E. (Eds.), *Global Practices on Effective Talent Acquisition and Retention* (pp. 126–144). IGI Global., DOI: 10.4018/979-8-3693-1938-3.ch008

Singh, A., & Sihmar, P. (2025). Higher Education Institution Sustainability: Role of Green Human Resource Management. In Adu-Gyamfi, M., Boateng, F., & Atiku, S. (Eds.), *Green HRM Awareness and Training in Higher Education Institutions* (pp. 1–14). IGI Global Scientific Publishing., DOI: 10.4018/979-8-3693-2956-6.ch001

Singh, J. P. (2000). Multinational corporations and technological change: Global melting pot or nation-state solutions? *Review of International Political Economy*, *7*(2), 225–253.

Singh, R., & Gupta, A. (2019). Non-performing assets in Indian public sector banks: Causes, consequences, and correctives. *Indian Journal of Finance*, *13*(4), 7–22.

Singh, S., & Singh, A. K. (2024). Role of Managerial Personality in Innovative Behavior at Workplace. *Journal of the Indian Academy of Applied Psychology*, *50*(1), 261–270.

Siomkos, G. J., & Kurzbard, G. (1994). The hidden crisis in product-harm crisis management. *European Journal of Marketing*, *28*(2), 30–41. DOI: 10.1108/03090569410055265

Solomons, J., Bekker, S., Groom, R., & Kraak, W. (2025). Insights into coaching effectiveness: Perspectives from coaches and players in South African Women's Rugby. *International Journal of Sports Science & Coaching*, *20*(1), 8–21. DOI: 10.1177/17479541241283625

Sommermann, K. P. (2025). Challenges for the Civil Service. *The Civil Service in Europe: A Research Companion.*

Soomar, Z. (2020). A framework for building and maintain trust in remote and virtual teams. *F1000 Research*, *9*(1187), 1187. DOI: 10.12688/f1000research.26626.1

Soon, C. C., & Salamzadeh, Y. (2021). The impact of digital leadership competencies on virtual team effectiveness in MNC companies in Penang, Malaysia. *Journal of Entrepreneurship. Business Economics (Cleveland, Ohio)*, *8*(2), 219–253. http://orcid.org/0000-0002-6917-2754

Soundariya, A., Behera, N. K., Chandel, P. S., Gupta, S., & Manjunath, T. C. (2025). AI and Environmental Ethics: The Role of AI in Addressing Climate Change Ethical Considerations in AI-Driven Environmental Solutions. In Chakraborty, S. (Ed.), *Human Values, Ethics, and Dignity in the Age of Artificial Intelligence* (pp. 321–346). IGI Global Scientific Publishing. DOI: 10.4018/979-8-3693-9035-1.ch013

Špoljarić, A., & Ozretić Došen, Đ. (2023). Employer brand and international employer brand: Literature review. *Corporate Communications*, *28*(4), 671–682. DOI: 10.1108/CCIJ-11-2022-0141

Sridharan, E. (2004). The growth and sectoral composition of India's middle class: Its impact on the politics of economic liberalisation. *India Review, 3*(4), 405–428. DOI: 10.1080/14736480490895769

Stadler, R., Fecker, D., & Huber, L. (2025). Co-branding alliances as an employer branding strategy. *Journal of Hospitality and Tourism Insights, 8*(11), 259–275. DOI: 10.1108/JHTI-03-2025-0358

Stawicki, C., Krishnakumar, S., & Robinson, M. D. (2023). Working with emotions: Emotional intelligence, performance and creativity in the knowledge-intensive workforce. *Journal of Knowledge Management, 27*(2), 285–301. DOI: 10.1108/JKM-07-2021-0556

Stewart, G. (1997). Supply-chain operations reference model (SCOR): The first cross-industry framework for integrated supply-chain management. *Logistics Information Management, 10*(2), 62–67. DOI: 10.1108/09576059710815716

Stor, M., & Haromszeki, Ł. (2025). Exploring employer branding and company performance results in non-crisis and crisis times: the mediating role of HRM outcomes in Central European MNC. *Journal of Organizational Effectiveness: People and Performance*, (ahead-of-print).

Suchman, M. C. (1995). Managing legitimacy: Strategic and institutional approaches. *Academy of Management Review, 20*(3), 571–610. DOI: 10.2307/258788

Supina, S., & Singh, A. (2024). Exploring the Presence and Adoption of Quality of Work-Life Dimensions in the Hotel Industry? *African Journal of Hospitality, Tourism and Leisure, 13*(2), 421–429. DOI: 10.46222/ajhtl.19770720.524

Suresh, P., & Paul, J. (2014). *Management of banking and financial services*. Pearson Education India.

Syamsir, S., Saputra, N., & Mulia, R. A. (2025). Leadership agility in a VUCA world: A systematic review, conceptual insights, and research directions. *Cogent Business & Management, 12*(1), 2482022. DOI: 10.1080/23311975.2025.2482022

Tahmasebi, R., & Nijs, S. (2024). A paradox perspective on talent management: A multi-level analysis of paradoxes and their responses in talent management. *International Journal of Human Resource Management, 35*(3), 507–562. DOI: 10.1080/09585192.2023.2250261

Tak, M., Deutsch, R., Kavanaugh, E., Lynch, M., & Tuakli-Wosornu, Y. A. (2024). Secure Sports Reporting Systems: A Qualitative Study of How Athletes Navigate Notification. *Journal of Global Sports Management.* https://doi.org/DOI: 10.1080/19406940.2024.2323011

Tamilselvi, M. (2024, April). Human facial emotion recognition using graphical cascaded convolutional neural network. In *2024 Ninth International Conference on Science Technology Engineering and Mathematics (ICONSTEM)* (pp. 1-8). IEEE. DOI: 10.1109/ICONSTEM60960.2024.10568797

Tang, W. G., & Vandenberghe, C. (2021). Role overload and work performance: The role of psychological strain and leader–member exchange. *Frontiers in Psychology*, *12*, 691207. DOI: 10.3389/fpsyg.2021.691207 PMID: 34093378

Tansley, C. (2011). What do we mean by the term "talent" in talent management? *Industrial and Commercial Training*, *43*(5), 266–274. DOI: 10.1108/00197851111145853

Teece, D. J. (2016). Dynamic Capacities and Entrepreneurial Management in Large Organizations: Towards a Theory of the Entrepreneurial Firm. *European Economic Review*, *86*, 202–216. DOI: 10.1016/j.euroecorev.2015.11.006

The People Management. (n.d.). Manipal Academy of BFSI and Axis Bank launch women-exclusive Young Bankers cohort to advance gender inclusion in banking. https://thepeoplemanagement.com/manipal-academy-of-bfsi-and-axis-bank-launch-women-exclusive-young-bankers-cohort

Theurer, C. P., Tumasjan, A., Welpe, I. M., & Lievens, F. (2018). Employer branding: A brand equity-based literature review and research agenda. *International Journal of Management Reviews*, *20*(1), 155–179. DOI: 10.1111/ijmr.12121

Thirunagalingam, A., & Selvakumar, P. (2025). Application of Automation and Robotics in the Oil and Gas Industry. In Abdullayev, V., & Khang, A. (Eds.), *Revolutionizing AI and Robotics in the Oil and Gas Industry* (pp. 229–244). IGI Global Scientific Publishing. DOI: 10.4018/979-8-3693-8156-4.ch011

Thunnissen, M., & Gallardo-Gallardo, E. (2017). *Talent management in practice: An integrated and dynamic approach*. Emerald Publishing Limited. DOI: 10.1108/9781787145979

Thunnissen, M., & Gallardo-Gallardo, E. (2019). Rigor and relevance in empirical TM research: Key issues and challenges. *Business Research Quarterly*, *22*(3), 171–180. DOI: 10.1016/j.brq.2019.04.003

Tichy, N. (2021). The Role of Transparency & Fairness in Performance Management-A Review and a Research Agenda. *In Academy of Management Proceedings (Vol. 2021, No. 1, p. 13230)*. Briarcliff Manor, NY 10510. *Academy of Management Journal*. Advance online publication. DOI: 10.5465/AMBPP.2021.13230

Times of India. (2025). IFFCO appoints KJ Patel as managing director. *The Times of India*. https://timesofindia.indiatimes.com

Today, C. X. O. (2024, December 17). Manipal Academy of BFSI and Axis Bank launch women-exclusive Young Bankers cohort to advance gender inclusion in banking. https://cxotoday.com/press-release/manipal-academy-of-bfsi-and-axis-bank-launch-women-exclusive-young-bankers-cohort

Triandis, H. C. (1995). *Individualism and collectivism*. Westview Press.

Tuakli-Wosornu, S., Mountjoy, M., & Budgett, R.. (2024). IOC Consensus on Interpersonal Violence Against Athletes. *British Journal of Sports Medicine*, *58*(9), 506–520. DOI: 10.1136/bjsports-2024-108766 PMID: 39586634

Turan, H. Y., & Cinnioğlu, H. (2022). Agile leadership and employee performance in VUCA world. In *Agile management and VUCA-RR: opportunities and threats in industry 4.0 towards society 5.0* (pp. 27–38). Emerald Publishing Limited., DOI: 10.1108/978-1-80262-325-320220003

Turner, J. R., Gray, B., & Bishop, W. (2023). The multifaceted theory of the formation of meaning. *Sistemas*, *11*(3), 145. DOI: 10.3390/systems11030145

Tushabe, M., Kyambade, M., Namatovu, A., & Oyella, S. (2025). Advancing gender diversity in leadership: The role of work-life balance and gender participation in Ugandan public universities. *Cogent Social Sciences*, *11*(1), 2486553. DOI: 10.1080/23311886.2025.2486553

Tushman, M. L., & Scanlan, T. J. (1981). Boundary spanning individuals: Their role in information transfer and their antecedents. *Academy of Management Journal*, *24*(2), 289–305. DOI: 10.2307/255842

Universum. (2023). *World's Most Attractive Employers 2023 Report*. Universum Global.

Unnikrishnan, D. (2022, November 21). *Banking Central | Why trade unions will stay in Indian banking*. Moneycontrol. Retrieved March 2, 2026, from https://www.moneycontrol.com/news/business/banking-central-why-trade-unions-will-stay-in-indian-banking-9571341.html

Upadhyaya, A. N., Debnath, P., Rani, P., Manjunath, T. C., & Bhattacharya, S. (2025). AI-Based Disaster Prediction and Early Warning Systems. In Mobo, F. (Ed.), *AI and Emerging Technologies for Emergency Response and Smart Cities* (pp. 55–74). IGI Global Scientific Publishing. DOI: 10.4018/979-8-3693-9770-1.ch003

Vaiman, V., Scullion, H., & Collings, D. G. (2012). Talent management decision making. *Management Decision*, *50*(5), 925–941. DOI: 10.1108/00251741211227663

Van der Wal, Z. (2017). *The 21st century public manager*. Palgrave. DOI: 10.1057/978-1-137-50744-0

Vandenabeele, W. (2007). Toward a public administration theory of public service motivation: An institutional approach. *Public Management Review*, *9*(4), 545–556. DOI: 10.1080/14719030701726697

Verhoef, P. C., Broekhuizen, T., Bart, Y., Bhattacharya, A., Dong, J. Q., Fabian, N., & Haenlein, M. (2021). Digital transformation: A multidisciplinary reflection and research agenda. *Journal of Business Research*, *122*, 889–901. DOI: 10.1016/j.jbusres.2019.09.022

Verma, A. (2024). Agile leadership in the VUCA world: combating challenges of the COVID-19 pandemic. In *VUCA and Other Analytics in Business Resilience, Part A* (pp. 267-285). Emerald Publishing Limited. DOI: 10.1108/978-1-83753-902-420241013

Wakefield, R. L., Leidner, D. E., & Garrison, G. (2008). Research note—A model of conflict, leadership, and performance in virtual teams. *Information Systems Research*, *19*(4), 434–455. DOI: 10.1287/isre.1070.0149

Walton, J. (1999). Human resource development and the corporate university. In Walton, J. (Ed.), *Strategic human resource development* (pp. 412–437). Pearson Education.

Weick, K. E. (1995). *Sensemaking in organizations*. Sage.

White, C. (2017). *Strategic management*. Bloomsbury Publishing.

Wilson, T. (2012). *A review of business–university collaboration*. Department for Business, Innovation and Skills.

Wong, S. I., & Berntzen, M. N. (2019). Transformational leadership and leader–member exchange in distributed teams: The roles of electronic dependence and team task interdependence. *Computers in Human Behavior*, *92*, 381–392. DOI: 10.1016/j.chb.2018.11.032

Worley, C. G., & Jules, C. (2020). COVID-19's uncomfortable revelations about agile and sustainable organizations in a VUCA world. *The Journal of Applied Behavioral Science*, *56*(3), 279–283. DOI: 10.1177/0021886320936263

Wright, P. M., & Haggerty, J. J. (2005). Missing variables in theories of strategic human resource management: Time, cause, and individuals. *Management Review*, •••, 164–173.

Wu, F. (2013). Corporate university development in China: A review of the literature and research agenda. *Journal of Chinese Human Resource Management, 4*(2), 134–149.

Xu, D., & Meyer, K. E. (2013). Linking Theory and Context: 'Strategy Research in Emerging Economies' after Wright et al. (2005). *Journal of Management Studies, 50*(7), 1322–1346. DOI: 10.1111/j.1467-6486.2012.01051.x

Yahaya, O. A. (2026). Information asymmetry as a moderator of intellectual capital disclosure and market valuation. *Journal of Business and Management Sciences, 13*(1), 1–54.

Yang, L., Holtz, D., Jaffe, S., Suri, S., Sinha, S., Weston, J., Joyce, C., Shah, N., Sherman, K., Hecht, B., & Teevan, J. (2022). The effects of remote work on collaboration among information workers. *Nature Human Behaviour, 6*(1), 43–54. DOI: 10.1038/s41562-021-01196-4 PMID: 34504299

Yasin, R., Bataineh, M. S., Atif, M., & Hossain, M. T. B. (2025). Green HRM and employer branding: Corporate environmental sustainability and organisational safety climate mediating role and moderating role of job experience. *Benchmarking*. Advance online publication. DOI: 10.1108/BIJ-01-2022-0052

Yeke, S., & Özveren, C. G. (2024). Enabling the management of diverse employees in the hybrid work model: A qualitative study. *Revista Brasileira de Gestão de Negócios, 26*(1), e20230128. DOI: 10.7819/rbgn.v26i01.4254

Yoon, B. S. (2019). The Role of Civil Service and the Human Resource Management Policies Required for the Government of the Future. In *Public Service Excellence in the 21st Century* (pp. 169–202). Springer Singapore. DOI: 10.1007/978-981-13-3215-9_6

Zakirova, A., Alff, H., & Schmidt, M. (2025). Unequal fields: Political ecology perspective on organic cotton production in Tajikistan. *Organic Agriculture, 15*(2), 183–198. DOI: 10.1007/s13165-025-00491-y

Zhang, Y., Weaver, R. G., Armstrong, B., Burkart, S., Zhang, S., & Beets, M. W. (2020). Validity of wrist-based photoplethysmography devices for measuring heart rate: A systematic review and meta-analysis. *Journal of Sports Sciences, 38*(17), 1939–1947. DOI: 10.1080/02640414.2020.1767348 PMID: 32552580

Zhao, H., Wayne, S. J., Glibkowski, B. C., & Bravo, J. (2007). The impact of psychological contract breach on work-related outcomes: A meta-analysis. *Personnel Psychology, 60*(3), 647–680. DOI: 10.1111/j.1744-6570.2007.00087.x

Zhao, K., Hsieh, W., Faulkner, N., & Smith, L. (2025). A systematic meta-review of organizational diversity and inclusion interventions and their associated outcomes. *Equality, Diversity and Inclusion*, *44*(9), 53–71. DOI: 10.1108/EDI-02-2024-0085

Ziegler, A., Naujoks-Schober, N., Vialle, W., & Stoeger, H. (2025). Analyzing National Talent Support Systems: The Case for a Resource-Oriented Approach. *Sustainability (Basel)*, *17*(13), 5896. DOI: 10.3390/su17135896

Zuboff, S. (1988). Dilemmas of Transformation in the Age of the Smart Machine. *Pub Type*, *81*, 17.

About the Contributors

Yusuf Hassan is an Assistant Professor of Business Management and Programme Director (MSc IBM Programme) at Heriot-Watt University, Dubai campus. Trained at the Indian Institute of Management (IIM) Indore and a fellow of the Stockholm School of Economics, he has held academic positions across leading institutions in the UK, USA, and India. His research integrates talent management, leadership, and sport particularly in marginalized contexts such as para-sports and the gig economy, employing both qualitative and quantitative methods. Dr. Hassan has published in ABS/ABDC-ranked journals, serves on editorial boards of several international journals, and has received multiple global research and travel grants. He has presented at premier conferences including EGOS, EURAM, AOM, and ANZAM. Known for his innovative and inclusive teaching methods, he employs simulations, gamification and popular culture-based learning to enhance student engagement. In recognition of his contributions, he has received numerous academic honors, including the Inclusion Champion Award and multiple Emerging Scholar Awards. Beyond academia, he has served in consulting and advisory roles across the UAE, India and Singapore, and continues to champion inclusive pedagogy and ethical leadership in business education.

***

Rahmath Nisha is a dedicated professional with comprehensive, hands-on experience in Human Resource Management (HRM), having successfully managed the entire employee life cycle—from recruitment and onboarding to performance management and employee engagement. She holds an MBA in Human Resource Management, where she was recognized as a Gold Medalist and awarded the title of Best Outgoing Student. Her academic journey began with a Bachelor's degree in Electronics and Communication Engineering, showcasing her diverse educational foundation. Currently serving as an Assistant Professor, she combines industry expertise with academic insight to mentor and inspire the next generation of HR professionals.

A.K. Subramani is a distinguished academic with a PhD in Business Administration from Manonmaniam Sundaranar University, Tirunelveli, India. With 18 years of teaching experience, he has made significant contributions to the field of human resource management and organisational behaviour. He has an impressive publication record with 80 articles in international journals, including two papers in the ABDC-A category, eight in the ABDC-B category, three in the ABDC-C category, 30 in Scopus-indexed journals, and eight in Web of Science journals. He has served as a resource person for various training workshops on SPSS and AMOS software packages

Neha Dhule is a dedicated and enthusiastic student at the Datta Meghe Institute of Management Studies, where she is pursuing her academic studies in the field of management. As an emerging management professional, she demonstrates a strong commitment to learning, personal development, and academic excellence. Throughout her academic journey, Neha has shown keen interest in developing managerial knowledge and practical skills essential for today's dynamic business environment. Her areas of learning include core management disciplines such as organizational behavior, marketing, human resource management, business communication, and strategic thinking. She actively participates in classroom discussions, collaborative projects, and academic activities that enhance analytical and problem-solving abilities. Neha is recognized for her positive attitude, teamwork skills, and willingness to explore innovative ideas. She engages in seminars, workshops, and institutional events that contribute to her professional growth and exposure to industry-oriented practices. Her participation in co-curricular and extracurricular activities reflects her balanced approach toward academic and personal development. With a strong aspiration to build a successful professional career, Neha Dhule continuously works on improving her leadership qualities, communication skills, and decision-making capabilities. She is committed to applying theoretical knowledge to practical situations and aims to contribute meaningfully to organizational and societal development in the future.

Vijay Kumar is a seasoned academician and management educator with over 23 years of extensive teaching experience across reputed universities and colleges in India. Currently associated with the Department of Management at Shoolini Business School, Shoolini University, Solan, Himachal Pradesh, he has established himself as a dedicated educator committed to academic excellence, student development, and institutional growth. Throughout his distinguished academic career, Dr. Kumar has contributed significantly to management education through innovative teaching practices, curriculum development, and academic leadership. His areas of expertise encompass core management disciplines, where he emphasizes experiential learning, industry-oriented pedagogy, and the development of analytical and leadership skills among students. Known for his student-centric approach, he actively mentors learners to bridge the gap between theoretical knowledge and real-world business applications. Prior to joining Shoolini University, Dr. Vijay Kumar served as the Head of the Department for MBA and BBA programs at LR Institute of Management, Solan, Himachal Pradesh. During his tenure, he played a pivotal role in strengthening academic programs, enhancing teaching quality, coordinating faculty development initiatives, and fostering an environment conducive to research and professional growth. His administrative leadership contributed to improving program effectiveness and academic standards within the institution.

Ankur Kushwaha is an assistant professor of Human Resource Management at FLAME University, Pune, India. He earned his PhD in Organizational Behaviour and Human Resource Management from Indian Institute of Management Indore. He has eight years of industrial experience in information technology and banking & finance. He also served as a student representative to the executive committee of the OB division at the Academy of Management (AOM) for 2022-2024. He is also Ambassador for India for MH division at the AOM for 2026-27. His research works have appeared in top peer-reviewed journals. His research interests include careers, gig work, work design, and sports management.

V. Lakshmi Prasanna is a distinguished academician and educator serving in the Department of Humanities and Sciences at Gokaraju Rangaraju Institute of Engineering and Technology, Hyderabad. With a strong foundation in interdisciplinary education, she has contributed significantly to the academic development of students by integrating humanities perspectives with scientific and technical learning environments. With extensive experience in higher education, Dr. Prasanna is committed to fostering intellectual curiosity, critical thinking, and effective communication skills among engineering and technology students. Her teaching philosophy emphasizes holistic education, combining theoretical knowledge with practical understanding to prepare learners for both professional and societal responsibilities. Her academic interests include language studies, communication skills, applied humanities, professional ethics, and personality development, particularly within technical education contexts. She focuses on enhancing students' soft skills, academic writing abilities, and global communication competencies—essential attributes for success in modern multidisciplinary careers. Dr. Lakshmi Prasanna has actively participated in research and scholarly activities, contributing papers to conferences, seminars, and academic forums. Her research engagement reflects an interest in innovative teaching methodologies, learner-centered pedagogy, and the role of humanities in shaping socially responsible engineers and professionals.

T.C. Manjunath was born on 6th February 1967. He did his B.E. from RV College of Engg. in 1989 (B'lore Univ), M.E. in Robotics & Automation from Govt.'s LD College of Engg., (Gujarat Univ., Ahmedabad) in 1992 with FCD-First Rank & PhD in Systems & Control Engg. from IIT Bombay in the year 2007, got best research scholar award for the entire IITB. He is currently working as the Dean Research (R & D) and as Professor in Dept. of Computer Science & Engg. with specialization in IoT, Cyber Security, Blockchain Technology in Rajarajeswari College of Engineering, Bengaluru, Karnataka. He has got a teaching (academic), research & administrative experience of more than 35+ years (10 years as Principal & 8 years as HoD, 1 year as Dean Research & rest as faculty) and has published more than 1500+ research papers in various national & international journals & conferences, with 175+ patents, 100+ book-chapters, 25 awards, 100s of Keynote talks and also published 25 text books in various field of science, engineering & technology, completed projects worth Rs. 9 Crores till date & guided 10 PhD scholars in VTU. He is a member of 30 Professional Society Chapters and is a fellow of IE, IETE, AMIEE, Sr. Member of IEEE and a chartered engineer.

P. Selvakumar is currently an Associate Professor in the Department of Science and Humanities at Nehru Institute of Technology, Coimbatore, Tamil Nadu, India. Prior to joining Nehru Institute of Technology, he held positions as an Assistant Professor in the Department of Science and Humanities various engineering colleges in Coimbatore, Tamil Nadu, India, spanning from 2011 to 2023. Dr.P. Selvakumar's academic and research interests lie primarily in the field of phytochemistry. He has made significant contributions to his field, with an impressive record that includes 30 journal publications, 12 patents, and 20 conference papers. Additionally, he has organized 5 seminars and conferences, further demonstrating his commitment to academic and scientific exchange. Throughout his career, Dr. P.Selvakumar has been recognized for his dedication and excellence in teaching, having been honored with several awards, including the Best Teacher Awards. He holds a prominent position in the academic community, contributing actively to research.

Jayesh Pandey is working as Assistant Professor in Organizational Behaviour & Human Resource Management area at Institute of Rural Management, Anand (IRMA), "Tribhuvan" Sahkari University. Previously he has worked for Great Lakes Institute of Management Chennai. He has pursued his PhD in Organizational

Behaviour & Human Resource Management from the Indian Institute of Management Ranchi. He has completed Post Graduate Diploma in Management from the Goa Institute of Management. His recent research has been published in Journal of Business Research, Journal of Technology Transfer, IEEE Transactions on Engineering Management, Journal of Retailing and Consumer Services, Journal of Global Information Management, Global Knowledge, Memory and Communication, and The Case Centre. His research interests are talent management, knowledge management, leadership, organizational restructuring, organizational politics, and motivation.

Vaishali Rahate is a distinguished academician and serving as Professor at the Datta Meghe Institute of Management Studies, Nagpur. With extensive experience in higher education, she has established herself as a dedicated educator, scholar, and mentor in the field of management studies. Her academic career reflects a strong commitment to excellence in teaching, research innovation, and institutional development. Dr. Rahate specializes in key domains of management education, including organizational behavior, human resource management, strategic management, and contemporary business practices. She is widely recognized for her learner-centered teaching methodology that integrates theoretical concepts with real-world managerial applications. Through interactive pedagogy, case-based learning, and experiential teaching approaches, she actively nurtures analytical thinking, leadership skills, and professional competence among students. Throughout her academic journey, Dr. Rahate has contributed significantly to research and scholarly activities. Her research interests encompass organizational effectiveness, employee engagement, leadership development, sustainable management practices, and emerging trends in business and management education. She has published research papers in reputed national and international journals and has presented her work at conferences, seminars, and academic forums, contributing to ongoing academic discourse. In addition to teaching and research, Dr. Rahate has played an important role in curriculum design, academic administration, and quality assurance initiatives within the institution. She has been actively involved in organizing faculty development programs, workshops, management conclaves, and student-oriented academic events aimed at bridging the gap between academia and industry.

José De Jesús Reyes-Sánchez, Ph.D. in senior management, has six master's degrees, in education, in management, professional soccer technique, in physical preparation, in professional soccer, in physical rehabilitation sciences, in sports sciences, as well as in coaching and integral well-being, who is a research professor at the TECNM Instituto Tecnológico Superior De Fresnillo, with more than 20 years of teaching experience, PRODEP profile and coordinator of the academic body with vast experience in conferences and workshops, currently novelist and writer.

Amrik Singh is working as Professor and HOD in the School of Hotel Management and Tourism at Lovely Professional University, Punjab, India. He obtained his Ph.D. degree in Hotel Management from Kurukshetra University, Haryana, India. He has published 115 Scopus-indexed publications. He has published 12 patents, and 01 patent has been granted in the inter-disciplinary domain. Dr. Amrik Singh participated and acted as a resource person in various national and international conferences, seminars, research workshops, and industry talks. He has published 20 books with IGI Global Publication, Emerald Publication, Bentham Publication, Nova Publication etc., on trending areas such as Food waste, Artificial Intelligence, Mountain Tourism, Virtual tourism, Healthcare Tourism, Guest behavior in tourism and hospitality. His area of research interest are Accommodation management, sustainability, Green practices, Human Resource Management in Hospitality, Artificial Intelligence, AR VR in hospitality, Hotel pricing, Employee Disability, Work life balance, women empowerment etc. He is currently guiding 8 Ph.D. scholars, and 5 Ph.D. scholars have been awarded Ph.D.

Deepthi.V.S. completed her undergraduate degree in bachelor of commerce(b. com) and post graduate degree in master of commerce(M.com) and is currently pursuing another post graduate degree in management. her curriculum honed her analytical skills, enabling to identify key trends, and fostering a meticulous attention to financial reporting, market dynamics and business operations, further her post graduate studies enhanced her research capabilities and strategic thinking. Her core competencies are her wide knowledge over commerce and management, which enables her to work with the industry better and give prominent solutions

Index

M

O

P

Q

R

S

T

V

W

www.ingramcontent.com/pod-product-compliance
Lightning Source LLC
LaVergne TN
LVHW081534300926
849161LV00006B/1425